Contemporary Portugal

For Augusto and Dias,
who just wanted to live a little better;
and for H.M.,
'il miglior fabbro'.

Contemporary Portugal
A history

R. A. H. ROBINSON
University of Birmingham

London
GEORGE ALLEN & UNWIN
Boston   Sydney

First published in 1979

GEORGE ALLEN & UNWIN LTD
40 Museum Street, London WC1A 1LU

© George Allen & Unwin (Publishers) Ltd, 1979

British Library Cataloguing in Publication Data

Robinson, Richard Alan Hodgson
   Contemporary Portugal.
   1. Portugal – History – 1910–1974
   2. Portugal – History – 1974–
   I. Title
   946.9'042   DP675   79–40004

ISBN 0–04–946013–7

Typeset in 10 on 11 point Times by V & M Graphics Ltd, Aylesbury
and printed in Great Britain by
William Clowes & Sons Ltd, Beccles and London

Preface

This book has modest pretensions. It is not intended as a work of original research for the specialist, but rather as a comprehensive general survey of the political, economic and social evolution of Portugal during the last half-century. Befitting its multi-functional purpose as an introductory text for students of contemporary history and politics, and as a background work for those primarily concerned with language and literature, it is intentionally long on information and short on interpretation. As also befits a book of this type, the scholarly apparatus of burdensome footnoting has been dispensed with; readers who wish to further their knowledge are provided with a bibliographical guide at the end of the text.

In any work for the English-speaking reader about a relatively little-known country not only is an introduction to land and people a necessity, but the writer also encounters the problem of what to translate and what to leave in a foreign language. In the present work no unfamiliar terms or phrases are left unexplained or untranslated; place names have been anglicised according to common usage (e.g. Oporto for Porto, Braganza for Bragança etc). Inevitably a large number of sets of initials are dotted throughout the text. An English translation of what these represent appears on the first occasion of use; thereafter any confusion on the reader's part may be quickly resolved by reference to the glossary, where the full titles of organisations are given.

While the author naturally takes full responsibility for his text (which is heavily indebted to existing secondary sources up to the 1970s), he nevertheless wishes to record his thanks to all those friends and academic colleagues in Britain, Portugal and North America who have stimulated, encouraged and sometimes unconsciously guided his interest in Portuguese affairs in recent years. Last, but by no means least, he thanks Mrs D. P. Leigh for typing quickly and accurately an often untidy and sometimes scarcely legible manuscript, and Mrs Jean L. Dowling for drawing the maps.

R. A. H. R.

Contents

List of Tables

1

Land and People

Portugal is Mediterranean by nature, Atlantic by position. Pequito Rebelo

My friends, what a sad fate to be born a Portuguese. António Nobre

Portugal is a small country, a very simple fact but one which must never be overlooked in any consideration of its history, its politics and its society. It covers an area of 35,383 square miles including the so-called Adjacent Islands, the archipelagos of Madeira (308 square miles) and the Azores (905 square miles) out in the Atlantic. Its total population was estimated in 1975 to be 8,762,000; censuses are taken every ten years and Table 1.1 gives the relevant figures for recent decades.

Table 1.1 *Population of Portugal, 1930–1970*

Year	Population
1930	6,826,000
1940	7,722,000
1950	8,510,000
1960	8,889,000
1970	8,668,000

(The fall in the population in the years 1960–70 was explicable by a high rate of emigration, an aspect of Portuguese society of considerable importance and about which more will be said later.)

As the map shows, Portugal has only two neighbours, the Atlantic Ocean with which it shares a coastline of 527 miles, and Spain. A narrow rectangular country some 350 miles long and on average 100 miles wide, taking up little more than 15 per cent of the surface of the Iberian Peninsula, it has no very convincing claims to national individuality on geographical, ethnic or linguistic grounds. Its 755-mile frontier with Spain is rather the product of historical development, beginning with the successful rebellion of Afonso Henriques, ruler of the County of Portugal, against his feudal overlord, the 'emperor' of León and Castile, in the twelfth century. The date 1140 is given by tradition to the proclamation of Portuguese independence, and at that time the County (or Kingdom) of Portugal comprised the northern half of the present-day state. By 1297 the southern half of the present territory had been conquered from its Muslim rulers and rival claims settled with Castile. Portugal's boundaries as a nation were therefore fixed before those of any other European country, even though the land was ruled by the Spanish Habsburgs from 1580 until 1640 and one small frontier change came about in 1801. By the Peace of Badajoz of that year Portugal ceded the nearby township of Olivença to Spain, in which country it has remained, despite the wishes of the Great Powers, expressed in the Treaty of Vienna of 1815, that the place should be returned to Portugal. The population of Olivença remains culturally Portuguese and the Portuguese claims to it are still outstanding, although these have never been pressed in the twentieth century in the lively manner in which Spain has called for the restitution of Gibraltar.

But, it may be asked, even if Portugal as a separate entity is the result of a series of historical accidents, to what extent do geographical, ethnic or linguistic factors reinforce or weaken the notion of national individuality? As one of the country's leading cultural figures of the present century, Jaime Cortesão, wrote: 'If we cast a quick glance at the most general geomorphological features of the Hispanic Peninsula, considered as a whole, no peculiarity seems to justify within it political fragmentation'. While there is no unity of natural conditions within Portugal, there are also no real signs of distinguishing features which coincide with the political frontier between Spain and Portugal. Beginning in the north-west, one notes that the River Minho marks the frontier with Galicia, but this holds true for only part of that river's course. Given the similarity of physical features, climate and forms of cultivation to north and south, only historical reasons can explain why the frontier does not follow, for example, the line of the River Lima farther to the south. The north-eastern part of Portugal – Trás-os-Montes and Beira Alta – is merely a prolongation of the Castilian plateau, the *Meseta,* while farther south Beira Baixa and the Alentejo region are geographically one with, and indeed socially and economically akin to, the Spanish region of Extremadura. The central mountain range of the Serra da Estrela divides northern from southern Portugal as its prolongation in the Sierras de Gata, Gredos and Guadarrama, divides Spain. The two great rivers of Portugal, the Douro and the Tagus, are also two of the great rivers of Spain. In the south, the Algarve cannot be differentiated from coastal Andalusia. Parts of the central coastal areas of Portugal, no more than a quarter of the land, could be called geographically different, but only in the same way as peripheral areas of Spain differ from its interior.

Geographically, then, Portugal is neither a homogeneous nor a peculiarly distinct unit. To ask whether Portugal is an ethnically homogeneous land is to put a rather old-fashioned question. The present population is descended from a historical mixture of ethnic groups, some of which are lost in the mists of prehistory. If one restricts oneself to going back no further than the first millennium BC, which would seem far enough, successive waves of settlement, conquest or partial colonisation may be noted: Celtic, Phoenician, Greek, Carthaginian, Roman, Germanic (especially Suevic), Arab and Berber. To this list may be added Jews, gypsies and black Africans imported as slaves before the final abolition of that institution on the Portuguese mainland in 1761. Twentieth-century ethnographic studies confirm the assimilation of all these elements, with the exception of some 92,000 gypsies who, as in other countries, remain nomadic social outcasts to be found chiefly in the Alentejo. They engage in begging, the buying and selling of animals and fortune telling, and have a bad reputation among the settled population for violence, theft and smuggling. Attempts have been made by the authorities to integrate them into the community by getting them to settle down, to go to school, to be law-abiding and to improve their standards of hygiene in the interests of others as well as themselves, but there are few indications of change in these respects.

Leaving aside these gypsies, there are no distinct 'nations' or sub-national groups in Portugal to correspond to the Basques or the Catalans in Spain, and so in this sense the Portuguese population may be termed homogeneous. There are no physical differences between the populations living on either side of the Luso–Spanish border, but this did not always deter some people earlier in this century from advancing the possibility of the existence of some sort of Portuguese ethnic type. The poet and political myth maker António Sardinha, in *O Valor da Raça*, written in 1914, advanced the idea (on grounds of 'anthroposociology' amongst others) that the aboriginal substratum of the Portuguese people was to be found, not under the labels *homo europaeus* or *homo mediterranensis*, but under that of *homo atlanticus*; the Portuguese were fancifully depicted as survivors from both Atlantis and the Homeric Aegean! More seriously, the ethnographer Leite de Vasconcelos noted that the Portuguese were one of the most homogeneous peoples in Europe with regard to physical characteristics because they contained the highest percentage of dolichocephalics. Both the significance and the validity of this conclusion have been disputed, but his other conclusions on physical characteristics are worth mentioning as they lend a certain dubious statistical support to simple, unscientific observation: 97·8 per cent of the population was found to be dark-haired, with the minority of fair-haired people coming from the north, from the Minho in particular; Portuguese with blue eyes came from the north, while south of Coimbra 77·8 per cent of eyes were dark; 12·3 per cent of Portuguese were tall (over 5 feet 8 inches), while 36·2 per cent were small (under 5 feet 4½ inches), the remaining 51·5 per cent being closer to the average national height of 5 feet 6 inches. In short, one may conclude, inhabitants of Portugal are more likely than not to be of medium stature and dark in complexion and therefore comparable to other European residents of comparable latitudes such as Spaniards, Italians and Greeks.

Having established that there is nothing peculiarly different geographically or ethnically about the Portuguese, there remains the question of language. Portuguese, which has been described as 'less harsh than Castilian and less musical than Tuscan', is spoken by more than 75,000,000 people, for it is also the language of Brazil. (Brazilian Portuguese differs in some respects from standard European Portuguese, based on the dialect of Lisbon: there are some sound changes and some variations in verb conjugation and syntax.) The Portuguese language arose as a synthesis in the twelfth century of the Galego-Portuguese of the Christian north and the Mozarabic-Lusitanian of the Muslim south; residual differences in dialect reflect these distant origins. Within the modern Portuguese language four principal dialects are said to exist: the northern or *interamnense* in the Minho and Trás-os-Montes; the central or *beirão*, in the Beiras; the southern, on the rest of the mainland (including Lisbon), and the insular, spoken in the Adjacent Islands and which could be said to include Brazilian. There are also further minor variations: a discernibly different dialect, really a Leonese *patois*, is spoken in Miranda do Douro on the Spanish frontier in the north-east, whilst in some of the villages on the north-western coast of the Azorean island of São Miguel the dialect seems Frenchifield, possibly reflecting settlement by Breton fishermen. Nevertheless, despite such differences of dialect, Portuguese is a distinct Romance language which also contains over five hundred words of Arabic origin, many of them describing clothing, furniture and utensils, agricultural tools and scientific devices. The Portuguese language could be said to provide evidence of the individuality of Portugal were it not that some 2 million people north of the frontier in Spain speak Galego, which is a dialect of Portuguese. Thus one is forced back to the notion that Portuguese individuality is the product of historical evolution and has precious little to do with linguistic, ethnic or geographical factors.

Having looked briefly at what does or does not differentiate Portugal from other lands, it is now time to consider differences between the various areas of the country. There are numerous ways in which the country can be divided. Following French precedents, the liberals of the 1830s divided Portugal administratively into *distritos* (districts) and these administrative units have continued to the present day, the last reform being the creation of the new *distrito* of Setúbal in 1926. The mainland is composed of eighteen *distritos*: Braganza, Vila Real, Viana do Castelo, Braga, Oporto, Guarda, Viseu, Aveiro, Castelo Branco, Coimbra, Leiria, Santarém, Lisbon, Portalegre, Évora, Setúbal, Beja, Faro; while the Islands are composed of four: Funchal (for Madeira), Angra do Heroísmo, Horta and Ponta Delgada (for the Azores). These administrative units do not always possess homogeneous geographical characteristics, and in 1936, a century after the liberal administrative division, a new administrative code superimposed on the eighteen *distritos* of the mainland eleven *províncias* (provinces). The boundaries of these *províncias* do not coincide with those of the *distritos* and were derived from the work of the geographer Amorim Girão, who believed rivers to be unifying rather than divisive factors in regional social and economic life. The *províncias* of 1936 also reflected – as their names make plain – an attempt to reintroduce into official life the traditional and pre-liberal regions. The way in which the *províncias* roughly correspond to the older regions, which continued – and continue – to dominate in popular speech, may be observed best in semi-tabular form (Table 1.2).

Table 1.2   *The Correspondence Between Regions and Provinces*

Old region	*Províncias*
Algarve	Algarve
Alentejo	Alto Alentejo
	Baixo Alentejo
Estremadura	Estremadura
Beira	Beira Alta
	Beira Baixa
	Beira Litoral
Minho	Minho
Trás-os-Montes	Trás-os-Montes e Alto Douro

There remain the two *províncias* of Douro Litoral and Ribatejo which straddle the older regional conceptions, the former being partly Minho and partly Beira, the latter partly Estremadura and partly Alentejo. There is, in fact, no single satisfactory way to divide up the country and at the same time cover all historical, social and economic eventualities, though Portuguese geographers keep on trying to find one and in the process come up with different and differing criteria for regionalisation.

In the attempt to explain regional differences which follows, we shall begin with an examination, part factual and part impressionistic, of the rural areas and then consider the cities, by which are here meant the Greater Lisbon area and Oporto, and their relationship with the rest of the country. Although the Minho is the historical cradle of Portugal, it will be more convenient to start our tour in the north-east, in the region of Trás-os-Montes (meaning literally the area lying 'across the mountains'), a name which originates in the popular usage of the people of the Minho in medieval times. Trás-os-Montes has the unfortunate distinction of being reputedly the poorest region in the whole of Europe. A vivid and somewhat dramatic image of the backwardness of the area was provided by two Spanish journalists who visited it in 1972. Having noted the enormous proportions of emigration away from the locality and that it borders the two poorest provinces in Spain, Orense and Zamora, they summed up their impressions like this:

> In Trás-os-Montes all hope is forbidden . . . Poverty, rather than seen, is divined, felt, kicked against, savoured in a thousand little details. There is hardly a car on the roads. We do not meet a single truck. The capital, Braganza, has only 8,000 inhabitants . . . We get to the *Pousada* (Portuguese state hotel) in Miranda do Douro and we are the only people there. The people are badly dressed and are even worse shod, when they have shoes at all. We pass through one, two, three, twenty or forty villages and always silence, emptiness follow us; the shops have nothing desirable in their windows – or the articles are just set out at the door or the clothes hung up outside . . . And the car covers kilometre after kilometre in the monotony of sadness and solitude. If the general impression of Portugal – of frontier Portugal – is one of sadness, this sadness reaches its obvious high point in this arid and mountainous region of the *trasmontano* north.

The Province of Trás-os-Montes e Alto Douro may be divided into two distinct climatic and geographical parts: in the north, the *terra fria,* or cold land, which shares the rigours of a continental climate – with hot summers but very cold winters – and in the south, in the Upper Douro valley, the *terra quente,* or hot land, which has a more temperate and Mediterranean climate with shorter and less harsh winters and hot summers made all the hotter by the sun being reflected off the schists.

The *terra fria* is an extension of the Castilian plateau and over 2,000 feet above sea level. Here the soil is generally infertile and the terrain rocky. Summits covered only with stunted vegetation serve as sheep fells and the few compact villages, with poor houses built of granite or shale, present depressing pictures. Rainfall is low. In the east, around Miranda, cattle are bred, while elsewhere sheep, goats and pigs are more common. A French sociologist of the Le Play School, Professor Paul Descamps, who did a survey of Portugal in the early 1930s, noted in the north-west of the area the survival of primitive communal societies, village communities with communal property and engaging in communal farming, whilst in other parts he noted that labour was rewarded in kind and not by monetary wages. Strong rivalries between communities are said to be a characteristic of the area and the cult of masculinity is reported by some to be exaggerated (one of the region's dances is that of the *pauliteiros,* which centres on stickfighting between the men). As in the neighbouring provinces of Spain, wolves roam about in the winter, killing animals and occasionally children. Though they live in a poor, bleak and undeveloped area, the inhabitants, the *trasmontanos,* have never been particularly noted for their religious feeling – a fact which some ascribe to ecclesiastical indifference in the last two centuries and others to the basic lack of interest in proselytising on the part of the military orders which dominated the area in earlier times. Nevertheless it is a conservative region and Descamps noted in the 1930s:

> Nowadays safety [from brigands] makes the clan less united, but the clan spirit continues to exist . . . What nowadays one can call a clan leader is a rich, influential man who lives locally and provides work for the *cabaneiros* [hut-dwellers], lends to financially inconvenienced farmers, helps the unfortunate, spends money on entertainments. A 'social authority' of this type guides public opinion, and when there were elections people voted as he did without bothering about which party he backed.

Moving south to the *terra quente* of the Upper Douro valley, a change is noticeable. Wheat, potatoes and chestnuts give way to arbutus, holm-oaks, rock roses, olives, almonds, oranges, apples and, of course, to intensive cultivation of the vine, for this is the port-wine country. Pinhão is an important production centre whilst, farther down river, Régua is the 'administrative capital' from where transport of the wine down to Oporto by rail is organised. Summer temperatures of up to 40°C help to ripen the grapes in the carefully terraced valley; the winter rain flows quickly off the slopes without leaving much moisture in the soil. The grapes are harvested in late September and October largely by migrant labour from Trás-os-Montes, Galicia and from farther south in the Beiras. Much of the treading of the grapes is done by people from the region as a sort of pastime; there is little employment at other times of the year, and in the 1930s Descamps observed that Régua was characterised in the summer months by temporary emigration, begging, indebtedness, drunkenness and wife beating. Before leaving the Province of Trás-os-Montes e Alto Douro, which also contains a more fertile flat area around Chaves, it is worth noting that this is one of the important mineral-yielding regions in a country poorly endowed with mineral resources. There are coal and iron-ore deposits at Torre de Moncorvo, whilst tin-bearing and other ores are mined in the *distrito* of Braganza.

To the west of Trás-os-Montes e Alto Douro lies the historic cradle of Portugal known as the Minho, a shorthand expression from the seventeenth century for the area Entre-Douro-e-Minho (between the rivers Douro and Minho), mentioned as a distinct unit by the ancient geographer Ptolemy. The Minho is divided from Trás-os-Montes by mountain ranges, the Serras do Gerês, da Cabreira, de Barroso and do Marão in the east, and bounded by the rivers Minho and Douro in the north and south respectively. The area thus takes on the form of an amphitheatre looking on to the Atlantic, divided by the beautiful river valleys of the Lima, the Cávado and the Tâmega which cross it from north-east to south-west. These, with the valley of the Lower Douro, provide possibly some of the finest scenery in Europe. The Gerês area is known, with little exaggeration, as the Portuguese Switzerland and is a national park. Climatically the Minho is quite different from Trás-os-Montes. It falls into the pluviose zone of the Iberian Peninsula and is one of the wettest areas in Europe, a fact reflected in the lush verdure of the countryside. The difference is noticeable also to anyone descending the Douro valley: around Régua there is a quite abrupt change in vegetation. A large part of the Minho receives between 40 and 80 inches of rain a year, compared to 30 to 40 inches in Trás-os-Montes. Whereas Trás-os-Montes is exposed to the high-pressure conditions of the *Meseta,* the Minho is subject to an Atlantic climate dominated by North Atlantic cyclones in the winter and the advance of the Azorean high-pressure system in the summer.

Whereas Trás-os-Montes has a very low density of population, the Minho, though also an area of high emigration, has a very high density. Even though the soil is not very fertile the high rainfall allows for intensive cultivation, the pattern being one of very small holdings (*minifúndios*) with many sharecropping arrangements, so that owners of some plots may also be labourers for part of the week on others. The density of population and the prevalent ideal of self-sufficiency leads to great competition for land and to countless disputes and endless litigation over such things as water rights. As a generalisation, it may be said that the hamlet is the usual unit of settlement, but individual houses, whether of the manor house type (*solares*) or of a much humbler variety, are almost as common in some parts. The overall impression of the Minho to the visitor is one of greenness, and appropriately it is from the Minho that one of the national dishes, *caldo verde,* a soup made from shredded cabbage, originates. Vines as well as vegetables are a characteristic of the region and it is the home of the *vinho verde* (green wine), a light and sparkling, rather bitter and refreshing beverage with a low alcoholic content. The fields in the region are often enclosed by hedges and climbing vines and two crops of cereals a year are not uncommon. On hillsides apple, orange and olive trees can be seen and hilltops are often crowned with trees (eucalyptus, pine or oak). On the narrow cobbled roads traffic, for the most part cars bought and registered abroad by migrant workers, is often halted or hindered by the ubiquitous long-horned oxen, which are used for ploughing and for pulling carts from a bygone age with solid wooden wheels. The yokes of the oxen are frequently intricately carved with a pattern said to be Suevic. The image of the *minhotos*, as the inhabitants are called, is, rightly or wrongly, very much that of the traditional peasant. Ownership of land, however small the holding, is considered highly desirable and the advancement of the family as a whole, whether by hard work in the fields or by remittances from members who have emigrated temporarily or permanently, is the norm. Attempts made by the state from the nineteenth century onwards, embodied in successive civil codes inspired by French examples, to insist on the division of properties among all the male children in the family, have been generally circumvented by one device or another. Given the traditionally high rate of male emigration, much of the work is done by the womenfolk and, despite the importance of family individuality, there is a communal element to cultivation in as much as groups of neighbours often get together, tending each other's crops in exchange for meals. The rhythm of rural life centres on the observance of numerous saints' days and there is rarely a Sunday on which there is not a *romaria* (a kind of pilgrimage, excursion or junketing) in one parish or another. *Romarias* are occasions for communal celebrations, with music, dancing and fireworks. The *minhotos* are the most religious of Portuguese but *romarias* and *festas* could fairly be described as predominantly secular occasions if one were to attempt to separate the religious and the secular. *Festas* (religious festivals as well as holidays in the modern secular sense) are also the occasions for the wearing of local costumes. In the Minho this is still a genuine manifestation of folkloric tradition, not just something to be revived for the tourist trade. The dances are vigorous and singing is much enjoyed, not least when working in the fields. The *minhotos* are often said to be the gayest people in Portugal, as well as the most talkative, the most docile and the most deferential. What store can be set by such a reputation is problematical: it has been suggested that the external gaiety compensates for inner griefs. One is on less uncertain ground in noting the high incidence of bronchitis, hardly surprising in view of the climatic conditions.

Not all the population of the Minho is engaged in agriculture. Apart from the city of Oporto and its activities, the inhabitants of the coastal areas include among their occupations fishing and tourism, and this mixture of activities can be found in Viana do Castelo and Póvoa de Varzim. Other notable towns in the Minho are Braga, famous as 'the Portuguese Rome' and whose archbishop contests with his opposite number in Toledo the title of Primate of the Spains; Guimarães, the old capital of the medieval County of Portugal; and Barcelos, a market town famed for the production of decorated ceramic cocks which have become a national symbol. The conservative and agricultural image of the Minho is well captured in a proverb from Braga: 'Every good house has its cattle and its tonsure.'

The central area of Portugal, south of the Douro and north of the Tagus, also bounded by an imaginary line running from just south of the mouth of Portugal's third river, the Mondego, inland to a point on the Tagus about 15 miles from the Spanish frontier, is known as the Beiras – the *províncias* of Beira Alta, Beira Baixa and Beira Litoral. Although the Beiras are said to constitute Portugal's centre of gravity, they raise in a particularly acute form the problems of regional differentiation. No very neat subdivisions can be made within the area which, taken as a whole, nevertheless constitutes a transitional zone between the north and the south of the country. The River Mondego, on which lies Portugal's third mainland city of Coimbra with its ancient university, is sometimes taken as the dividing line between north and south in a general sociological as well as a geographical sense. However, it could better be argued that the northern parts of Estremadura and the Ribatejo, which geographically are also central, have much more in common with the north than with the south. Having noted the complexities and dangers of generalisation, an attempt must nevertheless be made to describe the Beiras, as the three *províncias* constitute a region.

In general the area is characterised by the small size of agricultural holdings and by a mixture of owner-cultivation, sharecropping and renting of land. Religious feeling is also strong. However, these generalisations are perhaps less true of the *distritos* of Guarda and Castelo Branco. These two areas, with low density of population, are geographically and climatically similar to their neighbouring Spanish provinces and have something in common with Trás-os-Montes: Guarda, in particular, is bleak and desolate, its hills topped with strange lunar-like rock formations, while there is labour migration southwards from the two *distritos* at harvest-time. To the south-west of the town of Guarda lies the Serra da Estrela (the Mountain Range of the Star, though why it is so called is a mystery), which divides the inland part of the region in two and constitutes the roof of Portugal, rising to 6,500 feet. In summer, the sheep reared for their wool and their milk from which cheese is made are brought up here for pasture from lower altitudes by shepherds who pass the time playing on fifes or, as in the Alentejo, carving wooden utensils to relieve the monotony. In winter there is now a ski resort at Penhas da Saúde near Covilhã. This small industrial town is sometimes grandiosely called the Portuguese Manchester because of its longstanding textile industry.

In the two inland provinces, Beira Alta and Beira Baixa, the population tends to congregate along the valleys of the rivers Vouga, Dão, Mondego and Zêzere, the latter a tributary of the Tagus. The Dão area, centred on the district capital of Viseu, has some features in common with the Alto Douro area to the north. It is famous for its wine, mostly sweet and red with a velvety texture roughly comparable to a Burgundy, and arguably the best in Portugal. Viseu itself is a pleasant provincial capital, which tends to attract the residence of many of the better-off people in the region. The villagers of the area also grow maize, rye and olives and many of the hillsides are wooded. The soil is better than farther north even though rainfall, except in the Serra da Estrela, tends to decrease as one moves south and irrigation from the rivers is necessary to ensure against the uncertainties of the climate in summer. Taking the region as a whole, pigs, sheep and cattle are reared, as well as the inevitable goats. The sheep, which find their summer pasture in the Serra da Estrela, are brought down to the lower lying parts of the region in winter. This transhumance often extends farther down to Beira Litoral, so that it is still possible to encounter flocks of sheep passing through Coimbra cluttering up the main Oporto–Lisbon road, the N1. The ownership of land is still a goal of the rural population in the Beiras, as in the northern parts of Estremadura and the Ribatejo.

The landscape changes as one moves towards the Atlantic, granite yielding to sandstone and limestone, and wooded hills giving way to rolling sandy hills which look increasingly desolate as one goes farther into Estremadura towards Lisbon. The division between the inland Beiras and Beira Litoral reflects a basic division between the interior of the country and the more densely populated and economically thriving coastal area of the Lisbon–Oporto axis (though it would perhaps be more correct to say Setúbal–Braga axis). In Beira Litoral there is a change in agricultural produce: to the growing of cabbages, beans, potatoes, etc., is added the growing of melons and rice. The area is in some places quite thickly forested, mainly with pines and holm-oaks. Midway along the coast, at the mouth of the Vouga, is the town of Aveiro with its *ria* (lagoon), an area sometimes called, with the usual love of foreign comparisons, the Portuguese Holland, because the environs consist of a completely flat landscape which sometimes floods in winter. Aveiro is known for its ceramics industry and its salt-pans as well as for its fishing industry: sea-eel and sea-perch are caught in the lagoon, sardines and skate inshore and cod off Newfoundland and Greenland, while special high-prowed sailing craft (*moliceiros*) gather seaweed.

The inland areas of the Beiras contain some mineral deposits, notably wolfram ore, mined chiefly at Panasqueira near Fundão, and uranium, to be found in the *distrito* of Viseu. To give an insight into village life in the inland parts, it is also worth quoting this rather jaundiced passage from Franz Villier's *Portugal:*

In Beira Baixa is Monsanto, the most Portuguese village in Portugal. It has borne this title since 1938, when a grand competition was held. The most serious rival was a village in the same province, Paúl. Monsanto being gloomier and harsher had to be selected as the most Portuguese ... The granite-built houses huddle under the rocks and seem to blend with them. A typical Monsanto house has a door and even one or two windows but no chimney, and the smoke eddies merrily about inside. There is a single room, with an alcove, and the water that condenses on the walls is collected in a primitive ewer. Above the bed hang garlands of pears and onions, for in Portugal the onion is considered a fruit. Potatoes are heaped under the bed. Thus every available space is fully utilised. Apart from the procession [on 3 May there is a procession of girls who throw jugs of flowers over the battlements], as an all-the-year-round attraction there's a hunchback who tells fortunes and brews love-potions.

Rural Portugal is not one of the most idyllic places in which to live.

Although, as has already been noted, some geographers see the River Mondego as the dividing line between the north and the south, the view that the Tagus is a better rough guide in this respect will be followed here. Those parts of the *províncias* of Estremadura and the Ribatejo that lie north of the river would seem to have more in common, in general terms, with the land and people to their north than with those to the south, be it in vegetation or agrarian structure: smallholdings are still characteristic of the area even if rather larger farms become more common in the Ribatejo. Similarly in the sphere of religion: although there is a tradition of religious indifference and anti-clericalism in the areas closer to Lisbon, the northern parts of Estremadura and the Ribatejo have a claim to be the religious heart of Portugal, for it is here that the great pilgrimage centre of Fátima is situated, where Our Lady allegedly appeared before three children on the 13th of each month from May to October 1917. Since then Fátima has become one of the greatest pilgrimage centres in the world and the Portuguese Lourdes has quite overshadowed its earlier rivals for the title in the Minho such as Monte Sameiro.

In northern Ribatejo there is mixed cultivation of olives, vegetables and vines; from the Ribatejo come what might be called the everyday wines, reds from Cartaxo and whites from Chamusca, while not far away in Estremadura red wines are produced at Colares in the Serra de Sintra and whites at Bucelas. From Estremadura north of the Tagus come lemons, strawberries, pears, quince, peaches, tomatoes, almonds, figs and olives, while cereals are often to be seen growing between the fruit trees. Pines and eucalyptus abound, but nearer the coast the landscape is barer and slopes are often crowned with the remains of windmills. Ceramics and timber are major provincial industries. Along the coast, as is the case in the Minho, fishing and tourism mix in places such as

Ericeira, Peniche, São Martinho do Porto, Nazaré and (in Beira Litoral) Figueira da Foz. Nazaré claims to be a curious Phoenician survival, its inhabitants still wearing their distinctive local costume, the women sporting up to seven different coloured skirts, whilst Peniche is famous for its crayfish and lace. To the north-west of Lisbon, and behind the residential and tourist spots of the Costa do Sol, lies the Serra de Sintra, an area of considerable natural beauty much beloved of poets, including Southey and Byron. (Somerset Maugham, however, thought Tomar in northern Ribatejo the most beautiful place on earth.) The villages north of Lisbon as far as Mafra are known as the *saloio*, apparently derived from an Arabic word for country dweller. They are known for their orchards and kitchen gardens while their inhabitants have a traditional reputation for greed, envy and craftiness: *saloio* has become a pejorative term over the centuries like *galego* in northern and central areas of the country, though in Brazil the latter (meaning literally a person from Galicia) is a pejorative term for a Portuguese.

Part of the Province of Estremadura, the Setúbal peninsula, lies to the south of the Tagus estuary but, like the northern and western approaches to the capital and since the opening of the bridge across the river in 1966, it is best considered now as part of the Greater Lisbon area. All that needs to be said here is that this part is famous for its oranges, sheep's milk cheeses and muscatel, while the scenically beautiful Serra da Arrábida is more reminiscent of the Mediterranean than the Atlantic.

The southern part of the Ribatejo may be included in the discussion of the two provinces of the Alentejo – the names of the two regions originate from the medieval period of conquest by the Christians from the north, Ribatejo meaning the banks of the Tagus, Alentejo, beyond the Tagus. Geographically the Alentejo is a prolongation of the *Meseta*: bounded in the north by the Tagus, the countryside is broken by outcrops of rock in the Upper Alentejo south of the Serra de São Mamede. This rolling countryside then gives way to the plain which is the heart of the region, a plain bounded in the west by the ocean and in the south by the Serra do Caldeirão. It is a poor and sparsely populated region with low rainfall. There is virtually no natural vegetation and the soil is light and infertile. However, the relatively mild, damp winters and the long, hot summers make the area suitable for cork- and holm-oaks, olive trees and eucalyptus. Other parts of the country also abound in these trees, but perhaps they are most characteristic of the Alentejo: the holm-oaks provide acorns for the black pigs which are numerous in the region, while the cork-oaks are an economic standby if the region's main crop, the wheat from the plain, has a bad year. The region also provides winter and spring pasture for transhumant flocks of sheep from farther north. The southern Ribatejo is an area of livestock rearing; the *lezírias*, the marshy southern bank of the Tagus, constitutes the main bull-breeding area where the *campinos* (cowboys) in distinctive garb and on horseback, drive fierce wild cattle with long spikey poles. In suitably swampy areas rice is also grown.

The Alentejo is historically characterised by large units of agricultural exploitation, *herdades* or *latifúndios,* the result of royal grants of estates to nobles, military orders and ecclesiastics in the period of Christian conquest. Ecclesiastical property however had to be sold off in the early nineteenth century and so the area was dominated by large private landowners until the agrarian reform of 1975. The intermediate level of society – between bigwigs and labourers – was always accordingly much smaller in the Alentejo than in the rest of the country. The population follows the southern Spanish pattern in that widely spaced townships are the norm, with labourers also living in at the *montes,* complexes of buildings (master's house, barns, stables, bakery, lodgings for permanent workers and accommodation for seasonal labour) that formed the centre of the estates. Further similarities with southern Spain that may be noted lie in the spheres of food and religion: *gaspacho,* a cold soup made from tomatoes, onions, cucumbers and pimentos seasoned with garlic and vinegar, is a regional speciality, while the population has a reputation for religious indifference. Whether the roots of this should be sought in an attitude of resistance to Christianity inherited from the distant Moorish past, or in a shortage of clergy following the dissolution of the religious orders in 1834, or in ecclesiastical lethargy over the years, is matter for dispute.

Family bonds are looser in the Alentejo than elsewhere, a reflection in part of popular attitudes to religion, and there is a tendency to be less concerned than elsewhere with the formalities of marriage. Also relevant are some of the economic features of the region. It has been argued that the communal life of migrant labourers in the crowded accommodation of the *montes* encourages promiscuity, but it has also been argued that the seasonal migration of males and females from the townships, often at different times of the year, militates against the institution of marriage. If bonds of kinship are weaker than elsewhere, bonds of patronage and spiritual kinship (*compadrado*) in the Alentejo are possibly stronger.

In the Alentejo houses are built to protect the inhabitants from the heat and glare of the summer and are generally single-storey constructions with lime-washed walls and small doorways and windows. Building materials in some areas are still based on dried clay or mud bricks. As one would perhaps expect from a region which has much in common with southern Spain, the inhabitants have a reputation for indolence and vanity; on the other hand *alentejanos* are also said to be taciturn, fatalistic and melancholy folk. Traditional dances are relatively slow moving and songs are often mournful and seemingly betray Moorish influences: one listener compared *alentejano* singing to someone weeping. Neither climate nor environment are friendly, however: in the words of one traditional shepherds' song:

> Alentejo has no shade
> Save that which falls from above.

Perhaps the word which sums up the region best is monotony, and in this connection two English visitors to the area in 1960 wrote: 'It is hard to imagine the poverty of life in a place where one of the major daily events is the arrival of the bus from Lisbon'. Finally it may be noted that the region contains copper deposits, notably at Aljustrel and at São Domingos between Mértola and the frontier, while marble is quarried in the Upper Alentejo.

To the south of the Serras do Caldeirão and de Monchique, which make an amphitheatre *província,* lies the Algarve, probably the best known region in the whole country to outsiders on account of the tourist developments of the last decade or so. On the western and southern sides the *província* is bounded by the Atlantic, while to the east the River Guadiana forms the frontier with Spain. Although it is obviously geographically in the south of the country, it is nevertheless sociologically different from the Alentejo with which the term south is so often implicitly synonymous. The separateness of the Algarve is reflected in the fact that it was the last area to be brought under Christian rule and the official title of the monarchs was always 'King of Portugal and the Algarve'. The name itself derives from the period of Muslim rule, being a corruption of *al-Gharb* (the west, that is the west of the Muslim region of al-Andalus, Andalusia). Its climate is also different from the regions north of the mountains since it is subtropical which, with sea-bathing from March to November and comparisons with Californian weather, accounts for its popularity with tourists. Lagos has an average annual rainfall of 15 inches in ninety days, compared with 24 inches in ninety-nine days in Lisbon. This climate helps to explain the richness of the vegetation: almond trees which transform the area with their blossom in January, groves of orange and lemon trees, rice and sugar cane, fig trees, palm trees and the distinctive carobs, camellias and oleanders in profusion. Many gardens are hedged round with agaves and cereals often grow in the fruit orchards. The North African influence can still be seen in the design of many of the chimneys, designs which have become popular also in the new colonies of villas at places along the coast, villas often owned by retired English people or British or German tourists.

Apart from the ever-growing importance of tourism, the region lives by agriculture or fishing. The size of holdings is generally small, as in the north and centre of Portugal, and the methods of land exploitation vary from owner-cultivation to tenancies and sharecropping arrangements.

There is perhaps less religious indifference than in the Alentejo, though it is said that fisherfolk are more religious (or superstititious) than the farming population. *Algarvios* have a similar reputation to Andalusians for being lively and loquacious in their social life but apathetic and indolent in other respects; it is said that 'the Algarvian bursts if he does not talk'. The traditional dance, the *corridinho,* is very lively indeed, partners being whisked round on one leg for part of the time.

Whereas the Atlantic coast of Portugal is dangerous for fishermen, being exposed to the worst weather and having really only Peniche, Cascais, Setúbal and Sines as sheltered harbours, the Algarve, being much more sheltered, can enjoy safe all-year-round fishing, whether for anchovy, sardines, mackerel, stickleback or for tunny, fished intensively since at least Muslim times. As elsewhere, the smaller fishing craft are often hired out to the fishermen, who take what is left of the profit from the catch after the owners of the boat and the nets have taken their shares. As at Aveiro, so at Faro, the capital, there is a lagoon (*ria*) from which salt is collected. Some of the old fishing villages, such as Albufeira, must now be considered primarily as tourist resorts, but Tavira, Portimão, Olhão and Vila Real de Santo António retain their original importance. Vila Real, it may be noted, was built in 1774 as a customs post and is a magnificent and striking example of the town planning of that time. Also of interest to the historically minded, but 85 miles away at the other end of the *província,* is the Sagres peninsula, the most south-westerly point in Europe, associated with Prince Henry the Navigator and the explorations and discoveries of the fifteenth century. The great sixteenth-century poet Luís de Camões, whose epic poem *Os Lusíadas* may still be considered the national literary masterpiece, wrote that Sagres headland was the place 'where the land ends and the sea begins'. This simple description sticks in the mind of anyone who has stood on the windswept promontory looking out on three sides from the high cliffs over the vastness of the ocean.

However, before setting off in the wake of the explorers to describe the Adjacent Islands, we must first consider urban Portugal, which means Lisbon and Oporto. Lisbon, the capital, is also the country's chief port and largest city, with 800,000 inhabitants, nearly 10 per cent of the whole mainland population. If the industrial zones outside the city boundaries with their workers' housing complexes are included, then one finds that about one in five Portuguese live in the Greater Lisbon area which, together with the city's political and administrative importance, fully justifies the description of Portugal as being, like Greece, a macrocephalic country. Oporto, which was economically the more important and the faster growing city in the nineteenth century, has a population of 300,000, but to Oporto should be added Vila Nova de Gaia on the south bank of the Douro as well as Oporto's *plage,* Foz do Douro, and the neighbouring town of Matosinhos with its port of Leixões, created to avoid the periodic silting-up at the mouth of the Douro. The *distrito* of Oporto contains 16 per cent of the mainland's population, and the *distritos* of Lisbon, Setúbal and Oporto together almost 42 per cent, a striking illustration of the way in which the population is distributed. Furthermore, the census figures of 1970 demonstrate clearly other facts about population distribution and density: the eastern and southern parts of the country (comprising the *distritos* of Braganza, Vila Real, Guarda, Viseu, Castelo Branco, Portalegre, Santarém, Évora, Beja and Faro) taken together cover an area of 24,436 square miles, which is 71·5 per cent of the total area of the mainland; however, their combined populations add up only to 2,541,000 or just under 30 per cent of all the people on the mainland. Populations of provincial towns are small compared with Oporto and Lisbon: thus the third mainland city, Coimbra, has 56,000 people; Braga has 49,000, Évora 34,000 and Aveiro 24,000, while other capitals of *distritos* are smaller still: Leiria with 7,500, Viseu with 17,000, Vila Real with 11,000, Viana do Castelo with 14,000, Beja with 18,000.

The second city, Oporto (*o porto*, the port), has the distinction of having given its name to the whole country, Portugal being derived from the Roman Portus (now Oporto) and Cale (Gaia) on the opposite bank. The inhabitants, the *portuenses*, have also had the nickname of *tripeiros* (tripe eaters) since the fifteenth century. Traditionally the city is associated with the port-wine trade with England and in the eighteenth century English merchants took over the trade from harvesting to bottling. Since then, however, many of the companies, while retaining their English trade names, have become locally owned. The trade centres on Vila Nova de Gaia where the port-wine lodges are to be found, some with *barcos rabelos* – square-sailed barges formerly used to bring the casks down the Douro – moored in the river. The other principal industries are textiles, food canning, iron making, chemicals, leather, ceramics and filigree work at nearby Gondomar. Despite Lisbon's pre-eminence, the city still has the air of a major commercial centre and a symbol of its past importance may be found in the extravagant pastiche of the Alhambra to be found in the nineteenth-century stock exchange building. In the nineteenth century it was a liberal and even radical city, but in the twentieth it has yielded these honours to Lisbon too, now having a reputation for conservatism and Catholicism as the capital of the north: in the present century the bishops of Oporto have been the most progressive in the country and their diocese the best organised. Nevertheless, ironically, the poorest (and oldest) part of this hilly conurbation lies in the area of the cathedral and episcopal palace. This area was well described in 1960 by two visitors, Peter Fryer and Patricia McGowan Pinheiro:

... This quarter is a confusion of the narrowest alleys and steep stone steps you can discover anywhere in Portugal. These passages are filthy with the refuse of households without sewerage; on either side are doors, the top halves opening inwards like stable doors, through which you glimpse tiny rooms filled with beds, stoves, cooking utensils ... It is clear that whole families live in these cramped hovels. It is also clear that in many there is no water supply, for now and then a woman or a child can be seen going in or out with a pitcher. Nor are there sinks. Dirty water, old cabbage leaves, potato peelings and fish bones are thrown in the gutters. Women sit on the doorsteps preparing food or sewing. Children cling about them, and skinny cats lurk against the walls or crouch apprehensively over pieces of rotting fish, ready to evade the inevitable kicks from passers-by ...

Children follow us about. Little, nimble, brown-skinned boys and girls in rags, dirty and thin-faced. Some of them have sores around their mouths and on their hands ...

This is still Europe – not a 'backward', colonial country whose wretchedness the imperial-minded love to explain away. All these children, fair and dark, are children of a western nation. They creep up beside us begging for coppers, whispering and cajoling in the hoarse, sing-song voices of gutter children everywhere. Though it is the middle of the afternoon there are hordes of them, and we wonder why they are not at school.

Oporto gives the impression at times in its architecture and in its social life and *mores* of still being in some ways a Victorian city. The *portuenses* have their pride and view Lisbon, 215 miles to the south and some four hours away by the fastest train, ambiguously called *O Foguete* (The Rocket), as a different world of which they do not altogether approve. For the inhabitants of Lisbon, the *lisboetos* as they style themselves (*lisbonenses* is the linguistically correct form), Oporto is a sad, dark town of granite and people with amusing accents. Lisbon certainly provides a contrast and seems more typical of the Mediterranean with its larger squares, broader avenues, greater spaciousness, light-coloured buildings, palm trees and jacarandas, and livelier and noiser street life. *Lisboetos*, even if they are youngish immigrants who have only been resident for a year or two, have an attitude of self-confident superiority towards the rest of the country, as if they breathed an enlightened air denied to the lesser mortals of the provinces or the countryside. 'Lisbon is Portugal!' says a character in one of the novels of Eça de Queirós, and people in the city happily accept the nickname *alfacinhas,* people living at the very heart of the lettuce which is the nation.

The heart of Lisbon lies open to the Tagus, a monument to the work of Pombal in having the city rebuilt on lines of classical town planning after the disastrous earthquake of 1755. Behind the Praça do Comércio (obstinately called Black Horse Square by the British) with its government ministries lies the main commercial centre, the Baixa (lower town), after which come the famous Rossio and Restauradores squares before the ground slopes upwards along the imposing mile-long Avenida da Liberdade to the Edward VII Park (so named after the state visit of that British monarch in 1902). To the east of the Baixa lie older quarters dating from Moorish times: the Alfama and Mouraria with their steep, narrow, winding streets dominated by the Old Cathedral, while to the west lies the Bairro Alto on another hill. Northwards from the Baixa the city has expanded along fine avenues often called after foreign parts (Rome, Berne, Brazil, United States); this area includes notable modern buildings such as the headquarters of the Gulbenkian Foundation and the university. To the north-west the city is overlooked by the wooded slopes of Monsanto. Lisbon, however, has nowadays no neat boundaries; new suburbs push out to the north and along the Tagus to the industrial zone of Sacavém and beyond, while to the west, after the old working-class quarter of Alcântara and the national monuments of Belém, stretches the Costa do Sol (Coast of the Sun) for 18 miles as far as Cascais. The equable winter climate of this coast, with Estoril as its best-known resort, has made it a fashionable holiday area for at least half a century. Now, however, it is as much a collection of commuter suburbs for Lisbon as a tourist haven and magnet for exiles (who have included King Carol of Romania, Admiral Horthy, King Umberto of Italy and the Count of Barcelona).

If Sacavém and the Costa do Sol must be included in the Greater Lisbon area, so must the other side (*outra banda*) of the Tagus estuary, stretching towards Setúbal at the mouth of the River Sado, 30 miles away. Setúbal itself is the country's third port (after Lisbon and Oporto) and is famous for its fishing, which includes oysters. Farther along the coast the fishing village of Sesimbra is now better described as a holiday resort, while the north coast of the Setúbal peninsula, from Montijo to Almada, constitutes the heavily industrialised *outra banda*. Here blocks of workers' flats stretch farther and farther inland to house those attracted to the country's premier industrial complex, pollution and all: the steelworks at Seixal, the chemical industry at Barreiro, the Lisnave dockyard at Margueira, etc. The Lisbon area is the economic centre of Portugal as well as its political and social capital.

In surveying Portugal one must not forget the Atlantic archipelagos of Madeira (population in 1970 253,000) and the Azores (population in 1970 290,000), not least because, as the figures show, one in twenty Portuguese lives there. The uninhabited Madeiran archipelago is traditionally said to have been discovered in 1419 by the Portuguese navigator João Gonçalves Zarco, who subsequently undertook its colonisation, but there is evidence to suggest that the islands were known to Genoese in the previous century. The archipelago, some 340 miles from the coast of Morocco and 675 miles from Lisbon, consists of Madeira itself (*Ílha da Madeira,* island of timber), 34 miles long and 14 miles wide; the island of Porto Santo, 26 miles north-east of Madeira; and the uninhabited Desertas and Selvagens, 11 miles south-east and 156 miles south of Madeira respectively. Porto Santo has a population of 3,600 who live by fishing and growing melons, vines, wheat and barley. This small island (area 16 square miles) is famous only for tourism, having an excellent 4-mile-long beach.

Madeira itself, with 98,000 people gathered in its capital, making the port of Funchal Portugal's third city, is also of course famous for its tourist facilities, and for its wine. The original vines came from Crete and throve in the rich volcanic soil but phylloxera struck in the nineteenth century and the vineyards were then re-established on American stock by Englishmen such as Charles Blandy and Thomas Leacock, whose families still have a major share in the industry. Sugar has always been and still is a major product; the canes were renewed by John Blandy with stock from Mauritius in 1873. British influence and settlement on the island is still noticeable, and the embroidery industry which employs 70,000 female workers was introduced by a Mrs Phelps in 1850. Wickerwork is mainly associated with Camacha. The climate is generally temperate, varying from means of 16°C in winter to 21°C in summer. However, low mists also make for a treacherous climate and the unwary moving from one altitude to another are quite likely to catch pneumonia. The land rises sharply from the coast to a height of 6,106 feet (Pico Ruivo) and settlement is usually at the mouths of ravines or on the gentler slopes. Over 2,500 feet pines and pastures are the norm, while between 1,000 and 2,500 feet grow the vines, cereals and fruit (including avocado pears and mangoes); the third level of vegetation below 1,000 feet is subtropical and includes sugar cane, bananas and Barbary figs. Agriculture predominates in the Madeiran economy and terraced plots, usually tenanted on a sharecropping basis, are hoed, not ploughed, while there is a complicated system of water allocation, water being brought down from the heights in open channels called *levadas.* The 'pearl of the Atlantic' is a paradise for naturalists with blooms introduced from all parts of the world including hydrangeas, hibiscus, orchids, bougainvillaeas and *Strelitzia regina.*

The *madeirenses* are, like northern Portuguese, fairly religious. They also have been unflatteringly described as passive in the manner of domestic animals and sanguine in temperament. As in the Azores, great poverty can be found and, within a stone's throw of the villas of Câmara de Lobos, naked children suffering from malnutrition are a common sight. Until the late eighteenth century many black slaves were imported as sugar-cane workers, but this element has now been completely absorbed into the European population, leaving only occasional traces in folklore.

The Azorean archipelago lies some 760 miles west of Lisbon and spans some 400 miles of ocean, the nine islands formed from a volcanic mountain chain being divided into three groups: the islands of São Miguel and Santa Maria in the east; Terceira, Pico, Faial, São Jorge and Graciosa in the centre; and Flores and Corvo in the north-west. The uninhabited archipelago is reputed to have been discovered by Diogo de Silves in 1427 and is said to take its name, *Açores* (goshawks), from birds espied by the early voyagers (though there is no evidence for such birds ever being in the islands); like Madeira, however, mid-fourteenth-century Genoese maps suggest that they were known before then. Colonisation began in the fifteenth century with Portuguese and Flemings. Volcanic activity is still far from unknown (Pico and Faial experienced severe earthquakes in 1926). Thermal springs are a feature on the largest island, São Miguel. This island, on which is the capital, Ponta Delgada, with a population of 20,000, has only been linked directly with Lisbon by air since 1971. Cattle and dairy produce, canned fish, and pineapples (grown under glass) are among the exports. Cereal growing and cattle raising are local activities, as is fishing, including whaling. Bananas, tea and tobacco are grown. The islands have a mild but, at most times of the year, wet and windy climate. Blue hydrangea hedges are a feature of São Miguel and Santa Maria. Agriculture is generally primitive and the people are for the most part very poor. As in Madeira, emigration is an accepted phenomenon. Azoreans are said to be hospitable, religious, patient and tenacious and, as in northern Portugal, it is the women who work hardest.

Having surveyed the regions of the country, noting their differences and their similarities, it is time once more to return to the national picture and to examine some factors which might reinforce the chief distinguishing feature of the Portuguese – their long life in common in one political unit. However, it should not be forgotten that in a country where illiteracy is still quite high – in 1970 one in four people in the country could still be described as illiterates – and where communications, especially in country districts, are poor – in 1959 1,200,000 people, some 13 per cent of the population, lived in small villages inaccessible by road – feelings of national solidarity may be less well developed than in countries where such factors do not obtain. For many of the rural population, and not just for them, 'the state' is a natural enemy, or at least a much resented bugbear; Lisbon and all that it means – centralised administration and education, bureaucratic regulations, collection of taxes, police functions and conscription – is to be both feared and kept at a distance, when not ignored. As in other southern European countries, local bodies may outwardly accept what is decided for them but then very often fail to carry out instructions. Thus small-circulation local weeklies may be much more important than the national daily newspapers of Lisbon which do not penetrate to many parts of the country. Broadcasting might be expected to overcome such divisions. However, although radio and television, the latter started in 1957, are a great social boon for entertainment, programme content and the political and social values transmitted from Lisbon (where these values are seen as positively beneficial to the rest of the nation) often act as sources of further alienation rather than as national cementing material. In this respect local values and ways of life remain important within the general consciousness of being Portuguese, even though the general tendency is, as elsewhere, for regional differences and customs to become less deeply felt as the process of modernisation advances. Thus genuine, traditional customs die out, to be resuscitated only for the benefit of the tourist industry. As the Portuguese ethnologist Jorge Dias put it before the tourist boom of the 1960s, the function of this renewed interest in regional dances was to seek 'to give illusions of things that no longer exist, just as in the museums of natural history there are stuffed animals which have disappeared from our forests and mountains as the result of the destructive fury of our civilisation'.

As in other southern European countries, what one may term the national culture is for historical reasons an urban culture, with which subjacent regional cultures to a greater or lesser extent contrast. It is impossible to be very precise in this area, but it would still seem to be true that the principal divisions are the rural–urban disjuncture and the perceived and felt differentiation between north and south as well between the mainland and the Islands. If it be conceded, as it must in the last resort, that there is a Portuguese culture, then the elements of this must be examined.

One of the salient features of Portuguese society – and one which does not differentiate it in kind from any other south European society – is the prevalence of networks of kinship and patronage. Lengthy and complicated laws and regulations may be constantly drawn up, promulgated and revised to settle the rules by which society is to operate, but in practice every Portuguese knows that such rules are there to be bent or circumvented as one's own needs dictate and in so far as means can be found to achieve this. For historical reasons, including the political instability of the last two centuries, it can be said that no concept of the objective legitimacy of law or government has ever taken root in Portugal. It is assumed that those who make law or govern do so to further their own interests rather than those of society as a whole, and therefore the taking of countermeasures in self-defence is a natural and legitimate activity. From time to time there is a breakdown of the governmental system, a change of political regime and new laws result, but these changes do not usually make much impact on the substructure of social relationships.

Thus, whatever the regime, individuals and families need to be well connected to survive, to prosper and, if possible, to advance their standing and interests. Since Portugal is a small country and therefore has a small élite – facts which perhaps differentiate it to a certain extent from larger south European countries – who is related to whom, who knows whom, who owes whom a favour, are the essential elements in social relationships. Whether it be in one of the government ministries or in some rural area, those in positions of authority and influence constitute the centres of patronage. The protection of one's interests or the advancement of one's career is to a considerable extent dependent on whose system or network of patronage one belongs to; clients give their support to patrons, whether the nexus be one of kinship or *compadrado* or of some other type, and patrons in return look after the interests of their clients. Portuguese society is in one sense little more than a large number of competing 'families' organised for survival and advancement. If a patron fails to produce results, then he risks losing his clients and this still further weakens his position. As is to be expected, those who lose in this competition are wont to denounce corruption and injustice, while those who are doing well either keep quiet or defend themselves on the grounds that careers are open to talent and they have proved themselves more able. There are rules of the game which must be observed and seen to be observed but after that point patronage is an important, if of necessity sometimes obscure, social fact, be it in politics or in simple economic transactions.

Such a fact is an obstacle to the creation of a national civic consciousness of the type associated with north European countries: in Portugal the concept of the orderly queue is unknown. At this more general level of social behaviour that individual self-interest which the Portuguese call *egoismo* again shows through, though again in ritualised form. In a crowded restaurant or railway station success in getting one's needs satisfied lies in manœuvring oneself into the best physical position and pleading *faz favor* (do [me a] favour) more soulfully than one's competitors; the less successful are treated by the victor to a polite and sometimes smiling *desculpe* (sorry) often accompanied by a gesture to show that no harm was intended, though this action also signals that the incident is considered definitively closed. *Exaltarse,* to show anger, would in any case constitute loss of face on the part of the less successful.

Here we begin to enter the realm of what sociologists call socio-cultural variables, or more simply national character. That peoples do have different customs and societies have different modes of operation, and that individuals have differing outlooks on life, are self-evidently true statements, but that one can generalise about the character or nature of a people is not self-evidently true. Many, indeed, would say that it is palpably false and yet, in the case of Portugal, a great deal of energy has been spent in attempting to define or draw attention to national virtues and defects and to generalise about the Portuguese way of life. Since this has been, and *perhaps* to a lesser extent still is, something of a national intellectual hobby, anyone interested in Portugal and the Portuguese has at some point to take note of such outpourings. A belief in a collective self-image – partieularly if held by the intellectual élite – must have some effect on the way things happen in that country. Obviously there is no way in which the effects of such an influence or such an exercise in self-conditioning could be quantified, but most writings on the subject convey a sense of pessimism and self-criticism even when they set out to praise the Portuguese. To illustrate this point and enter further into this speculative realm, the views of two distinguished Portuguese ethnographers, a French sociologist and a major Portuguese literary figure, will be cited.

Addressing a foreign audience in 1959, Professor Jorge Dias said:

To describe the traditional national character in a phrase, we can say that the Portuguese is a mixture of dreamer and man of action, or better still, an active dreamer, who has a certain practical and realistic basis. Portuguese activity does not have its roots in cold-blooded will, but is nurtured on imagination and dreams, since the Portuguese are idealistic, emotional and imaginative, rather than deeply reflective. They share with the Spanish the aristocratic disdain for smallminded gain, for pure utilitarianism and comfort, and the paradoxical taste for ostentation of wealth and luxury. But they do not have a strong abstract ideal like the Spanish, or a pronounced mystic tendency. The Portuguese are above all, profoundly human, sensitive, loving and generous without being weak. They do not like to cause suffering, and avoid conflicts, but can be violent and cruel when pride is hurt ...

There is, in the Portuguese, an enormous capacity for adaptation to ideas and people, but this does not imply lack of personality ...

They do not have the exuberance and noisy spontaneous joy of the other Mediterranean peoples. They are more inhibited because of their great sense of the ridiculous and fear of the opinion of others. They are, like the Spanish, strongly individualistic, but have a profound basis of humanitarian feeling. The Portuguese do not have a strong sense of humour, but a critical and mocking spirit which can be sarcastic and destructive.

In his multi-volume study of the Portuguese, Professor Leite de Vasconcelos noted that samples had found Portuguese children above the American, British or Belgian averages in verbal and abstract intelligence, but their practical intelligence where long periods of concentration were necessary was not as good. Portuguese children were quicker in their reactions, but worse at keeping their attention fixed for long periods. Accordingly the Portuguese were quick in comprehension but showed little persistence in sticking to one thing. In Portugal the impartial spirit of inquiry was rare: people preferred to be either for or against. The Portuguese, a poetic nation who considered themselves amorous, liked to succeed without effort and shine before their friends. A lively intelligence was ruined by emotion, sentiment and a great lack of system. Although he deemed the Portuguese people as a whole to be gentle, sociable and quiet, he nevertheless thought loquaciousness and the use of hyperbole characteristic, whilst volitional characteristics included patience, passivity, fatalism, a desire for profit, carelessness and neglectfulness. Leite de Vasconcelos also believed that irony, disenchantment, sadness, *saudades* (a melancholy yearning and nostalgia) and individualism were· characteristic. Foreigners thought Portuguese hospitable, smiling and docile people who worked as little as possible for easy money and to gain a superficial sense of importance; while northern Portuguese were harder working and more serious, everywhere there was a non-European sense of time. He noted that others added to the list of national defects: parasitism; extreme credulity coupled with a certain fatalism; megalomania; moral insensitivity; a spirit of indecision coupled with a proclivity to contradictory actions; and a spirit of routine coupled with a love of novelty and change. Finally, Leite de Vasconcelos also found that since the sixteenth century his fellow countrymen had a strong tendency to think anything foreign, particularly French, better than anything indigenous, and were consequently imitative.

For his part, Professor Paul Descamps found in the 1930s that French influence was most marked in political and intellectual matters. He noted that disciplined children always had foreign tutors and ascribed the national propensity to sadness and *saudades* to sensitivity and nervousness resulting from the permissive upbringing which most children received in a society which was in some respects matriarchal. Children were spoiled at home and always got round their mothers through flattery – so had the tendencies to have limitless wants and to lack civic discipline. The Portuguese, he thought, were not lacking in initiative but in perseverance; they had no sense of time or of the consequences of their actions and were generally idle – letters were never answered, even by the fully literate. Though he detected a tendency towards anarchic individualism, he concluded that the Portuguese were 'unstable communitarians rather than true individualists': the main bonds of social solidarity were based on family, clan and patronage.

Possibly the greatest of the country's literary talents of recent times,

Fernando Pessoa (who died in 1935) wondered, on the other hand, whether his compatriots were not characterised by 'their excess of discipline', in the sense that

> [a] Portuguese never acts on his own, breaking with his *milieu,* turning his back on his neighbours. He always acts in a group, always feels in a group, he always thinks in a group. He always waits for others in everything . . . Here, as in Germany, one never knows who is responsible; there is always a sixth person responsible when only five participate in an action.

For Pessoa, however, the flight from responsibility and the fear of nonconformity were less important than 'the greatest Portuguese evil', provincialism.

> Provincialism consists in belonging to a civilisation without taking part in the higher development of it – in following it mimetically, with a happy and unconscious submissiveness. Love of progress and modernity is another form of this provincial characteristic. The civilised create progress, create fashion, create modernity; therefore they attach no more importance to them. Nobody attaches importance to what he produces. The admirer of production is the one that does not produce . . . The provincial is awed by what he does not make, precisely because he does not make it; and he prides himself on feeling this awe. If he did not feel that way, he would not be provincial . . . The provincial feels the artificiality but loves it for this very reason. For his awakened, but not completely awakened spirit, the new artificiality that is progress is attractive as a novelty but is still felt to be artificial. And, because it is felt to be artificial and at the same time attractive, it is the artificial that is loved. The love of big cities, new fashions, 'the latest novelties', is the distinguishing characteristic of the provincial . . . [whose] mentality bears a perfect resemblance to that of the child. The reaction of the provincial to his artificialities, which are the social novelties, is just like that of the child to his, which are his toys. Both love them spontaneously, because they are artificial.
> Now what distinguishes the child's mentality is, with regard to the intellect, the spirit of imitation; with regard to the emotions, little liveliness; with regard to the will, unco-ordinated impulsiveness. These are the characteristics which we shall find in the provincial; the fruit, in the child, of a lack of civilised development, and thus both effects of the same cause – the lack of development. The child is, like the provincial, an awakened spirit, but not completely awake.

What one should make of such pronouncements as this is rather puzzling but the Portuguese intelligentsia, if not the Portuguese people, has for a long time demonstrated an ability to take up foreign, particularly French, ideas with alacrity but without always considering their applicability to local circumstances. Given a certain gap which exists between theory and practice among people who have a tendency to believe that to write an arresting newspaper article on a subject is to go a long way towards the solution of a real political or social problem, this is sometimes perhaps just as well. When it is clear that the problem has not gone away, the intellectuals' response is usually either to move on to something else or to move from enthusiasm to pessimistic fatalism, rather in the manner of a manic-depressive personality. (Readers seeking confirmation of this view need only read the Portuguese press over a fairly short period.)

If reflecting upon and writing about the national psychology is a pastime of the intelligentsia, the Portuguese people as a whole have other leisure time activities which have unkindly been summed up as the three Fs: *fado,* football and Fátima. Portugal is known for *fado* as Spain is known for *flamenco* music, though neither genre is typical of the whole country: nevertheless the *fado* is to its admirers 'the most Portuguese of all songs and the liturgy of the nation's soul'. *Fado,* meaning fate, is the name given to popular poetry sung by a man or a woman to the accompaniment of a Spanish and a twelve-stringed Portuguese guitar. One student of the genre has adequately described it as follows:

Both words and music reflect the abrupt turns of fickle Fortune, the evil destiny of the unfortunate, the irony of fate, the piercing pangs of love, the poignancy of absence or despair, the profound sobs of discouragement, the sorrows of *saudade,* the caprices of the heart, and those ineffable moments when the souls of lovers descend to their lips and, before flying back on high, hover for an instant in a sweet embrace.

The origins of the *fado* have been much disputed, but it seems certain that it goes back no further than the 1830s and originated as the song of lower-class *lisbonenses.* It seems likely that it derives from the *lundum,* an African dance kept alive by slaves in Brazil and Lisbon, and that the songs of sailors and gypsies also played some part in its formation. It became generally popular in Lisbon in the second half of the last century, when a student variant, generally more melodic and less harsh, arose in Coimbra. The *fado* is still popular and has given rise to at least one artiste of international repute, Amália Rodrigues, though it has always had its critics in those who feel that tourist enthusiasm for it is a sign of national humiliation.

Another 'traditional' Portuguese phenomenon is the bullfight, though it would be wrong to think of bullfighting ever having held in Portugal the place it once held in Spain. Bullfighting centres on the bull-breeding area of the Ribatejo and on the ugly nineteenth-century Praça de Touros do Campo Pequeno in Lisbon, where the season lasts from Easter to October. In contrast to Spain, the bulls are not killed in the ring but encounter their moment of truth afterwards in the slaughterhouse. In the Portuguese bullring the chief figures are the *cavaleiro,* the mounted bullfighter who shows off his horsemanship, and the *forcados* whose collective task is to grab the bull by the (sheathed) horns and tail and immobilise it. Finally a number of cows with bells are sent into the ring to lure the bull out. In July, during the festival of the *colete encarnado,* bulls are run loose through the streets of Vila Franca de Xira.

Though bullfights are televised, it would be incorrect to say that bullfighting is a typical Portuguese sport. Just as the *fado* has yielded to modern international pop music, so bullfighting pales in its popularity before football, which can more accurately be termed the national passion. Internationally Portuguese football came to prominence in the 1960s – in 1966 their team was third in the World Cup competition and the black star Eusébio became an international as well as a national hero. Football was introduced into mainland Portugal in the 1880s by the English-educated Pinto Basto brothers (it had appeared on Madeira over a decade earlier). The principal clubs were founded in the first decade of the century – Benfica, Sporting (in the Lisbon area) and FC do Porto – and there are now many others organised in a two-division league, with Division 2 subdivided into North and South. Along with the game go the pools (*totobola*) which outdo other lotteries in popularity. Apart from football other popular sports are hockey, hockey on skates, basketball, cycling, swimming and athletics, while motor sport, sailing, golf, rugby and tennis also have their enthusiasts.

Less energetic pastimes include cinema going and the frequenting of cafés. Given the climate, Portugal, like other southern European countries, can be described as a café society, though only in Lisbon is one likely to see unaccompanied women in these places; as an old saying puts it, 'the woman at home, the man in the square'. The habit of going out for one's entertainment has hardly been affected by the advent of television, for sets are usually present in cafés. Billiard rooms, too, retain their popularity for the young in Lisbon and the rest of the country. If the climate leads to a lot of sitting outside cafés and on beaches and strolling about in the summer, the damp winters produce another phenomenon, the *constipação,* that seemingly permanent heavy common cold which everyone travelling on the Lisbon Metro always seems to have. Foreign visitors are likely also to note that the habit of spitting is still quite widespread.

Another feature of Portuguese life (particularly in the north) is the celebration of saints' days, *festas*, often accompanied by communal eating, fairs and fireworks as well as the decoration of churches. The pre-Lent carnival is also still a national institution: in country towns there are often processions and festivities, the pagan element showing through with people knocking members of the opposite sex over the head with little plastic hammers. In the capital, however, there is little organised activity, which leads disdainful Brazilians to comment on the whole affair as 'typically Portuguese' in that only a forced and 'sad' happiness is manifest. In country areas many feast days are observed, which led a French writer fifteen years ago to conclude 'that in Portugal the church and its festivals are the only entertainment that poor people have'.

Portugal is a Catholic country (even though church and state have been separated since 1911) in as much as there is no rival to Catholicism. It is much stronger as a social force and as a religion in the northern and central parts of the mainland and in the Islands than it is in Lisbon and the south. In 1960 96·5 per cent of the population officially declared themselves Catholic (less than in Italy, Spain or Belgium but more than in Austria, France or Ireland). Such statistics, however, do not offer much guidance as to the actual practice of religion. A public opinion survey conducted in 1971, based on a sample of 1,000 people on the mainland, found that 84·6 per cent of this sample identified themselves as Catholics (the difference between men and women in this respect being negligible), but only 52·5 per cent of these actually attended church at least once a week (compared with 83 per cent in Spain). The same survey found that 11 per cent of Portuguese Catholics never attended mass and 70 per cent never went to the social or cultural activities organised by their church. It is possible that these figures give too favourable a picture of religious realities in Portugal, as some answers may have been prompted by a desire to conform, just as some people are said to go to mass for social rather than religious reasons – but no one can know.

Professor Jorge Dias has written that 'their religious feeling shows the same basic humanity peculiar to the Portuguese. It does not have the abstract, mystical or tragic character of the Spanish, but it does have a strong belief in miracle and miraculous solutions.' For his part, Leite de Vasconcelos found that the myths of religion and Catholicism were very influential, but he thought Portuguese Catholics formalistic and inwardly indifferent, while Fernando Pessoa, in an essay on Portuguese Catholicism, opined:

> Among the Portuguese, in whom, in my view, emotion surpasses passion . . . Catholicism naturally assumes what we may call the Franciscan look, which is, so to speak, the essentially emotional aspect of Catholic Christianity. . . . Our Catholicism is formless – a religious affection, slothfully uncertain of what it really believes in. So our true

God-made-Manifest is not the one and triune God or any of the Persons of the Trinity, but a Catholic Cupid called the Child Jesus. So we pay no attention to the Virgin Mary, but only to Mother Mary.

So our real saints are St John Baptist as a child – that is, long before he became the Baptist – or a St Antony who is irremediably thought of as an infantile adolescent whose distinctive function – mending jugs – is a toy miracle.

As for the Devil, no Portuguese ever believed in his existence. Emotion would not permit it.

Whatever one makes of these assessments, it is a fact that Portuguese Catholicism has produced anti-clericals but no mystics.

Anthropologists have, of course, noticed that the line between Catholic religiosity and pagan superstitions is not always easy to draw, particularly in the remoter country areas. These traditional superstitions – belief in the evil eye and in *bruxas* (sorceresses) – would seem to be declining as education and medical services improve and contact with the outside world increases. (Some American anthropologists on the other hand maintain that *bruxas* are increasing in number, but this increase may be linked to the increase in the number of anthropology students doing Portuguese fieldwork.) Nevertheless the old ways have not yet disappeared and a reminder of what could happen not so very long ago was recorded by Descamps:

The belief in the power of the *bruxas* or anti-witches still sometimes causes crimes, like the one that occurred at the end of February 1933 in the hamlet of Oliveira, parish of Soalhães, municipality of Marco de Canavezes, to the south of Amarante [Douro].

To cure one hysterical woman, a *bruxa* had another killed; the latter, being possessed of the devil, was presumed to be the cause of the illness of the former. After the death of the unfortunate woman her body was burned on a heather pyre at night while a long prayer was said asking Jesus and Mary to forgive . . . the victim! For it was not she who had been the real cause of her neighbour's illness, but the devil who had taken possession of her body.

The criminals were astonished at being arrested as they thought they had carried out a meritorious act. It is proper to add that the parish priest fights these superstitions and that these deeds occasioned great revulsion in the surrounding area. It is an extreme case.

Despite indifference, Portugal may be considered a homogeneous community in religion, as in language and nationality, though there are small minorities. There are about 38,000 people in mainland Portugal who adhere to religions other than Roman Catholicism, a legal right since 1911. Most of these are organised in small Protestant communities in Lisbon, Oporto, Coimbra and coastal areas; there are also communities in the Azores and Madeira, originally founded by English people. There are Presbyterians, Methodists, Lutherans, Congregationalists, Episcopalians and some Jehovah's Witnesses, but the more important sects are the Baptists (supported from the United States and Brazil), the Pentecostalists (supported from Sweden), Seventh Day Adventists and Plymouth Brethren. In addition there is a Jewish community with synagogues in Lisbon and Oporto and its own cemetery. It would seem that Jewish communities survived the persecutions of the fifteenth and sixteenth centuries in such towns near the Spanish frontier in Trás-os-Montes and the Beiras as Castelo Branco, Penamacôr, Covilhã and Braganza (where a synagogue was opened in 1927). In these areas Leite de Vasconcelos noted that some inhabitants thought the Jews avaricious and unscrupulous and that in Trás-os-Montes Judaism was popularly associated with red hair. Immigration in the last two centuries would seem to have centred on Faro and Ponta Delgada (in the Azores) as well as Lisbon and Oporto. The Jewish community can be considered fully assimilated. There are also small communities of foreign residents – British, German, Franco-Belgian, Brazilian etc. – who do not occasion any noticeable hostility, though the Portuguese use the phrase *para inglês ver* (for the Englishman to see) to mean 'just for show'. There are also several thousand Spaniards, mostly from Galicia.

This introduction to the land and people of Portugal demonstrates the variety which lies behind their unity, a unity which is the product of historical evolution. Inevitably the assertion of a Portuguese sense of individuality has historically come from the struggles to maintain independence from Spain. Although there have always been proponents of Iberian unity in Portugal, popular sentiment would still seem to find an echo in the old saying,

> Neither good winds
> Nor good marriages
> Come from Spain.

2

Government and Opposition in Salazar's Time

To entrust to one person, no matter how able and trustworthy he may be, the whole future of a collective undertaking is not politically advisable. Oliveira Salazar (in 1929)

The Portuguese are not a very intelligent people. Oliveira Salazar

Students of modern political history searching for what is peculiar to the Portuguese political culture would probably decide that three inter-related 'isms', even if present under other names in other national political cultures, have a tendency to recur: Sebastianism, regeneration-ism and situationism.

Sebastianism is the term given to a popular yearning for sudden, miraculous political and social solutions to be brought about by a great man. It is the Portuguese variant of messianism, dating from the late sixteenth century when Portugal was ruled by the Spanish Crown, in the popular myth that the quixotic King Sebastian, killed in battle in Morocco in 1578, would return as a saviour to inaugurate the millennium of national grandeur when the people would be liberated from all oppression. Though here the term is of course used figuratively, the essence of Sebastianism can be seen in the exaggeratedly high hopes put by many in the changes of regime in the twentieth century: the advent of the Republic in 1910, the *coup* of Sidónio Pais in 1917, the military movements of 1926 and 1974. By the very nature of the psychic phenomenon, Sebastianism can never succeed. The hopes, the fantasies, the impossible wishful thinking can lead only to disillusionment, angry frustration or embittered apathy, as mania gives way to depression, excitement to routine.

Regenerationism, though not unrelated to Sebastianism (and a term beloved by both Spanish and Portuguese politicians and intellectuals), has, however, a greater empirical content and accordingly some chance of success. Passing into political usage in the early nineteenth century and primarily associated with the introduction of liberalism, regeneration signifies the ousting of decadence, the demolition of political and socio-economic structures that have outlived their usefulness; and the feeling that the nation must cease living in the past and be mysteriously reborn so that a collective effort can be launched in an atmosphere of optimistic determination that will both put the country in the forefront of 'modernity' and recover for it the glories of times past. Whereas Sebastianism suggests that solutions to problems will appear like rabbits from a conjurer's hat, regenerationism suggests rather the harnessing of popular energy to realise a preconceived programme or plan, imprecise though this may be. Sebastianism needs no hard work or popular participation; regenerationism assumes both, even though guidance from above is seen to be necessary. In reality, these ideal types usually intermingle, so that the installation of the Republic, the New State of 1933 and the Liberation of 1974 all have both regenerationist and Sebastianist features.

Situationism represents the other side of the political and social coin. Sebastianism and regenerationism concern the nation as a collectivity, but situationism concerns the individual. It signifies at worst his survival and at best his advancement. 'The situation' is the term given in Portugal to the prevailing political regime or government and, just as an individual needs a patron, so patron and client need to be 'on the side of the situation' at any rate in times of political stability. In times of uncertainty, on the other hand, there is an increased feeling of anxiety. When 'the situation' is unstable and may (or may not) soon change, then the art of survival and the opportunity for advancement lie in taking a gamble on the future. If one plays safe, it is as well to keep a low profile and not to be conspicuously 'on the side of the situation' so that one has a good chance of fitting into the 'new situation' if it arises. If one gambles for higher stakes, then one must anticipate the 'new situation' by publicly breaking with the old, in which case the failure of the 'new situation' to arise can have unfortunate personal consequences. Basically, however, in a small country with a small élite, where alternative personnel qualified to carry out important duties often do not exist, situationism represents the element of continuity. Thus when the regime changed in 1910 many Monarchists kept their jobs and their influence, adapting to the 'new situation'; Republican activists indignant on this score were met by the reply: 'We are always on the side of the government ... Is it our fault if the government changes?' In 1974 a former minister in the New State ruefully remarked that Portugal had doubled its population overnight: on 25 April 8 million democrats appeared in a country in which before that date there had only been 8 million fascists.

If this seemingly excessive situationism – a phenomenon scarcely unknown in other countries – may be considered a function of a small society in which patronage plays a major role, the same cannot be said of Sebastianism or regenerationism. The former would seem rather to be a function of a low level of political understanding and the historical lack of sustained political mobilisation among the people as a whole, while the latter is perhaps historically related to the relative socio-economic backwardness of modern Portugal combined with its intelligentsia's sense of national humiliation. The rise of Salazar to the position of Premier in 1932 ('with all the prestige of a messiah' as one of his opponents put it in his memoirs thirty years later) and the longevity of his regime cannot be understood without bearing in mind the Sebastianist and situationist elements in the Portuguese political culture any more than they can be understood without at least a cursory examination of the preceding failure of the regenerationism of the Republicans between 1910 and 1926 – a subject to which we must now turn.

In a general sense the Republic of 1910, like the 'National Revolution' of 1926, may be seen as a product of the increased sense of nationalism prevalent in Europe from the last quarter of the nineteenth century. In Portugal, as in other European Latin countries, this recrudescence of nationalism may symbolically be dated from a major humiliation by an Anglo-Saxon great power: Lord Salisbury's ultimatum of 1890, which dashed Portuguese dreams of possessing a continuous stretch of territory from the Angolan to the Mozambican coasts, corresponded to Italy's defeat in Ethiopia in 1896, Spain's loss of its remaining colonies to the United States and France's humiliation by Britain at Fashoda in 1898.

The ultimatum of 1890 and the major financial crisis which followed discredited the liberal constitutional monarchy of King Carlos in the eyes of many and led to an attempted republican *coup* in Oporto in 1891. Though the regime survived, the monarchist political élite became more and more divided, factionalism making stable government based on a two-party system increasingly difficult. King Carlos attempted to restore efficient government by giving wide powers to the politician João Franco in 1906-7. The political establishment resented the dictatorial new course and became alienated from the king. Some of its members made common cause with a longer-standing party of protest, the PRP (Portuguese Republican Party), which since 1891 had styled itself the party of national salvation and whose propaganda harped on corruption in high places, humiliation in international affairs, the evils of oligarchy and Jesuitism, and the hopeless decadence of the liberal monarchy in general. João Franco's experiment in administrative dictatorship was ended before his alternative of revolution from above could be tried. On 1 February 1908 King Carlos and the Crown Prince were assassinated in Lisbon and the short reign of his second son, Manuel II 'the Unfortunate', proved a futile attempt to return to parliamentary liberalism. The monarchy collapsed like a house of cards in the face of the republican revolution of 5 October 1910 in Lisbon.

In the eyes of its supporters, the advent of the republic not only returned Portugal to the mainstream of history overnight but actually put the country in the vanguard of modernity, for at that time France and Switzerland were the only other republics in Europe. Though nationally very much a minority movement with its strength among 'the people', i.e. the lower-middle and labouring classes of the capital, republicanism was accepted by the rest of the country in the same way as any other change in government: Lisbon, like Paris in 1789, set out to impose the enlightened ideals of democracy, laicism and reform on an apathetic nation. It was not long, however, before the quasi-millenarian hopes of the activists turned to disillusion and the republican leadership's dreams of rapid regeneration collided with harsh realities. To replace the blue and white flag of the monarchy by the red and green of the republic was easier than finding qualified republicans to staff the administration: thus monarchists had to be allowed to adhere to the republic even though this alienated the urban activists. In order not to be political prisoners of the urban radicals organised in the 'secret society' of the *Carbonária* who had helped make the revolution, those in power now placed greater reliance on the republican members of the officer corps, who had been only a small minority in the generally neutral armed forces in October 1910. The fate of the new regime, like that of the old, was dependent on the armed forces rather than the popular will.

The First Republic of 1910–26 is also known as the Democratic Republic, but this title reflects less the functioning of democratic institutions than the dominance of Afonso Costa's Democratic faction in national political life, this faction having emerged as the majority tendency in the PRP in 1911. Costa and his followers understood democracy as their right to exercise power: thus party and regime became identified in the eyes of supporters and opponents. In Jacobin style the Democrats saw themselves as the true democrats. Those in political disagreement were therefore monarchists or 'reactionaries' even though they might call themselves republicans: to oppose the Democrats was to be an enemy of democracy. This semantic confusion, deliberately fostered by Costa and his like, served abroad to disguise the quasi-authoritarian nature of the regime and give it democratic respectability while at home it made even genuinely republican constitutional opposition virtually impossible in the Republic's early years. In the longer run it devalued the whole concept of democracy in Portugal to little more than the level of a confidence trick.

The framework of political life was provided by the constitution of 1911, drawn up by a Constituent Assembly to which only PRP candidates were elected, most of them unopposed. The constitution created a bicameral system, the Chamber of Deputies and the Senate being elected by popular suffrage and the President of the Republic being elected by both chambers meeting together as the Congress. The Democratic Party machine never lost an election when in power and, though governments fell because of factional alignments within the group, the lack (until 1919) of a presidential power of dissolution meant that Democratic rule could only be ended by revolution, i.e. by military intervention, as in January 1915 and December 1917. The Democrats then saw that their way back to office lay by the same route (in May 1915 and 1919). The importance of Lisbon in the political system was reflected in the fact that, until May 1926, only *coups* originating in the capital were successful.

Government in the First Republic was a precarious thing. There were forty-five administrations between 1910 and 1926, lasting on average four months, with some five hundred individuals holding ministerial office, while only one of the six Presidents of the Republic completed his constitutional term of office. The number of *coups,* attempted *coups* and projected *coups* is difficult to estimate, but certainly averaged well over one a year, so that by the 1920s it had become a standing diplomatic joke internationally to compare Portugal's political gyrations to the seventy-eight revolutions per minute of the gramophone. *Coups,* counter-*coups* and rumours of *coups* kept the prisons busy and endangered freedom of the press. Governments could rule only through the inefficient bureaucracy which was always situationist, though it, too, developed its grievances. Outside the capital the regime was seen as rule by Lisbon for Lisbon, while in the capital economic difficulties killed off the initial enthusiasm of the lower-middle and labouring classes as their interests diverged. The Democratic Republic had no very firm or consistent social base and could never mobilise nationwide popular support. Governments might act in the name of the people, but the people as a whole were not to be trusted. The Republic ended the tax qualification of the Monarchy's electoral laws, but limited the suffrage to males over 21 who could read and write – only one Portuguese in four was literate at the start of the regime. By no means all of these bothered to register and rates of abstention in Lisbon always exceeded 50 per cent. From the Democrats' point of view the enfranchisement of women (allegedly susceptible to clerical influence), the urban lower orders (allegedly a prey to demagogy) or the rural masses (allegedly manipulable by reaction) was undesirable. People dependent on the apparatus of government voted for the party in power, almost always the Democrats, who also operated in the provinces through *influentes* and *caciques* (local notables and bosses) who became republicans to make sure nothing much changed. Thus the level of political mobilisation and popular involvement in government remained very low. When universal male suffrage was temporarily introduced by the 'Bonapartist' Sidónio Pais in 1918 the level of abstention among the enlarged electorate was still 40 per cent.

Given the need of the nascent Republic to absorb the liberal-conservative personnel of the Monarchist politico-administrative apparatus in order to survive, it is difficult to see how the Democrats could have embarked on a sweeping programme of reform of the social and economic structure to create a solid social basis of their own. In any case they did not want to for ideological as well as material reasons. The republicans were nationalists in the manner of French nineteenth-century republicans: what mattered was the absence of legal privileges, the semi-mystical sense of solidarity and fraternity between Portuguese and the freedom of the individual and private bodies from state intervention. As a token of its appreciation of the role played by workers in the republican movement and revolution, the new regime legalised the right to strike: the result was not, however, an increase in social harmony but a wave of strikes which reflected working-class disillusionment with the Republic as a harbinger of social reform in city or countryside. Since the number of industrial workers was quite small, Democratic governments saw such activities as sabotaging the new order and the solution of such conflicts principally as police matters. Arrests and the lack of significant social reform led to more violent attitudes on the part of workers whose unions became increasingly anarchosyndicalist-oriented. Deteriorating economic conditions led to a deepening of the chasm between government and unions, so that the UON (National Workers' Union, founded in 1914) adopted an attitude of benevolent neutrality to the anti-democratic takeover by Sidónio Pais in 1917. Nevertheless the confrontations, general strikes and violence continued and the UON's successor, the CGT (General Confederation of Labour, founded in 1919) affiliated to the Anarchist International Association of Workers in 1924. Alienated from 'bourgeois' politics and the Democratic Republic, the CGT adopted a position of 'proletarian neutrality' towards the movement of 28 May 1926.

The opium which Afonso Costa provided for the increasingly frustrated PRP rank and file in 1911 – and which enabled him to come out on top in the leadership struggle – was anti-clericalism. Here, too, the inspiration came from France: clericalism, there was the enemy. Inspired by positivist ideals, PRP propaganda before 1910 had played on the dangers of clerical domination of the state, finding evidence of such a threat in the revival of Catholic organisation, in which Jesuits were prominent, during the last decade of the monarchy. With the new regime installed, eighteenth- and early nineteenth-century laws expelling the Jesuits and dissolving all other religious orders and confiscating their property were reintroduced, while religious teaching in schools was ended, the wearing of cassocks forbidden, and divorce and civil marriage permitted. The main attack came with Costa's decree-law of 20 April 1911 for the separation of the state from the churches, inspired in large part by the French Law of Separation of 1905. The aim was to put the Catholic Church in Portugal firmly under state control: all ecclesiastical property was nationalised; ecclesiastical discipline was to be the state's affair; cemeteries were secularised; many seminaries closed; acts of worship were to be approved by state employees, and priests were not to sit on parish committees and were to become state servants. Costa's intention was to remove any international clerical influence in the new Portugal and clear the way for the progressive and natural withering away of religion before the advance of science and reason.

Elated though anti-clerical republicans might be, the law in fact proved counterproductive in as much as it further stimulated a revival of religious feeling and brought about an increased sense of urgency among Catholics concerning the problems of building up the organisational structures of religion. Far from bringing greater unity to the nation, it divided society by reinforcing political and ideological divisions, further alienating the populations of the north, centre and Islands from the leadership of Lisbon. The Pope and episcopate refused to co-operate and counselled passive resistance to the law, but acceptance of the republican regime as such. Bishops were exiled from their dioceses; four out of five priests refused to be paid by the state or accept lay control and government agents found themselves faced by hostile demonstrations when trying to enforce the law, the more sweeping provisions of which indeed proved unenforceable. From 1915 onwards there was a gradual retreat by the secular authorities from the position of 1911. In 1918 relations with the Vatican were resumed and the most offensive parts of the law repealed. Though church and state seemed to be moving towards a *rapprochement* by 1926, the tough content of the law of 1911 unnecessarily alienated a large part of the population from the Democratic Republic and played its part in stimulating a reaction against the regime.

If the First Republic failed to regenerate the country politically and socially, the same conclusion must be reached in the material sphere. The regime, however, cannot itself necessarily be held fully responsible for the way things turned out. Portugal was a poor country with slender financial resources and the need to put the national finances in order meant that the implementation of grandiose plans was impossible. Though the Republic switched its priorities to such things as education (for good national citizenship) from the stress on public works in the last years of the monarchy, the number of illiterates declined only from 75 per cent in 1911 to 68 per cent in 1930. From the point of view of expenditure, the decision of Portugal to enter the First World War on the Allied side in 1916 was disastrous, just as were the effects of the war on many aspects of the economy. These factors, combined with the chronic political instability, led to widespread dissatisfaction and exacerbated social conflicts, even though there were signs of improvement from 1923. The foreign trade deficit rose from £6·9 million in 1910 to £16·94 in 1926; the budget deficit, £60 million in 1910–11, stood at £1,281 in 1925–6; the rate of exchange of the escudo, 4·85 to the £ in 1911, was 113·03 in 1925. The cost-of-living index soared from 100 in 1914 to 2,286·4 in 1925, but by 1925 agricultural and factory wages in real terms had moved slightly ahead (indices of 2,682·7 and 2,330 respectively). Salaries of public employees fared less well: in the higher grades their purchasing power in 1925 was around 45 per cent of what it had been in 1914 and in the middle grades around 57 per cent.

The Democratic Party retained its dominance over political life in the First Republic until the end: it brought down General Pimenta de Castro's regime in 1915, blocked Sidónio Pais's attempt to found a New Republic in 1918 and helped foil an attempt to restore the monarchy in 1919. However, as the 1920s progressed, the Democratic grip was loosening, partly through the growth of opposition and partly through factional rivalries leading to more and more departures. In the Parliament of 1919 the Democrats had 122 seats to other groups' 112; in that of 1921 they were in a minority (76 seats to 141 – they had not held power at the time of the election); in that of 1922 they had 111 to various other groups' 115 and in that of 1925, 119 seats to the others' 99. The opposition groups were formed mostly from dissidents from the PRP who quarrelled among themselves and it was not until 1925 that many of them got together to form a conservative group, PNR (Republican Nationalist Party), while others moved off to the left of the Democrats to form a socialistic group influenced by the ideas of progressive intellectuals associated with the publication *Seara Nova*. In addition there was an uneasy coalition of royalists in the Monarchist Cause (*Causa Monárquica*) and a small Catholic Centre loyal to the constituted regime but hostile to the anti-clerical laws.

Probably the most important developments were, however, extra-parliamentary. A broader spectrum of the officer corps became more involved in politics and saw the armed forces as the harbinger of national salvation, whose duty it was to clean up political life and oppose self-seeking politicians, though this did not mean that political alliances were shunned. Sections of the officer corps, like the PNR, were much impressed by new trends abroad, notably by General Primo de Rivera's takeover in Spain in 1923. Some, particularly junior officers, were also susceptible to new creeds which seemed to have captured the hearts and minds of university youth. Just as from 1890 to 1910 the educated younger generation had manifested their generational conflict by opposition to the old men of the monarchy and espousal of neo-Jacobin republican ideas of nationalism, so in the 1920s younger Portuguese were catching up with the sea-change that had overtaken their French counterparts twenty years earlier. Now university activists were against the republic and democracy and for a new and integral version of authoritarian and Catholic nationalism influenced by Barrès, Maurras and other French rightists. The tide of Democratic and republican nationalism had ebbed; integral nationalism was to be the creed of the new postwar world. This change in fashion regarding political values was probably, given the small size of the Portuguese élite, the most important factor undermining the Democratic Republic.

The source of this new creed was a group of intellectuals – notably António Sardinha, Luís de Almeida Braga, Alberto Monsaraz, Hipólito Raposo and José Pequito Rebelo – who in 1913–14 set about reinvigorating Portuguese nationalism along traditionalist, illiberal and monarchist lines under the label of Lusitanian Integralism. Like Maurras, they believed that only a dynasty could provide the continuity for and transcend the centrifugal tendencies of the nation; however, the king must rule as well as reign in the manner of the pre-liberal age: to restore the liberal monarchy which fell in 1910 would be no solution to national problems. The Integralists were social and political romantics seeking to apply aesthetics to national government and were motivated by the myth that all would be well if Portugal could only return to its traditions of corporative socio-economic organisation, if religion and the sanctity of the family could again become the basis of national life. They set out, like their French counterparts, to convert the élite, particularly the young, to their doctrines as the surest path to national regeneration, while also taking part in any attempt to overthrow the Democratic Republic. Their conception of national-traditionalist monarchy represented the new Sebastianism; the exiled Manuel II, who remained basically loyal to liberal-constitutional ideas of his role, seemed never convincingly to fit the part they wrote for him and thus their sympathies tended to lie with the rival Miguelist branch of the House of Braganza, ousted in the 1830s and headed from 1920 by the young Dom Duarte Nuno, The monarchist movement, indeed, was always split: should Manuel or the Miguelist claimant be king? Should the pre-1910 constitution be restored or an authoritarian or traditionalist regime be installed? Should the monarchy return by *coup de force* or by legalist and democratic methods? In 1926 these questions remained unresolved, but the basic ideas of Integralism, positive and negative, had nevertheless taken firm root among the young. A review edited by a Lisbon law student, Marcelo Caetano, and called *Ordem Nova*, appeared in 1926 as if to epitomise the growing trend among the best minds of the younger generation: it proclaimed itself 'anti-modern, anti-liberal, anti-democratic, anti-bourgeois and anti-Bolshevik . . . ; counter-revolutionary and reactionary; Catholic, Apostolic and Roman; monarchist, intolerant and intransigent . . .'.

The Democratic Republic was brought to an end by the movement of 28 May, subsequently known as the National Revolution, though not all who took part in the *coup* did so to inaugurate an anti-republican or anti-democratic new order, but simply to oust António Maria da Silva's unpopular Democratic government which owed its existence to another triumph for the party's electoral machine in 1925. Opposition republicans of tendencies to the right and left of the Democrats saw military intervention as the only road to power, and ideas of a 'non-partisan' and 'national' government were widespread. Monarchists also obviously hoped that a military movement would pave the way for a restoration. For all these political tendencies, as for landowners and businessmen, who had recently founded a political party, the Union of Economic Interests, and who complained of social disorder and the activities of the anarchist-oriented trade unions campaigning for a six-hour day, the armed forces represented the real will of the nation and the quarter from which national salvation would come. In the officer corps, influenced by anti-Democratic feelings and foreign models such as Primo de Rivera's *pronunciamiento* of 1923, discontent was widespread despite a lavish but inappropriately spent military budget. The feeling that the officer corps itself should take over government to clean up public life as well as to end political interference in professional matters was particularly well developed among junior officers. Yet when General Gomes da Costa, the former commander of the Portuguese Expeditionary Corps in Flanders in the First World War, pronounced against the government in Braga on 28 May, there existed neither military nor civilian unity within the movement.

As usual, the aim of the conspirators was to announce that they had revolted against the government in the national interest and then trust that their preparations in various garrisons would not be upset by opponents. With the government deprived of military support the conspirators then counted on its rapid capitulation with the minimum of bloodshed. In fact no one rallied to the government side, for the key Lisbon garrisons were already dominated by the conspirators. However, the President of the Republic, Bernardino Machado, on 30 May handed over power not to General Gomes da Costa, a republican figurehead for a conspiracy of authoritarian and even anti-republican tendencies, but to the leader of a rival branch of the conspiracy, Naval Commander Mendes Cabeçadas who was a staunch republican, indeed a hero of the revolution of October 1910.

Though the common aim of conspirators was to install a stable patriotic government, the divisions within the movement as to what sort of government led to two months of extreme instability. With the Lisbon garrisons under the influence of the main pro-monarchist strand in the movement, headed by General Sinel de Cordes (who had led an unsuccessful *coup* in April 1925 and was ideologically close to the authoritarian-minded junior officers) Mendes Cabeçadas formed a duumvirate with Gomes da Costa on 1 June in the hope of turning the movement away from the dangers of authoritarianism and monarchism. However, it was Sinel de Cordes and the junior officers who were in key positions and they found an ally in a late adherent, General Carmona, Commander of the Southern Military Region. On 17 June, Mendes Cabeçadas was ousted, dealing a serious blow to the proponents of conservative republicanism such as the rising political star Cunha Leal, leader of the Republican Liberal Union (ULR) of which Cabeçadas was a member. Now Gomes da Costa seemed to be on top, but he was unpredictable and suffered from amnesia. After clashes in Cabinet he was removed from office and exiled to the Azores (returning with the rank of marshal before his death in 1929). On 9 July the non-partisan but Catholic General Óscar Carmona emerged as Head of Government and War Minister, with Sinel de Cordes as Finance Minister. With the administration in the hands of the military, especially pro-monarchist junior officers, and with Cabeçadas and Gomes da Costa ousted, it seemed that a monarchist restoration might be the next step. However, quite apart from monarchist political disunity, the need to appease republican sections of the officer corps and republican feeling in the country ruled out an immediate restoration. Carmona was respected by most factions and, while as Head of Government he was courted by both monarchists and republicans, as War Minister he could see that a balance was kept in the armed forces. The pragmatic 57-year-old soldier had become the new 'non-partisan' situation.

The new situation, with, in the view of some republicans, its threat of an eventual restoration of the monarchy, did not go uncontested. The constitution of 1911 had been suspended, censorship introduced and some concessions made on the religious question with a view to nationalising the republic, but on 3 February 1927 the Oporto garrison under General Sousa Dias, who had opposed the 28 May *coup,* revolted, a movement seconded by naval and police units in Lisbon. The government's determination not to give way was shown in its use of artillery and air power. Its victory over this civilian and military attempt to go back to the Democratic Republic came after six days of fighting which left 120 dead and 650 wounded. In fact, despite this outbreak, the armed forces remained basically united and many republicans still supported the government. Integralist monarchists impatient for a restoration still had the dynastic schism to contend with, but this did not prevent some of them envisaging a *coup de main,* a threat which the government squashed by preventive action in August 1927. Many monarchist hopes centred however on General Sinel de Cordes, the Finance Minister and chief organiser of 28 May, but these were dashed by his fall in prestige. He had set out to improve the country's financial situation, but state expenditure instead rose by 40 per cent from 1925-6 to 1926-7, while the budget deficit increased 38 per cent in the same financial years. He had to seek a foreign loan, but bankers insisted, partly because of the continuing political uncertainty, that a condition be League of Nations' supervision of the national finances. Feeling against such international control and disillusion with Sinel de Cordes was widespread, even within the ranks of the original conspirators, and so General Carmona removed him from office in April 1928. The question of which political tendency would come out on top after all the infighting and manœuvring remained open.

Meanwhile it was thought necessary to give the military dictatorship a less *ad hoc* appearance and the minds of the military leadership and its civilian advisers turned back to the presidentialist ideas of Sidónio Pais's New Republic of 1918, under which they had served. From 1927 the government began to organise its supporters into a rudimentary political organisation loyal to 28 May and on 25 March 1928 the Head of Government was the only candidate in a poll, conducted on a system of direct universal male suffrage, for the vacant presidency of the republic. General António Óscar de Fragoso Carmona was naturally elected in what was designed as a plebiscite to give democratic legitimacy to the new situation: 761,730 votes were cast in his favour.

In fact the continuation of the republican form of government, whatever its content might be, was now assured. Colonel José Vicente de Freitas, known to be staunchly republican, was entrusted with the premiership in April 1928 and the most pressing problem now seemed financial rather than political. The role of economic Sebastian was to be filled by a widely respected Catholic Professor of Political Economy from Coimbra, António de Oliveira Salazar, who had been publicly critical of Sinel de Cordes, and who now agreed to take the Finance Ministry only on his own terms: that he would have full control over the expenditure of all government ministries. This condition was accepted and his prestige rose when the 1928-9 budget envisaged a surplus, the first since 1913-14. His budget balancing was initially achieved not just through increasing revenue through higher taxation imposed by a political dictatorship, but also by a change in book-keeping methods which the League of Nations' statisticians found unacceptable and his opponents considered sleight of hand: pluri-annual items of expenditure were moved from 'ordinary' to 'extraordinary' expenditure. Nevertheless morale rose as the financial situation genuinely improved and Salazar took on an increasingly messiah-like quality in the political sphere for those seeking a more permanent solution than military dictatorship – and these included Carmona.

Salazar remained as financial dictator as governments came and went.

In July 1929 he backed his old friend Mário de Figueiredo over a minor rectification of the anti-clerical laws, with the result that Carmona appointed General Ivens Ferraz as Premier. In January 1930 came the showdown as to who was to mastermind future policies. Salazar's main rival was the ULR leader Cunha Leal, a man of ambition and talent who had hoped at 38 to come out on top after 28 May. The pro-monarchists who held the initiative in 1926–7 had kept him out because of his republicanism, but the appointment of Vicente de Freitas had been seen by some as improving his political prospects. After the 1929 crisis it seemed that the pro-Salazar tide, which liberal-conservative republicans like Cunha Leal saw as too reactionary even though they themselves wanted religious reconciliation and corporativism, had to be stemmed at all costs. A military *coup* – the last one attempted had been in July 1928 – was no longer a possibility, so Cunha Leal attacked Salazar for being lukewarm on imperial issues and giving insufficient priority to expenditure in Angola. The Premier, Ivens Ferraz, sided with the Cunha Leal line in Cabinet, with the result that Salazar resigned. Carmona and others by now saw Salazar as essential to any government: an effort to get the latter and Cunha Leal to work together under Colonel Passos e Sousa failed, so that General Domingos de Oliveira's government of 21 January 1930 marked a triumph for Salazar over a political rival he feared, for he was now Colonial as well as Finance Minister. Having failed to turn the movement of 28 May in his direction, Cunha Leal went into what was to be lifelong opposition, writing of Salazar in 1930: 'To try to turn this hypochondriac, this voluntarily castrated monk, into a statesman . . . is more of a danger than an absurdity.'

Nevertheless, given disunity among monarchist leaders and the discrediting of liberal-conservative rivals, Salazar more and more came to incarnate the political as well as the financial solution for the nation and command the allegiance of most of the nationalist younger generation in both armed forces and public life. Armed revolts were no more successful than political manoeuvring in trying to remove him or the dictatorship. In April 1931 there were revolts in the Adjacent Islands and from May 1931, encouraged by the overthrow of the Spanish monarchy (April 1931) and its replacement by a republican-socialist government. Opposition forces, including Admirals Mendes Cabeçadas and Tito de Morais, set out to create a single front, the Republican-Socialist Alliance, under a former war minister of the First Republic, General Norton de Matos. They were not allowed legal rights, however. As usual in such a situation, force was seen as the alternative but the civilian-military revolt staged in Lisbon on 26 August was suppressed. On 5 July 1932, after the collective resignation of Domingos de Oliveira's government, and three days after the death of the exiled King Manuel II in London, Salazar became the first civilian Premier since 28 May: the military dictatorship was about to be transformed into the New State.

The man who as Premier (President of the Council of Ministers) was to be the effective ruler of Portugal from 1932 to 1968 was born on 28 April 1889 in a cottage in the hamlet of Vimieiro near Santa Comba Dão (Beira Alta), the only son of Catholic parents. His father divided his time between the family plot and being the agent of a local landowner while his mother, the dominant influence on him, ran the local café. At the age of 11 he entered the seminary at Viseu, where he was noted for fastidiously sticking to the rules, reading a lot and being bored by games. He took minor orders but did not proceed to the priesthood, going instead to the university at Coimbra in 1910, where he studied law and economics and in 1918 became Professor of Political Economy. As a student he was active in the CADC (Academic Centre of Christian Democracy), a non-partisan group founded in 1901–3 to propagate Catholic social doctrines and reconvert the élite, but not, as Salazar was later to emphasise, to propagate political democracy. He helped to revitalise the group, together with Father Gonçalves Cerejeira and Mário de Figueiredo, with whom he shared lodgings, during the high tide of republican anti-clericalism. Loyal to the church and an ardent follower of the hierarchy, he accepted the republic as the established system of government without ever declaring himself a republican. He was active, too, in the CCP (Portuguese Catholic Centre), a group started in 1915 to intervene in politics in defence of the church, being elected Deputy for Guimarães in the short-lived Congress of 1921. Within the CCP he defended the papal policy of *ralliement* after 1919 against monarchists. In 1918 he had declined to become Secretary of State for Finance under Sidónio Pais, but was for a few days Minister of Finance in Mendes Cabeçadas's post-28 May government in 1926.

Undoubtedly the dominant influence on Salazar was Thomism and from this he derived his basic ideas on the nature of society, corporative organisation and distributive social justice. Papal encyclicals, especially Leo XIII's *Rerum Novarum* (1891) and Pius XI's *Quadragesimo Anno* (1931), were taken as guidelines for the building of a Christian society. However, the clarity and logic of Maurras's writings also had a strong influence on him, appealing, it is said, to his cold personality and his sense of always being in the right, even though, like others, he was to relegate the need for monarchy to a secondary level and follow the church in condemning the primacy of politics over religion. The Christian regeneration of Portuguese society was always his aim, but the practical examples of the brief administration of João Franco and Sidónio Pais also attracted him. It may also be noted that the CADC before 1910 had links with, and the CCP of 1915 was in part a continuation of, the Nationalist Party founded in 1903, which, under the slogan 'Country and

Religion', had also sought the regeneration of Portugal through the application of Christian social principles.

'I know quite well what I want and where I am going', said Salazar in 1928 on accepting the Ministry of Finance. The phrase perhaps reflected less a serene confidence in his own abilities than his determination to succeed, for fear of failure seems to have been something that haunted Salazar. The embitterment caused by his not being permitted to marry his patron's daughter was probably a factor which caused him to aim at even greater self-discipline, hard work and asceticism. His nervous temperament was something to be overcome by his own willpower. The outward modesty was compensated internally by the conviction that he alone was right, yet in his early political career he was unsure of his capacity to demonstrate the fact in practice. Revealing of the tensions which plagued him was his later account of accepting the Ministry of Finance in April 1928: 'I hesitated all night . . . I was afraid. I foresaw the possibility of failure. Imagine, if I had failed to put the finances in order, what would my students have thought of me?' Once fully engaged in public life there could be no going back: only by going on to do more and more, which entailed acquiring more and more power, could he prove his abilities to others, which meant also to himself. Criticism always seemed difficult for him to take, as if it raised his own buried doubts about himself, and opposition, whether in politics or manifested in petty personal disagreements with old friends, seemed to reveal a paranoid streak in him. Somewhat delicate in health as a young man, his strong emotions and frustrations were constantly repressed for fear others might think him weak or unstable. It seemed as if inner insecurity corresponded to his love of order, *his* order, the imposition of which would free him and the nation from anxiety. His political rival, Cunha Leal, saw him as a 'hermetic man . . . with a tendency to austere severity . . . , a model of the good professors of the bygone days of *magister dixit*'.

When 'the saviour' came from Coimbra in 1928, he joined the government not as a member of the CCP but as an independent technocrat. It was clear from the first that his conception of putting the finances in order and reorganising economic life necessitated strong and stable government; therefore he was quickly airing his views on the best ways of bringing this *desideratum* about on a more permanent basis. Though Catholic social doctrine provided him with his general guidelines, it was Maurrassian organising empiricism rather than the French thinker's full-blown ideological blueprints which inspired him. For Salazar, as for many other supporters of 28 May, a return to the constitution of 1911 was out because such a move would make impossible any schemes for national regneration based on the minimal principles of order, authority, stability and continuity. It was necessary to be pragmatic in seeking a way out from the transitional military dictatorship, and it was necessary to hold together on essentials the reaction against the Democratic Republic represented by the movement of 28 May: integral nationalists, pragmatic military men, monarchists of various brands and republicans of varied liberal and conservative views.

Already, in October 1927, the government had approved the organisation of the civilian supporters of the military dictatorship in a national union, known as the League of 28 May, to co-ordinate political support and represent local interests. Like General Primo de Rivera's Patriotic Union in Spain, it was to be open to all men of goodwill; it was also to accept the disinterested collaboration of existing organisations (which at that time meant monarchist groups, the CCP and conservative republican parties). In October 1929 Salazar declared that 'the constitutional reorganisation of the state must rest on a stable, wise and conciliating nationalism, which will assure the existence and regular activity of all the national, traditional and progressive elements of our society, especially the family, ethical and economic institutions, the parish and the municipality'. In May 1930 he spoke of the need for 'a new constitution incorporating the nation within the state', and of 'the erroneous conception' of those who thought in terms of a purely administrative dictatorship without a political philosophy. In July 1930 he declared that 'it is our intention to establish the social and corporative state in close correlation with the natural constitution of society. The families, the parishes, the municipalities, the corporations wherein all citizens coexist in possession of their fundamental juridical liberties, are the organic components of the nation'. The new order he envisaged would be based on 'a moderate nationalism' and on 'the substitution of individualism, whether pure or tainted with socialism', by corporativism. 'In such a long speech . . . little was said regarding liberty, democracy and the sovereignty of the people, but a good deal about order, authority, discipline, social co-ordination, the nation and the State. This is quite true . . . ; there are certain expressions and ideas which have been used so often and to such little purpose that they are now practically meaningless.' Salazar was not alone among Portuguese politicians in using opaque language, but the message, that he and his associates had power and intended to keep it, was clear.

This speech of 30 July 1930 came to be known as the Manifesto of the National Union, the UN (National Union) being the political coalition in support of the increasingly Salazarist situation officially approved a year later, not as 'a political party', but as an 'independent political association of the state'. In December 1931 a National Political Council, consisting of right-wing civilians (including Salazar) and military men, was created to advise on the new constitution, administrative and electoral codes and the 'organisation of the corporative regime of the state'. The draft of the constitution appeared on 28 May 1932, but with Salazar as Premier a new version was concocted which showed a further swing away from liberalism and towards corporativism. This shift was epitomised by the wording of one article: No. 6 of the 1932 document read: 'The Portuguese state adopts the respresentative and democratic republic as its form of government', but No. 5 of the 1933 document stated: 'The Portuguese state is a corporative and unitary republic.'

The constitution of the New State was put to the vote in a plebiscite on 19 March in which heads of families formed the electorate, it being previously decreed that abstentions would be counted as votes in favour. 1,214,159 electors were registered (by no means all entitled to did or were allowed to), and of these 719,364 voted in favour (to which were added the 488,840 abstentions), while 5,955 voted against. After this exercise in popular legitimation, the constitution officially came into force on 11 April 1933. Together with the Colonial Act of 1930 and the National Labour Statute of September 1933, it provided the formal framework for political, social and economic life. Since Salazar's primary aim was the regeneration and corporative organisation of social and economic life, the constitutional provisions with which we are here concerned represented only the political superstructure of a more profound socio-economic policy. Political superstructures, however, have a habit of determining much more than purely political life.

The constitutional text, which drew on sources as disparate as the constitutional charter of the monarchy, the constitution of 1911 (and Sidónio Pais's presidentialist and semi-corporativist modifications to that document), the Weimar Constitution of 1919, and the experience of the military dictatorship with its social-Catholic and authoritarian nationalist corporativist trends, was a compromise between liberal and corporativist principles. The Portuguese Nation was defined as 'an independent state, whose sovereignty only recognises morality and law as its bounds in the internal sphere' (Article 4), while Article 5 defined the state as 'a corporative and unitary republic, based on the equality of citizens before the law, on the free access of all classes to the benefits of civilisation and on the intervention of all the nation's structural elements in administrative life and law making'. Article 6 said it was the state's function 'to promote the moral unity' of the nation, 'to co-ordinate, stimulate and direct all social activities, causing a just harmony of interests to prevail within the legitimate subordination of particular interests to the general', and 'to take care of the betterment of conditions of the least favoured social classes, preventing these conditions falling below the minimum for a humanly adequate existence'. Among the 'individual rights and guarantees' of the citizen were listed freedom of worship, freedom of expression, education, choice of job, freedom from arbitrary imprisonment, freedom of association and meeting, the right to resist orders infringing the individual's guarantees etc. – but the same Article 8 went on to say that these freedoms and rights would be regulated by 'special laws'. Section III of the text stressed the defence of the family as an institution, while Article 20 stated that it was the state's function to defend public opinion from 'all the factors that turn it from truth, justice, good administration and the common good'. Military service was to be obligatory (as under the First Republic – Article 54), while the state undertook to 'promote, protect and help civilian institutions whose purpose is to train and discipline the youth to prepare it for the fulfilment of its patriotic and military duties'. These general provisions were a mixture of pious hopes and phrases susceptible to sinister interpretations.

In Part II the Head of State, National Assembly, government and courts were defined as the organs of national sovereignty. The President of the Republic was to serve for seven years and be 'elected by the nation', i.e. by direct popular suffrage. However, after the near fiasco of the 1958 presidential campaign, presidents of the republic from 1959 were chosen by an electoral college of members of both parliamentary chambers, plus delegates from each *distrito* and the overseas provinces. In theory at least, the President of the Republic was the man with the power for he could appoint and dismiss his President of the Council of Ministers (Premier). He was advised by a ten-man Council of State which included the Premier and also five presidential nominees, appointed for life.

The government consisted of a Council of Ministers individually responsible to the Premier (President of the Council) and its function was to govern (under the President of the Republic) regardless of votes in the National Assembly. The National Assembly was elected by popular suffrage every four years and consisted of 90 deputies, a number raised to 120 in 1945, 130 in 1959 and 150 in 1971; its function was to make, interpret and repeal legislation, vote the annual budget and generally act as a watchdog. Since no opposition deputies were ever elected, its functions may in practice be described as honorific. The second chamber, the Corporative Chamber, was a technical advisory body on legislation, consisting of *procuradores* – usually around 150 – representing local government bodies, branches of public administration and the moral, cultural and economic corporations. Since, as will subsequently be explained, most of the organisms to be represented there were never created or never functioned properly, the Corporative Chamber was in essence an amalgam of committees of government-appointed specialists. The judiciary represented another factor in the balance of powers but, though it enjoyed theoretical independence, its personnel were in practice subject to the prevailing 'situation' and, of course, it could only carry out the laws which others decreed.

With a strong executive – on paper the President, but in practice under Salazar the Premier – and a legislature consisting only of government supporters, the political constitution turned out to be little more than the figleaf covering the nakedness of authority. Special laws and the political atmosphere of the regime suppressed such liberal features as the constitution embodied. Essentially it represented the continuation of dictatorship by other means. Carmona was willing to play William I to Salazar's Bismarck, while the revision of the constitution in 1959 created a vicious circle in which the President of the Republic became a nominee of the existing government representatives.

The constitution of 1933, it may be noted, reflected both the strengthening of Salazar's position and the shifting to the right of the centre of gravity of the coalition of forces supporting 28 May. It came too at a time when liberal and democratic ideals were in retreat in most parts of Europe and authoritarianism of one brand or another seemed to be the spirit of the age. The only legal political-civic association in the New State was the UN, which began in 1930–1 as the political support organisation of the situation. It was a body which selected lists of candidates for the National Assembly, but it never had any constitutional status. Its statutes were officially approved in May 1932 and in November 1932 Premier Salazar himself became President of its Central Committee. According to the Minister of the Interior, Albino dos Reis (a one-time follower of Cunha Leal), the UN was incompatible with the party political spirit and acted in the service of the community; no groups were to be recognised within it nor parties outside it. A member of its consultative committee denied, however, that it was a 'combat group; it is an organisation of nationalist and patriotic defence aiming at putting the nation on the side of the state and not against the state'. The spokesman of the declining liberal current in the 28 May coalition, General Vicente de Freitas (who had brought Salazar to the Finance Ministry), a critic of anti-individualist tendencies in the Salazarist constitution, pointed out that, contrary to the verbiage of its members, it was 'precisely what was always called, and must be called, a political party'. The hegemony of the UN was likely to be worse than that of the Democrats as their former *de facto* monopoly of power would now be replaced by the UN's *de jure* monopoly. Vicente de Freitas was promptly dismissed as president of the Lisbon municipal administration.

If Salazar's victory over the old conservative republican tendency now seemed secure, there remained Catholic and monarchist political bodies. Salazar's speech to the UN on 23 November 1932 made it plain that these bodies were now superfluous. The CCP, whose leaders included close friends of Salazar, dutifully wound itself up. The Monarchist Cause was still in existence but was in a state of confusion after the death of the childless Manuel in July, many members not wishing to accept the succession of Duarte Nuno (of the Miguelist branch) who had come of age in 1927. Like the CCP, the Monarchist Cause (and Manuel) had advocated support for Salazar, putting aside the question of regime. After Salazar had given Manuel a state funeral, a similar attitude prevailed. Some monarchists saw Salazar as the instrument of an eventual restoration, but in November 1932 Salazar's reference to Manuel leaving 'no descendants, no successors' made it clear that he was not going to upset republicans' or indeed some monarchists' feelings by bringing in Duarte Nuno. The final estrangement with the monarchist Integralists backing the banished claimant came in November 1933 with the nationalisation of the House of Braganza's property. The Central Committee of Lusitanian Integralism had dissolved itself a little earlier, still attacking monarchists who accepted the republic. Afterwards most of the old Integralist leaders moved into opposition, though their rank-and-file following had already decided that the national cause was best served by a career in the higher echelons of the New State. On the whole the anti-republican activists of the younger generation decided with Salazar that there were more important things than a restoration, which would create more problems and divisions than it would solve: 'the crux of the matter is not dependent on external forms, but on a true conception of authority, of government, as well as of the organisation of the powers of the state', was how Salazar expressed this view.

However, there were Integralists who gave rather more trouble for a time, attracting students – and some army officers – to a more dynamic brand of nationalist revolution. The Integralists Rolão Preto and the Count of Monsaraz were the leaders of the blue-shirted ONS (National-Syndicalist Organisation) which emerged in 1932. Paralleling Georges Valois's earlier evolution from Maurrassism to fascism, they sought to attract the young to a violent and 'anti-bourgeois' nationalist revolution: 'the National Revolution of the Workers' was to be the work of a 'structurally and permanently revolutionary' ONS. Identifying themselves in a European context with early Italian fascism or the radical face of nazism, and equating Salazar with the ill-fated Austrian Christian social leader Seipel, they sought to propagate a violent and radical mystique; stating that 'only totalitarian formulas succeed in inflaming the peoples', 'the New State belongs to the young', 'throughout the old land of Europe there resounds the ceaselessly growing new rhythm, the virile and indomitable rhythm of the Nationalist Revolution on the march'. For them Salazar was 'a man of the centre' whose rational and academic language and style could never summon up the revolutionary spirit necessary to introduce 'organic syndicalism'. They were probably more of a nuisance than a threat for Salazar. Their paper *Revolução* was suspended in July 1933 and their propaganda banned.

There followed a split in the ONS, the less 'radically totalitarian' in 1934 deciding to join the UN to work for 'national grandeur', while Preto and Monsaraz were exiled. Preto returned in 1935 and his National-

Syndicalist followers joined military and other opposition elements in an unsuccessful *coup* to remove Salazar in September. Preto was left to muse on how in Portugal, as in Italy and Germany, the bourgeoisie had robbed the national revolution of its heroic idealism. Later he joined other opponents of the regime.

The National-Syndicalist episode proved an aid towards the classification of the New State as a conservative, authoritarian, bureaucratic regime rather than as a radical, totalitarian, fascist one. Just as in Vichy France, Horthy's Hungary, King Carol's Romania or the Austria of Dollfuss and Schuschnigg, the national revolution took on some of the language, style and outward trappings of fascism and the regime employed fascistic elements in subordinate positions; but despite the anti-democratic sentiments of the younger generation, it was the old élite which retained political and social control and used the existing state apparatus as its principal instrument. In Portugal, unlike Germany or Italy, the aim of the regime was depoliticisation rather than mass mobilisation within a single party seeking completely to identify with or to transcend the state.

A disinclination to bestow the fascist label on the New State is not intended to suggest that the system was not authoritarian or completely untouched by developments elsewhere. Salazar coined the Mussoliniesque slogan 'Nothing against the nation. All for the nation!' as early as 1929; the National Labour Statute owed much to Italian experience; Roman salutes were often used; and in the 1930s Salazar kept a photo of Mussolini on his desk. Nevertheless Italian fascism, with its statolatry, was 'pagan Caesarism'. Salazar's aim was not the 'deification of the state', but 'a strong state'. 'We wish to organise and strengthen the country by means of principles of authority, order, and national tradition in harmony with those eternal verities which are happily the inheritance of humanity and the sustenance of Christian civilisation'; the aim was 'perfect unity' without 'an exclusive totalitarianism'. Yet strong states needed strong governments not dependent on parliamentary votes or changes in public opinion: 'opposition parties . . . are things of the past . . . There is no place for them within our political system.' 'Portuguese nationalism is the indestructible bedrock of the New State', said Salazar; 'we are anti-parliamentarians, anti-democrats, anti-liberals . . . We are opposed to all forms of internationalism, communism, socialism, syndicalism . . . We are against class warfare, irreligion and disloyalty to one's country . . . We are antagonistic to all the great heresies of today.' 'To govern', he added on another occasion, 'is to protect people from themselves.'

The means by which Salazar protected people from themselves varied from the inherited to the innovatory. For the routine business of day-to-day administration his government could rely on the apparatus of the bureaucracy and a centralised system of government. Portuguese methods of bureaucratic administration had been modelled on the centralised system of revolutionary and Napoleonic France since the 1830s. This system, in which orders came from above and which allowed no initiatives at the lower levels, may be called, as in France, Italy or Spain, authoritarian. The system would hardly change even if the personnel adapted to the changed situation as they had to previous changes of regime and governments. Centralised governmental control of local government – 'the local autarchies' as they are called – was, if anything, tightened up after 1926. The basic and ancient unit of local government was the *concelho* (council), administered by the president of the municipality (*câmara municipal*) who was often government-appointed. The *concelhos* were themselves formed from a number of *freguesias* (or parishes) whose committees (*juntas*) were elected by heads of households – though in practice they were usually appointed by the president of the muncipality. The *concelhos* were grouped into provinces, administered by councils, while the government retained more direct control over local life through its appointment of civil governors of the *distritos*. Whatever elective elements there were supposed to be in the system were in practice nullified by centralised bureaucratic control coupled with the influence of local notables and their hangers-on (*influentes* and *caciques*) who participated in the UN. A further dimension of the generalised system of client-patron relationships must be added, for under the New State as under other regimes individuals needed a *cunha* (wedge) within the system in order not to lose out completely, and this method of operation led to the exertion of covert moral pressure. Given the increasing rigidity of the governmental system in the widest sense, it is possible that such limited bargaining power as clients at the lower end of the scale once enjoyed effectively disappeared.

Apart from using the existing authoritarian state apparatus and getting the most out of the patronage system, the Salazarist government also had at its disposal the forces of law and order which it had inherited, namely, armed forces and police. The police consisted of the ordinary PSP (Police of Public Safety) and the GNR (Republican National Guard), the former chiefly urban, the latter a chiefly rural *gendarmerie*, both normally commanded by army officers. In the last resort, however, the regime depended on the armed forces which had brought it into being. Although there were occasional attempted *coups* and almost perennial conspiratorial talk within the officer corps, Salazar was never ousted by the armed forces. At first, in the 1930s, his success lay chiefly in keeping the military happy with flattery and sizeable military budgets. Most officers saw him as the best political solution; it was nice to hear from the civilian Premier that 'the army has the secret of perpetual youth, and like a great and ancient family of noble descent it maintains and passes on its traditions so unimpaired and alive that it always forms one and the same moral unity'. However, there was no particular reason, in view of Portugal's modern historical evolution, why military sentiment should not turn against him at a later stage; by such a later stage, however, the armed forces had lost some of the freedom of manœuvre that they had formerly enjoyed. After the enthusiasm of junior and many senior officers in the late 1920s and early 1930s for authoritarian solutions, the external threats posed by the Spanish Civil War and the Second World War caused something of a patriotic closing of ranks and subordination of grievances and doubts.

By 1945 indirect civilian, i.e. regime, control over the armed forces had become more apparent. The years 1936–45 had seen the rise of para-military organisations which, though usually commanded by army officers, nevertheless detracted from the armed forces' monopoly of fire-power. The same period had also seen an intrusion of political considerations into the career structure, the dominant figure here being Colonel Fernando dos Santos Costa, a monarchist friend of Salazar from CADC days, who was successively Under-Secretary for War, War Minister and Defence Minister between 1936 and 1958 (Salazar was himself War Minister from 1936 to 1944). These developments, together with the increasing activities of the PIDE (secret police) within the armed forces, tended to diminish any sense of supra-political *camaraderie* which existed and make expressions of opposition or conspiracy more difficult. It would be wrong, however, to suggest that the armed forces quite lost their sense of internal autonomy; the rewards for the loyal in promotion, sinecures and directorships also played their part in stifling dissension. Disillusioned officers thinking in terms of *coups* in the 1950s and 1960s found that such undertakings were not as easy to prepare as they had been three decades or so earlier. The growing civilian control over the armed forces was epitomised in Decree No. 25317 of May 1945 which allowed the government to dismiss officers for disloyalty to established institutions. Civilian control in a non-party regime meant that the possibility of its overthrow was decreased.

The most notorious repressive instrument of the regime was its secret police. Originating under the First Republic, when it was scarcely noticeable, the PVDE (Vigilance and State Defence Police) was really a creation of the 1930s when, in keeping with the usual mania for aping what was new abroad, German and Italian advice was sought in organising and training the force. The name was changed to PIDE (International and State Defence Police) in 1945 when its powers were legally defined by Decree Law No. 35042: the force was under the jurisdiction of the Minister of the Interior and was empowered to arrest and hold anyone without charge for three months, extendable to six months at the minister's discretion. By Decree Law No. 37447 a Council of Public Security was established, consisting of the heads of the PSP, GNR and PIDE, to co-ordinate police activities: the PIDE itself was always quite small in numbers, but relied on a large number of informers, at one time estimated at one person in ninety. In March 1956 (by Decree Law No. 40550) its powers were extended: imprisonment of detainees 'may be extended by successive periods of three years as long as they continue to show themselves dangerous . . . The indefinite nature of the imprisonment permits it to be said to the prisoner that it is in his hands to be free, which can be an effective means of stimulating salutary reactions in his mind.' The PIDE's victims were stated to be 'those who found associations, movements or groups of a communist nature, or who carry out activities of a subversive nature', to whom were added members of, or collaborators with, such groups, indeed any who 'follow their instructions, with or without prior agreement' or helped them in any way, including 'promoting their propaganda'. The powers were sweeping, even though they were rarely applied in full; the intention behind publicising them was to deter and to intimidate and, given the uncertainty as to who was or was not an informer, to create an atmosphere of institutionalised anxiety among opponents of the regime.

Like comparable institutions elsewhere, the PIDE's lower echelons included thugs, criminal elements and sadists while its leaders were sometimes men of education fanatically dedicated to their job. For hundreds of opponents of the regime there were deportation centres in the Azores and Timor, as well as a penal colony (or concentration camp) at Tarrafal in the Cape Verde Islands between 1936 and 1956 where inmates lived in appalling conditions and suffered beatings and punishments which sometimes led to their deaths (though the 1933 constitution kept the provision of the Civil Code of 1867 outlawing the death penalty). With headquarters in Lisbon, Oporto and Coimbra, the PIDE used as their main prisons Caxias, Aljube and Peniche. The interrogation of suspects could be accompanied by various forms of psychological and physical torture, notably being made to stand without sleep for days; death resulting from torture was not unknown. The purpose of all this was to counter subversion of the regime, and in particular to crack communist clandestine organisation; however PIDE activities also extended to enforcing the censorship, policing the work force and vetting people for jobs. Their modes of operation were discreet – very rarely were people assassinated – and this lack of visibility kept oppositionists in a constant state of fear and led to rumours of their efficiency and omnipresence which exceeded the reality: the *coup* of April 1974 cast considerable doubt on the witticism that 'in Portugal nothing works except the PIDE'. Among the politically active and the educated – and workers were generally worse treated than intellectuals – the myth as well as the reality of the PIDE was the key to the regime's survival. Shameful though the deeds of the PIDE were, the regime strove for what has been termed 'an optimum of terror rather than a crude maximum': in a small country in which rumour was a characteristic form of transmission of information, a relentless 'economy of terror' proved more effective than mass terror or recurrent bouts of large-scale purging. Nevertheless it must also be recorded the PIDE never affected the lives of most Portuguese and the existence of this state within a state was apparently unknown to many until April 1974.

The PIDE was not of course the only instrument which the New State gave itself for its self-preservation. Censorship is a very traditional device for maintaining control and, as expected, the New State used it in a more systematic way than previous regimes. By a decree of July 1926 the military dictatorship gave itself the power to suppress newspapers found guilty of defamation on three occasions. The key document in this respect was however Decree No. 22469 of 11 April 1933 which created censorship committees nominated by the government to operate a system of 'prior censorship' as a measure 'indispensable to a labour of reconstruction and moral cleansing'. Article 3 proclaimed 'the only purpose of the censorship will be to prevent the perversion of public opinion in its function of a social force'; it would be used to 'defend public opinion from any factors which may misguide it against truth, justice, morality, good administration and the common good, and to prevent the fundamental principles of the organisation of society being attacked'. This was followed by another decree (no. 23203 of 6 November 1933) which defined as 'crimes of rebellion committed by the press', punishable by fines, imprisonment or deportation to the colonies, attacks on the established system of government or on members of the government, incitement to strike, spreading rumours prejudicial to the regime etc. The system of censorship was designed principally to muzzle the press. 'Newspapers', said Salazar, 'are the spiritual food of the people, and, like all foods, must be controlled', but it was extended to cover other communications media such as the theatre, cinema, radio and television. It was not extended to books, but these could be taken off the market on police instructions and their authors and publishers punished. Attempts were also made to ban foreign books and periodicals.

The extent to which the system was enforced and the rigour with which regulations were applied varied from censor to censor and from area to area. In this respect its operations were like those of the PIDE, haphazard and unpredictable, which meant that it was all the more effective. As the distinguished historian, Oliveira Marques, has explained:

> The ultimate consequences of a censorship extended for so long a period [forty years] were to self-discipline authors, journalists, impresarios, and all those concerned with public media, and to force upon them a self-censorship, in order to avoid having their production constantly

harassed and mutilated. This self-censorship has often led to extremes of caution with little real justification. It has also led to the rise of a highly original crypto-writing on the part of authors and to a sharp understanding on the part of readers and listeners. Another obvious result for the public was a hypercriticism of everything and a widespread doubt of what was read and said.

The press remained in private hands and, in addition to the official broadcasting network (Emissora Nacional/Rádio-Televisão Portuguesa) there were private commercial and religious radio stations (Rádio Clube Português, Rádio Renascença). Authors naturally found the repressive system stifling; the communist novelist Alves Redol just before his death in 1969 compared it to 'intellectual solitary confinement. They never allowed me to write down what I wanted to say.' On the other hand, as an opposition newspaperman remarked, censors and journalists came to be on cordial terms through habit, 'like the prisoner who gets used to his cell and his guards and jailers and who talks to them with familiarity'.

Just as censorship became more systematised than under preceding regimes, so the New State demanded formal displays of loyalty from public servants and sought to supervise the content of education more thoroughly for its own ends. By Law No. 1901 of 21 May 1935 all military and civilian employees of the state had to swear that they were not members of secret societies or clandestine organisations (e.g. Freemasons) and these societies and organisations were dissolved. Decree Law No. 25317 (May 1935) said that public employees (which included school and university teachers) showing 'a spirit of opposition to the fundamental principles of the political constitution, or who do not guarantee co-operation in achieving the higher aims of the state, will be suspended or retired . . . or . . . will be dismissed'. Decree Law No. 27003 threatened higher grades of public employees with the same fate 'if any of their respective officials or employees subscribe to subversive doctrines and it is ascertained that they did not use their authority or did not inform their superiors'. Thus the New State suspended a legal sword of Damocles over all its employees, and dissidents were sacked – for example, purges of university teaching staff occurred in 1936, 1946–7 and 1962.

No educational system is, of course, entirely value-free. Under the First Republic the idea of education for good citizenship prevailed as in the Third French Republic; the ideals of the state educational system could be described as 'humanitarian', laicist and republican. With the advent of the New State there was the usual change of approved textbooks and the stress was shifted towards more traditionalist indoctrination incorporating the imperial and Catholic outlook. Primary school reading primers pointed out to 7-year-olds that C stood for Carmona as well as other things, while Decree No. 27279 declared that 'elementary primary education would betray its mission were it to continue to place a sterile, rationalist Encyclopaedism, fatal to the moral and physical health of the child, above the practical and Christian ideal of teaching well how to read, write and add up and how to practise the moral virtues and a lively love of Portugal'. One pre-war Director of Secondary Education announced: 'The school's mission now can only be the creation of a single, holy, Catholic, universal and personal method of comprehending and developing this temporal life as a function of and preparation for eternal life. The opposite of this, at once the door to treason and the way to the abyss, was the foreignisation of education in Portugal.' To spare any embarrassment, university history syllabuses stopped at the Napoleonic invasion. When António Sérgio sought to apply his 'pedagogy of criticality' to the regime's official historiography, this was termed 'opposition politics': the nationalist-traditionalist interpretation was the only one acceptable. As Álvaro Ribeiro, leader of a pro-regime school of philosophy, put it: 'We can do without modern philosophy.' Perhaps because they themselves had been rebels against the establishment as students, the political élite of the New State were fully aware of the appeal which new ideas could have for the young. The only antidote they knew, it seems, was a heavy dose of educational indoctrination combined with cultural isolation; as in other places at other times, so in Portugal it became clear in the postwar years that there was no cure for the disease.

Changing the content of education, insisting on outward compliance with 'the situation' and hunting down 'subversives' were not, however, in the 1930s thought to be sufficient. What may be described as the fascist vertigo was felt in Portugal as in other countries and so fascistic trappings were added to life in the New State, trappings introduced at least in part to provide an outlet for the dynamic feelings of many Portuguese of school and university age, who might otherwise have found the regime rather boring and insufficiently modern in its outlook. One outlet for the energies of the dynamisers, as well as being another instrument of politico-social control in the armoury of the political élite, was the official youth movement, the *Mocidade Portuguesa,* founded in October 1936 to give reality to Article 56 of the constitution. Dependent on the Ministry of National Education, it was a compulsory organisation for schoolchildren and university students to 'stimulate the integral development of their physical capacities, the formation of their character and devotion to country, through the feeling for order, the taste for discipline and military duty'. The *Mocidade* succeeded AEV (*Acção Escolar Vanguarda*), set up in 1934 to be a vanguard for the New State composed of 'frankly revolutionary' youths. The *Mocidade* took over from the AEV its dark green shirts and Roman salutes. Belt buckles included a large S which stood for the motto *Servir* (but could also be taken to mean Salazar) and meetings began with the catechistic ritual usual in such organisations: 'Portuguese, who lives?' 'Portugal! Portugal! Portugal!' 'Portuguese, who leads us?' 'Salazar! Salazar! Salazar!' Originally compulsory for all young people, it was soon compulsory only from 11 to 14 and in fact was never a great success. Particularly after 1945 much of the overtly political content was dropped and most adolescents did not take it seriously. Nevertheless it survived – the Minister of Education still saluting into the 1950s – and subsequently became a youth welfare body.

For older citizens suffering from 'fascist vertigo' the Portuguese Legion was founded on 30 September 1936. Like the *Mocidade* this added to the fascistic trappings of the regime and the volunteers of the Legion included former followers of Rolão Preto's ONS. The Legion (unlike Preto's militia schemes) was under military command and dependent on the War Minister (Salazar himself from September 1936) although it wore Italian-style uniforms, green shirts and forage caps. Indeed in one sense the 'political' appearance of the armed formation was rather deceptive. Although only those loyal to the regime volunteered (or those who felt their career prospects could be adversely affected if they did not), the Legion was designed as a kind of 'home guard' unit. The Spanish Civil War had broken out in mid-July 1936 and there were fears of a Spanish leftist invasion in the event of a republican victory. Nevertheless, in a country where regime and nation were so closely identified, it was also bound to be a militia in the service of the situation, 'the living expression of the moral conscience of the nation' and 'clear affirmation of faith and of the doctrine of the national revolution' as Salazar put it in 1939.

Like the *Mocidade,* it was largely the creation of an academic, João Pinto da Costa Leite, and in its heyday (1936–45) had 120,000 members organised in armed military formations. The élite sections of the Legion were composed of the FAC (Motorised Shock Force, but often also called Anti-Communist Force) and the Commandos, renamed much later the GII (Immediate Intervention Group). There was also a section dependent on the Ministry of the Navy, the Naval Brigade, associated with Commander (later Admiral) Henrique Tenreiro. During the Second World War the Legion was engaged in civil defence work and for two or three years after the war another dependency, the FEN (Nationalist Students' Front), was active in universities and colleges. Finally there were women's social service and information sections. After the Second World War the Legion was largely stood down, but a certain resuscitation took place under the influence of Góis Mota in the 1950s when this body for the defence of 'God, country and family' became more clearly a militia of the regime, useful in case of military dissidence or opposition activities. As well as being an auxiliary for the ordinary police and the UN at election times, its information service collected data on a million citizens, data made available to the PIDE with whom it collaborated but by whom it was sometimes seen as a rival. On paper it retained a membership of 80,000 to the very end of the regime and was usually nicknamed the Rheumatic Brigade, though after 1968 some attempts were made by *ultras* to revivify it against Caetano's wishes. The latter indeed reduced it to impotence by making it leave its firearms in police barracks.

The other signs of attempted 'fascistisation' included the creation of a women's movement (*Movimento Nacional Femenino*) and the employment of 1930s-style dynamisers in the SPN (National Propaganda Secretariat), created in September 1933 under the journalist and official biographer of Salazar, António Ferro. The name was later changed to the more neutral-sounding SNI (National Secretariat of Information), and this was absorbed eventually (in Spanish style) into the new Ministry of Information and Tourism. For all the fascistic trappings, however, the Salazarist New State remained an authoritarian state with a Catholic and nationalist traditionalist ideology. Despite all the repression, the use of intimidation as a weapon of government and the whole apparatus of corporativism – institutions of a socio-economic nature more conveniently discussed at a later stage, although they also fulfilled the functions of social and political control – no attempt was made to wipe out dissidence provided it did not hinder the work of government. In short, there existed a dictatorship even when, as after 1945, attempts were made to present it as an 'organic democracy'. Not everything had to be rendered unto Caesar.

The military movement of 28 May 1926 was generally welcomed by Catholics, in the hope that the anti-clerical legislation of the First Republic would be repealed and that the social and political systems would be reformed in such a way as to approximate to the Thomist doctrines then prevalent in the church and interpreted in such encyclicals as *Rerum Novarum* and *Quadragesimo Anno*. Although the anti-clerical ambience of the years before 1926 quickly disappeared, significant rectifications of the law in favour of the church were slower in coming. A decree of 6 July 1926 was intended as a gesture only: it recognised the 'juridical personality of the churches' but reasserted the state's control over the composition and activities of parish committees, while allowing ministers of religion to form part of these provided they had not been deprived of civil or political rights and had not been suspended by their hierarchical superiors. Though the powers of the bishops over their clergy were strengthened, there was no wholesale return of ecclesiastical property confiscated in 1911. Religious instruction was now officially permitted in private schools. The episcopate saw the decree as a step in the right direction, but was not satisfied.

With the rise of Salazar to power there were hopes that the church's situation would improve, even though on becoming Finance Minister he told his fellow Catholics not to make demands on him which he could not fulfil. Catholics nevertheless knew that Salazar's devotion to religion meant that national regeneration was bound to work in favour of the church and have a religious content. Also, as it happened, the Patriarch of Lisbon from 1929 until his retirement in 1971 was Manuel Gonçalves Cerejeira, the mentor of the CADC during the First Republic who had shared digs with Salazar. They had been close friends, but from the late 1920s this personal friendship cooled somewhat as each set about his appointed task. While Salazar was still loyal to Catholic sociological concepts and very much in favour of religion, nevertheless as a secular ruler he was also determined to maintain the power of the state in the tradition of the monarchs of old. Symbolically, as it were, Salazar and Cardinal Cerejeira represented the two spheres, temporal and spiritual, of the Thomist conception of society. There would therefore be a retreat on the part of the state from the old republican belief in the absolute sovereignty of the state and the introduction of a harmonious relationship between the lay and ecclesiastical authorities. Separation of church and state would therefore continue, but now in an atmosphere of what one French commentator was to call 'moral union with economic and administrative separation'. Catholic Action was organised in 1933–4 to channel the energies of lay activists into social rather than political directions, the hierarchy winding up the old CCP on the grounds that it had now lost its *raison d'être*. While disgruntled Democrats complained of the advance of clericalism, veteran Catholic activists declared that 'theocracy, in today's purified meaning of the word, must be born', Catholic Action styled Our Lady of Fátima Queen of the Portuguese and Salazar was seen as a providential man.

The political constitution of 1933 did not turn Portugal into a confessional state. Article 46 said that 'the state maintains the regime of separation in relation to the Catholic Church and to any other religion'. While other articles proclaimed freedom of worship, the continued secularisation of cemeteries, that 'the education supplied by the state is independent of any religious cult' and that the church should be represented in the Corporative Chamber. However, in May 1935 part of Article 43 was redrafted to read: 'The education supplied by the state aims at ... the formation ... of all the civic and moral virtues, these being guided by the principles of Christian doctrine and morality traditional in the country'. In 1951 Article 45 was redrafted to describe the Catholic religion as 'the religion of the Portuguese nation', while Articles 45 and 46 of the 1971 revision proclaimed freedom of religion, with the caveat that sects' doctrines should not conflict with 'the fundamental principles of the constitutional order nor attack the social order', Roman Catholicism still being 'considered the traditional religion of the Portuguese nation'. The constitutional text as a whole reflected the social teaching of the church and a British Catholic biographer of Salazar, Hugh Kay, concluded that 'in the realm of theory . . . Salazar cannot be easily faulted in terms of papal teaching on workers' and employers' associations, the rights of the family, and the relation of the state to subordinate groupings'.

If the text of 1933 seemed to have little to say about religion, this was in part due to the absence of any concordat between Portugal and the Holy See. Before a concordat was signed, however, concessions were given to the church in the vital area of education. Law No. 1941 (of April 1936) ordered the crucifix to be returned to primary schools 'as a symbol of the Christian upbringing decided upon by the constitution', and Decrees Nos. 27084 and 27085 (14 October 1936) established the post of teacher of moral education in state secondary schools (*liceus*), teachers being selected by the Ministry of National Education from lists drawn up by the ecclesiastical authorities. In 1941 religious instruction was extended to technical education, and by 1942 religious oaths had been restored to courts of law.

The key document in church–state relations was, however, the concordat with the Holy See of 7 May 1940, which was chiefly negotiated on the side of the Portuguese state by a CADC luminary, Mário de Figueiredo, who, like Cerejeira, had shared digs with Salazar for a long period. Part of the purpose of this concordat was to safeguard Portuguese missionary rights overseas, but as far as the church in Portugal was concerned, the state formally recognised its juridical personality and the freedom of the clergy to obey and communicate with the Pope without any state *placet* (such as had existed under the monarchy and the First Republic). The church was permitted to buy and sell property like any other property owner, but it was not to get back all that it had lost in 1911. Property such as churches, vicarages, seminaries and church ornaments was to be handed back if it was not in use by public services or classified as national monuments or as 'of public interest'. Churches and seminaries were to be tax-free. In the matter of the appointment of bishops, the Holy See was to tell the Portuguese government the name they had in mind and the government had thirty days in which to raise objections 'of a general political character'. Priests were liable to military service, but only as chaplains. The church or its dependent bodies were permitted to have private schools, in parallel to the state system, which the state would have the right to inspect and which it could subsidise. Regarding seminaries, the state was not to interfere, but the ecclesiastical authorities promised that, in teaching history, 'legitimate Portuguese patriotic feeling would be taken into account'. Religious instruction was to be given by ecclesiastically approved persons in schools to anyone who did not ask to be excluded. The state, contrary to previous republican practice, now recognised canonical marriage as legal marriage so long as it was legally registered; Article 24 said the civil authorities recognised that there could be no divorce in Catholic marriages, unless the ecclesiastical authorities found good reason in canon law. Finally, Portugal was to be represented by an ambassador at the Vatican, a rank then also given only to Portugal's representatives in London, Madrid and Rio de Janeiro.

The concordat was appropriately signed on the eighth centenary of national independence, thus stressing the intertwining of the Catholic and national traditions. In his speech to the National Assembly Salazar referred to 'the primary reality' of 'the Catholic formation of the Portuguese people' as 'a constant of history': Portugal, indeed, had never experienced collective apostasy and constituted 'the rare example of the identity of religious consciousness'. For his part, Cardinal Cerejeira saw the concordat as 'reintegrating Portugal into the sources of its spiritual life' and 'opening a new age in the relations of church and state': persecutory Jacobinism was a thing of the past, but so was the state church of the monarchy. 'Honour and glory' were due to the New State for its zealous watch over the spiritual patrimony of the nation. However, he also noted that some had hoped for rather more state aid: with much of its wealth not restored to it and the state not providing stipends or allowing tithes, the church in Portugal was left fairly poor. However, this had the potential advantage of stimulating increased contact with the faithful, and the clergy of the Patriarchate of Lisbon were told: 'You can no longer gather the fruit without tending the tree'. Nevertheless the church's recovery of position in the educational field was noticeable and here the interpenetration of the national and religious traditions of eight centuries was most obvious; as Cerejeira put it: 'The Portuguese state, which allows freedom of religion and sustains no official church, is not neutral in moral and doctrinal matters . . . Portuguese education cannot cease to be Catholic without Portugal giving up being Portugal'.

Salazar no doubt intended the concordat to be the amicable and definitive settlement of the vexed religious question, and he proudly kept a photograph of Pius XII on his desk from 1940. 'I think it dangerous for the state to acquire the idea that it has the power to do violence to Heaven', he said in 1940; 'but I think it equally unreasonable that the church, basing itself upon the superiority of its spiritual interests, should seek to broaden its activity to influence what the gospel itself sought to entrust to Caesar . . . The state will abstain from playing politics with the church in the knowledge that the church will abstain from playing politics with the state . . . because politics corrupts the church.' For high-ranking ecclesiatics who recalled the pre-1926 situation Salazar seemed, in the words of Cerejeira in 1940, 'the instrument of Providence', a view which most members of the hierarchy retained throughout the regime: for the Archbishop of Braga he was still in 1959 'the bold and tenacious man at the helm who restored the nation's unity around the sacred symbol of the redeeming Cross'.

However, times changed and from the 1950s younger Catholic activists began to find the regime's repressive policies in the political and social spheres unacceptable, while some older Catholic activists began to feel more deeply disillusionment with the social achievements of the regime. The demarcation line between the temporal and spiritual spheres accordingly again came into question, some Catholics supporting the opposition candidate, General Delgado, in the presidential election of 1958 because the New State was using Catholicism to cloak the personal interests of its rulers. The most striking example of this movement towards opposition to the regime came in the form of a letter to Salazar from Mgr António Ferreira Gomes, Bishop of Oporto, on 13 July 1958. In it the bishop claimed that the best Catholics were becoming alienated from the church because of the government's demands for united Catholic support against communism, especially when the regime's attitude to social problems seemed increasingly out of harmony with papal doctrines, notably the prohibition of the right to strike. The bishop asserted the right of Catholic Action to spread the church's social doctrine (which conflicted with the New State's interpretation) and the right of Catholics to form their own politico-civic associations to contest elections. The bishop went into exile until after Salazar's death. Although the rest of the hierarchy did not support the bishop's personal initiative, the letter was a symptom of growing dissatisfaction with the regime on the part of the Catholic élite, a tendency encouraged by the pontificate of John XXIII and the proceedings of the Second Vatican Council.

For the traditionally minded Salazar, *aggiornamento* in the church, with its inevitable political and social consequences, was an unmitigated disaster and the growth of opposition among Portuguese Catholics equivalent to a stab in the back, or at least ingratitude for 'the respect and loving care lavished on the church during the past thirty years'. For the ageing Salazar of 1960 developments within the church were just part of a more general decline of Western civilisation: 'The world is mad! . . . Common sense has ceased to exist among the peoples!' The 1960s were to see more and more Catholic laymen move into opposition as well as the growth among some younger radical priests of a belief in a non-institutional Christianity and even a theology of revolution. The regime tried to draw some comfort from the visit of Pope Paul VI to Fátima in 1967, though it had been upset by his earlier visit to India after the latter's seizure of Goa. Fátima itself was to some extent used by the regime: not only were the apparitions of 1917 said symbolically to mark the beginning of a national renaissance, but later revelations in the 1930s and 1940s about what Our Lady allegedly said about the dangers of communism fitted in well with the regime's outlook. The regime, for its part, was prepared to use its powers of censorship against critics of religion: thus, for example, Tomás da Fonseca's attack on Fátima *Na Cova dos Leões* (1958) was banned and, though the Lisbon National Library possessed a copy, the reference card was overstamped in red Prohibited Work. By the time of his stroke in 1968 the devout Salazar was rueful about the church's value as a political ally – but as he knew, the church was eternal and all political regimes transitory.

Opposition activities among Catholics in the later stages of the New State were nevertheless largely the work of members of the élite, just as the organisation of opposition activities against the New State in general was for the most part the work of members of this social élite. Discussion of these activities may be arbitrarily divided into three periods: up to 1937; the years from 1945 to 1958; and the decade after 1958. The second and third periods, covering the years of legally defined security measures as well as an outward loosening up of the formal political system, reflected another sea-change in Portuguese intellectual fashions. Just as 'the best minds' of the 1920s had for the most part been carried away by integral nationalism of one variety or another, so from the 1940s the initiative among the young, in tune with events outside the country, lay with democratic ideas – liberal-democratic, social-democratic, Christian democratic or Marxist. Indeed Salazar denounced the fashion for Communism, 'the great heresy of our times', in terms which democratic republicans might well have used earlier about the fashion for integralism: 'In this communistic effervescence there is, in the first place, an element of snobbery, a dominating pose which overawes and at the same time provokes the respect of "poor people" such as we are; it is defended by gentlemen who, in silken array and immaculate attire, anticipate a future Utopia ...' Nevertheless, for all its security measures, the New State was powerless to stop the spread of ideas which it deemed heretical.

The first period of opposition activities (up to 1937) may be said to have represented the last phase of the efforts to prevent the installation of the New State system. We have already noted the failure of the old politicians in the Republican-Socialist Alliance to overthrow the dictatorship in 1931, as well as the abortive *coup* of 1935 which involved the National-Syndicalists. To these must be added three other episodes of significance. The proclamation of the National Labour Statute in September 1933 was followed by an attempted *coup,* led by the aviator Sarmento Beires, backed by a revolutionary general strike organised by a broad front of reformist socialists, anarchists and communists. Trade unions had been temporarily banned in November 1927 because of fears that the anarchist-dominated CGT was about to engage in revolutionary violence. The movement of 18 January 1934 was largely the work of the anarchists and of the communists of the PCP, who were beginning to grow in influence after the reorganisation of their movement (founded in 1921) by its Secretary-General, Bento Gonçalves, in 1929. PCP supporters rose in arms and declared a _soviet_ in the glass-manufacturing town of Marinha Grande (near Leiria). The movement was however quickly suppressed; some 350 militants were arrested and many of these were deported to a camp in southern Angola. After 1934 the strength of the anarchists began to ebb away at a faster pace than it had been since 1923, this being to the relative advantage of the PCP.

Almost inevitably the Spanish Civil War had an effect on the Portuguese situation, with the Portuguese government aligning itself with the nationalist insurgents while supporters of the pre-28 May situation sided with the republicans and revolutionaries. On 9 September 1936 the crews of three warships mutinied in the Tagus with the aim of joining the Spanish republican navy, but the ships surrendered when fired on from the land. The rebel sailors, who had apparently been principally organised by PCP activists, were deported to Tarrafal with other revolutionaries. This first phase of overt and violent opposition came to an end on 4 July 1937 when Salazar survived a bomb attack organised by a small group of anarchists. Whereas the mutiny of 1936 was quickly followed by the creation of the Portuguese Legion, Salazar in 1937 simply said: 'There can be no doubt about it, we are indestructible because Providence has willed it so'.

From 1937 to 1945 there was a lull in opposition activities aimed at overthrowing the regime, though this did not mean that opposition activities ceased altogether. There were strike movements in the autumn of 1942 and the summer of 1943, the former involving 20,000, the latter 50,000 workers in the Greater Lisbon area. In May 1944 came more strikes, this time including a widespread movement among southern agricultural workers, particularly in the Ribatejo, which were exercises in mass mobilisation organised by the clandestine PCP. These movements were, of course, suppressed; in the latter instance General Jorge Botelho Moniz arrested several hundred strikers and kept them in the bull-ring at Vila Franca de Xira for a time.

The PCP was the backbone of the opposition, the anarchists having disappeared from the scene and the old republicans either dying in exile or perpetuating old divisions and personal rivalries of the type which in the 1920s and 1930s had led to factions picturesquely known as _bonzos_ (hypocrites) and _canhotos_ (left-handers), _budas_ and _antibudas_ (Buddhas and anti-Buddhas). The PCP organisation had received quite a hammering from the authorities after the arrest in 1935 of its Secretary-

General, Bento Gonçalves, who died in the Tarrafal camp in 1942. Although its organisation was largely destroyed by 1941, the PCP (like other Communist parties after the German invasion of the Soviet Union) began to recover, reorganise and attract anti-regime militants into its ranks or as collaborators in broader opposition fronts. The policy of the new secretariat, one of whose leading members was the lawyer Álvaro Barreirinhas Cunhal, was to ally with other anti-fascist oppositionists and to use both illegal and legal means for propaganda, notably the infiltration of the state-sponsored syndicates. Though there had been attempts to form united opposition fronts and popular fronts in the 1930s, it was only in 1943 that signs of unity began to emerge with the PCP-sponsored MUNAF (National Anti-Fascist Unity Movement), which gained adherents among the young as well as the old opposition political class. Officially presided over by the former Republican War Minister, former Governor of Angola and leading Freemason, General Norton de Matos, its national council included PCP, socialist and various old republican party representatives; its unity however was always somewhat in question, non-PCP members seeing the overthrow of the regime in terms of a military *coup* and PCP members, who helped form Anti-Fascist Combat Groups, seeing it rather in terms of a national uprising after careful preparation. Suspicions within MUNAF always remained as to who was trying to use whom.

Hopes that things would change were raised by the Allied victory in Europe (8 May 1945) which was celebrated by a crowd estimated in hundreds of thousands in Lisbon with cries of 'Victory!' 'Liberty!' 'Democracy!'. Feeling the need to adapt to the new international climate, Salazar now set about giving a more 'democratic' face to the New State. There were now to be elections 'as free as they are in the free land of England', he said in October 1945. Prior to this the elections for President of the Republic – Carmona was re-elected in 1935 and 1942 – and for the National Assembly in 1934, 1938 and 1942, had been of a purely plebiscitary nature, all candidates being nominated by the UN. The suffrage was nevertheless rather wider in the New State than it had been during the First Republic: those entitled to vote were adult males (over 21) who could read and write or who paid more than a minimal amount in annual taxation and women with at least a secondary educational qualification. Not all entitled to register as voters ever did so, whether out of apathy, caution or dissuasion by the authorities, and not all who registered bothered to go to the polls. Thus the level of political participation in the New State remained low (as under the First Republic) as the table of elections (Table 2.1) to the National Assembly demonstrates (in 1925 there had been a total of 574,260 registered voters). This did not worry Salazar, who believed people needed to be governed rather than choose their governments and whose aim was a healthy level of depoliticisation among the population at large. Elections with opposition candidates who were never elected and with a short period of 'sufficient liberty' (i.e. less censorship) before polling day (which could help the regime to identify its opponents) were a somewhat farcical ritual, but they did allow the regime a degree of international acceptability; Portugal did have elections, even if the government's candidates did always win. Elections were *para inglês ver*; but then Salazar was on record as believing that 'in politics, what seems to be, is'.

Table 2.1   *Voting Figures in New State General Elections, 1934–1965*

Year of election	No. of voters going to polls	No. of voters expressed as\% of total population
1934	506,575	7·6
1938	743,930	10·6
1945	909,456	12·0
1949	1,140,000	14·6
1953	1,161,932	14·4
1957	1,213,381	14·5
1961	1,236,000	14·5
1965	1,278,387	14·8

It may seem surprising that the opposition should even have attempted to take part in electoral procedures which were so heavily loaded against them and thus have given the regime a spurious degree of legitimacy. Nevertheless the one-month pre-electoral period, with its relaxation of censorship, was seen as providing the only opportunity for reminding people that opposition existed, for propaganda and swaying the uncommitted, as well as an opportunity for releasing pent-up feelings of frustration. No opposition group had any organisation behind it except the PCP and this always presented a dilemma: should non-PCP groups go it alone, thus providing evidence that there was no united alternative to 'the situation', or should they ally with the PCP, thus giving limited credence to government charges that opposition was no more than the sinister manœuvring of the communists and their 'dupes'? To this dilemma were added others: was contesting elections in the hope that next time things might be different the way to destroy the regime? Would it not be better to seek salvation through a constitutional *coup d'état*, i.e. by somehow persuading the President of the Republic to use his power to dismiss Salazar as Premier? Was not the most hopeful way to success to concentrate on a military *coup,* with or without civilian (including or excluding PCP) support? In general terms, as Dr H. Martins has written:

One may distinguish four types of opposition in the Portuguese experience during 1945–68, the two cross-cutting criteria being legality and time-perspective (short-term or long-term). (1) 'Opposition' in a narrow sense, i.e. anti-regime behaviour oriented to the legal or semi-legal opportunities for political conflict. (2) Conspiracy, hallowed by the Portuguese praetorian tradition, illegal and short-term by definition. (3) 'Resistance': underground opposition with a long-term, strategic perspective. (4) *Paideia*: manifest long-term action such as the 'metapolitical' strategy for modernising the thought-forms and culture-mentality of the Portuguese intelligentsia adopted by A. Sérgio . . . and the *Seara Nova* group.

In 1945 there was still a rather naïve hope that the system could really be changed. In the weeks preceding polling day (18 November) MUNAF reorganised itself for semi-legal existence as the MUD (Movement of Democratic Unity), and issued a statement critical of the regime and asking for minimal electoral guarantees, such as freedom of the press and of assembly, and the right to found political parties. It asked, too, for the fair supervision of the elections and a political amnesty. Soon the MUD claimed 50,000 supporters in Lisbon and a 20,000-strong membership for its youth movement, the MUDJ. The MUD, which was not joined by the more conservative oppositionists around Cunha Leal, apparently was not quite sure whether it wanted to conduct a purely electoral campaign, to lobby Carmona to sack Salazar or to engage in conspiracy with military elements. As it turned out, the Minister of the Interior, General Júlio Botelho Moniz, announced that neither bullets nor ballot papers would shake the regime, and so the opposition in the end abstained.

After the election repressive measures were taken against some MUD members, but, in the twilight zone between legality and illegality, it still organised the odd demonstration and did its best to prevent Portugal being able to join the United Nations Organisation. Its official leader was a former minister of the First Republic and a distinguished academic, Mário de Azevedo Gomes, who accordingly lost his university job. Electoral activities were but one method to be used and, from the early months of 1945, Captain Fernando Queiroga tried to put a conspiracy together involving Admiral Mendes Cabeçadas (of both 1910 and 1926 fame), General Norton de Matos and civilians such as the former First Republic minister João Soares (father of the present socialist leader). Queiroga apparently planned simultaneous *coups* in various barracks up and down the country, but on 10 October 1946 his only supporters came from the 6th Cavalry Regiment in Oporto. No one else moved and so he surrendered to loyal units at Mealhada, just north of Coimbra, on the main road to Lisbon on which he was advancing.

Although this particular attempt was a miserable failure, conspiracy continued under the mantle of the JMLN (Military Junta of National

Liberation): the general idea was that military discontent with the War Minister, Santos Costa, could be channelled into a movement under Mendes Cabeçadas's leadership which would sweep away the New State and its institutions, set up a transitional government and prepare for free elections for a new constituent assembly. Whether or not this was to be done with the consent of the existing President of the Republic, Marshal Carmona, was not apparently quite clear to anyone, but it was believed that Carmona at this time had indicated a possible willingness to dismiss Salazar, given greater freedom of manœuvre. However, the more or less elaborate plans came to nothing on 10 April 1947, the most sensational incident being the destruction of part of the air force at the Sintra base by two mechanics, one of them Hermínio da Palma Inácio.

After the 10 April 1947 episode the government seemed to recover some of its nerve and proceeded to dismiss army officers and public employees and further harry the MUD, which, though officially suppressed, nevertheless formed the support organisation for the candidature of General Norton de Matos in the presidential contest of 1949. Norton de Matos was backed by a broad spectrum of opinion from the PCP to some monarchists but tried to dissociate himself from the Communists while making it plain that, if elected, he would dismiss Salazar. Though he himself apparently wished to contest the election, advisers persuaded him to withdraw for lack of freedom to campaign before polling day in February 1949. The withdrawal of the 81-year-old general left only one candidate in the field, the perennial Marshal Carmona, aged 80. Carmona therefore started on his fourth term of office since having himself elected President in 1928 and, though he was said to have compared himself as President to a bird in a gilded cage, Salazar was still Premier when Carmona died on 18 April 1951. The question of the succession had at last arisen.

One possible solution to the succession problem was the restoration of the monarchy in the person of Duarte Nuno. Perhaps under the influence of his War Minister, Santos Costa (who as a lieutenant had proclaimed the Monarchy at Castro Daire [Beira Alta] during Paiva Couceiro's attempt to restore it in 1919), and perhaps also with an eye to furthering his international respectability (Franco's Spanish State had declared itself a monarchy, albeit without a king, in 1947) Salazar in 1949 lifted the ban on the claimant's setting foot in Portugal, and in the following year Duarte Nuno, at the age of 43, entered the country for the first time to take up residence at the Casa de São Marcos near Coimbra. Despite their disappointment at the lack of a restoration in the 1930s many monarchists, even those exiled by the regime such as the stalwart Paiva Couceiro, expelled in 1937, had hoped that the New State would culminate in a restoration. Salazar, whether because of his own private monarchist sentiments or to play the monarchists along, had always taken care not to dash monarchist hopes completely. Apart from the UN (which included some monarchists), the Monarchist Cause was the only tolerated political association in the New State. Duarte Nuno had discreetly been given an allowance out of the funds of the Foundation of the House of Braganza; in 1938 Salazar had personally intervened to give the royal family passports so that they could move from Austria to Switzerland, while members of the royal family other than the claimant who visited Portugal in the 1940s were warmly received by the authorities. In 1950 Salazar hinted that the monarchy could be a 'national solution', and indeed the ideology of Duarte Nuno's supporters seemed to present no insuperable problems. While there might be disapproval of the practice of Salazarism in monarchist ranks, the Monarchist Cause had announced at the time of Duarte Nuno's acclamation in 1932 that its programme would be analogous to that of the UN until *Côrtes Gerais* (a traditional assembly convoked by the king) should decide otherwise. Duarte Nuno agreed and expressed his belief in 'a Christian monarchy, founded on the family, [a monarchy] corporative and representative, at one and the same time authoritarian, on account of its attribution to the king of the function of government and of the supreme sanctioning of laws, and liberating on account of the recognition of all legitimate liberties and autonomies – a monarchy that may truly be the guarantee of the common good and the safeguard of the national interest and honour against the corruption of internal politics and, especially, against the threat of the external enemy'.

On Carmona's death, however, Salazar and most of the UN still considered a restoration more trouble than it would be worth because of the divisions it would produce. The Santos Costa faction was defeated in the UN by those in favour of a continuation of the 'second' Republic, led by Marcelo Caetano, an ex-Integralist luminary of the New State, and Dinis da Fonseca, a CADC stalwart. Caetano and others thought that the best solution would be for Salazar himself to become President of the Republic, possibly with Caetano as Premier; but Salazar thought otherwise and an Air Force General, Craveiro Lopes, was chosen as the regime's candidate. In the presidential election of 1951 there were two opposition candidates, reflecting the schisms which had already become apparent in the elections for the National Assembly in 1949. Admiral Quintão Meireles, who had served alongside Salazar in Vicente de Freitas's government of 1928–9 but who now believed Salazar had betrayed 28 May, stood for the liberals, and a professor of mathematics from Oporto, Rui Luís Gomes, represented the Left in the shape of the MND (Democratic National Movement), a successor to the MUD composed of the PCP and others who thought a unitary opposition more important than anti-communism. Meireles's aim was to try and attract the more moderate or disillusioned supporters of the regime into an alliance with moderate oppositionists; hence his manifesto declared that he would have nothing to do with the MND camp and that he wanted evolution within the regime, not its overthrow. Nevertheless both opposition candidates' campaigns were harassed; the MND candidate was disqualified by the Council of State as a communist and Meireles gave up the unequal struggle and withdrew before polling day on 22 July. General Craveiro Lopes was therefore elected and, as expected, retained Salazar as Premier.

After 1951 the opposition entered into a phase of relative lassitude, 'an ebb tide' as the young oppositionist Mário Soares was to put it. The PCP had been weakened by the arrest of part of its leadership, including Cunhal, in 1949 and in any case, as a loyally Stalinist organisation, it also suffered from the effects of the Cold War and the growing awareness among oppositionists who had up to this time collaborated with it of what was happening in the countries of the so-called socialist camp. In Portugal young activists, realising what happened to fellow travellers in people's democracies, began to rethink their positions, while Khrushchev's revelations about the Stalinist era in the Soviet Union came as a further blow to the PCP. Nevertheless in the 1950s it managed to organise some strike activity among southern agricultural labourers and fishermen, as well as peace movements and disturbances in the universities. In 1956-7 fifty-two people, mostly students, were tried in Oporto for subversion and conspiratorial organisation. The majority of student activists tended to co-operate with the PCP, if they were not actually members. Nevertheless the PCP, which held its 5th Congress in 1957, remained the only opposition group with a definite programme.

The 1950s also saw previous pro-regime activists come out into open opposition. The public relations side of Admiral Meireles's campaign of 1951 had been handled by Captain Henrique Galvão, a quixotic character who had been involved in an attempt to restore the monarchy in 1927, had written a manual on guerrilla warfare for the Portuguese Legion and had subsequently been something of a confidant of Salazar; but in 1947-8, when a member of the National Assembly, he had attacked conditions in Angola and given evidence in favour of opponents of the regime. With former luminaries of the First Republic, including Cunha Leal, he formed a semi-clandestine OCN (National Civic Organisation) and began to indulge in conspiracy with disgruntled military men, but his activities were curtailed when he was arrested by the PIDE and imprisoned in 1952.

Desultory opposition nevertheless was manifested, chiefly by the Democratic-Social Directory, a group of intellectuals gathered around such prestigious academic figures as Mário de Azevedo Gomes, António Sérgio and (after his return from exile in 1955) Jaime Cortesão, who provided a link between the days of the First Republic and the younger, non-PCP, activists. The elections for the National Assembly in 1953 and 1957 were contested, though opposition candidates were subject to the usual harassment and roused little popular enthusiasm. In 1953 candidates were put up in Lisbon, Oporto and Aveiro, but none was returned although they got a fifth of the vote in the latter two constituencies. In 1957 most of the opposition called for abstention and nearly all non-UN candidates withdrew. Meanwhile petitioning of Craveiro Lopes for the restoration of full civil rights was kept up and some oppositionists were imprisoned for saying that the government should give way to India over the issue of Goa.

Just as some members of the opposition were beginning to despair, however, there came the presidential election campaign of 1958, and with it the revelation of a new Sebastian in the form of Air Force General Humberto Delgado. Delgado was in some ways rather like Galvão, whose treatment as a prisoner of the authorities was a key factor in making the general an outright oppositionist. Delgado had been an enthusiastic participant in the 28 May Revolution, a military adviser to the Legion, the author of a radio play dedicated to Salazar, a key negotiator with the Allies during the war, Director-General of Civil Aviation in 1944–6 and again in 1957 (in the interval he had been Military and Air Attaché in Washington and Portugal's representative on the Military Committee of NATO). With the imprisoned Galvão and António Sérgio he had apparently been involved in conspiratorial activities in 1956 and so agreed to become a candidate for the presidency in 1958. General Craveiro Lopes was by this time thought to be none too reliable as President by Salazar and the UN, and so the regime's candidate was the Minister for the Navy Admiral Américo Tomás.

At first there were two opposition candidates. The PCP and its collaborators were critical of Delgado's past and considered him reactionary, fascist and a candidate of the US and UK embassies – in fact a 'Coca-Cola' general. The communists therefore sponsored the lawyer Arlindo Vicente after trying unsuccessfully to reach agreement with Cunha Leal, a man they had previously denounced as a reactionary, who in any case withdrew his candidature in favour of Delgado on 20 May. Nine days later, in view of the enthusiasm Delgado's campaign was arousing, Arlindo Vicente also stepped down on certain conditions set out in the so-called pact of Cacilhas with Delgado. All the sections of the opposition, including the monarchist Rolão Preto, rallied to Delgado, who had begun his campaign on 10 May by stating simply that his intention was to sack Salazar and dismantle the repressive apparatus of the New State. Between then and polling day (8 June) the 'General Without Fear' received enthusiastic mass receptions up and down the country, which were attended by police intervention, rioting and shooting. His style of campaigning, which led Salazar to the conclusion that he was a rabble rouser of genius, was direct, simplistic and passionately populist. Though he never made it clear what he would do with power, the short-term goals were plain: 'It's time for them to go. We are sick of them. Out with them! Throw them out!' Given the government's mobilisation of all the forces at its disposal – the PIDE and the Legion, non-registration of oppositionists, electoral malpractice of all kinds, restrictions on campaigning – the final result could hardly be in doubt though the regime of Salazar and Santos Costa was manifestly shaken. In the event, though Delgado carried constituencies in Angola and Mozambique, the official figures gave him 236,258 votes to the victorious Tomás's 758,998, i.e. 31 per cent of the vote. Neither before nor after his defeat, however, was 'General Without Fear' prepared to be simply the Pierre Poujade of the Portuguese polling booths; he was, after all, a member of the Athenaeum Club.

Knowing that his campaign was doomed to defeat, Delgado had opened negotiations before polling day for a *coup d'état*. He appealed to former friends and colleagues still in positions of command, including President Craveiro Lopes who was known to have become restless with Salazar, and it seems that a *coup* was planned; but, as so often, no one actually moved on 2 June. The Defence Minister, Colonel Santos Costa, got to know of these plans and stymied a post-electoral attempt. On 27 July Delgado approached Generals Júlio Botelho Moniz (Chief of the Armed Forces' General Staff), Lopes da Silva (President of the Military Supreme Court), Costa Macedo (Chief of the Air Force General Staff) and Beleza Ferraz (Chief of the Army General Staff), appealing to them at least to oust the unpopular Defence Minister. He sought to shame the military leaders into action by telling them they had allowed the armed forces to become a Praetorian Guard for 'the hermit of Belém' (i.e. Salazar). He suggested a *coup,* which he believed Craveiro Lopes was already preparing, before Tomás became President on 9 August: 'the hour of national liberation has arrived . . . This is the moment to save the nation's honour and fulfil the army's duty towards it'. His former colleagues from the 28 May movement were non-committal, while Beleza Ferraz more pointedly replied that 'we have different conceptions both of politics and of loyalty, and therefore we cannot meet on the same ground nor follow the same paths'.

On 9 August Admiral Tomás was duly sworn in as President and five days later there came a major government reshuffle, Salazar retiring the leaders of two quarrelling factions within the regime, namely, the Monarchist Defence Minister, Santos Costa, and the Minister of the Presidency, Marcelo Caetano. Santos Costa was replaced by the republican General Júlio Botelho Moniz, who advised Delgado to drop political activity and go abroad at the government's expense. But

Delgado was not to be bought off and he continued to organise his MNI (Independent National Movement), 'a civic organisation of individuals ... opposed to all dictatorial or totalitarian concepts and to the inclusion in its own organisation of any group, sect or party'. The government naturally banned the MNI. A demonstration broken up by the police on the forty-eighth anniversary of the republic, a congratulatory telegram to Pope John XXIII asking for his help in liberating the Portuguese people and an invitation to Aneurin Bevan to lecture, all in October 1958, led to the arrest of his collaborators Azevedo Gomes, Cortesão, Sérgio and the monarchist Vieira de Almeida. Delgado himself, who had told the *Daily Mail* 'We shall even use guns to get what we want', was dismissed from the armed forces on three-quarters pay and, fearing further charges if not assassination, sought asylum in the Brazilian Embassy on 12 January 1959 'on the grounds of coercion and imminent imprisonment'.

Before this Delgado had conspired with, among others, the former Catholic youth leader, Manuel Serra, and the confidant of ex-President Craveiro Lopes, Captain Almeida Santos – but again, on 18 December 1958, the movement had to be called off. Further embarrassment to the government came with Galvão's escape from hospital on 16 January 1959 and his request, after a month's clandestine activity, for asylum at the Argentine Embassy. The government's fear of military dissidence was reflected in a decree at this time raising military pay: whereas generals got an extra 1,000 escudos a month, captains (key elements in any military movement) were given a relatively handsome extra 900 escudos. By May 1959 both Delgado and Galvão were in South America, but while Delgado was in the Brazilian Embassy the PIDE had at last discovered some conspirators. A *coup* had been scheduled for the night of 11–12 March but military nerve had again failed. Some, like Manuel Serra and Major Luís Calafate, escaped to South America, while others like the nominal leader Major Pastor Fernandes, and Father Perestrelo, were arrested, the latter with guns under his cassock. On May Day there were clashes and during the summer the PCP caused widespread stoppages. The Delgado phenomenon had indeed come close to toppling the regime. Henceforth there were to be no more elections for the presidency by popular vote, while the extent of the opposition movement, particularly in Catholic and military ranks, was a serious worry for Salazar. This was made as clear as his oblique style would allow in his end-of-the-year address of 1959: 'I cannot say that times are favourable . . . Quite the contrary: they will be very heavy, at least until we are able to awaken the sleepers, encourage the hesitant and rekindle faith everywhere.'

This was not to be the end of the regime's troubles though it survived its ordeal with a mixture of good luck and good management to emerge at least temporarily strengthened. The year 1960 was a quiet one but 1961 – which saw the outbreak of violence in Angola – was not. Portugal returned to the international headlines with the hijacking of the 21,000-ton Portuguese cruise liner *Santa Maria* by Spanish and Portuguese exiles on 22 January 1961, among them Henrique Galvão. In Brazil Delgado had made Galvão Secretary-General of his MNI, which failed to arouse much enthusiasm among Portuguese communities in Latin America. With a few Spanish exiles organised in DRIL (Iberian Revolutionary Directorate of Liberation) Galvão hit upon the idea of Operation Dulcinea, so called 'because we were romantics fighting for our lady, Liberty': the plan was to seize the liner and sail it to the Spanish island of Fernando Po, set up rival governments in Africa and hope for risings in the Peninsula. Despite a heart attack, Galvão boarded the liner at Curação and the two dozen commandos duly seized the ship which, after an officer on the bridge had been shot, became, under the new name *Santa Liberdade*, 'the first liberated portion of Portuguese territory'. Certainly as a publicity stunt Operation Dulcinea was a success and after thirteen days, short of water and fuel, the ship was surrendered in Recife harbour to the Brazilian authorities by the hijackers in exchange for political asylum. How far Delgado was involved remains a matter for speculation, but Delgado expelled Galvão from his MNI not long afterwards for treason, exhibitionism and theatrical propaganda. Before this, however, Delgado and Galvão had made it very clear that they were as anti-communist as they were anti-Salazarist. The MNI aimed at a representative democratic system for Portugal within a 'federal republic of the united states of Portugal' which, while recognising the principle of self-determination for the colonies, nevertheless would be a kind of Lisbon-dominated Portuguese Commonwealth.

Meanwhile sixty-three oppositionists in Portugal drafted a 20,000-word *Programme for the Democratisation of the Republic* to try to give the lie to the regime's charge that the opposition was disunited and could agree on no objectives. Dated 31 January but released only in May 1961 – an event which led to all its signatories being arrested – it had some practical use in the elections for the National Assembly in November, a month which saw a Portuguese airliner hijacked by Palma Inácio and used to drop leaflets on Lisbon, Beja and Faro. In the elections the opposition as usual withdrew before polling day for lack of minimal guarantees.. The Programme of *Democratisation* called for political and social reform and administrative decentralisation in the colonies. As a British writer hostile to the regime put it: 'It is essentially a list of desirable reforms, some of them very costly; nothing is said about how these measures are to be paid for; the economic expansion envisaged is all predicated on the continuance of Portuguese sovereignty overseas'. The moving force behind the document was the Republican Directory of whom the same author, Peter Fryer, wrote:

their ideas are very old-fashioned . . . For the most part they are romantics, still steeped in the liberal ideas of the nineteenth century. The acute problems facing Portugal . . . bewilder them; they have no answer except to blame Salazar and clamour for liberty. Not in all the three and a half decades they have been outside official life have any of them succeeded in drawing up a comprehensive plan that would show their countrymen how the liberty they clamour for might fruitfully be used.

The real threat in 1961 came not from the civilian opposition but, as was bound to be the case, from within the ranks of the armed forces. The attempted *coup* of 13 April 1961, coming a few weeks after the outbreak of hostilities in Angola, was probably the closest Salazar came to being removed from power. Pressed into action by the Air Force Chief, General Albuquerque de Freitas, the Defence Minister, General Júlio Botelho Moniz, who had been linked with conspiracies since 1958, decided with other officers that a motion of no confidence in Salazar should be passed when the Defence Council met on 8 April. Apparently a change of government rather than regime was envisaged and Salazar would be packed off to Switzerland (which Salazar later thought was a nice idea but beyond his economic means). Possibly tipped off by the Army Commander, General Câmara Pina, Salazar did not attend the meeting. On 11 April Botelho Moniz and others went to see President Tomás, but the latter said he would not dismiss the greatest statesman of the century after Churchill. Salazar alerted the PIDE, the GNR and the Legion and prepared for confrontation with the plotters, who included the Chief of the General Staff, Beleza Ferraz, the Army Minister, Colonel Almeida Fernandes, and the Military Governor of Lisbon. On 13 April Botelho Moniz and his fellow conspirators met and agreed to move on government positions at 16.00 hours that day. In the event no one moved for by then Botelho Moniz had received his letter of dismissal from the Premier's chauffeur. The relevant people were detained – including ex-President Craveiro Lopes with his marshal's uniform already packed in his suitcase – and put under surveillance. All that ensued was the inevitable government reshuffle.

With the failure of Botelho Moniz to oust Salazar from within the system, the initiative once again passed to the exiled Delgado, who was able to pick up the strands of earlier conspiracies and also to make contact with PCP elements, previously rather hostile to insurrectionism. In the summer of 1961 in Brazil he conceived the idea of starting a movement with a small group of people who would take over a military unit and therefore one region of the country. On the assumption that the regime would be able to rally little support, the use of one radio station would be enough to instigate other takeovers culminating in the fall of the regime through mass insurrection. The plans were prepared and Delgado moved to Morocco. He arrived in Lisbon in disguise, having missed the Ceuta–Algeciras ferry, only on 30 December. The revolt had been supposed to start on the 3rd, then on the 8th. It eventually began at 02.00 on 1 January 1962, but without Delgado's knowledge, when about thirty men led by Captain Varela Gomes (close to the PCP and an opposition candidate) and Manuel Serra, scaled the walls of the barracks of the 3rd Infantry Regiment in Beja. Chaos ensued, the colonel in command wounding Varela Gomes before fleeing and alerting the GNR and Lisbon. Troops from Évora who were supposed to support the revolt surrounded the barracks and the whole episode ended in further fiasco when the Under-Secretary for War, Colonel Felipe da Fonseca, was accidentally shot by his own troops on his arrival from Lisbon. Sixty-five people were subsequently given prison sentences, including Varela Gomes and Serra, while Delgado, who had gone to Beja, escaped across the frontier after ten days in Oporto.

It was to be the last military revolt until 1974. Delgado moved the centre of his activities to Morocco and then Algeria, where he had the use of a radio station and was President of the FPLN (Patriotic National Liberation Front). However, although he wanted a revolution supported by all the opposition, he fell out with the PCP, whom he feared were taking over the FPLN, and then with nearly everyone else. Nothing if not a man of imagination, he then announced the existence of another (unipersonal) FPLN (Portuguese National Liberation Front) and talked of plans for Operation Oranges – a scheme to take Macao with Chinese connivance, where he would set up an internationally recognised government for Portugal. He increasingly lived in a fantasy world and it cannot have been difficult for agents of the PIDE (who were incensed at looking foolish for not catching him in 1961–2) to persuade him to journey to the frontier in the belief that another revolution was in the offing. In February 1965 he and his Brazilian secretary were assassinated by men of the PIDE somewhere in the Spanish province of Badajoz. From the regime's point of view his death – there are suggestions that the original plan was for a kidnapping – was utterly counter-productive since it created an international scandal and made a martyr for the opposition of a man who, alive, would probably have constantly disrupted and embarrassed it.

With the hope of military action gone, the opposition reverted to its work of organisation and petitioning and also to propaganda among the younger members of the élite. There was a strong anti-regime current in the universities from the 1940s and demonstrations and clashes between student activists and the regime were frequent. As early as 1944 students in Coimbra had tried to hold free elections for their management committees and student activism reached peaks in 1957 and 1962. In the latter year a student strike was staged in the three universities of Coimbra, Lisbon and Oporto and this was put down by expulsions and the dismissal of some teaching staff. The Rector of Lisbon University, Marcelo Caetano, resigned in protest against police activity on the campus and thus gained some credibility for the future in opposition circles. Though arrests and disturbances continued during the 1960s, 1962 nevertheless marked the end of a phase of opposition activity that had begun in 1958. As long as Salazar remained in power and the opposition was divided, it seemed that nothing would happen.

While abroad Delgado and the Algiers-based FPLN faded from the scene and Galvão's FAPLE (Anti-Totalitarian Front of Free Portuguese in Exile) failed to pull off any spectacular incidents, the opposition within the country kept on reforming and reshaping itself, the trend among the spectrum of opinion to the right of the PCP being at last for the third force (those who had grown up with the regime) to cast off the tutelage of the venerable figures whose memories went back to the First Republic. In 1963 all opposition factions except the communists, monarchists and Catholics united in ADS (Democratic-Social Action) and failed to gain recognition as a loyal opposition within the New State. Its leaders were Azevedo Gomes and Cunha Leal but the leading activists were younger men such as Mário Soares, who drew up the 'Manifesto to the Nation' for the elections to the National Assembly in 1965. It called for full electoral guarantees and self-determination for the colonies. The candidates put up in five constituencies as usual withdrew before polling day, though not before many Catholics had shown their support for the ADS stand.

With the death of Azevedo Gomes in 1965 ADS began to split, socialists like Soares being anxious to form a democratic left-wing movement with PCP dissidents and progressive Catholics whose oppositionist tendencies were reinforced by the events of the Second Vatican Council and papal critiques of colonialism. In May 1965 these tendencies led to the foundation of the MCAD (Christian Movement of Democratic Action). Its manifesto called for a society based on Christian humanism and for political and social democracy. 'The Portuguese social situation is anti-Christian ... Personal power which surpasses the occasionally necessary need for it is by definition anti-Christian . . . A totalitarian state of a conservative type is the most anti-Christian social situation ... Christ can never be on the side of shock police, suffocation of thought, violation of law . . .'; 'a policy of Truth, Love and Liberty', in the words of John XXIII, was what was needed. From 1965 there was increasing collaboration between Catholics and socialists in anti-regime activities and the process of disengagement from the regime by individual Catholics continued: in 1965 for example, a leading economist and Catholic lay activist who sat in the Corporative Chamber, Francisco Pereira de Moura, protested against the validity of Tomás's re-election as President by an electoral college.

To the ranks of the still basically fragmented opposition of the 1960s must be added monarchists, who were divided into more than a dozen tendencies to the left and the right of the regime, their leading figure still being Rolão Preto. On the left there were also small factions with revolutionary ideologies springing up among the young, many of them originating as splinters from the PCP: such were the pro-Chinese Portuguese Marxist-Leninist Committee and FAP (People's Action Front) of 1964. Social banditry as a form of opposition also lived on in the person of Palma Inácio who in 1967 founded the Paris-based LUAR (League of Revolutionary Union and Action, but also meaning moonlight) and relieved the Bank of Portugal's Figueira da Foz branch of some 30 billion escudos.

The backbone of opposition nevertheless remained, as ever, the PCP based in Prague, even though it was a less fashionable body for the young to join by the 1960s. Having gone through a phase of what was later called right-wing deviationism in 1956–9, PCP hostility to the violent overthrow of the regime had been somewhat modified from 1959; however, it continued to believe in using legal as well as illegal means to weaken the regime – including the organisation of an agricultural strike in the south in 1962 – in preparation for the great day and also aspired to a hegemonic position within a united democratic opposition such as it had enjoyed in the days of the MUD. Its clandestine organisation, complete with clandestine press, was still really the only one of note and it received a certain fillip with the escape from Peniche gaol in January 1960 of Álvaro Cunhal, and of other leaders in 1961 from Caxias in the armoured Mercedes Hitler had once presented to Salazar. Cunhal, who became Secretary-General of the PCP in 1961, seemed to bring about greater cohesion (at least among those who remained) and the 6th Congress of 1965 clarified its programmatic position. PCP strategy was one of preparation and waiting. The regime, said Cunhal in 1965, could only be overthrown by insurrection, but 'that insurrection can only take place when the masses are to be found in open struggle against the regime, when a considerable part of the army is won over to the cause of revolution, when the revolutionary movement has an organisation strong enough really to direct the development of popular struggles and to begin successfully the final battle'. In the meantime people had to live in hope that this day would not be far off.

When the regime in 1966 celebrated the fortieth anniversary of the National Revolution of 28 May, it still seemed secure. Salazar was getting older but the instruments of control and repression still seemed to be working with enough efficiency to prevent the civilian opposition from expanding much outside the élite. The threats of military intervention, although not apparently detected by the PIDE until the last minute, seemed to have passed. Among the educated, young and old, it might seem that 'the best minds' were against the regime, but they had been for some time. In Africa there were colonial wars, but in 1966 the threat these posed to the stability of the regime seemed insignificant; indeed, after the initial shock of 1961, there had been something of a patriotic closing of ranks. Catholicism might be now a questionable prop of the regime but, on the other hand, despite increasing emigration and heavy military expenditure, economic progress was becoming more apparent and there were doubtless some in the regime who saw its future as a kind of technocratic developmental dictatorship made more secure by the alleged global trend towards the end of ideology.

It was indeed in the realm of ideology that the New State was now dangerously vulnerable. The new corporative man talked of in the 1930s had not emerged and the continuation of opposition and the need for repression pointed to the failure of a non-partisan national consensus in favour of the regime to emerge. Most might be apathetic and many indifferent about politics but the élite had stubbornly refused to be converted *en masse*. In one of his increasingly rare speeches, Salazar himself in 1965 admitted failure in two 'essential' respects: 'to convince our rulers that they need political support for their actions, and that this support can only come from the National Union; to convince the National Union that political formation cannot just be left to gambling on what is read or on family influences, but must be the subject of a process of systematic and persistent doctrinal education'.

The New State, then, was ideologically bankrupt, institutionally petrified and powered only by inertia, but this was enough for its survival faced with a divided opposition, a tamed officer corps, an expanding economy and a lack of military disasters. In 1968 President Tomás reluctantly brought Salazar's thirty-six-year reign to an end, but the dictator's removal took place when he was unconscious and no one dared tell him before he died on 27 July 1970 that he was not Premier. The fall of the dictator had been precipitated not by military intervention or civil disturbance, but by the collapse of the deckchair in which he was sitting on 6 September. The shock produced a clot on the brain and inevitable hospitalisation for the 79-year-old Salazar, feverish politicking in the higher echelons of the regime, and cautious inhibition amounting to total inaction on the part of the opposition.

There was acrimonious argument in the Council of State as Tomás sought general agreement on the name of a successor from among the competing factions. Names mentioned as possibles included the Foreign Minister, Franco Nogueira, the son of a shepherd but now a wealthy lawyer; another lawyer, Adriano Moreira, the son of a policeman who had once defended oppositionists but subsequently made a name for himself as Overseas Minister in the early 1960s; and generals such as Deslandes and Kaúlza de Arriaga. Despite the opposition of *ultras,* who still included Santos Costa, it was the latter's old rival who was chosen.

The man appointed Premier on 25 September 1968 was the son of a primary school teacher, a lean and ambitious lawyer, Marcelo das Neves Caetano, who looked younger than his 63 years. His background suggested that he was very much a man of the regime. As a student journalist he had espoused the extreme right-wing ideas then fashionable and at the age of 23 had become legal adviser to the Finance Ministry then occupied by Salazar. He had been a professor of law at Lisbon University in 1933 and had played an important role in drafting the New State's laws, especially the administrative code of 1936. From 1940 to 1944 he was National Commissioner for the *Mocidade* and from then until 1947 Minister for the Colonies. A leading member of the UN, he became President of the Corporative Chamber in 1950 and Minister of the Presidency, with overall responsibility for economic planning, in 1955. However, he was dropped in the 1958 reshuffle and made Rector of Lisbon University, a post from which he had resigned in 1962. He had spent the intervening six years officially out of politics as a lawyer and academic, but he had given indications that, as an empiricist in politics, he was in favour of the modernisation and liberalisation of the regime, including a federal solution for the overseas problem which would go some way towards self-determination for the colonies.

Caetano, therefore, was looked upon favourably by the younger technocratic members of the regime and his appointment sent a wave of hope through the ranks of the opposition: if he were not exactly Sebastian, expectations of change were nevertheless raised. His first public statements were ambiguous. He was succeeding 'a man of genius', he said, but he also referred to 'seeking to establish highly desirable communication between the government and the nation' and to 'the generalisation of a spirit of living together where reciprocal tolerance of ideas would break down hate and antagonisms' (though liberty had to be defended from 'communism' and 'anarchical impulses'). In time there would be 'necessary reforms' within the 'major outlines' of 'the situation'; he would 'guarantee continuity', but this 'implies a notion of movement, sequence and adaptation. Faithfulness to the doctrine brilliantly taught by Dr Salazar should not be confused with stubborn adherence to formulas or solutions that he at some time may have adopted . . . A thought must be living if it is to be fruitful. Life is a constant adaptation.' How far such 'adaptation' would go remained to be seen. It was by his actions that both the opposition and the apprehensive *ultras* would judge him.

3

Foreign and Colonial

Holland makes cheese, Switzerland condensed milk, while Portugal goes on standing on tiptoe trying to make itself seen in the gathering of Great Powers. Gilberto Freyre

Not merely a European but a World Power. President Carmona on Portugal in 1939

For English readers no doubt the best-known fact about Portuguese foreign affairs is the existence of the Anglo-Portuguese alliance, declared by Churchill to be 'without parallel in world history' since it has lasted for six centuries. The first treaty of alliance between the Crowns of Portugal and England was signed in St Paul's Cathedral on 16 June 1373; the second and more important was concluded at Windsor in May 1386 and read in part:

There shall be inviolate and endure forever between the above Kings now reigning and their heirs and successors, and between the subjects of both kingdoms a solid, perpetual and real League, Amity, Confederacy and Union, not only on behalf of themselves and their Heirs and Successors, their Subjects, Vassals, Allies and Friends whatsoever, so that either of them shall be bound to succour and afford aid to the other against all men that may live and those who shall attempt to violate the peace of the other, or injure his state in any way.

After 1386 the alliance had its vicissitudes but was reaffirmed in 1643, 1654, 1660, 1661, 1703, 1815 and on 14 October 1899, by the so-called Secret Declaration of Windsor, in which Great Britain undertook 'to defend and protect all conquests or colonies belonging to the Crown of Portugal against all his enemies as well future as present'.

In fact, like all diplomatic arrangements, the alliance was interpreted or ignored by either partner according to convenience: thus the declaration of 1899 was aimed, on the British side, at getting the Portuguese to stop arms supplies to the Boers passing through Mozambique, while on the Portuguese side it was an attempt to get

Britain to drop contingency plans for the partition of the Portuguese empire with the Germans. In so far as the alliance survived or had any reality this was because of certain constant interests on either side. Portugal needed an ally to ensure its independence from Spain and, in modern times, Britain as the dominant maritime power was the ideal choice from the Portuguese point of view. From the British standpoint a friendly Portugal was an asset since the mainland and the Islands could provide threatening bases if in unfriendly hands: Portugal was an important key to the security of Atlantic traffic and the route to the East, whether this was seen as going through the Mediterranean or round the Cape of Good Hope – in the latter case who held the Cape Verde Islands, Angola and Mozambique was of some importance. From the restoration of Portuguese independence in 1640 the British were always very much the senior partner and took advantage of the fact. Portugal's need for political security for itself and its colonies had to be paid for by economic concessions to Britain and, after the Peninsular War and the loss of Brazil, Portugal and its overseas possessions became in a sense an informal colony of Britain. Britain, as in 1890, could set the limits to Portuguese African expansion – 'England treated us like the chief of the Matabele or the sultan of Zanzibar', commented the Portuguese imperialist António Enes – and talk of partition with the Germans because she had the naval and economic power. Portugal still had to cling to Britain, however much this might be resented, because to go against it could mean not only loss of empire but absorption into Spain. Portuguese dependence on Britain was reinforced by financial and economic weakness in the century of free trade, a concept which, as one Portuguese writer bitterly remarked, constituted 'a chain prepared for the simple . . . an excellent doctrine for the strong against the weak'.

By 1914 one could say that Portugal still needed Britain, but Britain had little need of Portugal. If Portugal were to play a more independent role it would have somehow to become more economically self-reliant and establish good relations with other Great Powers to counteract the dominance of Britain – and this the realities of Great Power relationships and the need to keep her colonies did not allow. Although, since Britain declared war on Germany in 1914, Portugal was not bound by the alliance to enter the First World War, prudence demanded that Portugal do so whenever Britain and France were agreeable. Were Portugal to remain neutral it was conceivable that its overseas possessions could become the basis for a compromise peace settlement between the Western Allies and Germany. In March 1916 Portugal duly entered the war after seizing German shipping at the request of the British and in the peace settlement which followed it emerged with its territories intact; indeed a small gain was made in the form of the Kionga triangle (taken by the Germans in 1894) in northern Mozambique.

Portugal's need for British friendship was still recognised as essential by Salazar in the 1930s. While, faced with the resurgence of Germany, France was unlikely to provide an alternative to Britain as protector, there was the theoretical possibility of more room to manœuvre given Anglo-German and Anglo-Italian rivalries. While Mussolini might be admired on ideological grounds and because he seemed to represent the revival of a sister Latin power, Salazar could not afford to alienate the British when the chips were down. Arms were purchased from Italy and some sympathy shown at the time of the Ethiopian War, but the Italians (who had once taken an unhealthy interest in Angola) were no alternative to Britain since they were a Mediterranean, not an Atlantic, power. Germany, too, could be a source for the purchase of arms but, despite Salazar's view of German usefulness as a barrier against communism, it became increasingly ideologically unacceptable as a close partner; and with talk of an Anglo-German settlement in the mid-1930s on the basis of colonial readjustments, Portugal, as in the period 1890–1914, found that reaffirmation of the alliance (and also closer relations with South Africa) were its best bets for the security of its African territories. So, despite Italophil and Germanophil sentiments among sections of the élite, and despite resentment at the cavalier way Britain treated Portugal, Salazar found that there was little room for manœuvre. As he put it in 1935: 'We believe that in accordance with the true interests of the Portuguese nation its foreign policy is always to avoid, if possible, any entanglements in Europe, to maintain friendly relations within the Peninsula, and to develop our resources as an Atlantic power.' In this connection the idea of an 'Atlantic alliance' of Britain, Spain and Portugal was floated by the Portuguese Foreign Minister on a visit to Spain in late 1935, but it came to nothing. Portugal remained a member of the League of Nations though Salazar mocked its supporters' 'belief in the innate goodness of human nature, in the good faith of nations, in the dream of a perpetual and universal peace'; and, of course, as a staunch anti-communist, he opposed the admission of Soviet Russia (with which Portugal had no diplomatic relations until 1974) to membership in 1934.

From 1936 to 1947 Salazar was his own Foreign Minister, which underlined, were that necessary, the importance of external relations for Portugal and for the regime which identified itself with the national interest, during the Spanish Civil War and the Second World War. The Salazarist government had been suspicious of the Spanish Second Republic from its installation in April 1931, fearing that some Spanish republicans would help Portuguese exiles in their struggle against Salazar. Though Spanish republicans showed sympathy for their Portuguese opposite numbers, nothing very much actually transpired. With the victory of the Popular Front in Spain in February 1936 and the growing disorder which ensued, the Portuguese regime became more worried again and clearly favoured the military revolt in July 1936; its leader, General Sanjurjo, who had spent two years in exile in Portugal and had attended military parades at President Carmona's invitation, was killed on 20 July taking off from a ploughed-up racecourse near Cascais. Salazar and his colleagues from the first hoped for the defeat of the republicans, whom they equated with communism, and the victory of the nationalists, whose cause they saw as analogous to their own National Revolution: as the German *chargé d'affaires* in Lisbon, Count du Moulin, reported, 'the Portuguese government determined on the clear policy of complete support for the rebels as far as it was possible to do so and maintain the semblance of formal neutrality'.

The Spanish Civil War divided Portuguese opinion as it did opinion in other countries. Captain Jorge Botelho Moniz, director of the commercial station Rádio Clube Português, effectively put his transmitter at the insurgents' service and subsequently organised *viriatos* from the Portuguese Legion to fight for Franco in their thousands: most were volunteers, some regular army officers. Insurgent agents organised propaganda and arms supplies in Lisbon, and with the insurgents in control of the whole frontier area, Portugal severed diplomatic relations with Republican Spain after its Legation had been sacked. Portugal reluctantly adhered to the British- and French-sponsored Non-Intervention Committee but never approved of it; aid continued to go to the nationalists and Portugal played an obstructive role on the committee. On the other hand opponents of Salazar sided with the republic: as already noted mutinies occurred on warships in the Tagus, while to the bomb plot against Salazar in 1937 must also be added anarchist sabotage of supplies for Spain and the blowing up of the Rádio Clube Português transmitter at Parede.

'Portugal and Spain are like two brothers, each possessing his own home in the Peninsula', said Salazar, but the brother was National Spain: republican refugees were often deported to face death. Salazar saw that his regime's future depended on a nationalist victory which he saw as 'the barrier between Portugal and Iberian communism'; on the other hand friendship with brother Spain was conditional on the latter's recognition of 'the immutable principle of the duality of the Peninsula which has survived the federal tradition of the two republics as well as the imperial tradition of Philip II'. Portuguese hostility to non-intervention and its support for the Axis-backed Franco led to some friction with Britain, whom Salazar wanted to support Franco. The opportunity was taken to remind the British that Portugal had her own interests and her destiny was not to be one of limitless obedience. Nevertheless Salazar's special agent and later Ambassador in Spain, Pedro Teotónio Pereira, arrived in Spain only at the same time as his British opposite number, Sir Robert Hodgson, while official recognition of the nationalists in April 1938 was coupled with another public reaffirmation of the British alliance and a welcome for a British military mission to see to arms deliveries and coastal defences.

Within the context of the British alliance, Salazar sought to increase Portuguese prestige and security by concluding the Treaty of Friendship and Non-Aggression ('the Iberian Pact') with Spain on 17 March 1939, by which the Iberian neighbours agreed to respect each other's frontiers and to refuse to aid any other power which attacked either. Portugal intended to affirm her position as a valued go-between in Anglo-Spanish relations and a magnet for drawing Spain away from overdependence on her Axis friends. The Iberian Pact, Salazar claimed, created a 'true zone of peace in the Peninsula' of benefit to Britain and her French ally, and thus represented 'the crowning of a great work and the keystone of a policy'. At the same time, as part of his Atlantic policy, Salazar set out to strengthen contacts with the daughter-nation of Brazil, a policy inherited from the First Republic but now made ideologically more promising with President Vargas's creation of his own New State in 1937.

London, Madrid and Rio de Janeiro were three cardinal points in Salazar's diplomatic outlook; the fourth, the Vatican, was added with the concordat of 1940. During the Second World War Salazar's policy was aimed at preserving the integrity of the mainland and its overseas possessions and at keeping the war out of the Iberian Peninsula while, as a neutral, benefiting from the needs of the nations at war. In all these aims he proved successful. As in 1914, it was Britain which declared war on Germany and so Portugal was not bound to support Britain. In September 1939, with the agreement of the British government, Portugal declared its neutrality, while the Germano-Soviet attack on Poland, which Salazar bemoaned, did much to disenchant Axis sympathisers within the regime. Salazar no doubt, like the Vatican, hoped for a short war and a peace settlement which would keep communism out of Europe and, as the leader of a small state, he took care not to offend either side: thus in 1941 he assured the German Ambassador that he approved of the reorganisation of Europe and he would resist British pressures. Nevertheless, whatever politenesses might be exchanged with German diplomats, he did not desire a German victory; as he put it to the Italian minister in 1940: 'My main worry is that Germany may obtain a crushing military victory over the Allies. Hitler, drunk with victory, would Germanise Europe. And if Napoleon's soldiers carried the principles of the French Revolution on the points of their bayonets, Hitler's carry a neo-paganism of mystic and racist origin that is contrary to our Roman and Catholic traditions.'

As War Minister and Foreign Minister as well as Premier, Salazar had the last word, while press and radio and members of the officer corps had differing views as to what the Portuguese attitude should be. Though stubbornly intent on defending Portugal's 'juridical neutrality' Salazar, if only out of self-interest, tended from the first to be co-operative with the oldest ally on at least some minor matters such as the sale of trawlers to the Admiralty, the denial of the coastline to U-boats and the suppression of weather forecasts.

The trickiest time for Portugal came in 1940 with the fall of France and the Spanish move from neutrality to non-belligerency. Salazar feared, with reason, that Spain might now join the war on the Axis side and try to pick up an easy victory by an invasion of Portugal in conjunction with the Germans; at the same time Churchill was restrained by the Foreign Office from trying to forestall the Germans by seizing the Azores and Cape Verde Islands, key points in Atlantic naval warfare. Since any effective help from Britain in the event of an Axis-Spanish invasion was unlikely, Salazar and his Ambassador, Teotónio Pereira, dealt with this threat by diplomacy, though the final negotiations of the Luso-Spanish Protocol of 29 July 1940 were the work of Franco's brother (Nicolás, Ambassador in Lisbon) and the Portuguese Foreign Ministry, behind the back of Franco's pro-Axis brother-in-law, Serrano Súñer. The Protocol to the Treaty of 1939, stressing the need for consultation in the event of a threat to either country, went some way to cementing a Peninsular Bloc, and therefore Iberian neutrality, provided no attack came from outside. However, in December 1940, when Franco parried a German demand for immediate intervention on the Axis side, Salazar opened staff talks with the British and agreed to move his government to the Azores after token resistance to any German invasion. By 1941 the strength of the Portuguese Army had been doubled (to 80,000), many units being stationed in the Islands, and early in that year Eden (British Foreign Secretary) sought to counter pro-Axis propaganda with the public promise not to bring down Salazar in the event of an Allied victory. In fact the threat of the war coming to mainland Portugal was over after Operation Torch (the Anglo-American landings in North Africa in November 1942), when the Spaniards became altogether more enthusiastic about the idea of an Iberian Bloc and the Western Allies assured both Lisbon and Madrid that they had 'nothing to fear' from the United Nations, while the Germans chose not to open another front in the Peninsula. The question of the Islands and colonial possessions was, however, far from over.

The Azores were, from the Western Allies' viewpoint, of great strategic importance and their occupation by the Germans would be disastrous. British policy was therefore to keep Portugal neutral, thus denying the islands to the Germans. Even before their entry into the war the Americans were themselves prepared to forestall any German move by occupying the islands, and to this end an expeditionary force was prepared and contacts made with pro-Allied Portuguese officers. From the Allied point of view naval and air facilities in the islands (where the Americans had had bases in the First World War) would help in the war against the U-boats and make possible quicker and cheaper air contacts between North America and Europe, a factor of increasing importance as the time for an invasion of the Continent approached. By early 1943 it seemed less likely that the Germans would take counter-measures against Portugal and so the British began to negotiate for naval and air facilities after invoking the old alliance, though the preliminary survey work had begun in 1942. Churchill had some sympathy with the American view of delivering an ultimatum and using force but was persuaded to accept the diplomatic course, which culminated in the Anglo-Portuguese agreement of 17 August 1943 allowing for British personnel to land on 8 October: Portugal, in Eden's view, was a more co-operative neutral than Éire or Turkey. The British intention was to broaden the agreement to include use of the bases by the Americans, but the latter, of whom Salazar was suspicious, unilaterally proposed to the Portuguese in September 1943 'a virtual takeover of the islands' (in the words of the American *chargé d'affaires,* G. F. Kennan). The British persuaded them to desist, however, in case Salazar should invoke the old alliance against an American invasion. Portugal, noted Eden, 'is not a second Guatemala, from whom anything the Americans desire can be obtained simply by threats or bribes'. Salazar, indeed, was determined to compromise his neutrality no further and American use was made conditional on the fiction that their personnel and equipment were 'on loan to HM government'; he would not budge on this point, threatening to use force against an overtly American presence until after D-day (June 1944). In addition to American use of the Lajes airfield on Terceira, the Portuguese agreed to the building of a further airfield in November 1944 on Santa Maria.

In fact the Azores issue did not exist in isolation and was linked to the question of Portuguese Timor (in the East Indies) and economic matters. One of the factors linked to the various Azores agreements was the Portuguese anxiety to recover Timor, and if possible to take part in operations in the Pacific War to this end. In November 1941 Salazar undertook to defend Portuguese Timor and to call in British help in the event of an attack, but in mid-December 1941 Australian and Dutch troops landed without any request from Portugal. Salazar was furious at this breach of neutrality, fearing Japanese counter-measures against Macao. The British were apologetic and agreed to withdraw when Portuguese reinforcements arrived, but before they did the Japanese took over the territory in February 1942 and Allied forces retreated inland to conduct guerrilla warfare. British–Portuguese staff conversations began in September 1944 with a view to its recovery but the

Americans were against direct Portuguese participation; instead they got the Santa Maria base agreement by way of indirect participation. In the event there were no Allied plans for operations against Timor when Japan surrendered and the territory reverted to Portuguese rule.

Economic relations with Portugal were almost throughout the war a complicating factor for the belligerents, especially as Portugal was the most important European producer of wolfram, much in demand by both sides for its uses in machine-tools and the making of armour-piercing shells. As a neutral and a poor country, Portugal naturally wanted to take advantage to the maximum extent of the upsurge in demand and consequent price rises. The wolfram issue was also connected to the wider economic effect of the war on Portugal, notably the Allied blockade. The constant and complex haggling which took place was, as Salazar put it, 'due in part to the impossibility of entirely reconciling the right that we claim as neutrals to trade with other neutrals and with the belligerents, and to look for our suppliers wherever we consider it convenient; the impossiblity of conciliating this right on the one hand with the conception and policy of the British blockade on the other; for that blockade is influenced less by principles of law and economy than by the place which is given to the blockade in British war policy, a preoccupation which entirely dominates those who have to carry it out'.

Though Portugal never officially suffered domestic rationing, the war did have a distorting effect on its economy. The reallocation of shipping and resources meant that Portuguese trade suffered, as did the imposition of the navicert system by Britain from July 1940; Germany had been an important trade partner and, until the fall of France, land communications with that country were cut. The British were naturally anxious to deprive the Axis powers of essential supplies and the acceptance of quotas for exports affected Portugal, especially as most of her prewar transit and re-export trade had been with Germany and Italy. Difficulties were encountered in disposing of colonial surpluses, but it was not until 1941 that agreement was reached over re-exports. The Portuguese resisted precise commitments wherever possible, but tin exports to the Axis were banned after April 1941. If the Portuguese gave way too much to what Salazar called Allied wrist-twisting there was the fear that Germany might be tempted into military action; as it was, there was a tacit understanding that Germany would not sink Portuguese shipping if trade in vital commodities such as wolfram continued. In such a situation Britain indulged in pre-emptive buying to deprive the Axis of supplies, an activity much facilitated by the banking agreement of November 1940 by which Portugal, unlike other neutrals, allowed Britain to purchase her currency with sterling credits (which totalled £80,000,000 by the end of the war) instead of gold. Pre-emptive buying was engaged in with regard to sardines (the price for a case of which rose from about 100 escudos at the start of the war to 280 by 1944) and, of course, wolfram, Portuguese supplies of which were vital to the German war economy after the latter's attack on Russia cut off Far Eastern supplies. The price naturally soared from £1,250 a ton in June to £6,000 a ton in November 1941. British-owned mines were the biggest producers and throughout the war the Allies bought most of the production; the aim however was to stop sales to Germany, which increased as more and more countryfolk deserted agriculture for the quick profits to be made from their own mining activities (fossicking), and production accordingly increased.

General Allied War Trade and Supply-Purchase agreements were negotiated in November 1942, but wolfram continued to be sold to Germany. The need to continue this trade with Germany diminished as the tide of war turned in favour of the Allies, who became able to supply the steel and fertilisers they had previously been unable to provide for the Portuguese. Though the Allies could bargain with petrol supplies, it was nevertheless understood by Churchill that Portuguese political benevolence to Britain had to be compensated for by the continued supply of some wolfram to Germany: thus Germany took no offensive action when the Anglo-Portuguese agreement on the Azores was implemented. In June 1944 Portugal finally agreed to a complete embargo on wolfram supplies to Germany when threatened with full-scale economic sanctions plus the invocation of the old alliance and Brazilian entreaties. The embargo meant a loss of £2,000,000 to the Portuguese treasury and tens of thousands unemployed as a result of the closure of mines. In the economic sphere Salazar's policy had been, in so far as circumstances permitted, 'business as usual'. In the diplomatic sphere his 'vigilant neutrality' had balanced pro-Allied and pro-Axis factions among the élite in the earlier part of the war, while his concessions to the Allies from 1943, and the guarantees for his regime and Portuguese territorial integrity in Europe and elsewhere which were given in exchange, made the continuance of the New State a reality and enhanced his and Portugal's prestige in some quarters. As a 'premature Cold Warrior' he deprecated the Allied policy of unconditional surrender and the advance of Soviet influence westwards and was to the end a stickler for the proprieties of 'juridical neutrality'. He and De Valera, both rulers of nations traditionally in the British orbit, asserted their independence by sending condolences to Admiral Doenitz on the death of Adolf Hitler. In 1945 Salazar was, with Franco, the last of the prewar dictators, but Portugal was never subject to the same pressures as its Spanish counterpart because, as Stalin explained at Potsdam, Salazar's rise to power had domestic roots unconnected with Axis aid. Nevertheless the Soviet Union opposed Portuguese membership of the United Nations Organisation.

After 1945, the Cold War and decolonisation were dominant features of the international scene. Until 1960 the main preoccupation of the New State was with the threat of communism, while after 1960 – the year in which the United Nations began to concentrate its attention on Portuguese colonial policies after the Belgians granted independence to the Congo – the attitudes of the Afro-Asian powers added to Portugal's worries. Soviet communism and the rise of the Third World were seen by Portuguese leaders, in their self-appointed role as defenders and, indeed, chief interpreters of the interests of Western civilisation, as two faces of the same phenomenon, the advance of the non-Western world.

Given the regime's anti-communist stance domestically and internationally, Portugal did not have the option of trying to play off the Eastern and Western power blocs in the 1940s. If the regime were to boost its prestige, gain greater respectability among the Western allies and safeguard its colonial interests, it therefore had to try and make itself indispensable to Western defence. The geographical position of the country, mainland and Islands, was of enormous advantage in this respect once it became clear that an American presence would remain in Western Europe. The American need for a transit base was recognised and various agreements prolonged American use of the Lajes Base until the bilateral arrangement was formalised in the Defence Agreement of 1951, renewed at intervals since. The need for the Azores base as a link between North America and Western Europe, together with Portugal's possession of the strategically situated Cape Verde Islands, led the United States explicitly to ask for Portuguese adherence to the North Atlantic Treaty in 1949.

Portugal, of course, joined, even though NATO was dedicated to the defence of democratic liberties. Membership bolstered the regime's position *vis-à-vis* the opposition at home, while Salazar made it clear that he dissented from the democratic verbiage of the Treaty's Preamble. For him it was simply an anti-communist alliance in which he thought Spain should also be included. In 1949 Franco visited Portugal and the Iberian Pact was reaffirmed (to continue in existence until allowed to disappear in 1975–6). NATO did not cover Portugal's overseas possessions, but the Portuguese clearly hoped that membership of the alliance would indirectly help their security. Portuguese foreign policy in the 1950s was in fact based on the assumption, as in the 1930s, that Portugal was essentially an Atlantic country and therefore good relations with Spain, Britain, Brazil and now the United States were essential.

In the 1930s Salazar had said that the Anglo-Portuguese alliance would last as long as the British Empire – and this proved to be the case even if the Portuguese government was slow to recognise it. Britain in 1947 withdrew from the Indian sub-continent, quickly followed by the French, and the Indian government no doubt expected Portugal to do the same. Portugal, however, saw no reason to give up the State of India (essentially the enclaves of Goa, Damão and Diu) and refused Indian requests to negotiate a withdrawal. When Indian troops invaded Goa in December 1961 Salazar invoked the old Alliance – last invoked by the British in 1943 and 1944. Britain, however, replied that the alliance did not apply in this case and, in any case, she could not act against a fellow member of the Commonwealth and therefore declined to give the Portuguese the air-staging facilities requested. For Salazar, who wept on television, the old alliance was as good as dead, and the Portuguese were henceforth disillusioned with Britain as an ally. Britain would not publicly and positively support Portugal's stand in Africa and in 1966 relations became even more strained when, during Anglo-Portuguese talks on the problem of the Rhodesian declaration of independence, Britain introduced sanctions in the United Nations. The result was the blockade of Beira, and sanctions (which in practice the Portuguese did not observe) were a severe blow to the central Mozambican economy. In the defence and development of her southern African possessions, Portugal increasingly saw South Africa and Rhodesia as her allies, not Britain.

The deterioration of Anglo–Portuguese relations in the 1960s was part and parcel of Portugal's stubborn refusal to recognise the existence of the winds of change in Africa. Diplomatically, the Third World's attack on the continued presence of Portugal in Africa predated the outbreak of hostilities in Angola (in 1961). In 1951 Portugal had renamed her colonies 'overseas provinces' and, as such, integral parts of Portugal, but the United Nations General Assembly of which Portugal became a member in 1955, in December 1960 nevertheless considered them 'non-self-governing territories' and soon went on to demand their independence and the increasing ostracism of Portugal. The Portuguese stuck to the line that the charter of the United Nations (Article 2[7]) prohibited intervention 'in matters which are essentially within the domestic jurisdiction of any state' – and since, for example, Angola was part of Portugal, this part of the charter was applicable. Thus the legalistic arguments were conducted on different premises. Nevertheless, with an Afro-Asian majority in the General Assembly, debates on Portuguese colonial matters were an embarrassment to Portugal's allies in NATO, who generally abstained when it came to the voting.

Portugal resented the lack of public support from its NATO allies and in the 1960s manoeuvred in several directions to prevent the fate of being, as Salazar put it, 'proudly alone'. The United States' ideas of withdrawing all support from Portugal during the Kennedy administration were effectively countered by Portuguese threats to terminate the Azores agreement at a time when Lajes was still essential in American military thinking. In NATO itself Portugal constantly argued for reform of the alliance to cover the global commitments of any member, and in particular argued for the revision of Article 6 of the North Atlantic Treaty which set the limit at the Tropic of Cancer. France was wooed with support for the Gaullist idea of the 'third force' which, in the Portuguese view, had to be based on a Eurafrican policy, while with West Germany good relations were cultivated from the 1950s. Portugal supported the idea of German reunification and in return received aid and weapons from the Federal Republic in the 1960s, as indeed it continued to do from France, Britain and the United States. The weapons, of course, were agreed to be for NATO, not African, use. In the 1960s the French were allowed to set up a missile-tracking station in the Azores and the West Germans an airbase near Beja. Portugal's 'isolation' in the 1960s was therefore far from total; what was resented was the lack of positive public support on the part of her allies, a point which led Portuguese propaganda to present the African wars as a heroic but misunderstood battle being fought on the West's behalf. Portugal, indeed, as the English-language broadcasts of Emissora Nacional made clear, was the true 'Voice of the West'.

In addition to courting NATO allies, Portugal continued her close relationship with Spain – though this cooled somewhat in the 1960s as a result of differing attitudes to decolonisation – and sought to get ever closer to Brazil. Brazilians were generally somewhat resentful of Portuguese claims that they were Portugal's greatest gift to the world, but there was some response to ideas of Luso-Brazilian community. In 1953 a treaty of friendship, the Treaty of Rio de Janeiro, was signed between the two countries: it spoke of mutual consultation in matters of foreign policy and moves towards assimilation of Portuguese living in Brazil and Brazilians living in Portugal. Relations were warm during Kubitschek's presidency (1956–61) but cool in the time of Quadros and Goulart (1961–4); after the military takeover of 1964 relations warmed again, as a joint agreement of 1966 showed. However, the Brazilians did not get themselves physically involved in the defence of Portuguese Africa, perhaps to the disappointment of Portugal's Foreign Minister Franco Nogueira (1961–9).

By the end of the 1960s, when there were signs of Portugal getting more support from the United States and other NATO allies as well as from South Africa and Brazil, it had become obvious that the Portuguese regime's sole aim in foreign relations' was self-preservation, which entailed diplomatic as well as military and economic backing for its African policies. The fate of a Portugal deprived of its overseas possessions was seen to be either that of a satellite of Spain or that of the Albania of the West – perhaps both. It is therefore time to turn to look at Portugal's colonial, imperial or overseas policies.

The territories ruled by Portugal in the twentieth century are shown in Table 3.1.

Table 3.1   *Portuguese Overseas Territories and Dates of Loss*

Territory	Area (in sq. miles)	Population in 1970	Date lost to Portugal
Asia			
State of India	1,537	638,000 (1955)	December 1961
Macao	6	249,000	—
Timor	5,763	609,000	December 1975
Africa			
Guiné	13,948	487,000	September 1974
Cape Verde Islands	1,557	272,000	July 1975
São Tomé e Príncipe	372	74,000	July 1975
Angola	481,351	5,674,000	November 1975
Mozambique	303,070	8,234,000	July 1975

To these should be added the Portuguese Territory of São João de Ajudá, which by 1960 consisted of a ruined fort and the governor's bungalow and garden, an enclave surrounded by Dahomey which became independent from France in that year. In 1961 Dahomey asked Portugal to give up the territory but received no reply from Lisbon; in August the governor burned down his bungalow hours before an ultimatum from Dahomey expired, and drove to the airport. This somewhat comic episode may nevertheless be taken as symbolic of the intransigent Salazarist attitude to decolonisation.

Though the origins of the Portuguese empire went back to the days of exploration and discovery associated with Prince Henry the Navigator in the fifteenth century, the twentieth-century imperial complex was principally a creation of the late nineteenth century. Portugal's first empire, maritime and commercial in character and centred on Golden Goa and the East, began its decline in the sixteenth century, to be replaced as the focus of attention in the seventeenth and eighteenth centuries by Brazil, with its slave-trading connections with western Africa. When Brazil became independent in the 1820s, Portugal ceased for a time to be a major imperial power. Only with the general European scramble for Africa towards the end of the nineteenth century did any widespread enthusiasm revive for the idea that Africa could be developed to compensate for the loss of Brazil, and that an African empire was a necessary part of Portugal's destiny as a great power, perhaps even of its survival as an independent nation. It was only in the last quarter of the nineteenth century that a large part of the élite came to accept the ideas of the country's modern imperial precursor, Sá da Bandeira, who had maintained from the 1830s that 'only colonies can give us in Europe the influence and position which otherwise would be denied us so justifiably because of the narrow boundaries of the Metropolis, and its situation in the [Iberian] peninsula'. Portugal could no longer lay claim to vast tracts of territory simply by virtue of the longevity of her coastal settlements and her indirect contacts with the interior. The criterion for ownership of land was now 'effective occupation' as the Portuguese were made to realise by the British ultimatum of 1890, and so the three ensuing decades saw the conquest and pacification of much of the area which was subsequently invoked to lend credence to the claim that Portugal was not, after all, a small country.

The third empire, centred on Angola and Mozambique, was then the creation of both monarchist and republican regimes employing the talents of a fairly small number of determined, adventurous and imperially minded individuals of the type of António Enes and Mousinho de Albuquerque. It was such men of the imperialist generation of the 1890s who sought to give the lie to the image of Portuguese 'boastful fecklessness' (in Lord Salisbury's phrase) by conquering native opponents and *'forcing* these rude Negroes in Africa . . . to civilise themselves through work'. In the last years of the monarchy and during the First Republic the policy of forced labour which was seen as an integral component of the 'civilising mission' was accompanied by a tendency towards administrative decentralisation from Lisbon and financial autonomy. The early republic, under the spur of French Republican example, preferred to call its overseas possessions colonies rather than provinces, a practice followed by the New State until 1951. The New State continued and re-Catholicised the imperial policies of its predecessors except that the trend towards decentralisation, which had given wide powers to colonial high commissioners that some said were abused (Norton de Matos was nicknamed by Cunha Leal Caligula in Angola), was sharply reversed.

The corner-stone of revised imperial policy was the Colonial Act of 8 July 1930 (Decree No. 18570), the work of Salazar and the Colonial Minister Armindo Monteiro, though drawing on the experience of decrees of 1926 and 1928. This Act was republished as an appendix to the political constitution of 1933 and, with minor modifications in 1935 and 1945, continued in force until 1951 as the charter of the Portuguese Colonial Empire. Its Article 2 boldly proclaimed: 'It is of the organic essence of the Portuguese nation to carry out the historic function of possessing and colonising overseas dominions and civilising the indigenous populations therein contained.' Effective government control was vested, through the Colonial Ministry, in the Lisbon government, represented by a governor or governor-general on the spot

In general terms the Act proclaimed that the rights of natives would be guaranteed, though the state could compel them to 'work on public works of general interest to the collectivity'. The state was to aid overseas religious missions as an 'instrument of civilisation and national influence'. Colonial economies were to be organised 'in harmony with the needs of their development [and] with the rights and legitimate convenience of the Metropolis and the Portuguese Colonial Empire'. Colonial budgets were to balance and be approved in Lisbon, and the state's right to control economic resources was asserted.

The need to anticipate and stymie the tendency to decolonisation which followed the Second World War brought about a change in the language of colonial rule, with French precedents again serving as conceptual inspiration. Just as the French Third Republic's example had prompted the use of the term colonies in 1911, so now the constitution of the Fourth Republic inspired the new formula of legal integration with the Metropolis. On 11 June 1951, Law No. 2048 revised the constitution of 1933 in such a way as to incorporate provisions previously enshrined in the Colonial Act. The Colonial Ministry became the Overseas Ministry, the colonies, overseas provinces, which were defined as an 'integral part of the Portuguese state'. The same provisions were made for the native inhabitants as in the Act of 1930 (though these were now said to be a 'regime of transition'). It was with this legal text that Portuguese spokesmen sought to defend their empire against charges that their possessions were non-self-governing territories ripe for decolonisation in the 1960s: the constitutional revision of 1959 specified that representatives of the overseas provinces were one component of the electoral college which selected the President of the Republic.

Until 1971 (indeed effectively till 1974) Metropolitan Portugal and its overseas possessions were governed as one unitary state, despite the creation of local legislative councils in Luanda and Lourenço Marques. For the colonies the Overseas Ministry and its staff performed the function of the civil administrative bureaucracy in the Metropolis. Though the overseas provinces were represented in the National Assembly and the Corporative Chamber, the hierarchical organisation of administration was dependent, as in the Metropolis, on the Lisbon government. Territories were subdivided into *distritos*, with Lisbon appointing the Governors, and below them were the *administradores* of *concelhos*. Often military men were governors of *distritos* but the reforms of Adriano Moreira as Overseas Minister in 1963 specified that half these posts were to be held by civil servants, hopefully byproducts of the Higher Institute of Social Sciences and Overseas Policy in Lisbon, the old colonial academy where the administrative élite of various ethnic origins was trained. In less advanced areas there were *circunscrições*, rather than *concelhos*, whose *administradores*, and the *chefes de posto* under them, were to represent 'in the middle of the native population, the sovereignty of the nation, the authority of the republic, the order, the dignity, and the justice of Portuguese civilisation'. Also under the *administradores* were government-appointed *regedores,* tribal chiefs or village headmen for the most part, who co-operated by collecting taxes and seeing that labour obligations were fulfilled.

Under the New State the pattern of administration varied from territory to territory and in Angola, Mozambique, Guiné and Timor the influence of the imperial generation of the 1890s, already felt during the First Republic, could be seen in the abandonment of traditional *theories* of uniform treatment of all people under Portuguese rule. In this respect the New State continued for Angola, Mozambique, Guiné and Timor the ideas set out in a statute of 1926 which divided the population into two categories to produce a policy which was a compromise between British colonial ideas of indirect rule and French ideas of assimilation. The mass of the population in the four territories were subject to the *regime do indígenato,* whose aims were described as twofold:

> One is to guarantee the natural and unconditional rights of the native whose tutelage is entrusted to us . . . and to assure the gradual fulfilment of his moral and legal obligations to work, to be educated, and to improve himself . . . The other is to lead the natives, by means appropriate to their rudimentary civilization . . . to the profitable development of their own activities and to their integration into the life of the colony, which is an extension of the mother country. The natives are not granted, because of the lack of practical application, the rights associated with our own constitutional institutions.

Under this policy there existed two judicial types: *indígenas* (unassimilated natives) and *não-indígenas* (whites and assimilated natives and people of mixed race). Though the aim of the whole policy was said to be 'to improve the cultural, economic, and social level of the Negro . . . to drag him from his ignorance and backwardness, to try to make of him a rational and honourable individual, worthy of the Lusitanian community', the fact remained that the numbers of *assimilados* (assimilated natives) was minimal – 0·75 per cent of the Angolan population and 0·076 per cent of the Mozambican in 1950. *Assimilados* had the advantages of freedom of movement and were exempt from contract labour and payment of the head tax; but against the advantages were set the financial and cultural difficulties put in the way of opting for this status, the payment of heavier taxes and the deprivation of the right to use reserved land, get free medical assistance or be recognised as a tribal chief. In reality these policies were aimed at the perpetuation of two categories of people. Nor were the *indígenas* left alone to pursue their traditional and primitive ways of life. All natives were forced to do work for the authorities if they were not engaged in other forms of labour – and how far the legal provisions on remuneration and other aspects of contract labour were realised were moot points. As one colonial minister, Vieira Machado, said in 1943:

> It is necessary to inspire in the black the idea of work ... If we want to civilise the native we must make him adopt as an elementary moral precept the notion that he has no right to live without working. A productive society is based on painful hard work ... and we cannot permit any exception because of race ... It is to be an unenlightened Negrophile not to infuse the African with the absolute necessity for work.

Given the changing international climate concerning colonialism, it was to be expected that changes in native policy would follow the change of terminology from colonies to overseas provinces in 1951. Modifications in the native labour regulations, aimed at removing some of their harsher provisions, and stricter and better enforcement of the existing provisions from 1955 led an International Labour Office Commission in 1961 to conclude that charges, brought in the ILO by the Ghanaian representative, about the continuation of forced labour in the Portuguese territories could not be substantiated. In 1961, the year of the outbreak of insurgency in Angola, a new code of rural labour was promulgated, firmer guarantees against the expropriation of land reserved for African subsistence farming were introduced, and, in September, the old Native Statute (i.e. the *regime do indígenato*) was abolished: all inhabitants of Portuguese territory now became full citizens, though the onus was still on the native to declare for full citizenship.

The legislation associated with Adriano Moreira as Overseas Minister therefore represented the adoption of French ideas on indiscriminate assimilation, while the Organic Law of the Overseas Provinces of 24 June 1963 reformed the administrative structure, without giving wider powers to all the newly created provincial assemblies as Moreira had intended. The legislation of 1961–3 was intended to make more of a reality of Portuguese claims to be one 'pluricultural and pluricontinental nation'. Full-scale integration and assimilation of peoples of all ethnic origins were now to give greater reality to the longstanding claim of Portuguese colonial policy that it was founded on the 'idea that there are no essential differences between races'. The underlying assumption, unpalatable to indigenous nationalist opponents, was, of course, that integration would take place on Portuguese terms and that assimilation meant becoming culturally Portuguese. Civilisation, as the rhetorical propaganda of the New State made clear, was Portuguese Christian civilisation.

The New State, indeed, saw itself not only as continuing the work of the imperial generation of the 1890s but as having the same sacred and civilising mission traditionally attributed to Prince Henry the Navigator and his contemporaries (the fifth centenary of the prince's death in 1960 conveniently provided the occasion to drive this point home). The *Leitmotiv* of the New State's policies, overseas and domestic, was traditionalist. The Portuguese were 'the legitimate heirs of a great tradition [and] entitled to invoke the past, not as a remembrance of dead things, but as a source of inspiration for the future'; they were 'a chosen people' with a peculiar talent for mixing with other peoples. Thus the regime could find ideological support in the ideas of the Brazilian sociologist, Gilberto Freyre, and his semi-mystical theories of Lusotropical civilisation, the interpenetration of races and cultures brought about by miscegenation and Christian socialisation; for Freyre Portugal's relationship to Africa represented a 'sort of bicontinentality, in an unstable and ill-defined population, corresponding to bisexuality in the individual'! Though it may be true, as Professor C. R. Boxer has said, that the Portuguese historically 'did mix more with coloured races than did other Europeans, and they had, as a rule, less colour prejudice', the Portuguese of the 1960s still saw themselves as a superior people raising up inferior ones. Nor did colour blindness extend to the economic sphere of competition for jobs where informal discrimination continued. If Portuguese rulers shared Freyre's dream of a multi-continental Lusitanian community, it was a dream encompassing the old Brazilian saying: 'White women for marriage, mulatto women for loving, Negro women for work.' For his part, Salazar held to the belief that without a European framework for guidance, non-Europeans would revert to a primitive condition. 'Let no one accuse me of racism because I say that the blacks do not have the same aptitudes as the whites', he said in 1964; 'it is an obvious discovery which is the fruit of experience.'

Spreading the faith was also an integral part of the Portuguese civilising mission from the beginning, and the New State sought to further this after the unsuccessful attempt of 1911–19 to replace Catholic with secular missions. The Missionary Statute of April 1941 was the main legal text in this matter, though it really only updated the Organic Statute of Missions of October 1926. The statute of 1941 defined Portuguese Catholic missions as 'institutions of imperial utility and eminently civilising purport' and gave their function as the creation and running of schools. Missions could have foreign Catholic missionaries to help them provided they were in every way subordinate to Portuguese control and could speak and write Portuguese. The missionaries received state aid, for they were not only spreading the faith but also, since they were entirely responsible for the rudimentary education of the *indígenas,* spreading

Portuguese civilisation. The aims of native education were stated to be 'essentially nationalist' and practical, i.e. preparation for future work, while native languages could only be used for religious instruction. From the state's point of view the missions' function was (in the words of the 1926 statute) 'to uphold the interests of the Portuguese colonial empire'; foreign and Protestant missionaries could not be left free to 'denationalise' the natives, and there was therefore always suspicion of, for example, Baptist missionaries. With the abolition of the *indígenato* in 1961 the rationale for a missionary monopoly of native education came to an end and the state concentrated more funds on schooling as part of its socio-economic developmental strategy.

Churchmen in general had been quite happy about the secular implications of the missionaries' role; as Cardinal-Patriarch Cerejeira put it in 1960: 'We need schools in Africa, but schools in which we show the native the way to the dignity of man and the glory of the nation that protects him . . . We want to teach the natives to write, to read and to count, but not make them doctors.' There were, however, those critical of colonial practice, perhaps most notably Mgr Sebastião Resende (Bishop of Beira, 1943–67) who denounced abuses, while in the 1950s colonial bishops took a stand against forced labour. In the 1960s and 1970s, with armed revolt in full swing and the influence of new ideas being felt within the church, some Catholics moved into opposition to a continuation of hostilities. For others, however, the struggle waged by the Portuguese was a just war.

In general terms, then, the Portuguese Empire in the period of the New State was intended as an instrument for enhancing the prestige and international status of the Metropolis by making the country seem a large intercontinental nation instead of a small European one. Within the framework of this overall geopolitical aim, the New State sought the gradual acculturation of the indigenous populations to Portuguese civilisation, an integral part of which was identified as the adoption of Catholic Christianity. However, as in the time of the discoveries, economic interests were interwined with power-political, cultural and religious aspirations. Salazar's aims were to make the overseas territories pay their way, to keep firm control over them by a bureaucratic administration based in Lisbon, and to develop them to the advantage of Metropolitan Portugal. The type of empire defined by the Colonial Act of 1930 did not aspire to complete self-sufficiency, though autarkic concepts were no doubt an influence on official thinking; instead there was to be, in so far as was possible, a mercantilist relationship between the Metropolis and its far flung possessions.

The economic conference of the Portuguese Colonial Empire held in 1936 called for the intensification of such a 'complementary' relationship, for 'the exchange of agricultural products and manufactures of the Metropolis for raw materials and food products of the colonies'. The development of colonial territories therefore meant the exploitation of their natural resources with the local populations providing cheap labour. The prime example of how this theory worked out in practice can be seen in the case of cotton: until 1961 purchasing monopolies were given to concessionary companies which had the power to force Africans in designated areas in Angola and Mozambique to grow cotton and sell their quotas to the companies at prices below the world level, so that the Metropolitan textile industry could benefit. The colonies were intended to be the chief market for the finished products. With a more rapid pace of development in Portugal and the overseas territories in the 1960s the degree of national economic control changed somewhat, but the basic principle, that colonies existed for the Metropolis and not *vice versa,* remained. If it was now necessary and desirable to invest more in the overseas provinces, Metropolitan interests were still paramount. Within a multi-racial polity the view expressed in 1954 by a former colonial minister, Marcelo Caetano, remained basically true: 'The blacks in Africa must be directed and organised by Europeans but are indispensable as auxiliaries [who] must be regarded as productive elements organised or to be organised in an economy directed by the whites.'

Another aspect of the New State's view of empire bore a striking resemblance to the Italian rationale for overseas expansion. This was the need, thought to be particularly acute in the 1930s when Brazil was virtually closed to Portuguese emigration, to absorb surplus population. During the New State period the white population of the southern African territories underwent a remarkable increase though colonial territories were never those most favoured by emigrants. Nevertheless, despite the failure to channel people into the Portuguese colonies, the aspiration remained of attracting poorer Portuguese to a better life overseas under the Portuguese flag. As the Preamble to the Second Development Plan (1959–64) stated: 'We must therefore people Africa with Europeans who can assure the stability of our sovereignty and promote the Portuguesation of the native population.' 'Africa', said Caetano in 1972, 'does not belong to the blacks, just as America does not belong to the redskins.'

The first threat to the continuation of Portuguese rule overseas came, however, not in Africa, but in the East, culminating in the loss of its Indian territories in 1961. The Portuguese State of India dated back to the exploits of Afonso de Albuquerque in the opening decades of the sixteenth century. By the twentieth century only three enclaves remained: Damão, on the Gulf of Cambay, taken by the Portuguese in 1558, which also included the tiny enclaves of Dadrá and Nagar-Aveli, entirely surrounded by Indian territory; Diu, an island off the Katiawar Peninsula ceded to the Portuguese by the Sultan of Gujerat in 1509; and the enclave of Goa itself, with its capital of Pangim, most of whose territory had been acquired in the eighteenth century though Portuguese rule dated from 1510. Also associated with the sixteenth century and the missionary exploits of St Francis Xavier were the Portuguese rights of ecclesiastical patronage (*padroado*) in the East, which, by agreement with the Vatican in 1950, were reduced to the boundaries of Portuguese rule, though they had been progressively curtailed over the previous century.

Since the eighteenth century Goans had had parity with other Portuguese citizens and had held office in the bureaucracy of Portugal and its empire. Emigration was traditional, particularly to East Africa and into the Indian hinterland. Two-fifths of the population were Catholic and had gone a long way to developing a 'Luso-Indian' Goan identity. Living standards were generally higher than in the neighbouring areas and Goa produced iron-ore and manganese for the world market. Nevertheless there was a somewhat decayed and stagnant air about the territory until the 1950s, when the Indians were claiming it: then greater efforts were made to improve roads and services and in 1955 a new Statute provided for greater autonomy in the administrative and fiscal spheres. Nevertheless the State of India remained, in Salazar's words, 'a portion of the national territory' and even though it was of little economic significance to the Metropolis the 'moral duty' of Portugal had to be done.

Three years after the British withdrawal, the Indian Union suggested negotiations for the peaceful incorporation of the State of India, but Salazar refused to consider any transfer of sovereignty. In 1954 Nehru, with the support of the Goan Archbishop of Bombay, Cardinal Gracias, and under pressure from Goan anti-colonial groups in the Indian Union, stepped up measures against the 'vestiges of a colonial past', and on 25 July Goan separatists and Indian Army elements occupied Dadrá and Nagar-Aveli; despite the subsequent verdict of the International Court at The Hague that both enclaves were Portuguese they were integrated into India in August 1961. In 1954 and 1955, after a decade of agitation by separatists who had more support outside Goa than within, *satyagrahis* (groups of Gandhian-style non-violent demonstrators) marched into the enclaves in their thousands and were repulsed with the loss of fifteen lives on one occasion. Indo–Portuguese diplomatic relations were severed and Nehru announced that India was 'not prepared to tolerate the presence of the Portuguese in Goa, even if the Goans want them to be there'. Apart from odd raids by activists of the Hindu extremist organisation *Azad Gomantak Dal,* the situation remained unchanged until 1961. With the Americans Britain pressed the Indians not to take violent action, but in 1954 Britain had indicated to Portugal that the alliance could not be invoked since a fellow Commonwealth country, India, was involved.

The final crisis came in 1961, Indian action being prompted by the outbreak of armed revolt in Angola. Early in December the Indians massed some 30,000 troops, supported by tanks, aircraft and warships, on the borders of the three enclaves. The Governor-General, Vassalo e Silva, had dispersed throughout the three enclaves 3,000 ill-equipped troops (fewer than in the mid-1950s) without air support or anti-aircraft defences, an aged frigate (appropriately *Afonso de Albuquerque*) and 900 Goan police (who were to desert when invasion came). Internationally Portuguese policy was to rally support against Indian aggression and unsuccessfully to invoke the Anglo-Portuguese alliance on 11 December. On the 14th Salazar explained to Vassalo e Silva that Portuguese forces were sufficient to force India to prepare a massive invasion in the international limelight; if the Indians were to go through with an invasion then resistance must go on for eight days to allow mobilisation of foreign support against India. If this were not to prove effective, then there was to be 'total sacrifice' to save Portuguese honour. In the event, Indian forces invaded Goa, Damão and Diu on 17 December. In Damão and Diu there was last-ditch resistance while in Goa, on the morning of the 19th, Vassalo e Silva gave up the useless struggle. Any Portuguese hopes of international help were dashed when the USSR vetoed a Security Council resolution demanding Indian withdrawal.

Thus the Portuguese State of India ceased to exist, though Portugal refused to recognise the 'temporary' reverse as permanent until 1974. Forty-five Portuguese had died in defence of Portuguese India, which was officially annexed to the Indian Union in March 1962. Thousands of Goans left the territory, many going to East Africa: in Mozambique the Portuguese expelled the existing Indian community as a reprisal and also to provide employment as traders for the refugees. In 1967, it may be noted, the populations of Goa, Damão and Diu rejected in a plebiscite incorporation into the neighbouring states of Gujerat and Maharashtra despite – or perhaps as a result of – increasing pressures for Indianisation. For Portugal the repercussions of the loss of Goa went beyond Salazar's tears on television. General Vassalo e Silva and other officers were dismissed from the army in 1963 in an effort to shift responsibility for the *débâcle* away from the government and, no doubt, to set an example for other military men. Many officers felt the punishments to be unjust and that comrades-in-arms had been made scapegoats for civilian shortcomings. Discontent and resentment over Vassalo e Silva's treatment was to continue throughout the colonial wars and was to feed military suspicions about politicians: it was significant that Vassalo e Silva and others were reinstated in 1974.

The loss of the State of India did not however remove the last traces of Portugal's first sixteenth-century empire from the map: there remained Portuguese Timor and Macao. The Portuguese presence on the East Indian island of Timor dated from the first half of the sixteenth century. In the twentieth century Portuguese Timor consisted of the eastern half of the island, including the capital Díli, and the enclave of Ambeno and a few offshore islands, the frontiers with the Dutch East Indies being fixed in 1904. Timor under the New State was the forgotten portion of empire, except when the victim of invasion during the Second World War. However, Portuguese rule survived the independence of Indonesia and that country's incorporation of West Irian (Dutch New Guinea). The degree of neglect by Lisbon, despite a grant to balance the local budget, was symbolised by the territory being in a juridical vacuum after the offical abolition of the *regime do indígenato* there in 1953. The number of European settlers was small (a few hundred) and there was little in Timor of any economic importance, and most of this in the hands of an 18,000-strong Chinese community. Much of the administration was carried on by *assimilado* Timorese, the population to be administered being backward and primitive and lacking in linguistic homogeneity. Apart from the fifteen or so local languages, 15 to 20 per cent spoke Portuguese, while missionary activity converted some 30 per cent of the population to Catholicism. From the Second World War until 1974 it is hardly an exaggeration to say that history passed Timor by. In 1975–6 the territory was incorporated into the Indonesian Republic, though the Portuguese, somewhat after the manner of Salazar and Goa, refuse to recognise the *fait accompli*.

Macao (or Macau) was to be the last Asian territory to remain in Portuguese hands. Portuguese rule dates from the cession of the town at the mouth of the Canton river in 1557 and it remains a transit trade centre. It avoided Japanese occupation during the Second World War. The continuation of Portuguese rule, which is formal rather than real, is dependent on Chinese goodwill and convenience. Mao Tse-tung noted that the Portuguese had never made war on China and that they were the only people really to have understood race relations, but the need for foreign exchange is probably the key to the surviving Portuguese presence. The Chinese maintain that Portugal remains only on sufferance and that Macao has never ceased to be part of China: thus celebrations for the fourth centenary of Portuguese Macao had to be abandoned and in 1966, during the Cultural Revolution, effective control of the territory passed out of the governor's hands. Thereafter the Portuguese authorities' sphere of action was curtailed and real power came to depend on the connections of local Chinese businessmen (including casino owners) with the Peking leadership. The vast mass of the population is Chinese and no serious attempt was ever made at integration with Portugal or acculturation of the local Chinese into being yellow Portuguese.

The pride of Portugal's twentieth-century empire was Angola, a territory fourteen times the size of the Metropolis and intended to be the new Brazil. The Portuguese presence in the region dated from 1482, the year in which Diogo Cão discovered the mouth of the Congo river and came into contact with the Kingdom of the Kongo, though the Angolan capital, Luanda, was not founded until 1575: the name Angola was derived from _ngola,_ the title of Kimbundu kings to the south of the Kongo. Chiefly famous for the supply of slaves to Brazil, Portuguese Angola in the late nineteenth century comprised only the coastal belt of the present territory, whose boundaries were agreed between the Powers in the 1880s and 1890s. Portuguese dreams of a continuous stretch of land from the Atlantic to the Indian Ocean were dashed and at the Conference of Berlin (1884–5) Portugal received the Enclave of Cabinda instead of ownership of both banks of the Congo river as she had wanted; nevertheless by the end of the nineteenth century vast stretches of territory in southern African had been recognised as Portuguese, only about a tenth of which were effectively occupied. Pacification of the land assigned to her in south-western Africa took at least the first two decades of the present century.

Within Angola about a hundred tribes can be counted but the most important groups among the 4·8 million Africans (taking figures for 1960) are the Ovimbundu (1,750,000 in number) living in the central highlands; the Kimbundu (1,050,000 strong) inhabiting the Luanda region; and the Bakongo (620,000 in Angola) in the north of the country, the legacy of the old Kongo kingdom and therefore in reality straddling the frontier with Zaïre (formerly Belgian Congo). By comparison the European population was quite small, rising from 44,000 in 1940 to 173,000 in 1960, and to over 300,000 by 1970, an immigration prompted by economic development and centring largely on cities such as Luanda (whose population increased between 1940 and 1970 from 60,000 to over half a million), Lobito, Nova Lisboa (Huambo), Malange and Carmona (Uíge). From the 1940s there were also official schemes to settle poor white farmers, the _colonato_ of Cela being started in 1952. Traditionally there was also a mixed population termed _mestiços_ (or mulattos), though contrary to what might have been expected from the propaganda about colour blindness, these were quite small in number: 15,000 in Angola in the 1930s, rising to 54,000 in 1960. Miscegenation tended to decrease with increasing white immigration and usually took place outside wedlock. Figures for marriages in 1957 among _não-indígenas_ are revealing in this respect: out of 218 marriages in that year 150 were between whites; 19 between white men and mulatto women; 1 between a _mestiço_ and a white woman, and the rest between *mestiços* and negroes. There was, of course, no colour bar but society tended informally towards stratification along ethnic lines. As the white population of the cities increased in the 1950s and 1960s whites tended to be preferred over blacks in employment even though wage differentials were narrowing (in Luanda in 1961 European cooks earned £41 a month compared to the African cooks' £6).

Nine-tenths of the population were engaged in agriculture and economic development in the first two decades of the New State was slow. The debts run up by the expensive policies of Norton de Matos in the 1920s meant that Salazar gave priority to balanced budgeting in Portugal and the colonies rather than to development. Shortage of funds for investment and a relative lack of interest in the colonies led to reliance on forced labour and to other abuses, conditions which were denounced in a secret report to the National Assembly in 1947 by the Supreme Inspector of Colonial Administration, Henrique Galvão. In his report he denounced the forced labour system, from which 'only the dead are really exempt', which was leading to depopulation through emigration; the lack of medical services, and the maltreatment of labourers by employers who, contrary to legal precepts, in practice rented them from the authorities. The authorities in fact discouraged voluntary labour as defined in the labour legislation and recruited contract labour without consideration of the effects on the traditional native economy, one of which was the growing of less food. Corruption, arbitrary punishments and abuses were rife and he calculated that up to 30 per cent of labourers contracted to work in São Tomé died. As already noted, efforts were made to end abuses and reform things in the 1950s and 1960s – in the latter decade with greater urgency following the revolt of 1961.

Until the coffee boom following the Second World War, Angola was perhaps best known in the economic sphere by two enterprises, neither of them wholly Portuguese: Diamang (the Angola Diamond Company), founded in 1917 and partly British, Belgian, French, American and South African owned, operating in the north-east, and whose production of precious stones constituted the mainstay of the economy until 1940; and the Benguela Railway Company, started by Sir Robert Williams of Tanganyika Concessions in 1902, whose 836-mile line (completed in 1931) opened up much of the hinterland and carried much of the copper production of Katanga and Zambia (Northern Rhodesia) to the fine natural harbour of Lobito. From the 1940s it was coffee production, centred on Carmona (Uíge) in the north, which became the mainstay of the economy, while in the 1960s other natural resources were tapped and came to the fore, including iron, from the central highlands and from Cassinga in the south (with the aid of West German capital), and oil, onshore near Luanda (exploited by a predominantly Belgian company) and off the shore of Cabinda (exploited by the American Gulf Oil).

Contrary to previous policies, foreign capital was encouraged in the 1960s to make speedy development possible, development from which the Portuguese would gain financial advantage and, possibly, political, given the need to keep such resources under Western control.

Some of these changes in Angola's economy can be expressed as follows. In 1938 coffee accounted for only 11 per cent of Angolan exports compared with 29 per cent (the largest item) for diamonds; by 1947 however coffee represented 26 per cent to 16 for diamonds. The value of coffee exports increased over six times between 1946 and 1960 and until the mid-1960s coffee constituted about half the annual exports by value. By 1969 however exports of iron, oil and diamonds combined had surpassed coffee exports in value, whereas the three commodities together had amounted to less than half the value of coffee in 1960. Between 1960 and 1969 total exports and imports roughly trebled.

The year 1961 has been described as the turning-point in Angola and in many ways this is true. However, it should not be forgotten that the process of economic development, accelerated after 1961, was well under way before then and that the drift of Africans to the cities was already a fact. Luanda already had, like so many cities elsewhere, its shanty town suburbs (*muceques*), with their primitive living conditions, which grew at a pace outstripping government housing schemes. Before 1961, too, white immigration had been on the increase and ideas of greater autonomy, inherited from the pre-New State period, among settlers and *assimilados* were far from unknown. Grievances against centralised rule from Lisbon, despite the introduction of a palliative in the form of a legislative council in 1953, were probably responsible for Delgado being credited with proportionately more votes in Angola than in the Metropolis in the 1958 presidential election. After 1961 these feelings no doubt persisted but were offset by the need to have Metropolitan support to survive the threat posed by the emergence of black nationalism, which in its modern forms dated essentially from the 1950s and was one of the causes of the 'confusion' of 1961.

Before the New State there had been black and *mestiço assimilados* who had called for a greater share in the running of the territory and these traditions revived and were transformed in the post-1945 world. Official reactions were perhaps epitomised by the statement of Colonel Sá Viana Rebelo, the Governor-General, in 1958 that 'the native's access to higher levels of society can be granted only with prudence'. By this time, however, the aim of at least part of the black and *mestiço* élite was no longer to become simply 'black Portuguese'. Symbolic of the change was the short-lived appearance in 1952 of the Luanda literary journal *Mensagem* in which poets such as Viriato da Cruz and Mário de Andrade set out 'to discover Angola', i.e. to create an indigenous Angolan African, rather than an *assimilado,* culture. This Angolan cultural nationalism, a product of the educated in the cities, soon took on political form and in December 1956 the MPLA (Angolan Popular Liberation Movement) was founded, with Viriato da Cruz as its Secretary-General. The MPLA was a fusion of various nationalist groups, including the Angolan wing of the Communist Party which sought to provide it with organisation and a Marxist ideology, though at this time other influences were also present, including that of Catholics associated with the Chancellor of the Archdiocese of Luanda, Fr Joaquim Pinto de Andrade (brother of the poet, Mário). The incipient organisation of the MPLA was to a large extent smashed by the PIDE, who arrested dozens of people in 1959 and 1960, including Fr de Andrade and the poet and physician Agostinho Neto who had recently returned from Portugal. With the chaotic coming of independence to the Belgian Congo (Congo-Kinshasa, now Zaïre) in June 1960 it was nevertheless likely that the Portuguese would face a testing time.

The first challenge to the colonial authorities may, however, have been non-political and occurred towards the end of 1960 in the Malange area: here Africans, weary of compulsory cotton-growing for meagre returns, went on strike. Violence ensued and a bloody repression took place by the military in which possibly thousands died. By March 1961 the disturbances were over in the Malange area, but by then more serious threats had been posed by nationalist forces. On 3 February 1961, the day which began 'the national revolution' in MPLA terminology, perhaps 200 armed Africans attacked the prison where MPLA prisoners were held, and other targets of strategic significance in Luanda. The attackers in this revolt of desperation were repulsed and in ensuing days a white backlash set in with shootings in the cemetery and the *muceques*. The revolt was unco-ordinated with other anti-Portuguese activities and was doomed to failure, though the rebels scored a psychological victory in as much as Luanda was turned into a city of fear divided along crude racial lines.

The major challenge came outside the capital, in the north-west, in the coffee-growing regions inhabited principally by the Bakongo, and it was in some ways a less modern challenge than that of the MPLA and the urban rebels. The massacres of whites, *mestiços* and blacks (often Ovimbundu contract labourers on coffee plantations as well as Bakongo) that took place on and after 15 March were the work of Angolan nationalists who were in reality Bakongo tribal nationalists. Among factors influencing the outbreak can be listed the confused situation in Congo-Kinshasa (and the Bakongo were a powerful force in Congolese politics); a certain tradition among the Bakongo for following messianic leaders; the indirect influence of the work of Baptist missionaries, and resistance to exploitation on some coffee plantations. The revolt was organised and led by an essentially tribal political grouping based in Léopoldville (Kinshasa) and one of its features was the invasion of northern Angola by non-Angolan Bakongo forces: the group was the UPA (Union of the Populations of Angola), led by Holden Roberto, which had emerged in 1958 from the UPNA (Union of the Populations of North Angola), a group dedicated to seeing a Protestant on the shadowy throne of the Kongo kingdom. The Portuguese, however, eventually came down on the side of a Catholic claimant in 1961, by which time Roberto's UPA had gained international contacts as an *Angolan* nationalist body, although it was contemptuous of MPLA *mestiços* and had no following outside Bakongo areas (and other Bakongo political groups were hostile to it).

On and after 15 March UPA followers, primitively armed, massacred perhaps 2,000 people, of whom about 300 were Europeans; often in a drugged state, the rebels went in for appalling atrocities, including dismemberment and disembowelling. Though foreign sympathisers were later to doubt survivors' accounts, UPA spokesmen themselves on occasion acknowledged such acts with apparent approval. Inevitably the bloody initiative of the UPA was followed by massive retribution at first carried out by local whites themselves in conjunction with Ovimbundu and Bakongo whose relations had suffered at the hands of the insurgents. How many people perished during this repression is not known with any degree of accuracy but possibly 30,000 dead would not be an exaggeration: villages were burned, atrocities committed and black Africans indiscriminately massacred regardless of tribal origin.

The quasi-exterminatory offensive of the settlers only began to abate in May with the arrival of reinforcements for the armed forces (which in February 1961 numbered some 12,000, about half of them African). Guerrilla war now began in the Kongo and Dembos areas, with perhaps 10,000 guerrillas in the field. The Portuguese, aided by aviation and the coming of the dry season, recaptured lost posts; by October they could declare that the main military operation had been successfully concluded. The guerrillas, short of food and orders and subject to napalm bombardment, had lost the initiative and up to 300,000 Bakongo crossed into Congo-Kinshasa to avoid the repression and the war in general and join their fellow tribesmen. Though the psychological, physical and international damage inflicted on the Portuguese had been great, the economy nevertheless continued to function and much of the coffee crop was harvested as usual. The blow dealt by the UPA had been stunning in the north-west but had not proved fatal to Portuguese rule in Angola as a whole; 1961, however, did prove fatal to the tolerance hitherto extended to British and American Baptist missionaries, who had 200,000 followers compared with over 2,000,000 Catholics: they were expelled.

The Portuguese response to the new situation was to follow counter-insurgency precedents set by the British in Malaya and, more especially, the French in Algeria. Repression continued, with at least 10,000 detained in camps and the PIDE active in running efficient networks of informers in the *muceques* of Luanda, in rural areas and among exiled groups outside Angola. These measures, coupled with the reforms of 1961–3, and with the strength of the armed forces increased to some 60,000, could not, however, suffice to ensure the retention of so vast a territory. Better communications – building airfields, building and improving roads – were given high priority, and this fitted in well with the needs of the economy. Together with the physical suppression of suspected nationalists went psycho-social warfare: the winning of the hearts and minds of the people through economic and social development. Just as terror was met with counter-terror, so the expectations aroused by nationalists were to be countered and given reality by the Portuguese, who now came into closer contact with and exercised closer control over more of the rural population than they previously had done. The aim was to contain the guerrilla threat at a minimal level while endeavouring to cement the loyalty of black Portuguese by material improvements.

The building of an economic infrastructure to support the increased pace of development was accelerated after 1961. By 1967 there were 2,200 miles of paved roads (and another 700 miles of all-weather dirt roads) compared with only 250 miles in 1960. Plans also went ahead to exploit hydro-electric power, though the Cunene river scheme was intended to benefit South-West Africa as much as Angola – hence South African co-operation. As part of the radical transformation of the social environment at which Portuguese policy aimed, endeavours were made to improve educational and health facilities. After 1961 educational expansion was most notable in the primary and technical spheres: numbers of pupils in primary education rose from 105,781 in 1960–1 to 392,809 by 1969–70, or just over half the children of primary school age. In secondary education, however, in some ways the test of the policy of assimilation through education, numbers only rose from 7,486 to 11,321 in the same period – and most of these were white. In 1966 it was estimated that 12 to 13 per cent of Angolans were literate, but a literacy rate of 60 per cent among Europeans compared with one of 10 per cent for Africans. Health services were also improved, though here again towns were better served than countryside even if the statistics showed up reasonably well by comparison with other African countries. In the period 1961–4 Angola had a ratio of 2·5 hospital beds per 1,000 of population, compared with 1·5 in Mozambique, 1 in Ghana, 2·8 in Zambia, 1·9 in Tanzania, 0·4 in Nigeria and 4·1 in Rhodesia. Between 1964 and 1966 there were 13,140 people to each doctor in Angola, compared with 17,990 in Mozambique, 31,250 in Congo-Kinshasa, 21,820 in Zambia, 18,240 in Tanzania, 44,230 in Nigeria and 7,570 in Rhodesia. Material progress there was, for which wits with unerring judgement thanked the rebels of 1961.

The theory of the Portuguese version of counter-insurgency strategy was to incorporate the Angolan population on equal terms in a prosperous, peaceful, non-racial society with an expanding economy. However, leaving aside the military question of quelling insurgency and the expenditure necessary for this, the practice indicated serious obstacles to fulfilment: how to Africanise administration without running up against white resentment which would exacerbate racial feelings; how to deal with the new expectations of the rudimentarily educated drifting from the land into the *muceques,* particularly when increased white immigration meant greater competition for employment; how to be sure that introduction to a market economy, if not a consumer society, together with alienation from tribal traditions, could be resolved by pride in being black Portuguese from Angola. Despite the doubts, Portuguese policy makers believed in a successful outcome provided they were given time for their policies to work.

One factor militating against their hopes was the guerrilla threat which had precipitated these policies in the first place. In this respect, as far as Angola was concerned, the Portuguese had little militarily to fear given the incessant factionalism among those claiming to represent the Angolan people, and tribal hostilities among the guerrilla leaders abroad could be exploited almost as much as they could within the territory. After 1961 continuous insurgent activity was confined to about 7 per cent of the country, to areas bordering Zaïre (Congo-Kinshasa) and the Dembos area (one of the last to be pacified in 1919).

The main elements of African nationalist activity operating in Angola were the following. Holden Roberto, with the backing of Congolese (Zaïrean), Algerian and American wellwishers, continued to lead the Bakongo-based UPA from Léopoldville but, despite the use of the Kinkuzu base nearby, his movement, which became the FNLA (Angolan National Liberation Front) in 1962 and set up GRAE (Revolutionary Government of Angola in Exile), went into decline in the 1960s through lack of success. For a time he had the blessing of the OAU (Organisation of African Unity) and looked as though he might unite other opposition forces around him. The pro-Chinese *mestiço,* Viriato da Cruz, forced out of the MPLA leadership, joined Roberto, but this was followed by the departure of GRAE's Foreign Minister, Jonas Savimbi who, disillusioned with inefficiency, nepotism and Bakongo dominance, went off to form his own UNITA (National Union for the Total Independence of Angola) among his Ovimbundu brothers in the south. Attacks on the Benguela Railway in 1966–7, however, effectively deprived him of Zambian goodwill as it interrupted the latter's exports, and the movement made little headway.

The rival which worsted Roberto's GRAE proved to be the MPLA, which has been temporarily knocked out by arrests in 1959–60. Jealous of

Roberto's position and viewing him as a tribalist opportunist demagogue, the intellectuals of the MPLA remained passive militarily (they had no forces) but built up their links with other colonial opposition movements. In April 1962 Agostinho Neto mysteriously escaped from prison in Portugal and arrived in Kinshasa, where he reorganised the MPLA, ousting Viriato da Cruz and downgrading Mário de Andrade. However, despite Eastern bloc sympathy, no progress was made until headquarters were moved to Congo-Brazzaville in 1964. Whereas the FNLA counted on support among the Bakongo and Savimbi hoped to build up a base among the Ovimbundu, Neto could only boast a following among a minority of the Kimbundu (from which he came) so long as the Portuguese held sway in the *muceques* of the capital. MPLA strategy was to try to begin activity among as many tribes as possible, and so with Zambian connivance operations began in eastern Angola in 1967. Though small-scale operations inconvenienced the Portuguese, by the end of the 1960s it seemed that no serious threat was being posed and, indeed, on occasion rival guerrilla bands clashed with each other. With Soviet backing and Congo-Brazza and Zambian goodwill, Neto's MPLA indulged in little significant military activity and potentially had support only in Luanda and among the Kimbundu, and possibly in some eastern areas. Roberto's FNLA, losing OAU goodwill to the MPLA, and virtually confined to the Bakongo, seemed more bitterly opposed to the MPLA than anyone else. Savimbi's UNITA was still pretty insignificant and likely to be as hostile to the MPLA as to the Portuguese. It might have been thought that Cabinda, cut off from the rest of the territory, was the most obvious place for liberation to begin: but the catch was, 'liberation by whom?' The UPA/FNLA/GRAE tried, as did the MPLA, but there was little response from the population, which was in any case courted by (in addition to the Portuguese) at least two 'liberation fronts' of its own. Ranque Franque's FLEC and the rival FLEC of the ex-UPA, anti-MPLA Taty. For the success of Portuguese strategy, however, it was not enough that the guerrillas be divided and militarily contained or that socio-economic development should proceed smoothly; as the less confident military men in Angola were wont to point out, there could never be a solution without all neighbouring states actively collaborating with Portugal to abolish the liberation movements. So the war would go on, sapping Portuguese strength and morale.

Portuguese contact with Mozambique dates from the voyage of Vasco da Gama and his visits to the mouth of the River Zambesi and Moçambique Island in early 1498. Despite movement up the Zambesi during the early sixteenth century and the Portuguese Crown's practice of granting land to some of its subjects (the *prazo* holders) in the Zambesi valley, Portuguese control of inland Mozambique did not start to become a reality until the end of the nineteenth century. The frontiers were delimited by 1891 (except for the addition of the Kionga Triangle in 1919) and conquest and 'pacification' were not complete until about 1921. Even so, until the 1930s the territory was largely controlled by concessionary companies: the Zambesia Co., founded in 1892, in Tete and Quelimane; the Moçambique Co., founded in 1888, in Manica e Sofala; and the Niassa Co. founded in 1891, in the north. Owing to the undercapitalisation of the companies, development was slow and early twentieth-century Mozambique owed much of its prosperity (relative to Angola) to its dependence on the transit trade from South Africa and British central African territories: in the centre the Beira–Umtali railway was built by Cecil Rhodes's company in 1896, while in the south the Lourenço Marques–Transvaal line was opened two years earlier. Thanks to French arbitration, Delagoa Bay had gone to Portugal and not Britain in 1875 and, with the development of the mineral wealth of the Transvaal, the focus of Portuguese interests had shifted south to the port of Lourenço Marques, the capital from 1897. Dependence on South Africa for revenues was well illustrated by the Mozambique–Transvaal Convention of 1909 (renewed in 1928 and 1940) which assured Lourenço Marques of at least 47·5 per cent of the Witwatersrand's trade in exchange for African labour. Up to 100,000 workers (the figure of the 1940 agreement) were to be recruited by the Witwatersrand Native Labour Association, who paid the Portuguese authorities a sum in gold bullion for each worker signed on and handed over half the wages to be paid out on the worker's return to Mozambique. The transit trade and the export of labour (to Rhodesia and East Africa as well as South Africa) were therefore two of the territory's economic mainstays, making it economically dependent on more advanced neighbours. In addition, despite Salazarist ideas of national economic control, foreign companies were well entrenched in Mozambique: the British-owned Sena Sugar Estates was one of the most important concerns, while it was only in 1948 that the authorities acquired the port of Beira from the Moçambique Co. and in 1950 that they bought the Beira Railway. To a considerable extent Mozambique was a middleman subservient to other people's economic interests.

Mozambique, eight and a half times the size of Portugal, was inhabited (according to the 1950 census figures) by over 5,600,000 Africans, of whom the biggest tribe was the Islamised Makua in the north (about 1·7 million strong); the next biggest northern tribe was the non-Islamised Makonde, often hostile to the Makua, and 136,000 strong in Mozambique, but with 300,000 other Makonde across the River Rovuma in Tanzania (Tanganyika). Tribes like the Nyanja, Ngoni and Chewa straddled the frontier with Malawi (Nyasaland), while farther south the Shona straddled the Rhodesian frontier and to their south lived the Thonga peoples (1·5 million) from whom most of the emigrant labour was recruited for South Africa (especially from the Shangana tribe). While north of the Zambesi most tribes tend to be Islamised, to the south most are animist or Christian: in 1964 it was estimated that only 15 per cent of the total population of Mozambique was Catholic and another 4 per cent Protestant. As in Angola about 90 per cent of the whole population was engaged in agriculture in the 1960s, while most of the trading was in the hands of Asians (Goans, Chinese, Indians and Pakistanis). The extent to which Mozambique was overtaken by Angola in development is crudely indicated by figures for *per capita* income in 1966: $100 in Mozambique, $170 in Angola (compared to $210 in Rhodesia, $180 in Zambia and $50 in Malawi). As in Angola, so in Mozambique, the New State period saw an increase in the white population: from 27,500 in 1940 to 48,000 in 1950, and from 85,000 in 1960 to 250,000 by 1973: Lourenço Marques, whose total population rose from 37,000 in 1928 to 184,000 in 1964, contained the largest white population though relatively large numbers also lived in Beira, Nampula and Quelimane.

Mozambique is not as rich as Angola in natural resources and the main exports in the mid-1960s were still cashew nuts, cotton (production of which had risen notably since the 1920s), sugar, tea and vegetable oil products. In addition there was some coal mining and some mineral extraction after prospecting in the 1960s. Natural gas and petrol refining also came to be added to the list of Mozambican assets. The rise in cotton production was largely the work of the Cotton Export Board, which from the 1930s was responsible for drawing up to 500,000 Africans in the north of the territory into growing this crop at cut rates for the benefit of the textile industries of Oporto and Braga. The effects of this policy on the native population were summed up as follows by the Bishop of Beira in 1950:

> After the cotton campaign was begun there, the fertile fields ceased to supply food for the neighbouring populations, and the people of the region itself also commenced to feel hunger. There belongs to my diocese a region in which for six months the black spectre of hunger reaped the lives of the inhabitants . . . I know of districts in which the native . . . received as payment for his harvest from 50 to 90 escudos. And in the same region, and in the same locality, if the native worked at planting other crops, he could grow in an equal area of land, and perhaps with less effort, from 2,000 to 4,000 escudos worth of products.

In this as in other respects the abuse and crude exploitation of native labour continued until the reforms of 1961–3, though improvements in labour conditions and remuneration were apparently slower and less widespread than in Angola thereafter. The abolition of compulsory cotton-growing for low returns was in part a response to a movement of mass protest among African farmers in northern Mozambique during the 1950s which culminated in the deaths of perhaps 500 farmers during a demonstration near Mueda in 1960. The experience of this protest movement and the bitter legacy left behind, especially among the Makonde, were to be a factor in the guerrilla war which began in 1964.

Politicised opposition was not, however, rural in origin. One strain of opposition was to be found among dockworkers in Lourenço Marques, among whom there was unrest in the late 1930s, and who staged strike movements in 1947 and 1948, the latter being a more violent episode countered by deportations to São Tomé. Another strike in 1956 culminated in the deaths of forty-nine stevedores and in 1963 strikes in Lourenço Marques, Beira and Nacala were suppressed. Thereafter, with PIDE activity widespread, the strike weapon was abandoned as an instrument of protest; the official workers' unions (*sindicatos*) were nevertheless stronger in Mozambique than in Angola and the apparatus of corporativism, officially extended to overseas territories in 1937, had rather more reality there too. Another strain of opposition was to be found among whites, the small number of *assimilados, mestiços* and Asians who resented the constriction of their commercial activities by government decision making in Lisbon, even though the reforms of 1953 and 1963 in theory allowed for greater consultation of local interests through the Legislative Council of Mozambique. Opposition went further than the purely economic sphere. The Association of the Mozambique Born in the 1950s was a non-racial body which favoured scholarships for Africans and greater independence for the territory, and as in Angola the 1958 presidential campaign showed that the sympathies of many settlers were with Delgado. In 1961 the MDM (Democratic Movement of Mozambique), essentially a movement of the white professional classes but advocating civil rights for all Africans, more education and an end to forced labour, was also closed down by the authorities after calling for a boycott of the elections. Though this strain of liberal opposition, often reflecting hostility to Metropolitan interests in the territory, such as the economic complex based on the Banco Nacional Ultramarino, continued clandestinely, the authorities also had to contend in the 1960s with another strain of opinion among settlers which favoured independence accompanied by a more South African-style policy of segregation.

The movement for independence which finally emerged with the founding of FRELIMO (Mozambique Liberation Front) in Dar-es-Salaam in 1962 under the leadership of Eduardo Mondlane, was a coalition of black opposition groups. Mondlane himself, the *assimilado* son of a chief in southern Mozambique and educated in South Africa and the USA as well as Portugal, was a prestigious figure who had helped to found an African high school students' association, NESAM, in 1949, and this gave him the basis for a national political network. However, he realised from the Angolan experience that armed resistance would have to be based abroad and the movement incorporated groups which had already been set up among Mozambican emigrant workers: UDENAMO (Mozambique Democratic National Union), founded in 1960 by Adelino Gwambe in Rhodesia; MANU (Mozambique African National Union), founded in 1961 by Matthew Mmole from Mozambicans in Kenya and Tanganyika; UNAMI (African Union of Independent Mozambique), founded in 1961 in Nyasaland. Mondlane's aim was to avoid the divisions among his Angolan colleagues and form a supra-tribal movement aiming at one-party democracy and enjoying OAU (as well as private American) support for the preparation of revolt. Though the leadership was intertribal most of the initial rank and file were almost inevitably Makonde refugees in Tanzania, a fact which was to alienate some other tribal groups, notably the Makua, when the armed struggle began. From the first there were faction fights among the leaders resulting in expulsions and the attempted creation of rival movements or coalitions. UDENAMO and MANU were refounded and the latter was the first to send a guerrilla group into Mozambique on 28 August 1964 in an attempt to upstage FRELIMO which began its more effective operations on 25 September. Gwambe (of UDENAMO) went on to head COREMO (Mozambique Revolutionary Committee) in Zambia as a rival coalition to FRELIMO, but soon Gwambe was expelled from COREMO and founded another splinter group. Though COREMO was responsible for some small-scale operations in the Tete region, it was FRELIMO which was the serious force.

Operating from bases in Tanzania, whose model for socialism FRELIMO tended to follow, the guerrillas were from 1964 active in the northern areas of Cabo Delgado, Niassa, Zambesia and Tete, though the main focus of concentration was on building up a proto-state in Cabo Delgado and Niassa. In March 1968, when FRELIMO controlled 5 per cent of the territory, sporadic operations were begun in Tete, the region in which the huge Cabora Bassa dam was to be built and in which prospecting for minerals was being carried out. With the war in Angola apparently proceeding satisfactorily, the Portuguese were able to put more troops (60,000 by the 1970s compared with 16,000 in 1964) into the field against perhaps 8,000 guerrillas and in 1970 the Commander-in-Chief, General Kaúlza de Arriaga, launched the tolerably successful Operation Gordian Knot to regain the initiative and strengthen the Portuguese position. For FRELIMO it was a war of ambushes; generally selective terrorism (especially against village headmen who were often still the main agents of Portuguese rule); mined roads and railways; and propaganda, internal and external. For the Portuguese it was another exercise in counter-insurgency, making full use of aviation, gathering the population into strategic villages (which gave the Portuguese greater control over the population and expanded the possibilities of social development, though the uprooting of people also increased the Africans' sense of alienation), and counter-terrorism which was sometimes indiscriminate, resulting in massacres of villagers. The short-term aim was to produce a military stalemate and containment of the guerrillas, which the Portuguese believed had been achieved after Operation Gordian Knot, so as to give free rein to the long-term aim of socio-economic development, the other face of psycho-social warfare.

Making use of their strategic villages attempts were made by the Portuguese to improve educational and medical facilities, with some success – ironically Mondlane himself had in 1955 called the health service 'one of the most forward looking and most successful in Africa'. In Mozambique (where 97·9 per cent of the population were illiterates in 1958, compared to 97 per cent in Angola and 98·9 per cent in Guiné), educational advance was observable in the statistics: 264,233 children attending primary schools in 1957; 510,170 in 1968. However, as in Angola the number of Africans in secondary and higher education was small and in 1972 only about 30 per cent of children of school age were receiving primary education. The most spectacular developments lay in the realm of economic infrastructure, though the road network remained inadequate, while the Lonrho oil pipeline from Beira to Umtali, finished in 1965, could not be used when sanctions were imposed on Rhodesia. It was in the hydro-electric field that development was most obvious, with the decision made in 1966 to dam the Zambesi at Cabora Bassa, upstream from the town of Tete. Construction by the South African-dominated Zamco consortium began in 1970 on a scheme which would allow Portugal to sell electricity to South Africa – it would produce more power than the Aswan dam – so as to pay off the cost of the project while also boosting agriculture by irrigation of some 3·7 million acres, allowing for the settlement of farmers in the Zambesi valley on the model of the Limpopo valley scheme where a mixed African and European farming settlement followed in the wake of that dam's opening in 1956. The Cabora Bassa scheme increased South African involvement in Portuguese Africa and also demonstrated that Portugal was dependent on foreign capital for large-scale development.

For the Portuguese Cabora Bassa became a symbol of their determination to stay in Mozambique while for FRELIMO it focused international attention on their cause, the aim being to hinder the dam's construction and make it more costly. Until 1972 the Portuguese forces seemed to be successful in containing the FRELIMO threat. Given Zambian and Malawian dependence on Portuguese rail links and ports, considerable pressure could be exerted on these countries to FRELIMO's disadvantage, but the same pressure could never be applied to Tanzania. FRELIMO's grip on parts of the north led to rumours of a possible Portuguese withdrawal from the northern part of the country the better to hold the centre and south, and some anti-FRELIMO nationalists in Malawi in 1969 set up a movement for an independent Rombesia; however, this would not have ended Portugal's problems in Mozambique, nor was it an option given the all or nothing outlook in Lisbon. FRELIMO itself underwent a number of leadership crises which the Portuguese doubtless welcomed when they did not themselves have a hand in them. In 1968 Mondlane's leadership was challenged by an attack on his Dar-es-Salaam headquarters, apparently the work of Lázaro Kavandame, leader of a section of the Makonde, who subsequently went over to the Portuguese. On 3 February 1969 Mondlane was blown up by a parcel bomb (allegedly sent by the PIDE) and a power struggle followed resulting in victory in 1970 for the Algerian-trained military leader Samora Machel, seconded by the increasingly pro-Soviet *mestiço* poet, Marcelino dos Santos, over the Protestant pastor Uria Simango, who had been an UDENAMO leader before joining FRELIMO, and whose pro-Chinese stance now led him into COREMO. In 1971 FRELIMO's roving ambassador, Miguel Murupa, went over to the Portuguese. Despite the schisms, however, FRELIMO still posed a more serious threat than any of the Angolan movements and had wide international support in the OAU, China, Russia, Scandinavia and the World Council of Churches. The war, with its increasing costs for Portugal, would, it seemed, go on.

A still more intractable problem faced the Portuguese in Guiné (this form will be used throughout for Portuguese Guinea/Guinea-Bissau to avoid any confusion with French Guinea/Guinea-Conakry). The first Portuguese contact with the territory dated from 1446 but its frontiers were not delimited until 1886, by agreement with the French who controlled neighbouring Senegal and Guinea. Pacification of Guiné, a triangular enclave two-fifths the size of Portugal, was completed by 1915, though there were further risings to be suppressed as late as 1936, in which year a British visitor noted that the colony was held down by 264 African troops under six white officers and eleven NCOs. Until at least the 1950s Guiné vied with Timor as possibly the most neglected outpost of empire. A fairly heavily populated land by African standards, it contains some twenty tribes divisible into seven major ethnic groups, of which the four largest (according to 1970 figures) are the non-hierarchically organised Balante (250,000), the strongly Muslim and hierarchically-organised Fula (100,000), the Mandjaque (140,000) and the Mandinga (or Malinke, 80,000). The very small European population and the mostly Cape Verdean *mestiços* were centred on Bissau, whither the capital was moved from Bolama in 1941. Most internal trading was carried on by Lebanese and Syrians as well as by the indigenous Dyulas whilst external trade and shipping were the monopoly of the Metropolitan CUF (Companhia União Fabril) – a fact which led some to call the struggle against the guerrillas in the 1960s the company's war.

Guiné is not a land endowed with many natural resources. Though a little bauxite was mined, the main products were peanuts, rice and coconuts: peanuts corresponded to cotton in Angola and Mozambique in that up to 50,000 families in the 1950s were compelled to cultivate this crop at low fixed prices for export. There were no railways and little in the way of roads, since much of Guiné could be classified as jungle or swamp and movement was difficult except by river.

The movement of opposition to Portuguese rule was largely the work of one of the most acute minds in the Third World, Amílcar Cabral, a half-Cape Verdean *mestiço* born in Guiné in 1924. Educated in the Cape Verde Islands (there was no secondary school in Guiné until 1958) and trained in Portugal as an agronomist, he was one of the founders of the PAIGC (Guiné and Cape Verde African Independence Party) in Bissau in 1956; most of his colleagues were Cape Verdean *mestiços* like himself. During his stay in Lisbon (1945–51) he was active in creating a Centre of African Studies for the 're-Africanisation of spirits' with Mário de Andrade and Agostinho Neto. Such contacts with other *assimilado* intellectuals were subsequently to take more overtly political form in the MAC (Anti-Colonialist Movement, 1957), FRAIN (African Revolutionary Front for National Independence, 1960) and CONCP (Conference of the Nationalist Organisations of the Portuguese Colonies, 1961), bodies designed to co-ordinate the struggle against Portuguese colonialism. The PAIGC initially thought in urban terms, recruiting port-workers, artisans and functionaries, but after the deaths of fifty dockers during a strike at the Pidjiguiti docks on 3 August 1959, it decided to give priority to organising the rural population for armed struggle, which was officially begun in January 1963, though acts of sabotage had been carried out since August 1961. The PAIGC headquarters was in Conakry, capital of Sékou Touré's Guinea, and guerrilla forces operated from there and from Senegal, though the latter's President, Léopold Senghor, had at least an initial preference for a rival group, itself a coalition of smaller groups, FLING (Front for the Liberation and Independence of Portuguese Guinea), dating back to 1953 and generally advocating non-violent struggle under the leadership of Benjamin Pinto Bull. As Secretary-General of the PAIGC, Amílcar Cabral became the internationally known leader of the struggle, particularly after the arrest in 1962 of its President, Rafael Barbosa (who came out in support of the Portuguese after his release in 1969).

For the Portuguese, who saw the opening of three fronts in the south, north and east in 1963–4 as another example of the invasion of part of their territory by outsiders, the war never went well; nor, in the absence of Guinean and Senegalese collaboration with them, could it because of the indefensibility of frontiers and the difficulties of communication. Within five years of the start of hostilities the PAIGC claimed to control about 70 per cent of the territory and up to half the population, and, even allowing for propagandistic exaggeration, this basic picture was never to alter significantly thereafter. The Portuguese continued to hold most of the coastal area (including the capital) and the grasslands of the Fula in the north-east, where conservative Muslim chiefs opposed to the 'revolutionary democracy' of the PAIGC 'vanguard' could be relied on. Given the mining of roads and the difficulties of the terrain, the maintenance of the Portuguese position was heavily dependent on aviation, the military uses of which were combined with the now-familiar policies of material amelioration in strategic villages, whose inhabitants were increasingly armed for self-defence to try and take the load off regular forces numbering over 30,000 by the 1970s (compared with about 5,000 in 1963). The creation of strategic villages apparently caused headaches among the PAIGC leaders and Portuguese pressure caused a change to more mobile military tactics in 1968. Nevertheless the guerrilla impact could be seen in the fall in peanut production and the need (in part due to the increase of the military establishment) to import rice, previously an export. Some of the rice crop, indeed, was marketed by the PAIGC in Guinea as part of its strategy of building up a politically democratically centralised and economically communalist alternative society, complete with medical, educational and economic facilities.

The case of Guiné illuminated in stark form the Maoist strategy of popular mobilisation through 'winning the hearts and minds of the people' adopted by both sides – though if only because of memories of past oppression it was a strategy with a built-in disadvantage for the Portuguese. Nor did napalm always kill only guerrillas. However, the 'policy of blood and smiles' (as PAIGC spokesmen saw it), begun by General Arnaldo Schultz as governor and military commander (1964–68) was continued by General António de Spínola in these capacities (1968–73). Thus the (badly needed) improvement of health and education services continued in Portuguese-held areas, now under the slogan 'For a better Guiné', while Spínola combined keeping up military morale in a war which could not be militarily won, with emphasis on 'a real social revolution' and 'popular mobilisation by means of persuasion . . . the real weapons in this war'. As evidence of 'a permanent dialogue' with the 'most representative elements' of 'the aspirations of the popular masses' he initiated a more thorough policy of boosting traditional authority, 'utilising the traditional with a view to their gradual change into administrative structures'. For Portuguese conscript soldiers, small numbers of whom deserted, as for regulars, this expensive struggle to hold an economically worthless territory devoid of white settlement made less and less sense. Why, then, did Portugal not abandon this territory the better to defend the others? The simple answer was given by President Tomás, visiting in 1968: 'We attach to it [Guiné] the same importance as to other sacred portions of national territory . . . It is a part of the same body, which to function perfectly must be kept intact.' So the war went on against the PAIGC, with its Cuban advisers and Eastern bloc support. The atmosphere of Guiné was succinctly described in August 1963 by an American visitor to Catió, 'a prison in which the Portuguese have sought shelter . . . No one moves outside the town during the day without a weapon. After dark the barbed wire gates are closed and floodlights illuminate the hostile jungle . . . Soldiers based in Catió live in continual tension.'

Some 560 miles to the north-west of Guiné lie the ten Cape Verde Islands, together with which Guiné was administered until 1879. Many of the leaders of the PAIGC advocated independence for the islands as well as the mainland territory. The uninhabited islands were discovered by the Portuguese in the 1450s and were subsequently populated by Portuguese from the homeland and Madeira, who imported large numbers of slaves so that the population was racially very mixed, *mestiços* being the majority. The high incidence of miscegenation led the Portuguese ethnographer Jorge Dias to refer to the islands as 'a magnificent manifestation of Portuguese culture', while Gilberto Freyre himself considered the Cape Verdean 'the most perfect Portuguese human being'. Though bananas, peanuts and coffee were exported, a struggling subsistence agriculture was the norm, an activity pursued against terrible climatic odds because of the natural aridity of the islands exacerbated by the tree clearing in which early settlers had indulged.

Drought is the dominant preoccupation for the inhabitants, and drought means famine and, given the high rate of demographic increase, emigration. The famines of 1940 and 1942–8 claimed some 50,000 victims and that of 1958–9 another 10,000, which no doubt partly explained why Portugal spent more *per capita* in the Cape Verdes in the years 1953–67 than in other colonial territories. Much of the expenditure was on irrigation and made little impact. As far as education was concerned, a rough idea of its condition may be gleaned statistically. The percentage of the Cape Verdean population in primary school in 1960–1 was 4·7 (compared to 3·8 in Guiné, 4·5 in Guinea-Conakry, 4 in Senegal and 2·4 in the Gambia); in secondary education the percentage for the islands was 0·8 (0·3 in Guiné, 0·5 in Guinea-Conakry, 0·3 in Senegal and 0·7 in the Gambia). In respect of medical services the ratio of doctors to total population was 1:14,000 in the islands in the early 1960s (compared to

1:20,000 in Guiné, 1:19,000 in Guinea-Conakry, 1:21,000 in Senegal and 1:16,000 in the Gambia). Figures for infant mortality show a similar comparability with West African countries: 91·7 per 1,000 in the Cape Verdes (1968), 80·2 in Guiné (1966), 92·9 in Senegal (1960–61), 140 to 145 in Liberia (1969).

Clearly there was not very much to keep the Cape Verdeans at home, even though the islands were never subject to the *regime do indígenato*. Emigrants went to Brazil, Argentina, Senegal and the United States, where the number of Cape Verdeans is greater than the population of the archipelago itself; others went to São Tomé and Príncipe and to Angola, while the better educated were often to be found as *chefes do posto* in various African territories. During Caetano's premiership, which coincided with a bad period of drought, some 25,000 went to the Metropolis to help fill gaps in the labour force left by Portuguese emigration to Europe; they were not afforded a warm welcome by the local population. Starting a guerrilla movement in the islands was virtually impossible given the lack of neighbouring territory from which to launch attacks. Accordingly the PAIGC gave priority to Guiné and indulged only in propaganda and occasional strike action in the Cape Verdes (such as the movement in the capital, Praia, in March 1962), while Dakar-based rivals wanting to keep the islands separate were apparently even less effective. Nevertheless the threat of the strategically important archipelago falling into hostile hands was a card Lisbon could play with its NATO partners: the airfield on the island of Sal and the fuelling station and good harbour at Mindelo, on São Vicente, were major assets in this connection.

The other component of Portugal's empire was formed by the islands of São Tomé and Príncipe, 275 and 125 miles off the African mainland in the Gulf of Guinea, uninhabited when discovered by the Portuguese in the 1470s. The history of both is linked with sugar and slaves, but with the end of slavery cocoa (the chief export) and coffee took over from sugar. The islands were the subject of international scandal before the First World War over the importing of tens of thousands of Angolan labourers who were effectively slaves. The import of African labour, essential for the cacao plantations given the greenhouse-like climate unsuitable for Europeans, continued, the contract labourers being brought from Angola, Mozambique and the Cape Verdes. The census of 1950 showed that 30 per cent of the population (16,750) were forced labourers subject to the *regime do indígenato,* which was never applied to the permanently settled population. The stratification of the population was complex: apart from about 1,000 Europeans the élite was best described as creole, the *filhos da terra* being of mixed European and African descent; in addition there were *angolares* (fisherfolk descended from survivors of a shipwreck in 1540), *forros* (descended from slaves freed at abolition), *serviçais* (temporary contract labourers) and *tongas* (children of the latter). As in the Cape Verdes there was a strong correlation between skin colour, social status and wealth.

The colony had been the world's largest cacao producer in 1919 but by the 1960s had declined to sixth position through a combination of manpower shortages, soil erosion and tree diseases. Efforts to increase the supply of manpower by forcing small cultivators into plantation labour by Governor Carlos de Sousa Gorgulho after 1945, and low wages paid by employers because of falling world prices, culminated in a threat of revolt being announced by local people in 1953. The native troops were disarmed and a wave of repression resulted in over 1,000 deaths in a week; after the massacre of Batepá the governor was replaced. As in the Cape Verdes, the creation of guerrilla movements on small islands proved impossible. Nevertheless a small group of *émigrés* set up a Liberation Committee in 1960 with the support of Nkrumah. The fluctuations of African politics forced them to move from Ghana to Congo-Brazzaville, then to Equatorial Guinea and finally to Gabon, where in 1972 under Manuel Pinto da Costa it was restructured as the more impressive sounding MLSTP (São Tomé e Príncipe Liberation Movement). In short, despite the sullen resentment of many among the population noted by deportees such as Mário Soares in the late 1960s, the Portuguese position in the islands was never threatened and they could safely be used for flying aid to Biafra in 1967–9.

When Caetano became Premier in 1968 he was known to have advised Salazar six years earlier, in his capacity as Councillor of State, that overseas policy should be aimed at the creation of a Portuguese United States, a federation of the Metropolis with the overseas provinces on terms of equality for each component. However, in order to gain acceptability in military circles as Premier, he had to commit himself to drop federalist experimentation and continue the integrationist policies of Salazar. Promises, he informed the Army Minister, Brigadier Bettencourt Rodrigues, could not be eternal, but 'we shall defend the overseas in so far as we are able'. In 1968 the situation was only militarily serious in Guiné and so, within the integrationist framework left by Salazar, he set out to keep options open by a policy of progressive autonomy for the territories overseas. This entailed assuring a Portuguese future for the populations: within a pluri-racial community the security of the whites would thus be upheld in the event of Angola or Mozambique choosing complete independence at some point in the future, while in the meantime there was to be increasing participation by all ethnic groups in the process of government. Notions of 'positive discrimination' in favour of blacks were, however, forsworn as contrary to the 'equality of opportunity' set up as the ideal.

Caetanist reformism was given legal form in the constitutional revision of August 1971, which stated that 'the territories of the Portuguese nation situated outside Europe constitute overseas provinces which will have their own statutes as autonomous regions'. The provinces, which could qualify for the title of states, were to become self-governing and more economically independent, but 'the exercise of the autonomy of the overseas provinces will not affect the unity of the nation, the solidarity between all portions of Portuguese territory, nor the integrity of the sovereignty of the state'. Lisbon, in fact, was still to have the final say, but even so the constitutional revision was unpopular with convinced integrationists. A new organic law was nevertheless passed (June 1972) and the new Statutes of the Provinces promulgated (December 1972), Angola and Mozambique receiving statehood. This policy of 'progressive autonomy', allegedly inspired in its details by Italian regional arrangements and the Spanish republican constitution of 1931, was, of course, dependent on a number of factors to have any chance of success, and the most important factor was time.

By the end of 1972 the military situation in Angola and Mozambique (despite FRELIMO activities in Tete) was well under control, though the importance of unchallenged air power was vital to communications as well as to strike capability. There was, however, no sign of Portugal's African neighbours ceasing to harbour guerrillas. Economic threats and occasional bombing of the frontier might keep countries like Zambia or Malawi in line, but there was little to be done in other cases. Bombing guerrilla bases in Tanzania would have been internationally counter-productive, while an attempt with local dissidents to topple the Guinea–Conakry regime of Sékou Touré in November 1970 by a commando raid failed. On the other hand the Portuguese position internationally improved somewhat with a shift in American policy in 1970 from a more or less neutral stance over southern African affairs to one more favourable to the *status quo*. Similarly relations with South Africa, which had opted for an 'outwardgoing policy' in the 1960s to create an economically South African-dominated zone of peace in southern Africa, became more intimate, although there were no treaty links and separate racial policies were maintained. Sanctions against Rhodesia, while bad for Beira, were nevertheless good for Lourenço Marques to which much of Rhodesia's export trade was diverted. While Scandinavian and Dutch as well as Vatican opinion showed increasing sympathy with the PAIGC and FRELIMO, Portugal was never deprived of arms supplies by other West Europeans: West Germany supplied Fiat G.91s, with a short take-off run suitable for ground attack operations in Africa, and France Noratlas transports and Alouette helicopters which had obvious relevance to the tasks in hand.

But if by 1971-2 the international and military situations could be viewed from Lisbon as satisfactory in the circumstances, the policy of progressive autonomy was still based on a continuation of the military effort, which inevitably put strains on Portuguese morale, society and economy. Indeed only with an expanding economy could the effort be maintained. Defence expenditure rose from 3,023 million escudos in 1960 to 14,699 million in 1971; from being 26·7 per cent of the budget in 1960 it accounted for 45·9 per cent in 1971. Expressed as a percentage of gross national product, military spending rose from 4·5 to 8·3 in this period. Understandably Caetano's policy was to shift as much of the burden of the wars onto the territories themselves, given the economic development which was taking place. By 1971 it was estimated that Angola was paying half the costs of the war there, but in Mozambique less than a fifth was paid locally. Similarly in terms of manpower the policy was to use more and more indigenous troops; in 1971 of about 142,000 troops deployed in Africa (out of a total army strength of 179,000) over 40 per cent were black (though there were few black officers). Nevertheless conscription, which was for two years in the case of the army, was naturally unpopular in Portugal, especially as two years more could be added on for service in a 'different part of the national territory separated by sea'. In 1972 the percentage of regular armed forces to people of military age was 11·2 in Portugal (3·4 in Britain, 6·1 in the USA, 7·2 in the USSR). Though the casualty rate was fairly light – from 1961 to 1968 3,579 Portuguese troops were lost in Africa, of whom 1,888 were actually killed in action – the effect of the war on recruitment to the Military Academy was proving serious. The military career had lost its glamour and its safety so that, to the disquiet of senior regulars, there was increasing reliance on conscript officers (*milicianos*) coming from those veritable centres of subversion, the universities.

The decision, really made in 1961, against decolonisation was therefore producing its strains a decade later, though many non-Portuguese had been surprised that Portugal was still in Africa at all. The reasons for going on paying out 'the expenses of sovereignty' were not entirely ideological or political. The colonial policies of the New State were intended to benefit the Metropolis economically and this in some ways they continued to do. The implications of the overseas territories for the Portuguese economy will be more conveniently discussed in the context of the next chapters. The economic potential of Angola and Mozambique was a major factor in Lisbon's determination not to decolonise. Though the Metropolis had to help finance overseas development and shoulder most of the military burden, in return economic 'solidarity' with the colonies meant purchasing commodities at less than world prices and, even if foreign capital had to be called in to exploit natural resources, taxation of the profits and a generally favourable trade balance with all colonial territories signified an important source of income helping to keep Portuguese international payments in favourable balance.

Caetano argued that 'if there were only big capitalist interests in Angola and Mozambique, we could certainly not have bothered ourselves about their defence, because powerful enterprises defend themselves very well and always find a way of coming to an understanding with whomsoever is in control. No. What we defend in Africa are the Portuguese, of whatever race or colour, who trust in the Portuguese flag.' Nevertheless, given the comparative weakness internationally of Portuguese capitalism, Portuguese control of the overseas was necessary if Metropolitan magnates were not to go to the wall. Politically important in the Metropolis and with large holdings in the overseas, the big Portuguese companies were not strong enough to contemplate turning colonialism into neo-colonialism. Portugal's empire, which at the beginning of the century could be cited as a case of uneconomic imperialism, had become by the 1970s in important respects an example of economic imperialism.

4

Economy and Society

I have always advocated an open and simple
administration, such as can be carried out by a good
housekeeper; a modest and easily understandable
policy which consists in knowing how to spend well
what one has, and not spend more than one's resources
can afford. Oliveira Salazar

When Salazar took over the Ministry of Finance in 1928, Portugal could
be classified as an underdeveloped country. Most of the population
earned their living from agriculture. The country possessed no heavy
industry and its manufacturing industries, chiefly textiles, were of
modest proportions. Its exports consisted for the most part of primary
products. There was little indigenous capital available for investment
and development, and the average *per capita* income was low by
European standards. Furthermore, parts of the national economy were
in foreign hands: this was expecially evident in wine producing, minerals
extraction, services (transport, telephones, power) in the cities, and in the
colonies. Communications were inadequate, medical services were poor
and illiteracy widespread. Salazar's overall remedy for this state of affairs
was to think in terms of slow but sure long-term development within a
nationalist economic framework, beginning with the creation of a proper
economic infrastructure. The national economy was to be made less
dependent on the outside world through policies of import substitution
and decreased international indebtedness. Economic reconstruction was
to be based on sound principles of financial orthodoxy applied both
internally and *vis-à-vis* the outside world.

In order to ensure the conditions necessary for such policies in the long
and short terms, political stability was essential under strong government
– hence the political constitution of 1933 – and the state had to have
greater control over social and economic affairs – hence the National
Labour Statute of 1933. Salazar's aim was the regeneration of Portugal by
means of a well-ordered economy. For the economist Salazar, as for
Marxists, political forms were subordinate to socio-economic priorities;
the corporative system was the product of ideological preconceptions, but

mere changes in political superstructure and institutions were not the all-embracing aim of the New State. The New State was rather to reflect and represent the national society after the preceding period of disorder and indiscipline. The aim, said Salazar in 1938, was 'a progressive revolution, which, having once brought within its scope all industrial, commercial, and agricultural activities, will change the aspect of our economic and social structure, thereby conferring on the state its own specific characteristics'. On the other hand 'the proposition that the nation's economic interests should be directed by the state is almost self-evident'. Although the 'substitution of individualism' as a social principle was necessary, state intervention should be limited: 'real progress can only be achieved when the state is prepared to abandon all forms of activity which can best be performed through private channels'. The distant ideal, indeed, was a self-regulating corporative economy and, true to papal social teachings, Salazar saw the role of the state as being that of a stimulant to the creation of such a corporative order. In practice, as the Portuguese historian Oliveira Marques noted in the 1970s, the 'complex system' that was created

> shaped a new Portugal, very much in the socialist way, [and] built up an economically organised country, an interventionist state essentially different from the liberal, *laissez-faire* Republican order. Almost forty years of actual performance have made the Portuguese accustomed to, and more and more dependent upon, the state.

The political constitution of April 1933 defined the state as 'a corporative and unitary republic' (Article 5) and went on to say that it was the state's function 'to promote the moral unity and establish the juridical order of the nation, defining and causing to be respected the rights and guarantees resulting from nature or from law, in respect of individuals, families, local autarchies and economic and moral corporations'. It was also the state's function to 'co-ordinate, stimulate and direct all social activities, making a just harmony of interests prevail within the legitimate subordination of particular interests to the general interest' (Article 6). The family was recognised as the basic social unit in Part I, Section III, while Section IV declared that it was for the state 'to promote and help' in the creation of 'moral or economic corporations and syndical associations or organisations', as well as to recognise the existence of these. Such bodies were to be concerned with literary and artistic affairs as well as welfare, 'technical amelioration' and 'solidarity of interests', and were to be fully represented in the upper house of the regime, the Corporative Chamber. The state, declared Article 31, was to have overall responsibility in the spheres of employment, labour relations, credit, wages and prices and emigration. Article 39 prohibited strikes and lock-outs. The state was to be responsible for public works (Articles 60–1). The function of the Corporative Chamber was to produce written opinions (*pareceres*) on legislation prior to discussion in the National Assembly (Articles 103–4).

The key document for corporative organisation was, however, the National Labour Statute, promulgated on 23 September 1933 and largely the work of Salazar's young Under-Secretary for Corporations, Teotónio Pereira. The Statute, inspired by papal encyclicals such as *Rerum Novarum* (1891) and *Quadragesimo Anno* (1931) but also influenced by the Italian Charter of Labour of 1927, repeated some of the generalisations of the constitution and filled in more details of the plan to create a corporative order based on class collaboration. As Teotónio Pereira wrote: 'The old idea of bourgeois and proletarian, separated by fierce rivalries and unbridgeable abysses, is one that we must remove from our path . . . The Portuguese state is neither bourgeois nor proletarian.' However, although in theory Portuguese corporativism retained its autonomy *vis-à-vis* the state, in practice the weakness, political unacceptability or non-existence of associations meant that the whole system was heavily dependent on the state and could be described as part of its bureaucratic apparatus.

Until Law No. 2086 of 22 August 1956 no corporations actually existed; the delay in setting up the organisms was in part due to the theory that they should be of organic growth and not simply creations of the state and in part due to the convenience which those ruling the state had found in prolonging the transitional phase. Thereafter eleven corporations, constituting (in the language of the Statute of 1933) the unitary organisation of the forces of production and integrally representing their interests, were set up: Agriculture, Transport and Tourism, Credit and Insurance, Fishing and Canning (1957); Industry, Trade (1958); Press and Graphic Arts, Entertainment (1959); Arts, Sciences and Letters, Social Relief, Physical Education and Sports (1966). Though enjoying their own 'collective juridical personality', they were, nevertheless, in practice still subject to the Ministry of Corporations and to the Corporative Council. The latter body, created in August 1934 as the 'organ of supreme orientation of corporative organisation', was a sort of inner Cabinet presided over by the Premier to control the development of corporativism and to appoint, in the absence of corporations, representatives to the Corporative Chamber. This council (which meant, in effect, the government) was at the top of an organisational pyramid, some of whose components existed only on paper. Membership of corporative organisms was not obligatory (except in the special cases of the Orders of medical practitioners, engineers and lawyers), but the Statute of 1933 proclaimed that the organisms were the legal representatives of employers and employees whether they were members or not, and the organisms had the monopoly of collectively negotiating wages and contracts.

At the base of the corporative pyramid were the primary organisms: the *sindicatos nacionais* (national unions) for workers in trade and industry, which were not in fact national in a geographical sense; the *casas do povo* and *casas dos pescadores* (mixed employer-employee institutes for rural workers and fishermen respectively); and, for employers, *grémios* (guilds) in trade, industry and agriculture.

The formation and activities of the *sindicatos nacionais* was carefully supervised by higher authority. The principle of one union per *distrito* for each type of work, though sometimes modified in practice, meant a large number of often quite small (and therefore weak) unions. There were generally around 300 unions under the New State and encouragement to join was given by a decree in 1939 saying that non-union members could be asked to pay dues. In 1942 more than half the dues were collected from non-members, but thereafter the numbers joining steadily increased as did the size of particular unions as industrialisation proceeded. In effect the function of the 'non-political' unions was the disciplining of the workforce, even though covert oppositionists sometimes got their lists of candidates for leadership elected; higher authority, however, could easily suspend leaders who stepped out of line, such as PCP collaborators out to storm the 'fortress of the fascist unions' from within from the 1940s onwards. The unions actually played little part in negotiating collective wage agreements but they were the basic units of social welfare schemes, as well as being linked to the FNAT (National Foundation for Happiness in Work), the function of which was to provide sporting, cultural and holiday facilities.

The *casas do povo* in rural areas were different: they aimed to attract rural workers into them, provide an insurance scheme and educational opportunities, and organise work locally. Employers of labour were members, too, and formed the leadership in the institutes, which were conceived of as 'families of families'. In general the institutes were less successful (or real) than the urban unions, though a greater density of organisation was initially observable in the south, where a rural proletariat existed and where in the 1940s some *casas* were closed for 'revolutionary agitation'. By 1959 only 555 *casas do povo* existed in mainland Portugal, though there were nearly 4,000 parishes which should have boasted one each. In the same year there were 433,000 members out of an active agricultural population of 1·4 million. The *casas dos pescadores* were also interclass institutes with broadly similar characteristics, except that harbour masters always headed the *casas* (twenty-eight in number in 1959) and membership was compulsory for fishermen.

The primary employers' organisations were the *grémios* (guilds): these existed in trade and industry, and also in the agricultural sector, which in 1959 boasted 237 *grémios* with 820,000 members (out of a grand total of 522 with 1·06 million members). The greater number of employers', as opposed to workers', organisms reflected the weight within the economy of agricultural smallholdings and small-scale trading and industrial firms. It may be noted that one of the purposes of corporative organisation was to protect the interests of the small man *vis-à-vis* large-scale interests, though corporativism was only partly successful in this aim. The *grémios* were supposed to act not only as employers' unions but also to be the basis of the self-regulation of the corporative economy, supplementing and indeed taking over some of the functions which the state would otherwise perform. In contrast to the workers' bodies, individual *grémios* often covered large areas of the country or more than one branch of economic activity; in some cases the primary organisms were consubstantial with the secondary or intermediate organisms. Unlike workers' bodies, the employers' organisations often had existed before the New State and now simply adjusted to the institutionalised framework the better to safeguard their legitimate interests. Though they might sometimes complain of too much state bureaucracy and regulation, they were nevertheless in a better position *vis-à-vis* government than the unions; despite the corporative schema the Portuguese Industrial Association continued to exist as a separate entity. On the other hand the state could use corporativism to bring pressure to bear on firms to adhere to its own economic policies; but these policies were often those favouring the larger enterprises which could dominate within various *grémios*. The baroque complex of employers' organisms led, in fact, not to a self-regulating economy but (in Caetano's words of 1959) to 'the excess of regulation and the excess of bureaucracy', to 'socialism without a doctrine' – albeit a 'socialism' far removed from the proclaimed intentions of the Statute of 1933 which repudiated not only the class war but also 'the predominance of plutocracies'. In the agricultural sector, too, it was the big landowner who dominated within the system.

Above the primary *grémios,* unions and *casas* in the corporative pyramid, and beneath the corporations eventually created, were the intermediate federations and unions. These organisms were sometimes regional or national groupings of *grémios* or federations of related *sindicatos,* such as the Lisbon Portworkers' Union; no plans to group *casas do povo* together, however, emerged until 1957. It was at the intermediary level of representation of producers that the state exercised most pressure to get its policies implemented and so government ministries came to have greater control over more dispersed groups of employers. Alongside and sometimes overlapping the theoretically independent intermediate groupings were pre-corporative state bodies of economic co-ordination – pre-corporative because corporations were envisaged as eventually taking over their co-ordinating functions. In reality, however, the organs of economic co-ordination were instruments of the government aimed at regulating production and trade. Thus most of these bodies dated from the early 1930s and were concerned with import and export policies – the Port-Wine Institute, the National Fruit Exporting Board, regulating committees for marketing cod and rice, the National Wheatgrowers' Federation etc. Too useful to the state to be abandoned, pre-corporative co-ordinating bodies were built into the corporative structure created after 1956.

The corporative system outlined in the Statute of 1933, though intended to be eventually independent of the state and a middle way between capitalism and socialism, was crowned by a state institution, the National Institute of Labour and Social Insurance (complete with an Under-Secretary for Corporations), whose function was to 'see to the execution of the laws protecting labour and others of a social character, and to integrate the workers and other productive elements in the corporative organisation'. However, the legislation on working conditions, together with the ban on strikes and lock-outs (including 'revolutionary lock-outs'), gave few advantages to the worker. Despite the panoply of labour courts, collective contracts and agreements, corporative commissions, etc., the achievements of the system in furthering social justice were meagre; improvements in the workers' lot usually stemmed from conjunctural factors in the labour market.

The system of social insurance outlined by Teotónio Pereira was based on the principle that the state was not a welfare organisation; somewhat as in France, workers and employers would jointly finance a social security system through their respective contributions, thus leaving the state free of the burden. The system that evolved was a corporative version of self-help which both Salazar and Teotónio Pereira publicly stressed would be of slow growth. From the figures already quoted for the spread of *casas do povo,* plus the fact that these were almost without finance, it followed that the rural population received no benefits until the reforms of the Caetano period.

The *casas dos pescadores* also had little money so that fishermen benefited little. Industrial workers were comparatively better off, but that did not say very much. Family allowances and sickness insurance took priority over the provision of old-age pensions or payments to the victims of industrial accidents. In short, the social insurance schemes of corporativism, while steadily increasing in terms of payments and numbers of people covered, increasingly lagged behind developments in other (admittedly richer) countries. Whereas the state was not a contributor it was a beneficiary since the funds of the savings banks (*caixas*) were largely invested in state bonds. The enthusiasm with which the National Labour Statute had originally been greeted rapidly faded after the usual Portuguese pattern, and those who had seen in the New State the promise of a more just society became increasingly disillusioned until the reforms of the Caetano period brought a new wave of hope. Intended as a 'corporatism of association' and not a 'state corporatism', the system in practice conformed in many ways to the latter model under the New State. As a report to the congress of the UN put it in May 1956: 'Corporativism has not created a special type of economy but rather an economic bureaucracy, organised, well or badly, by the state'.

The corporative system was seen by Salazar as ideologically the best solution to the 'social question' since it was the one advocated by the teachings of the church. It also had the advantage in practice of preserving a private enterprise economy while at the same time legitimising moderate government intervention permitting overall control of the economy. When he became Finance Minister in 1928, however, corporativism lay in the future. His first task, as he saw it, was to put the finances in order so as to stabilise the economy. Then, when order had been restored and confidence returned, there could be economic development which would lead to social improvement provided that political stability was maintained, a condition fulfilled with the introduction of the constitution of 1933. As already noted, Salazar, albeit initially with a certain sleight of hand, quickly succeeded where others had failed. By changing and improving methods of accounting, curbing expenditure and introducing new taxes to boost revenue, the budget moved from deficit to surplus and remained in positive balance thereafter. The change may be illustrated by a few figures as in Table 4.1 (1 conto = 1,000 escudos).

Table 4.1   *Budget Balances of 1925–1928 and 1931–1934*

Financial year	Revenue	Expenditure	Balance
	(in thousand contos)		
1925–6	1417	1539	—122
1926–7	1468	2109	—641
1927–8	1722	1903	—181
1931–2	2007	1857	+150
1932–3	2031	1948	+ 83
1933–4	2200	2070	+130

Other outstanding financial problems were tackled with a new vigour and these, too, produced renewed confidence, reflected in a fall in interest rates. The national debt, which stood at 7,448,908 contos in June 1928, had been reduced to 6,580,756 by the end of 1936; in the same period the floating debt was brought down from 2,114,000 to 36,522 contos. The exchange rate of the escudo, 4·85 to the £ in 1911 and 113·03 in 1925, was stabilised at around 110 to the £ in the 1930s. Portugal briefly returned to the gold standard in 1931, but had to follow Britain in abandoning it within a few months. The deficit on the balance of trade continued but the gold reserve nevertheless increased (from £1,926,138 in June 1931 to £8,339,000 at the end of 1937). The cost-of-living index, 100 in 1929, stood at 81 ten years later. Unemployment increased slightly but was never generalised owing to the public works undertaken by the regime, and in real terms wages seem to have remained stable. Thus the vigorous pursuit of financial orthodoxy within an authoritarian political system produced economic results and, with the cumulative index of economic activity rising (1932 = 100, 1936 = 123·5 according to the Bank of Portugal), it was time to embark on a more general economic plan.

The first of the regime's plans, the fifteen-year Plan of Economic Reconstruction, was set out in Law No. 1914 of 1935. Though in reality a number of sectoral programmes co-ordinated only at the financial level, it envisaged the expenditure of 6,500,000 contos, for the most part on infrastructure: railways, roads, airports, ports, telegraph and telephone services, hydro-electric works, land reclamation, schools, etc. Given its relative success, indicative planning was continued from 1953 with the first of a series of development plans for the Metropolis and the colonies, which again stressed the development of infrastructure and also aimed to boost production and consumption. The Second Plan (1959–64) emphasised industrialisation, the Interim Plan of 1965–7 production for export and the Third Plan (1968–73) again industrial development. Expenditure envisaged was as shown in Table 4.2 (in millions of contos).

Table 4.2   *Envisaged Development Plan Expenditure, 1953–1973*

First Plan	16·5	(70 per cent of it in the Metropolis)
Second Plan	31	(71 per cent of it in the Metropolis)
Interim Plan	49·18	(71 per cent of it in the Metropolis)
Third Plan	168·5	(72 per cent of it in the Metropolis)

While the importance to be attached to these plans as a factor in producing economic development is problematic, Portugal's economy certainly changed in the New State period. Taking 1953 = 100, the general index of industrial production was 43 in 1933 and 192 in 1962; United Nations statistics taking 1963 = 100 showed an increase from 92 in 1962 to 154 in 1969. Statistics for employment of the labour force by sector are also revealing (see Table 4.3; percentages).

Table 4.3   *Employment of the Labour Force by Sectors, 1930–1970*

Sector	1930	1940	1950	1960	1970
Primary (Agriculture)	56·5	49·3	48·4	42·8	29·8
Secondary (Industry)	20·5	20·4	24·9	29·5	36·7
Tertiary (Services)	23·0	30·3	26·7	27·7	33·5

The proportion of the national product by sector of origin changed as shown in Table 4.4 (percentages).

Table 4.4   *Changes in GNP Proportions by Sector, 1953–1969*

Year	Agriculture	Industry	Construction	Transport and communications	Commerce
1953	32	27	4	5	12
1960	25	30	4	5	12
1969	18	36	5	6	13

In the economic philosophy of the New State development was to be essentially the work of society itself, i.e. of private enterprise, but the state was assigned the role of providing the conditions in which private enterprise could operate in the national interest. In the period of reconstruction and afterwards it therefore fell to the state to undertake public works schemes to build up the country's infrastructure, thereby preventing unemployment in times of stagnation or depression and also providing tangible evidence of national progress.

In the sphere of communications it was a question of modernisation rather than starting from scratch. There were 3,225 kilometres of railway line in existence in 1926; 3,582 in 1939 and 3,617 in 1969, the relative lack of development being attributable to the growing preference for road transport. Like Spanish railways, the track was of wider gauge than in the rest of Europe, but it may also be noted that approximately a fifth of the railways were narrow gauge. The New State governments made efforts to improve rolling stock and plans for electrification were launched; by 1968 some 900 kilometres of line were electrified (compared with 25 in 1926). Attempts to co-ordinate rail and road transport were never very successful and the various private railway companies got into increasing difficulties. In 1946 all the companies were amalgamated into one, with state participation, and this Companhia Portuguesa de Caminhos de Ferro was granted the operating monopoly in 1951 when the state gave up its share in railway ownership. The volume of freight traffic declined from 7·8 million metric tons in 1930 to 3·5 million in 1969, though there was a small increase in terms of ton/kilometres during this period. The number of passengers carried increased from 30 million in 1927 to 144·7 million in 1969. As in other countries, just what to do with the railways was something of a problem and by the early 1970s strange contrasts remained. The electric line along the Costa do Sol and the Lisbon Metro, opened in 1959, were models of modernity and efficiency, while mainline expresses, running on the broad-gauge tracks, were still slow by European standards. Ancient steam locomotives were still in use alongside the new diesels while the arrivals indicator at Beja station still consisted of a blackboard with the hand-painted heading 'Probable times of arrival of trains'.

Road building and road repairing were major priorities of the New State. The total road network increased from 13,000 kilometres in the mid-1920s to 26,000 by 1950 and to over 32,000 by 1970 (of which some 2,000 were dirt roads). By the late 1950s Portuguese roads were good by European standards but the accelerated economic development to which they contributed caused relative inadequacy in the 1960s. The increasing use made of the road network, which still did not reach many villages, was reflected in the increase in the number of vehicles. There were 7,900 commercial vehicles in 1931; 26,000 in 1949; 48,700 in 1959 and 106,000 in 1969. The number of private cars rose from 25,100 in 1931 to 56,500 in 1949, to 145,000 in 1959 and to 493,000 in 1969. (Incidentally it may be noted that the number of private cars per head of population in Portugal was 1:17·5 in 1969, which may be compared to the United Kingdom's 1:4·8 or Spain's 1:17.) Together with the development of the road network went bridge building: the most impressive examples were those over the Douro at Oporto opened in 1963 and over the Tagus at Lisbon opened in 1966, the latter, Salazar Bridge (now renamed the 25 April Bridge), being the longest suspension bridge in Europe.

Efforts were also made to improve port facilities, notably in Lisbon and at Leixões (near Oporto). Apart from obviating congestion, the hope was also to capture a share of the ship-cleaning and repair trade by taking advantage of low-cost labour and the country's position on the Middle East–Northern Europe tanker route. The New State also aspired to renew the outdated merchant navy and provided state credit for the purpose after the Second World War. Tonnage of Portuguese merchant shipping, which had sunk from 254,000 to 163,000 between 1931 and 1947, rose thereafter to 272,000 in 1959 and to 428,000 tons in 1969, while the number of ships registered steadily declined from 270 in 1948 to 141 in 1969. Airports were constructed at Portela (Lisbon), Pedras Rubras (Oporto) and later, to help tourism, at Faro and on Madeira and São Miguel. A government-owned national airline, TAP (Transportes Aéreos Portugueses), was created in 1946 which by the 1960s, with a modest fleet of Caravelles and Boeing 707s and 727s, had a good international reputation for reliability (although when delays did occur its initials provided an ideal target for English-speaking wits who dubbed it 'Take Another Plane').

Apart from aspiring to provide adequate transport facilities the state also sought to provide another prerequisite for industrial growth, a reliable supply of energy. The means chosen to accomplish this were the construction of dams which were expensive to build but had the advantage of also providing water for irrigation schemes and reducing dependence on the import of foreign fuel, thereby saving foreign exchange. As with the development of roads and bridges, the building of dams was begun in earnest after the Second World War, which had seen an accumulation of funds for extraordinary expenditure, i.e. development. The hydro-electric schemes, in which the state took the lead, were a success: the output of electric energy rose from 260,000 kilowatt hours in 1930 to 940,000 in 1950; 3,260,000 in 1960 and 6,840,000 in 1969. Dependence on foreign fuels for the production of energy dropped from 85 per cent in 1937 to 50 per cent in the late 1950s. In 1936–8 67 per cent of electricity produced came from thermal sources and 33 from hydro-electric; by 1960–2 the percentages had been dramatically reversed to 6 and 94 respectively. In the 1960s however the high cost of distribution and the disadvantage of dependence on the weather for keeping up hydro-electric production led to some rethinking in favour of thermal sources and eventually to thoughts of nuclear energy in the longer term.

The creation by the state of a sound infrastructure in the fields of communications and energy was undoubtedly a major factor making for accelerated industrial growth from the 1950s. Budget surpluses during the wartime period and the effects of the war in reducing imports, which produced the abnormality of a surplus on visible trade in 1941–3 due to the minerals boom, further boosted confidence nationally and internationally and brought about a tenfold increase in Portuguese gold and foreign exchange holdings between 1938 and 1947. The wartime dislocation of trade patterns also stimulated import substitution – an economic priority of the regime – and industrialisation. In the immediate postwar period there were short-lived booms in some export industries but private investment was not always wisely placed from the point of view of future demand. As was to be the case later, the economic advantages of low-wage policies were offset by low productivity per worker and the lack of a pool of skilled labour. Again, as later, there was a lack of entrepreneurial skills and a small domestic market. In 1948 the postwar boom, with its dangers of increased inflation and a big influx of imports, now combined with poor crops and fishing, led the (as ever) cautious government to curtail expenditure and restrict credit and imports from the dollar area, thus slowing development by a deflationary policy which lasted until 1950, when demand for Portuguese minerals again picked up and worldwide economic recovery got under way during the Korean War. Portugal then shared in the general economic expansion and also started to receive American aid from 1950. Although such assistance obviously must be classed as an aid to development – as well as rearmament, American aid did not play the significant part in the process of development that it did in other European countries, as the figures in Table 4.5 (in millions of US dollars) indicate.

Table 4.5 *US Economic and Military Aid to Six European Countries, 1946–1965*

	Portugal	Spain	Greece	Turkey	Italy	Denmark
US Economic Aid 1949–52:	51·2	52·8	733·4	225·1	1,520·4	273
US Military Aid 1949–52:	10·6	—	323·5	235·9	169·6	73·7
US Economic Aid 1953–7:	12·4	494·8	273·6	457·8	435·6	7·7
US Military Aid 1953–7:	228·8	224·4	433·7	916·5	1,417·1	307·8
Total US Aid 1946–65:	516·7	1,863·9	3,669·9	4,755·2	6,053·7	923·1

But if American assistance was not quantitatively significant, it did help to bring about a more positive attitude towards investment on the part of the state. The aid had to be allocated and so the National Development Fund was set up which grew into the semi-public Development Bank in 1959, an investment bank for long- and medium-term credit. The Development Bank could allocate credit in line with government policies and give a lead to private investment. Further attempts to overcome the rather sluggish investment of the 1950s criticised by economists were made by the state savings bank, the Caixa Geral de Depósitos, which had previously generally only lent funds to local authorities. Nevertheless, despite disappointment at the level of investment and the government's continued emphasis on price stability, the 1950s did see something of an economic breakthrough and the foundation of a national steel industry, Siderurgia Nacional, at Seixal was a turning point. Between 1953 and 1960 non-traditional industries, such as cement, paper, chemicals, metal working, machinery, transport equipment and plastics, grew at a faster pace (1953 = 100, 1960 = 246) than traditional industries, such as leather, textiles, food processing, beverages, cork and resin transformation (1953 = 100, 1960 = 136). Older industries, such as textiles, built up on cheap colonial cotton, suffered from undercapitalisation, outdated production techniques and small units of production: textiles were the biggest employer but in the early 1960s just over half the workers were employed by 1 per cent of the factories and 19 per cent by 84 per cent of the units of production.

The overall rate of growth of the Portuguese gross national product in the decade 1950–60 – which speeded up towards the end of the period – was not outstanding by southern European standards: the figure was 4·5 per cent, compared with 5·0 for Spain, 3·8 for southern Italy, 6·2 for Greece, 5·6 for Turkey and 10·7 for Yugoslavia. Some indication of the relative wealth of the country can be gauged from the figures (Table 4.6) for *per capita* GNP (in US dollars).

Table 4.6   *GNP* per capita *for 1960–1961 in Six Southern European Countries*

Country	Year	Per capita *figure*
Continental Portugal	1961	270
Spain	1960	274
Southern Italy	1960	280
Greece	1961	364
Turkey	1961	180
Yugoslavia	1961	246

The model employed for national development was described by one leading economist, Francisco Pereira de Moura, a Catholic activist who moved into the ranks of the opposition in the late 1960s, as follows:

Private enterprise would carry out industrialisation, whether by substitution of imports or by exporting; the state would help out with the planning and realisation of infrastructure and with the legal framework, by guaranteeing markets (tariff protection and industrial regulation) as well as low costs (wage restraint by corporative *sindicatos*, depressed prices for raw materials from the primary sectors and the colonies, and also financial benefits of various kinds).

Right or wrong, just or unjust, it was a logical model.

In the 1960s, despite an initial setback due to a crisis of confidence in the wake of the outbreak of hostilities in Angola and increasing military expenditure, the country continued to experience a period of faster growth than at any time in its previous history. The old problems remained: poor management, lack of a skilled labour force, a disappointing level of private investment – which tended to be increasingly speculative, cheap labour advantages offset by the high cost of importing raw materials and by low productivity due to technological backwardness, a small domestic market in which increases in purchasing power were offset by buying imported goods. To try to counter these drawbacks Portugal joined EFTA (European Free Trade Association) on its creation in 1960 on preferential terms and, accommodating itself further to what were seen as international trends, shifted the emphasis of its policies away from economic nationalism towards neo-liberalism by encouraging foreign investment.

Annexe G of the Stockholm Convention of 1958 which created EFTA recognised that Portugal's was a young economy and permitted the country to keep protective tariffs for its new industries for a long period, while benefiting from the rapid abolition of customs duties in its trade with other member countries. The result was to be increased trade with EFTA countries, but hopes of a general stimulation of the economy as a result of an enlarged domestic market were not fully realised as national investors held back because of fears that Portuguese firms would be unable to compete. The benefits of Portuguese membership of EFTA came rather from the encouragement that low labour costs and a liberalised policy towards foreign investment gave to outsiders, who could set up subsidiary companies in the EFTA country with the lowest wage levels and at the same time make use of advanced technology and know-how.

In theory the introduction of foreign capital and foreign firms entering into partnership with Portuguese entrepreneurs was supposed not only to speed up industrial growth through increased investment, but also to modernise Portuguese entrepreneurial attitudes by improving local acquaintanceship with up-to-date management and marketing methods and technological expertise. In these spheres the policy was to prove partially successful, but no machinery was successfully devised to channel foreign investment into sectors of the economy where it would be of lasting benefit to Portuguese national development. Foreign investors, said Caetano in 1969, 'will be welcome when they seek effectively to aid internal development and not to exploit us'. Nevertheless, for his Secretary of State for Industry, Rogério Martins, the nightmare remained of the foreign investor realising a quick profit on the basis of low wages and then simply closing down his firm in a time of recession when, as he put it, 'the entrepreneur folds up his tent like a Bedouin and goes home to his country of origin with the profits he has made, leaving behind him only a souvenir of scarcely admirable selfishness'.

The changeover in attitudes towards foreign investors was manifested in Decree Law No. 46312 of 28 April 1965, which said that authorisation for foreign investors would always be given in certain ill-defined areas of the economy which included mining, improvement in agriculture, industrial installations and structures, transport, energy production and the infrastructure of tourism. In some areas, for instance those connected with public services and defence, there was restricted access to foreign capital and an insistence that majority capital must be Portuguese. Other areas were left unclear. In fact a legislative maze grew up which encouraged the would-be investor to use at least some local talent: in the words of a leading student of foreign investment in Portugal, Luís Salgado de Matos, the businessman from abroad needed to recruit Portuguese, not just to improve his image, but

> on account of the complexity of Portuguese economic bureaucracy, which demands a special, unique know-how in which the Portuguese have a decisive advantage over other countries . . . The bureaucracy is very developed, needing as a rule a quantity of paper (and not just paper . . .) which is beyond the comprehension of an average European.

Nevertheless, for those able to play the bureaucratic game, the Law of 1965 promised 'just and equitable treatment', no discrimination, full and prompt compensation in the event of nationalisation, freedom to send profits abroad and the possibilty of tax exemptions. Rightly or wrongly, the Law of 1965 became known as the most liberal foreign investment law in Europe, itself an encouragement to outsiders.

The liberalised legislation on foreign investment of the 1960s partially reversed the earlier and more nationalistic aspirations of the New State, though it should be noted that Salazar had always been a pragmatist where foreign capital was concerned. In 1931 he explained that he was not opposed to foreign capital on principle; it would have a role to play alongside native capital so long as the Portuguese government retained 'the right of choice and the opportunity for intervention', a view reiterated in 1955. The Law on the Nationalisation of Capital of April 1943 – in force until 1961 – drew a distinction between established foreign firms (of which there were many) and future investors. The main provision of the Law of 1943 was the insistence that Portuguese firms (defined as 60 per cent Portuguese owned) alone could run public services or engage in other activities 'of fundamental interest to the defence of the state or the economy of the nation'. Though Portugal had to control the 'key positions of its economy', it was never made clear exactly which these were, so that things proceeded much as before. Intended, as Salazar put it, as 'evidence of confidence in Portuguese capital', the Law's effect was not to increase the state sector of the economy by nationalisation but rather to get some enterprises to augment their share capital to bring about Portugalisation. Thus the new legislation of the 1960s represented an attempt to attract new investment on favourable terms rather than completely to change the direction of previous policy.

There are no statistics on the extent of foreign ownership of firms before the 1960s (and those thereafter are not very informative on new investment), but foreign holdings up to that time may be described as fairly substantial, particularly in mining and exporting industries. A survey in the 1930s would doubtless have noticed that the copper mines at São Domingos were exploited by Mason and Barry, the mines at Panasqueira and Fundão by Beralt Tin and Wolfram, those at Aljustrel and the marble quarries at Vila Viçosa by Belgian firms. The trams, telephones, and water supply of Lisbon and the telephones of Oporto were British-owned, the gas and electricity of the capital Belgian-owned. Petrol refining was in Romanian hands. Franco-Belgian capital had a large share of the tobacco industry. In 1936 British companies did 28 per cent of the country's insurance, and other foreign companies a further 9 per cent, while some banks were British- or French-owned. Foreign capital had a considerable stake in railway companies, while British firms dominated the wine trade, the biggest export trade at that time. The SAPEC chemical firm was Belgian-owned, while the important cork trade was in foreign hands. On Madeira it would be little exaggeration to say that all industries were British, while between 1870 and 1936 over half the capital invested in Portugal's colonies was British – and there was Belgian and French investment as well.

The boost given to foreign investment by the liberalised policy of the 1960s was reflected in the figures for the entry of long-term capital into the private sector: 20 million contos between 1961 and 1967 compared with just over 2 million for 1943–60. In 1971 alone private foreign capital entering the country was three times the total figure for 1943–60. (It may also be noted that the state, which had nationalised the foreign debt in 1940 and set its face against foreign borrowing, again started to borrow abroad.) The first figures collected on foreign investment covered the years 1969–71 and showed that the USA was the biggest single source (23·8 per cent), while EEC countries (West Germany foremost among them) accounted for 28·9 per cent, Portugal's EFTA partner Britain for 13·3 per cent and other European OECD countries for a further 25·5 per cent. For the decade 1961–71 it seems likely however that British investment was rather greater than the 1969–71 figures would suggest. It has been estimated that Britain, the USA, West Germany and Belgium together accounted for three-quarters of the foreign investment in Metropolitan Portugal, followed by France, Spain, Sweden, Switzerland and the Netherlands, who together accounted for a fifth, followed by Denmark, Finland, Italy, Austria, Brazil and Japan. It has also been estimated that foreigners owned 10 per cent of the capital in Portugal by 1970, but the estimate did not include entries of capital prior to 1943. While it would be wrong to say that foreign capital dominated the Portuguese economy at the end of the 1960s – it was predominant only in mining, dyes, electricals and pharmaceutical products – Portugal was nevertheless quite heavily dependent on foreign capital for continued growth and to offset the drain on funds brought about by the colonial wars. In 1969 a third of private investment was financed by outside sources. Portuguese industrialists generally welcomed the participation of foreign capital in their firms in public, but in private they feared that in the longer term they would be unable to compete.

Whatever the longer term fears, foreign investment played a positive role in the 1960s in aiding Portuguese economic growth and foreign investors were attracted by high profit rates and quick recouping of investments. Though respectable rates of growth were achieved in the industrial sector (seen in the average annual growth rate of over 8 per cent between 1953 and 1970), the economy was getting into increasing difficulties in the late 1960s: Portuguese businessmen were ceasing to invest because of lack of confidence in the political as well as economic future; they were finding it difficult to compete for markets; accelerated rates of emigration were undermining the reliance on cheap labour and the shortage of trained technical personnel was being increasingly felt. In addition the longstanding government aim of price stability, successfully maintained except during the wartime period, could no longer be realised: the rate of inflation, measured in consumer prices, rose from 1·7 per cent in 1963 to 5·5 per cent in 1967, 8·8 per cent in 1969 and 11·7 per cent in 1971. In terms of economic performance in the 1960s the Portuguese achievement, as in the previous decade, was not outstanding by southern European standards: the overall annual growth rate of gross domestic product was 7·8 per cent from 1960 to 1969, compared with 10·4 per cent in Spain and 10·7 per cent in Greece (GNP) and 6·35 per cent (net material product, 1960–7) in Yugoslavia. In terms of GNP *per capita* (in US dollars) the position was as shown in Table 4.7.

Table 4.7   *GNP* per capita *for 1970 for Five Southern European Countries*

Country	Year	Per capita *figure*
Portugal	1970	660
Spain	1970	1020
Greece	1970	1090
Turkey	1970	310
Yugoslavia	1970	650

Portugal had moved in the years 1930–70 from underdevelopment to semidevelopment but showed few signs of being able to narrow the gap between itself and the developed countries, which had been a long-term policy aim.

A phenomenon of Portuguese industrialisation was a process of increasing concentration, social, economic and geographical. Between

1950 and 1970 the number of employers of labour decreased from 241,661 to 73,155. Alongside this development went the expansion of a small number of large industrial or financial-industrial groups, often in the 1960s in partnership with foreign concerns, to the extent that it became normal for critics of the regime to speak of the political as well as economic domination of oligopoly or monopolies by the end of the 1960s. Since the development model made industry the motor of progress, what was observable from the 1950s was 'the rise of the industrial-financial bourgeoisie (or of the secondary sector, if one wants to use that terminology) within the Portuguese economy and society, tending to replace the predominantly agrarian and trading forces, *ancien régime* in style, in political power' (in the words of Pereira de Moura). In 1971 it was calculated that 168 companies, many of them interlinked or belonging to the same group, or 0·4 per cent of all the companies existing in Metropolitan Portugal, held 53 per cent of the total capital.

The biggest and best-known Portuguese company, sometimes compared to ICI or Unilever, was CUF, which originated as a soap manufacturing firm at Fontainhas, near Lisbon, in the late nineteenth century, and was largely built up by Alfredo da Silva, a ruthless tycoon sometimes likened to Henry Ford; Silva's personal fortune was reputed to be the sixth largest in the world when he died in 1942. In 1971 CUF itself, not to mention its subsidiaries, accounted for 4·4 per cent of the capital of all industrial concerns in the country. It practically owned the town of Barreiro (on the south bank of the Tagus) and in partnership with Dutch and Swedish capital held a large share in the Lisnave ship-repair company. The CUF group had widespread interests in shipping (49 per cent of all capital in 1971), textiles, mining, the food industry, cellulose, paper, ship building, electricals, petrol refining and petrochemicals, not to mention insurance (it owned the biggest company), tobacco, banking (it owned the Totta e Açores, one of the big six), supermarkets (owning Pao de Açúcar, the biggest chain), office blocks, hotels, restaurants and casinos. Overseas it had interests in Guiné, Angola and Mozambique. Associated principally with the Melo family, who had a direct interest in twenty companies in the group (representing together 40 per cent of its capital), the CUF complex was also associated with the Portela family, directly interested in ten companies within the group.

Perhaps the second best-known name was Champalimaud, whose group had begun as the Casa Sommer, a successful cement-manufacturing firm, which bought the Banco Nacional Ultramarino (one of the biggest commercial banks in the Metropolis and the issuing bank in Mozambique) in 1944. The Champalimaud group had the biggest share in the steel industry, owning Siderurgia Nacional. In addition to extensive colonial holdings, the group had interests in mining, insurance, paper, electricals, cellulose, resins, some of them resulting from the group's acquisition of another of the big six banks, Pinto e Sotto Mayor, in 1961. In contrast to the CUF group, which had a policy of forging links with foreign concerns (e.g. ICI in dyes, Billeruds AB in paper pulp, Ludlow Corp. in textiles), the Champalimaud group generally steered clear of foreign partnerships but itself went in for investment abroad.

Another of the biggest groups was that of the Espírito Santo family, founders of the bank of that name. The group well illustrated the links between the financial and industrial worlds, for the Banco Espírito Santo owned insurance companies, coffee and sugar plantations in Angola and Mozambique and had big holdings in petroleum (at home and in Angola), cellulose, tyres (in conjunction with Firestone), tobacco, brewing, hotels, agriculture and telecommunications. Other large economic 'groups' centred on other big banks, including the Banco Português do Atlântico (with interests in petroleum, cement, glass, brewing, cinemas, insurance, tourism, etc., at home as well as in Africa); the Banco Borges e Irmão (founded by the family of that name in Oporto in 1884); the Banco Fonsecas e Burnay group, of partly Belgian origin, with African interests and links with Belgian and American big business (notably ITT); and the BIP (Banco Intercontinental Português) group of Jorge de Brito with widespread interests in insurance, transport, real estate and road building.

If there was increasing concentration of capital in fewer hands, industrialisation became increasingly geographically concentrated, which led to talk in the later 1960s of correcting regional imbalances and plans to develop whole new areas, such as that around Sines in coastal Alentejo. As already noted (in Chapter 1), and as the population figures show (see Table 4.14), the effect of industrialisation was to increase the importance of the coastal areas from Braga to Setúbal. Figures for 1955 show that the northern industrial zone centred on Oporto, was, with its heavy dependence on textiles, relatively stagnant and contributed much less to GNP than the southern, centred on Lisbon and containing the chemical industry, despite the employment of roughly the same number of workers in each zone. The increasing importance of the southern zone was a constant tendency. With further regard to industrial concentration, it may be observed that already in 1955 over 80 per cent of industrial workers and of firms' incomes, as well as 86 per cent of the industrial product, were concentrated in these two zones combined.

What happened in the industrial sector of the economy, where there was an average annual growth rate of between 8 and 9 per cent from 1953 to 1970, was in marked contrast to developments in the agricultural sector, where the Portuguese annual growth rate of gross domestic production between 1953 and 1961 was 0·9 per cent (compared with between 2 and 3 per cent in Spain, Turkey and Yugoslavia and over 3 per cent in Greece). The intractable problems of agriculture were seen as a powerful brake on general development. Nevertheless change in the agricultural sector did take place, as can be seen in the fall in the number of employers of labour from 142,100 in 1950 to 18,500 in 1970; however, these figures must be put into perspective, for an official report in the early 1950s concluded that 80 per cent of Portuguese units of exploitation were family affairs and only 18 per cent of farmers could be classed as employers. Many of Portuguese agriculture's problems stemmed from geographical factors, exacerbated by a structure of land ownership which had changed little since the fifteenth century. Figures for 1968 showed that 72 per cent of the units of exploitation, covering 30 per cent of the land farmed, could be classified under subsistence farming; while another estimate put at one-fifth the proportion of the agricultural product produced for the market. Of some 1·3 to 1·45 million people engaged in agriculture in the 1950s nearly a third were isolated in 8,000 villages inaccessible by road at the end of that decade.

The structure of exploitation of the land may be seen in statistics for 1968: 23 per cent of farm units, covering 0·7 per cent of land farmed, were between 0·05 and 0·5 hectares; 73 per cent, covering 36·8 per cent of the area, were between 0·5 and 20 hectares in size; 2·7 per cent, covering 16·2 per cent, were between 20 and 100 hectares; 0·5 per cent, covering 22·9 per cent, were between 100 and 1,000 hectares, and 0·06 per cent, covering 20·6 per cent of land farmed, were over 1,000 hectares. (It is worth bearing in mind that units of 25 hectares and less are usually classified as 'small'.) The variations in size were not uniform throughout the country. *Minifúndios* predominated in the north and larger estates were to be found in the south as an analysis of average size by *distrito* indicated: less than 3 hectares in Viana do Castelo, Aveiro, Coimbra, Oporto, Braga and Leiria, but 30·7 in Portalegre, 39·4 in Beja and 62·3 in Évora. Farming units varied from tiny holdings perched on mountain ledges in the north to the great *latifúndios* of the south, where four owners (Posser de Andrade, Santos Jorge, the dukes of Cadaval and Palmela) between them accounted for some 95,000 hectares (235,000 acres, or 1·8 per cent of the total area farmed in mainland Portugal).

Implicit in these statistics were many of the reasons for the disappointing performance of Portuguese agriculture – and agronomists believed that much land unsuitable for agricultural use was being farmed: one estimate put the percentage of land suitable for utilisation at 27·6 per cent north of the Tagus and 29 per cent south of that river, while the actual figures for area of exploitation were 49·9 and 61 per cent respectively. Portugal had not carried out the technological revolution in methods that had occurred in northern Europe, but many smallholdings were too small and/or too poor in terms of quality of land to benefit from mechanisation and/or more intensive cultivation. Quite apart from the reluctance of many farmers to change their methods of exploitation, most owners – and two-thirds of farms were owner-cultivated – were too poor to invest in irrigation, fertilisers or better seeds. While mechanisation was certainly appropriate for cereal cultivation on larger holdings, and was stimulated by the drift from the land in the south in the 1960s, it was not appropriate for small plots on steep slopes or for olive harvesting or cork stripping, which had to remain labour-intensive activities. Migration from rural areas in the 1960s meant getting rid of disguised unemployment due to relative overpopulation, but whereas in the south in particular this phenomenon in combination with strikes for higher wages did bring increased mechanisation – the number of tractors rose from 13,353 to 32,075 and of combine harvesters from 934 to 2,830 in the years 1965–71 – it also led throughout the country to a situation in which 45 per cent of farms were run by people over the age of 55. Fears were expressed that the rural exodus would result in diminished production rather than increased efficiency.

Among the methods used to improve agriculture over the years were irrigation and land reclamation, both of these expensive and therefore slow to progress. The part played in irrigation by the dams built primarily for hydro-electric schemes was reflected in the fact that nine-tenths of this irrigated land (some 12 per cent of the total area cultivated) was to be found in the north and centre of the country, while in the Alentejo, where aridity indices were high, things proceeded slowly: by 1968 only 11,000 hectares of the 170,000 planned had been irrigated. Land reclamation did play a part in boosting rice production. Neither of these costly techniques could however come near to producing a solution to the agrarian conundrum, and the settlement of 3,500 smallholders in the Alentejo by the Board of Internal Colonisation was hardly a great success: financial and technical help was inadequate for them and they often ended up working for larger owners. In the north a policy of reparcellation, i.e. regrouping very small holdings to overcome the non-contiguity of the various plots, was soon abandoned because of lack of success due to local hostility: the Second Development Plan had spoken of creating 6,000 rationalised units, but only 450 materialised. Nor were governments very successful in encouraging co-operatives: in 1973 there were 628 on the mainland and in the Islands, with some 275,000 members, compared with 441 with 143,000 members in 1962. Enmeshed in the corporative structure they did not function very well, though milk and wine were perhaps exceptions to this rule.

The large number of middlemen, like low productivity, remained a headache for planners, who also complained of the shortage of credit for small farmers to offset the drawbacks of undercapitalisation. Rural psychology often meant that recourse would be had to banks or other money-lenders only *in extremis,* which left economists fuming about farmers' lack of productivity-consciousness. Though resistance to change persisted, there was some improvement – particularly among larger owners – in the extent to which herbicides, insecticides and fertilisers were employed in the 1960s. Food and Agriculture Organisation figures for 1961–3 showed that Portugal's index of value of agricultural production was at a Third World level, being only about half that of Spain, Greece, and Yugoslavia and lower than Turkey's though the country used proportionately more fertiliser than the latter two. Rates of agricultural growth fell behind Spain and Greece and, to quote but one agronomist, 'in the period 1957–70 the agricultural sector remained almost stagnant, it being clear that its production was a long way from satisfying the demand that the rise in living standard in other sectors and the consequent change in diet provoked'. The 3 per cent annual increase in gross agricultural product set as a target in the Third Development Plan (1968–73) was not achieved.

Apart from the techniques mentioned to try to improve the performance of agriculture, the New State's traditional method of obtaining results was pricing policy. The most important and best-known endeavour in this sphere was prompted by the need to save some £2 million a year in foreign exchange by making the country self-sufficient in wheat. The wheat campaign, reminiscent of contemporaneous Italian policies, was launched in August 1929 with subsidies for land brought under wheat, but the policy proved only partially successful. As with the increased demand for wolfram during the Second World War, the response to financial incentives was to increase production: everyone wanted to share in the high prices. However, this led to an embarrassing surplus by 1935 which, because of the high cost of production in Portugal, had to be disposed of at cut prices on the international market. In that year, too, steps were taken to cut down the area under cultivation, which had included olive and cork groves and sub-marginal land. Sowing in 1936 was 25 per cent down on 1931–5, years which had seen a third more acreage devoted to wheat than 1926–30. In general, the wheat campaign illustrated some of the shortcomings of incentives and subsidies, for assured good prices did little to stimulate improvements to increase yield per hectare; they also produced distortions, through decreases in production of other commodities, and put more money into the pockets of wealthy large landowners in the south as well as small marginal growers. In the long run the campaign was unsuccessful in achieving self-sufficiency, and kept food prices fairly high. In 1960–9 the average area under wheat was 646,300 hectares, compared with 556,400 in 1931–5, but the yield per hectare for the same periods actually fell slightly – and according to one calculation had not significantly changed since the thirteenth century. Comparative figures for average crop yields of cereals suggested that Portugal was falling behind other south European countries, as Table 4.8 shows (figures are in 100 kilogrammes per hectare).

Table 4.8   *Comparative Crop Yields in the Periods 1934–1938
and 1959–1962*

	1934–1938	1959–1962
Portugal	7·1	7·5
Spain	10·7	11·1
Greece	9·1	14·4
Turkey	10·7	11·0
Yugoslavia	13·7	19·2

One consequence of the wheat campaign was erosion on non-irrigated land brought under wheat, and it was to counter this that the state undertook a plan of reafforestation after the Second World War, planting 190,000 hectares, with the result that by the early 1960s, adding in the 2 million hectares of private and natural forest, there had been a 7 per cent increase in the total afforested area. Apart from improving the land, the afforestation policy also anticipated the important industrial demand for wood pulp. On the other hand, in social terms, the consequences were sometimes negative, for the need to protect saplings meant the exclusion of sheep and goats from traditional grazing, thus adversely affecting the local food supply. Forest fires, a feature of the Portuguese summer, were not always started accidentally.

The stress on cereals, guaranteed prices for rice and olive oil and the subsidised export of excess wine production were government policies, but by the 1960s, with improving living standards in industrialising areas and changes in dietary habits usually associated with these, agriculture could not satisfy the increased demands for meat and dairy produce. The density of Portugal's livestock population was one of the two lowest in Europe. In the 1950s only a fifth of this population consisted of horses, mules and asses, the implication being that much of the cattle herd was used for draught purposes, thus explaining the low levels of milk and meat production. In this respect supply was not adjusted to demand, with the usual negative consequences for the balance of payments. The 1960s witnessed only a gradual rise in pork, beef and milk production, but a better performance, due to the use of industrial methods, was observable for poultry and egg production. Production of crops, on the other hand, was generally stagnant except for rice, tomatoes and orchard fruit.

The stagnation of the agricultural sector, 'largely a pre-capitalist survival' in the words of the economist Pereira de Moura in the early 1970s, extended also to fisheries. Sardines were traditionally associated with Portugal and sardine-canning was introduced from France in the late nineteenth-century. The industry, important in the export field, was chronically undercapitalised and backward in its techniques, as well as being dependent on the quirkish habits of the fish themselves. In general, the New State period saw the decline of the sardine as an item in the economy. Cod fishing (off Newfoundland and Greenland) was also in relative decline and more and more foreign exchange had to be expended on the purchase of foreign cod to satisfy local demand for dried cod, a traditional national dish. Nevertheless, landings of fish nearly trebled in quantity from 1927–31 to 1965–9.

The development of and changes in the economy as a whole were reflected in trade figures. The relationship between the volume of a nation's external trade and its national product is not a good guide to national development, but the figures do have the advantage of showing the extent of external dependence. The growing relative importance of foreign trade may be illustrated by Table 4.9, where the volume of trade is expressed as a percentage of GNP.

Table 4.9   *The Growth of External Trade as a Percentage of GNP, 1938–1970*

Year	Total trade as % of GNP	Imports as %	Exports as %
1938	23·3	15·6	7·7
1950	29·7	17·7	12·0
1960	38·7	24·2	14·5
1970	39·6	24·8	14·8

The value of foreign trade increased five and a half times between 1950 and 1970, over twenty-one times between 1938 and 1970. In this period, too, there was a continuation of the longstanding deficit in the visible balance of trade (except for 1941–3, exceptional because of the value of wolfram exports): this phenomenon is illustrated in Table 4.9. However, the overall balance of payments was kept healthy by emigrant remittances, income from tourism and favourable trade balances with the outside world on the part of overseas provinces which were within the escudo zone. Together with the large gold and foreign exchange reserves built up by Salazar, particularly during the Second World War – gold reserves increased from 1,437 million escudos in 1939 to 10,707 in 1946 – the escudo was maintained as a hard currency from its stabilisation in the early 1930s; until it began to slide in the mid-1970s it was only devalued once, in 1949, by 10·5 per cent against the US dollar. This hard currency policy helped to minimise the increasing cost of imports – be they essential foodstuffs, raw materials, manufactured goods or luxury products – as did the supply of colonial produce at low prices (notably cotton, sugar, coffee). Except for the wartime period, when minerals were much in demand, the terms of trade were generally unfavourable: there was little increase, for instance, in the price of cork, of which Portugal was the world's largest producer, because of its increasing replacement by plastics and other synthetic products. The preferential relationship with the colonies provided markets for Portuguese manufactured goods which, on grounds of cost or because of tariffs, could not have been sold elsewhere.

The extent of the help given to the balance of payments by income from tourism, which increased over nine times in the years 1960–70, and by emigrant remittances, which went up nearly eight times in the same period, may be calculated by expressing these sources of foreign exchange as a percentage of the cost of imports (Table 4.10).

Table 4.10   *Contributions of Two Sources of Foreign Income to the Balance of Payments, 1936–1970*

Year	Cost of imports (in millions of escudos)	Tourist income as % of cost of imports	Emigrant remittances as % of cost of imports
1936	1,997	4·3	7·5
1950	7,882	3·2	6·4
1960	15,695	4·3	11·9
1965	26,553	17·8	12·7
1970	45,494	14·0	31·5

Some idea of economic change is provided by a comparison of the composition of imports and exports in 1937 and 1970, taking the six major items in value (Table 4.11).

Table 4.11   *Changes in the Composition of Imports and Exports, 1937–1970*

A. Imports

Year	Percentage of total and item
1937	10·1 = iron and steel; 8·3 = coal, coke and lignite; 8·1 = cotton (raw, ginned and corded); 3·9 = dried cod; 3·4 = sugar; 2·8 = industrial machinery and apparatus.
1970	14·0 = machinery (other than electric); 10·0 = chemicals; 7·4 = petroleum and petroleum products; 7·4 = motor vehicles; 6·9 = electrical machinery and appliances; 6·8 = textile fibres.

B. Exports

Year	Percentage of total and item
1937	20·4 = wines (chiefly port); 16·7 = fish (chiefly sardines in oil); 13·8 = unmanufactured cork; 4·9 = cotton tissues; 4·3 = cork manufactures; 3·6 = resin.
1970	17·0 = textile yarn, fabrics etc.; 8·4 = clothing (except fur); 7·3 = alcoholic beverages; 7·3 = chemicals; 5·3 = fruit and vegetables; 5·0 = pulp and waste paper.

The general trend was for industry to play a much bigger role in exporting.

Britain was Portugal's main trading partner until the 1920s, a position increasingly threatened thereafter. The geographical pattern of Portuguese trade and the changes therein, which show the importance of colonial territories, may be illustrated by looking at the origin of imports and the destination of exports. In 1937, 18·3 per cent of imports came from Britain; 15·1 from Germany; 11·2 from the colonies; 10·4 from the USA and 8·9 from Belgium; in 1970, 15·5 came from West Germany; 14·0 from Britain; 13·9 from Angola and Mozambique; 7·1 from the USA, and 7·0 from France. With regard to exports, in 1937, 21·5 per cent went to Britain; 12·9 to the colonies; 10·8 to Germany; 10·2 to France and 7·7 to the USA; in 1970, 21·6 went to Angola and Mozambique; 20·4 to Britain; 8·7 to the USA; 6·3 to West Germany, and 5·3 to Sweden.

The importance of the British export market was one obvious factor necessitating Portugal's membership of EFTA, and it is worth noting that Portugal's exports to her EFTA partners went up from 18·3 to 32·4 per cent of the total from 1959 to 1970. Though not growing as quickly, her trade with the six EEC countries also increased in this period; they took 18·3 per cent of her exports in 1970. With the decision by Britain and Denmark to enter the EEC from 1 January 1973, it therefore became all the more important for Portugal to conclude a trade agreement with the EEC. In fact Portugal had in 1962 asked for the opening of negotiations, but these did not proceed when Britain failed to enter in that year. Conversations at ministerial level began in 1970 and an accord was signed in Brussels on 22 July 1972, which the Portuguese described as disappointing. The accord stipulated general mutual tariff reductions until their disappearance in mid-1977 on industrial products, though EEC countries put restrictions on Portuguese paper exports, as well as some textiles and cork products, while Portugal was allowed to continue with some industrial tariffs into the 1980s. The EEC also made tariff reductions for Portuguese tinned tomatoes and fish and fortified (but not ordinary) wines; Portugal was to keep up levels of imports for EEC meat, dairy products and cereals.

The accord with the EEC was yet another step along the road away from the imperial and nationalist economic ideas of the 1930s. The balance of trade between Portugal and its colonies moved from a deficit for the Metropolis in the 1930s to an export surplus in the 1950s. After 1961 foreign capital was encouraged to exploit the natural resources of Angola and Mozambique and sizeable investments were made by West German, American and Belgian concerns, as well as South African and Japanese: figures for 1970 valued Belgian investment holdings in the colonies at 775 million escudos, American at 158 million, South African at 105 million, British at 53 million and West German at 19 million. Portuguese development aid to the African territories was proportionately (in term of GNP) as great as the foreign aid programme of the United States in the 1960s, but this was compensated by the transfer of profits by Portuguese capitalists to the Metropolis, an important source of capital accumulation for the big economic groups, and by the advantages accruing from the complicated workings of the exchange system of the escudo zone, which enabled the Metropolis to take advantage of Angola's favourable trade balances with non-escudo countries; Mozambique's trade balance was, however, consistently unfavourable, though because of invisibles the overall balance of payments was as often as not in surplus, at least until the mid-1960s.

Caetano's policy of 'progressive autonomy' meant a shift away from the Salazarist conception of centralised imperial rule in the economic as well as political spheres, but talk in the years 1968–72 of a choice between European and African futures for Portugal was in some respects unreal. The big-time capitalists wanted an approximation to Europe, but without losing the African interests which allowed them to accumulate capital. For the maintenance of these interests a neo-colonial relationship with the overseas territories, failing continued Metropolitan rule, was a *sine qua non*. The trouble was that, without Portuguese political control, Portuguese capitalist enterprises could well prove too weak to survive foreign competition. In the early 1970s Portugal therefore continued to fight to hold on to its colonies while the profits went to its wealthier citizens.

The colonial wars with their high cost in terms of money and manpower were not, however, the only drain on national resources. Like Ireland, Portugal has traditionally been a country with a high rate of emigration abroad: the historian Alexandre Herculano referred in the 1870s to this 'herd of human cattle . . . the most important Portuguese export industry'. Between 1860 and 1930 some 30,000 Portuguese a year went abroad to seek their living, and an analysis for the period 1890–1940 shows that 92 per cent of legal emigrants came from northern parts of the country and that the destination of 83 per cent was Brazil. After 1930, with restrictions on immigration by Brazil and other countries prompted by the world depression, the emphasis was on internal migration, to find jobs in industry and the big cities, so that the rate of emigration fell: the annual average dropped from 33,519 in 1926–30 (it had been 54,255 at its highest level in 1911–15), to 7,492 in 1931–5, rising slightly to 8,849 in 1936–40 as the world economy recovered somewhat. During the war years 1941–5 the annual average was lower still (3,840), but then it began to pick up again, to 14,214 in 1946–50. Until the 1960s Brazil was the destination of the vast majority of emigrants, but thereafter its place was taken by Western Europe: this change of direction is dramatically illustrated by the fact that whereas 41,518 went to Brazil in 1952, only 1,669 did in 1970.

From the late 1950s Portugal, like other Mediterranean countries, became a supplier of labour to the more advanced countries of Western Europe, as can be seen in Tables 4.12a and 4.12b, based on the work of Dr Eduardo de Sousa Ferreira, which also illustrate the relative failure to attract settlement to the colonial territories.

Table 4.12   *Emigration Patterns from Portugal, 1950–1970*

(a) Year	No. of emigrants (legal + illegal to France)	No. going to colonies	No. to France (legal + illegal)
1950	41,301	19,409	314
1955	57,740	27,593	1,336
1960	67,187	32,028	6,434
1965	131,332	39,395	60,267
1970	209,632	31,000 (est.)	135,667

(b) Year	Total of legal emigrants (excluding colonies)	Principal destination as % of total	
1950	21,892	Brazil (64·6);	Argentina (8·5);
		USA (4·3).	
1960	32,318	Brazil (38·5);	USA (17·6);
		France (11·1).	
1970	64,927	France (33·8);	West Germany (30·5);
		USA (15·0).	

As can be seen, the majority of emigrants went to France, and by the 1970s Paris had become the second Portuguese city after Lisbon. Emigration to the United States was a phenomenon much associated with the Azores and, to a lesser extent Madeira; the centres of settlement were New England and, to a lesser extent, California. Canada was also a major destination for Azoreans in particular in the 1960s, while Madeirans favoured Venezuela and South Africa. As for the mainland, emigration was principally a phenomenon associated with the north-west until the 1950s when it became general to the whole country. It became more attractive for rural workers to go in search of the higher wages of France and Germany than to migrate to Greater Lisbon or Oporto; better wages were also a lure for urban workers, skilled and unskilled, while for those of military age illegal emigration had the added attraction of avoiding conscription.

Some idea of the social spread of the emigratory phenomenon can be gathered from statistics (Table 4.13) on the occupational composition of *legal* emigration (in percentages).

Table 4.13   *Types of Emigrants from Portugal, 1951–1970*

Year	Workers in agriculture, fishing, etc.	In industry and construction	Domestic employment	Employment in trade, etc.
1951	14·6	15·4	19·0	15·0
1965	21·9	25·9	22·8	6·5
1970	22·6	13·2	29·8	6·0

Emigration abroad or to the colonies – and between 1950 and 1970 some 2 million Portuguese emigrated, equivalent to 60 per cent of the labour force in the latter year – was connected with a more general shift in population away from the agricultural areas to the developing *distritos* of the coastal Braga–Setúbal axis, though the pull of Greater Lisbon as well as the wider world is also reflected in the statistics. Table 4.14 shows the difference in the population figures for each *distrito* expressed as a percentage of the previous figure (the *distritos* of the Azores are grouped together as one unit); population density is in inhabitants per square kilometre.

Table 4.14   *Population Shifts by* Distritos, *1930–1970*

Distrito	1930–1950	1950–1960	Population density in 1960	1960–1970
Aveiro	+23·2	+ 8·1	194	+ 4·6
Beja	+19·8	− 7·6	27	−24·9
Braga	+31·9	+ 8·8	219	+ 3·9
Braganza	+21·9	+ 0·9	36	−23·0
Castelo Branco	+24·0	− 4·3	47	−19·0
Coimbra	+16·4	− 1·1	110	− 8·8
Évora	+24·0	− 3·2	30	−18·1
Faro	+10·8	− 4·6	62	−14·7

Distrito	1930–1950	1950–1960	Population density in 1960	1960–1970
Guarda	+13·8	− 6·8	51	−23·2
Leiria	+27·7	+ 1·0	118	− 4·3
Lisbon	+16·8	+33·0	501	+14·9
Oporto	+30·8	+13·1	523	+10·3
Portalegre	+14·5	− 2·6	32	−21·2
Santarém	+21·7	+ 0·4	69	− 5·8
Setúbal	+39·9	+15·3	73	+23·4
Viana do Castelo	+19·7	− 1·4	132	− 9·1
Vila Real	+24·6	+ 1·3	77	−18·0
Viseu	+12·0	− 3·6	96	−12·4
Madeira	+27·4	− 0·7	337	− 5·6
Azores	+24·7	+ 3·1	140	−11·6
NATIONAL TOTAL	+25·1	+ 4·0	97	− 2·1

A demographic study by Professor Livi Bacci noted that the size of families was larger in the north and the Islands, where seven or eight children was the norm in 1940, than it was in the capital, where three or four was usual. In 1960 the north and the Islands were still the areas where families were largest, but the diminishing size of families in the south had brought down the national average from 5·2 to 3·9 in twenty years. Nevertheless, the birth rate remained high, decreasing from 30·2 per thousand in 1930 to 24·3 in 1960, though still 21·3 in 1971 (compared to 16·3 in Greece, 19·5 in Spain, 18 in Yugoslavia and, in 1967, 39·6 in Turkey).

Most statistics on the economy and society of Portugal are indicative of underdevelopment and the general rule is not broken when one comes to look at standards of living, health and education. With regard to living standards, it is as well to bear in mind, in the words of Pereira de Moura in 1969, that

Portuguese industrialisation was based on the sacrifice of the labouring classes (low wages, high price levels for consumer goods, weak state intervention with regard to redistribution [of wealth], be it direct or indirect through public investments and expenditure of a 'social' type, such as education, housing, health, social security and rural advancement). It was a capitalist process, albeit with the State intervening to an important extent, but in the sense of helping the private sector, and not compensating for or correcting the latter's abuses and shortcomings in a human perspective.

While the proportion of national income paid to labour is usually of th
order of 60 to 70 per cent in a developed country, the Portuguese figur
was still 39 per cent in 1950; it rose to 47 in 1965 and 52 in 1971.

Very crude figures suggest that real agricultural wages rose slightly i
the 1930s, and the index (100 = 1929) stood at 227 in 1948; in the sam
period (1929–48) the cost-of-living index had moved from 100 to 168
Taking 100 = 1955, the cost-of-living index rose from 95 in 1948 to 110 i
1968, while agricultural wages rose from 104 in 1948 to 304 in 1968 an
industrial wages from 99 in 1953 to 209 in 1968. If, overall, real wage
rose, there were regional variations: average northern industrial wages i
the mid-1950s, for instance, were only two-thirds of those in the souther
industrial area, although the northern cost of living was higher. Wage
varied from industry to industry. In 1972 it was estimated that rura
wages were about 60 per cent of the urban-industrial level; both typica
families selected spent about half their earnings on food and could sav
nothing. Some idea of the gap between Portugal and other countries ma
be illustrated (Table 4.15) by a very rough comparison made of take hom
earnings adjusted in terms of purchasing power (figures in Germa
marks).

Table 4.15   *Comparative Take-Home Earnings in Europe, 1971–2*

Denmark (1972)	13820
France (1972)	12660
West Germany (1972)	12560
Britain (1972)	9750
Italy (1972)	7000
Ireland (1972)	6840
Spain (1972)	4590
Greece (1971)	4360
Portugal (1971)	2880

Herein one observes one spur to the high emigration of recent years.

Another crude indicator of living standards, as of health, is the averag
daily *per capita* caloric intake: this increased from 2,270 in 1950 to 2,93
in 1969. Bearing in mind that this is an *average* and that the FAC
recommended minimum requirement is 2,580, the Portuguese level in th
latter year was more or less comparable with Greece (2,900), Spai
(2,750), Turkey (3,150) and Yugoslavia (3,130). Life expectancy at birt
in Portugal by the end of the 1960s was 67 years (compared with 62 ¡
decade earlier); it was 70 in Greece and Spain, 65 in Yugoslavia and 54 i
Turkey. The infant mortality rate improved from 144 per thousand i
1930 to 57 in 1969, but it was still almost the highest in Europe; the figur
for 1969 for Greece was 32, for Spain 30, for Yugoslavia 56. In Portuga

the rate was higher in the north than the south. Yet another comparison with other south European countries can be made for health (Table 4.16).

Table 4.16 *Comparative Health Services for Five Southern European Countries, 1968–1971*

Country	No. of persons per doctor	No. of persons per hospital bed
Portugal	1,050 *(1970)*	159 *(1971)*
Greece (1969)	638	163
Spain	746 *(1970)*	218 *(1968)*
Turkey (1969)	2,267	69,413
Yugoslavia (1970)	1,000	177

There were the usual regional differences: for example, the number of persons per doctor in Lisbon was 620, but 2,310 in the Algarve, 2,830 in Trás-os-Montes, 2,700 in the Alentejo.

As with health services, so with education: progress was steady, if slow. The proportion of illiterates in the population (7 years and over) fell from 58·1 per cent in 1930 to 40·4 in 1950 and was 25 per cent in 1970 despite the national adult education campaign begun in 1952. The level of illiteracy was not evenly spread. In 1968 it was estimated that only 7·9 per cent of those aged under 40 were illiterate, while figures for 1960 showed that, while illiteracy among males over 15 stood at 26·4 per cent, the figure for females was 39·8. Whereas, in 1960, the proportion of illiterates in the *distritos* of Lisbon and Oporto was 20·6 and 25·2 per cent respectively, it was 32·9 to 34 in the Minho, 36·9 in the Algarve and 38 to 44·1 in the Alentejo. Although expenditure was stepped up in the late 1960s the Portuguese level of literacy lagged behind those of Greece, Spain and Yugoslavia, but was well above the Turkish level. A report of the Education Ministry showed that 36 per cent of those over 7 were illiterate in 1960; 28 per cent were literate but had no educational qualification; 32 per cent had completed primary education; 3·14 per cent had a secondary education and 0·74 per cent had had higher education. According to UNESCO figures, in 1968 there were 418 students per 1,000 in higher education in Portugal, compared with 490 in Spain, 844 in Greece and 427 in Turkey. The need to try to improve the educational position led to the reform programme of Veiga Simão (Education Minister 1970–4), mentioned in Chapter 5.

In general terms, one can say that the period of the New State saw a steady rate of economic and social development in Portugal, though not one fast enough to lift the country from the bottom end of the European statistical league table. One might extend to Portuguese society and the economy as a whole the verdict of the Secretary of State for Industry, Rogério Martins, in 1970: 'the industrial system which has existed in our country for the last twenty-five years has not permitted an approximation to the economically developed European countries . . . nor improved our position relative to others'. While the political system remained static and seemingly monolithic between 1933 and 1969, the society over which it ruled exhibited increasing contrasts between change and continuity. The urban-rural disjuncture between the northern and southern industrial areas and the rest of the country became more marked with the concentration of population in the former exacerbated by the depopulation of the latter through emigration. Nevertheless the difference between different country regions were maintained: north of the Tagus population was still more dense than to its south, religion still stronger, infant mortality rates and deaths from infectious diseases still higher, but the level of illiteracy lower. Only the Algarve was injected with a certain modernity in the form of national and international tourism. While in the north the distribution of property remained more even, in neither part could the growth of an important middle class be observed. The amenities of life, whether better wages, higher living standards, better medical facilities, greater educational opportunities, wider opportunities for social advancement, were increasingly and more obviously becoming concentrated in the two industrial areas. Change, in rural areas, was principally associated with people leaving them – and the same could be said of the Adjacent Islands where the pull of emigration was also strong.

In the developing Portugal of the two industrial zones, the tendency for Oporto to be eclipsed by Lisbon was accentuated. Both cities suffered the effects of accelerated urban growth – inadequate housing, pauperism, vagrancy, increased alcoholism, etc., though begging diminished – but the advance of Greater Lisbon was reflected in the fact that by 1960 the tertiary sector had become the biggest employer of labour there, whereas in Oporto, with its older industries, smaller enterprises and more conservatively minded business world, the secondary sector remained the biggest employer. Psychologically provincial, *portuenses* observed with mixed feelings the growing concentration to the south of industrial financial and political power. In the long term it seemed that Greater Lisbon might be left as the only oasis in the Portuguese desert. In Lisbon and its environs were to be found most of the upper class, a term applicable (it has been suggested by Hermínio Martins) to between 0·5 and 1·2 per cent of Portuguese in the 1960s, and most of the middle class, between 15 and 25 per cent of the active population. In Lisbon, and to a lesser extent in Oporto and other centres, the emergence as a result of economic development of a new social stratum, the lower-middle class, was evidenced by the end of the 1960s in the increased number of private cars, used at weekends for rural picnicking, visiting nearby seaside resorts and going hunting, as well as in the advent of supermarkets. But if this stratum sought to follow in the footsteps of more advanced consumer societies and ape the fashions introduced to it by tourism, films and television, it was at the same time affected by the general social malaise occasioned by a sense of uncertainty. Could African problems be resolved? Could Portugal catch up with the more advanced countries? Could the political system evolve to permit greater freedom?

It has already been observed that the New State period saw Portugal change from an agricultural to an industrialising country (see Table 4.3) and that this change was accompanied by the increased importance of a number of financier-industrialists. Nevertheless changes in the composition and outlook of the upper class and governing élite should not be exaggerated. In the small country of Portugal the governing élite and upper class were thoroughly identified and interlinked. The upper class has been defined by H. Martins as comprising 'latifundists, financiers, leading industrialists and other businessmen; the upper echelons of the officer corps, the civil service and the professoriate; the Catholic episcopate and the top ranks of the liberal professions'. These different segments, however, were often interlinked by marriage, overlapped, shared common educational (especially university) backgrounds, and were convergent in values and life-style, which tended to 'aristocratic conspicuous consumption' rather than to 'bourgeois rationality'. Access to this élite was not closed, though in the 1960s over half the controllers of large enterprises (over 500 employees) were their founders or their heirs. On the other hand, given good luck in the operation of patronage, someone of ability but non-upper-class birth could rise in the university world, church or armed forces and be co-opted into the élite, Salazar and Caetano being examples. (The extent of professorial prominence in government can be judged from the fact that over half the civilian ministers were academics – of these over half graduated in law.) There was then a close interlinking of different élites to form a remarkably cohesive national élite which had many opportunities for reinforcing itself through what Hermínio Martins has termed 'kleptocracy: the use of public office for gain, or conversely the purchase of political and administrative favours, in a systematic and sustained fashion'. The balance of power within the élite shifted from the big southern landowners to the big capitalists under the New State, but the former were still strong enough to block structural agrarian reforms which might have seemed to be in the interest of the industrialists in the 1960s. But, as the Italian theorist of the élite, Vilfredo Pareto, said, 'history is a graveyard of aristocracies': revolution was not far distant.

If the Lisbon of the 1960s thought of itself as European or cosmopolitan by Portuguese standards, with signs of progress all around, it was still provincial by international standards. The old ways were disappearing slowly, as seen in the persistence of flowery manners and conservative modes of dress. Among the middle class there was nostalgia for a traditional way of life made possible by low-wage domestic service. Two British writers, Peter Fryer and Patricia McGowan Pinheiro, at the beginning of the decade found Portugal the last European survival of the Edwardian era: 'Opponents of Salazar condemn every sort of intellectual obscurantism. At the same time many of them take for granted practices that are downright feudal.' They described how:

a young man who had been in jail for his activities in the *MUD Juvenil* – a left-wing youth movement – astonished us when we visited him by punctuating the conversation with peremptory summonses to the maid. She was obviously busy in the kitchen preparing dinner, but he called for her for the most trivial things: to pick up a newspaper he had dropped on the floor and would not permit us to stoop for; to answer the telephone, which was at his elbow (the calls were invariably for him); to bring his cigarettes from the room he had left them in. And this boy was no *fidalgo,* or aristocrat, nor an heir to wealth... Nor was he the arrogant young prig one might expect from this kind of behaviour. On the contrary, he was gentle, unassuming and humorous, and not at all lacking in intelligence. It had clearly never occurred to him to treat servants otherwise...

The wife of a cultured liberal complained:

Servants are not what they used to be. Just imagine, I've caught one of my girls taking my cast-off nylons. She wanted to go out in nylon stockings! Really, the next thing, we shall see the servants wearing hats, just like us!

As mores changed and opportunities for female industrial employment increased, the servant problem became more acute and the war between *donas de casa* (housewives) for good maids intensified.

There remained those who served God, not man, woman or Mammon, but their numbers also seemed to be decreasing. Despite the Catholic revival of the first third of the century and the rechristianisation of public life under the New State, ecclesiastics continued to complain of the formalism of religious life in the country. The church seemed unable to keep pace with the movement of population to the cities and its strength continued to lie north of the Tagus. Thousands of the faithful made the pilgrimage to Fátima each year and further anti-communist revelations by Sister Lucia, the only survivor of the three children to whom the Virgin was said to have appeared in 1917, in the 1930s and 1940s brought a further convergence between the causes of church and state. The attempt to rechristianise the Alentejo, including making the diocese of Beja a missionary area, was a failure. The religious indifference of *alentejanos* was reflected in high illegitimacy rates and low marriage rates in the south: in the 1950s one observer noted that in parts of western Alentejo illegitimate births often exceeded legitimate, while in Setúbal and Évora in 1950 just under half the marriages performed were followed by a religious rite. For the southern poor, urban and rural, religious marriage was expensive and made divorce very difficult. The Portuguese overall illegitimacy rate was among the highest in Europe, being 16 per cent in 1937, falling to 7·5 by 1966; in 1960, with 10 per cent, Portugal trailed behind Iceland, Austria, East Germany and Sweden (25·3, 13, 11·4 and 11·3 per cent respectively) in the European illegitimacy league, but contrasted markedly with other Mediterranean countries: the Italian, Spanish and Greek rates were 2·4, 2·3 and 1·2 per cent respectively.

Though, as events after 1974 were to demonstrate, it would be wrong to think of the Portuguese Church as a spent force, its internal crisis was by the 1960s becoming acute. Catholic Action, which had a flourishing membership of over 50,000 in 1940, folded up in the late 1960s, while the joint lay/ecclesiastical Courses in Christianity made little impact. The Second Vatican Council accentuated the tendencies for Catholics to divide on political, social and, in the 1960s, even theological issues. Though the hierarchy had its own Rádio Renascença from the 1930s and its own Catholic university in Lisbon from the 1960s, and there were Catholic secondary schools, the number of seminarists, which had recovered by the 1930s from the anti-clerical ravages of the First Republic, declined markedly from 1962. The Portuguese Church, which was not exceptionally well provided with clergy (in the 1940s there was one priest for 1,773 believers in Portugal compared to one per 593 in Ireland), was in danger of running out of personnel. The number of seminarists fell from 1,873 in 1961 to 1,098 ten years later; in 1962 there were 126 ordinations, in 1967 only 64. Most seminarists still came from the north and the Islands and something like four out of five were of humble rural origin. By the end of the 1960s most Portuguese Catholics favoured a revision of the concordat of 1940 and were in favour of divorce being permitted between Catholic spouses.

In the sphere of culture, trends also seemed to be set against the philosophical basis of the regime. From the first, a considerable proportion of the intelligentsia was in opposition to the New State: the neo-realist reviews *O Diabo* and *Sol Nascente,* reacting against the abstract and metaphysical tendencies popular in the 1920s, were suppressed in 1940–1. Intellectuals had to contend with the internal censorship and with the ban on some foreign books (which included works by Malraux and Lorca); yet despite a sense of cultural isolation, literary production and criticism was not stifled by the authorities. In poetry the New State period opened with Fernando Pessoa, the greatest Portuguese literary figure since Camões, still alive. By the time of his death in 1935 he had moved towards 'English-style conservatism' and away from his earlier messianic imperial nationalism; his discovery by educated Portuguese in general dated from the 1940s and made a major impact on the literary world which is, however, difficult to gauge. Poetic output was kept up by José Régio, a founder of the *Presença* movement of the 1930s which concentrated on psychological themes; Alexandre O'Neill, Jorge de Sena and the Catholic poet, Sofia de Melo Breyner Andresen.

In the realm of prose writing the dominant trend was neo-realist, especially from about 1950 when French, Brazilian and American influences became particularly obvious, and authors seeking to portray social realities often ran into trouble with the censors. The precursor of neo-realism was Ferreira de Castro, whose *A Selva* ('The Jungle', 1930) is the most translated Portuguese novel. In general the new realism tended to focus on the lower classes rather than the upper and middle, the subject of nineteenth-century realism. Writers of note included Alves Redol, whose *Fanga* ('Bushel', 1943) dealt with social conflicts in the Alentejo, while his *Uma Fenda na Muralha* ('A Gap in the Wall', 1960) presented a more realistic account of life among fisherfolk in Nazaré; Aquilino Ribeiro, whose *Quando os Lobos Uivam* ('When the Wolves Howl', 1959) concerns the problems of northern peasants; Carlos de Oliveira, whose anarchistic *Alcateia* ('Pack of Wolves', 1944) was banned; Fernando Namora, whose *Casa de Malta* (1945) was concerned with homeless casual labourers; Miguel Torga, whose stories reflected his love of rural simplicity and penchant for social criticism; Virgílio Ferreira, whose *Vagão J* (1946) deals with migrant workers in a cattle wagon in search of employment, and José Cardoso Pires, whose *O Anjo Ancorado* ('The Anchored Angel', 1958) concentrated on generational conflicts among oppositionists and whose *Dinossauro Excelentíssimo* ('Most Honourable Dinosaur', 1972), a satire on the Salazar regime, was a best-seller under Caetano. Historians who challenged, directly or indirectly, the nationalist-traditionalist interpretations beloved of official circles could also be in difficulties and some had to go abroad, such as Vitorino Magalhães Godinho and A. H. de Oliveira Marques, as well as the sociologist H. Martins.

In the visual arts the foundation of the Portuguese Information Secretariat in the 1930s provided a source of patronage and created a national style which pervaded the arts till the 1950s. However, the leading painter, Maria Helena Vieira da Silva, best known for her abstract

'Golden City' (1956), lived abroad from 1928. After 1945 neo-realist influence was felt in the artistic world alongside surrealism and the artistic world increasingly fell out with the regime. From 1957 the Gulbenkian Foundation took over the role of patron of the arts once held by the SNI/SPN. The national style can be seen at work in the monument to Henry the Navigator at Belém (built in 1960, but designed in 1940), while the influence of totalitarian architecture can be detected in the University of Coimbra and the Lisbon National Library. On the other hand the Lisbon church of Our Lady of Fátima betrays the influence of Gropius, while the headquarters of the Gulbenkian Foundation, the leading centre of high culture, provides possibly the best example of contemporary architecture in the country.

The symbolic divorce between the intellectual world and the regime can also be observed in the case of the former's most distinguished representative, the neurologist Egas Moniz, whose moderate opposition stance in the 1940s and 1950s was particularly embarrassing since in 1949 he was awarded the Nobel Prize. His scientific treatise *A Vida Sexual* ('Sexual Life') could only be obtained by the medical profession because of the ban on pornography.

To critics of the regime the New State by the late 1960s seemed to be a hopeless anachronism. While important social and economic changes had and were taking place under the regime, these changes seemed either to make its ideals less relevant to contemporary concerns or increasingly falsified them in reality. In the international boom years of the 1960s it seemed strange that the country should still be ruled by the same man who had proclaimed in April 1937:

We are not seduced by or satisfied with the acme of technique, or the machinery that lessens the man, or the delirium of the mechanical, or the colossal, the immense, the unique, the brute force, if the wings of the spirit do not touch them and subject them to the service of a life every time more beautiful, more high and more noble. Without losing sight of activities which may provide for all a greater amount of goods and with them greater material comfort, the ideal is to flee from the materialism of today: to make the fields more fertile, without silencing therein the merry songs of the girls; to weave cotton or wool in the most modern looms, without interlacing with the thread class hate and without banishing from the factory or the workshop our old patriarchal spirit.

From a civilisation which is returning scientifically to the jungle we are separated, unceasingly, by spiritualism – fount, soul, life of our History. We shun feeding the poor with illusions, but we want at all costs to preserve from the wave that is rising in the world the simplicity of life, the purity of customs, the sweetness of feelings, the equilibrium of social reactions, this familiar air, humble but dignified, of Portuguese life . . .

While to the aged Salazar the times were now out of joint, the clamour for higher growth rates, structural reforms, greater social expenditure continued. Some saw these as impossible without decolonisation and democratisation, others advocated socialism. But at least one opposition leader, the economist Pereira de Moura, seemed aware that the number of options was strictly limited: were the working classes to take power by revolution, he wrote in 1971,

were this to happen in isolation and with a neo-capitalist Europe (leaving aside the political viability of this hypothesis), it would permit wage increases and social advancement, though these would quickly be limited; in fact, once the tasks of redistribution had been achieved, it would run into economic stagnation because of the small and poor nature of the economy; stagnation and instability, the response to which would be authoritarian political forms – the working classes would finish up beneath the control of a state apparatus which would escape from their hands into those of the bureaucratic 'new class' (supplied by the present technocrats).

If things could not go on as they were, it was difficult to see exactly how things could be changed for the better.

5

Caetano and the Revolution of the Flowers

This country outwardly gentle and smiling, but tormented and tragic within. Miguel de Unamuno

The appointment of Marcelo Caetano as President of the Council of Ministers on 26 September 1968 opened a new phase in the history of the New State. While he always emphasised that changes could only come slowly, the new Premier's change of style, ranging from meet-the-people tours in Portugal itself to visits to the overseas territories and Brazil and fireside chats on television, aroused expectations among the educated and the uneducated alike. As one old peasant woman in the south was reported to have said: 'this looks a much nicer Salazar than the other one was!' Certainly the image projected by the new Premier stressed movement rather than *immobilisme* and the great propaganda slogans of his premiership were 'renewal in continuity' and 'evolution without revolution'. For non-Portuguese seeking reference points for the new trend, Caetanist reformism was often termed, perhaps inaccurately but conveniently, liberalisation (after the image of Spain in the 1960s projected by its Minister of Information, Fraga Iribarne) or thaw (in the manner of the Soviet Union under Khrushchev). No one could be sure, however, perhaps not even the pragmatic Caetano himself, where the road of reform would lead. Was the long-term aim a reinvigorated 'Salazarism without Salazar', or was it the transformation of the regime into something approaching conventional Western European democracy, perhaps along the lines of the Fifth French Republic? Such questions remain unanswered, but the historical reality was that within five and a half years the reformist experiment had come to a halt in a *cul-de-sac*. As the *ultras* of the regime had feared and the opposition had hoped, liberalisation was the prologue to the extinction of the regime of 1933.

In the realm of politics, Caetano's premiership can be divided into two parts: the days of hope, hope that changes would be real and far-reaching and that a new page of history would be turned, lasting until 1970–1, followed just as quickly, with the seemingly normal swing of the Portuguese political and emotional pendulum, by the increasingly bitter disillusionment of 1972–4.

Caetano's short-term political aims in 1968–9 were to gain credibility with moderate opposition forces; to broaden the basis of support for himself and the regime; to avoid a sudden counter-productive confrontation with the *ultras* or Salazarists still entrenched in positions of power; and to gain internal and international respectability by acts of liberalisation. Thus there was no sudden and complete change of governmental personnel though the *ultra* Foreign Minister, Franco Nogueira, who wondered where the new course would end, resigned in October 1969. The opposition lawyer and leader of the small ASP (Portuguese Socialist Action, founded in Switzerland in 1964), Mário Soares, was brought back from a spell of deportation to São Tomé in November 1968, and the Bishop of Oporto was allowed to return. Censorship of the press was relaxed somewhat so that in May 1969 newspapers could report on a national manifesto issued by the socialists, and on a republican congress in Aveiro at which calls were made for the freeing of political prisoners (of whom there were officially stated to be 187 in November 1968) and open discussion of overseas policies. Another sign of the new times was the appointment in December 1968 to the leadership of the UN of José Guilherme de Melo e Castro, a progressive Catholic known to favour political pluralism and a free press, who set about trying to revitalise the 'civic association' with new men and to attract oppositionists into dialogue, if not into the UN itself.

The first real test of Caetano's sincerity so far as the opposition was concerned came with the elections for the National Assembly in November 1969. The electoral law was changed so that literate adults, male and female, were entitled to the vote, thus making for the widest suffrage known in Portuguese history to that date. However, discriminatory provisions against the opposition's use of the media and large assembly halls were maintained, while a mixture of indifference and local bureaucratic and political pressures meant that fewer than half those entitled to register as voters actually did so. For Caetano, as for oppositionists, widespread indifference to political issues was at that time an obstacle to increasing popular participation in the electoral process, whether this be used for the strengthening of the existing system or for its transformation. Despite the danger that Salazarism without Salazar might legitimise itself in the freest elections yet held, the opposition decided to take part in the process. Since the regime could not be overthrown by civilian insurrection, here was an opportunity for repeating the Delgado experience of 1958; as Soares put it in a subsequent memoir: 'In a country that was politically asleep, the point was not so much to win as to wake it up.' In 1969 19·5 per cent of the total population were registered voters, compared with 14·8 in 1965. In the event, 42·5 per cent of the voters abstained (51·9 per cent in Lisbon) for various reasons, of which, according to Soares, 'the lack of unity among the opposition was unquestionably one of the most important'.

While on the government side there was rather more evidence of pluralism among the candidates, two-thirds of whom were new, including some in Oporto who declared that they were not bound by official UN policies, on the opposition side there was division. Leaving aside a very unsuccessful monarchist list in Lisbon (which included Rolão Preto), the decision of Cunha Leal's increasingly fictional ADS to withdraw left the candidates of the CED (Democratic Electoral Committee) and the CEUD (Electoral Committee of Democratic Unity). In Lisbon (where the principal CED leader was the now left-Catholic economist, Pereira de Moura), in Oporto and in Braga, the opposition provoked dismay among wellwishers by failing to agree on one list: in these three constituencies a rather motley collection of left-wing Catholics, communists and others projected a radical image for the CED, while a less radical image – and one firmly opposed to 'totalitarian socialism' – was projected by the socialists led by Soares. In other constituencies unity was achieved among the different oppositionists, confusingly under the CED label. Official figures recorded that some 88 per cent of voters had endorsed the UN lists – and therefore Caetano – compared with 11·8 per cent for the CED/CEUD lists. Wits said that the opposition had had its campaign, but the government its election.

For oppositionists the election campaign 'sowed the seed of ideas which [would] bear their fruit in the future' but for some 'this comedy of the voting booth' also showed that 'the political springtime heralded by [Salazar's] departure [had] withered on the bough' (in the words of Soares, who went into French exile after attacking government policy in New York in 1970). Other oppositionists were more cautious: they waited to see how Caetano would act with his position *vis-à-vis* the *ultras* strengthened and with a presidential election due in 1972, and how much impact the so-called liberal wing of UN deputies, about 20 in number out of the total 130, could make in changing the regime from within.

After the elections of November 1969, which he interpreted as a triumph for 'renewal in continuity', Caetano proceeded along what he saw as 'the road of reform'. In January 1970 he formed a new government with fewer ministers for greater administrative efficiency. Younger men, often technocrats with a Catholic Action background, were brought in, who would be personally loyal to the Caetanist 'new course'. The Foreign Minister, Rui Patrício, was the Premier's godson; the Minister of Corporations, Health and Welfare was the talented Baltasar Rebelo de Sousa; the Minister of Education, charged with expansion and

democratisation, the Cambridge-trained nuclear physicist, Veiga
Simão. Among the secretaries of state were well-known economists who
had been critical of the regime's performance in the past, such as João
Salgueiro (Planning), Rogério Martins (Industry) and Xavier Pintado
(Trade), while Maria Teresa Lobo, as Under-Secretary for Health and
Welfare, became the first woman to be included in a Portuguese
government.

Along with the changes of personnel in government, aimed at
providing a younger, more dynamic and politically neutral image for the
regime, went some changes in nomenclature. The powers of the PIDE were
curbed and some of its personnel retired: from November 1969 it
became (following Spanish practice) the DGS (Directorate-General of
Security). The UN was restructured, at least in the cities and on paper, and
from 1970 went by the new name of ANP (People's National Action –
probably a Venezuelan-inspired title). Having failed to attract into the
ANP (of which Caetano became President) some of the younger
intellectuals whom he had hoped to win over, the Premier permitted
limited political pluralism by authorising the formation of another civic
organisation, SEDES (Social and Economic Development Study Group),
which became a tolerated centre of criticism of the government and
regime rather than a second governmental support organisation.

By the autumn of 1970, when the question of constitutional revision
came to be debated, there had been no real institutional changes in the
regime even though the country was in a real sense freer than it had been
under Salazar. The press, especially the opposition evening daily
República, was rather less dull; the public could now sample books, films
and plays which would earlier have been deemed subversive; and the
atmosphere of suspicion and unease had given way to a more relaxed
climate in which people were less afraid of voicing criticisms in public. So
far Caetano had lived up to the first part of the witticism that he signalled
left but turned right. The debates on amending the constitution showed
that, intentionally or otherwise, he lived up to the second part. The
debates, in which Caetano had apparently expected to be supported by
the ANP's liberal wing, in fact proved the occasion for an irreparable
breach between the genuine liberalisers and the government, which was
always mindful of a backlash from *ultras.* The constitutional
amendments, taken together with the much vaunted new Press Law,
suggested to the opposition and to members of the liberal wing that the
whole policy of renewal in continuity was no more than a facelift for the
regime. The censorship was liberalised, but since there was a state of
emergency because of the wars in Africa, prior examination of texts
continued much as before.

From late 1971 the process of liberalisation was at a standstill; if people
claimed that it was being reversed, this was to be explained more by

people having become accustomed to the idea of constant progressive change under Caetano, however limited and slow, rather than to any serious attempt on the part of the government to put back the clock – which in the political sphere had not admittedly been very far advanced. Estranged from centrist opinion represented by leaders of the liberal wing, Caetano's hopes of broadening the regime's basis of support and shifting the governmental centre of gravity away from the Right faded. Although then aged 78, President Tomás, seen as a guardian of the old order by the *ultras*, decided to have himself elected for another seven-year term. Ironically Caetano had earlier described the Portuguese regime as being characterised by 'the presidentialism of the Prime Minister', but now he was apparently powerless to prevent the old man having his way. Members of the liberal wing, who had wanted to return to presidential election by direct suffrage, were unsuccessful in getting the Governor of Guiné, General Spínola, to allow himself to be nominated by them. Out of the electoral college of 669, 616 voted for Tomás.

After Tomás's re-election to the presidency of the republic it was clear that there would be no further liberalisation. Either the *ultras* were too well entrenched to be shifted or Caetano was unwilling to press hard for further changes: either way Caetanist reformism was fatally paralysed. Early in 1973, after the government had sacked half a dozen civil servants for taking part in a vigil against the colonial wars in a Lisbon church on New Year's Day, one of the leaders of the liberal wing, Francisco de Sá Carneiro, renounced his seat in the National Assembly. In conjunction with members of SEDES and with the support of *Expresso* (a critical weekly started in January by another member of the liberal wing, Francisco Pinto Balsemão, which almost immediately established itself as the country's leading journal), Sá Carneiro set about the organisation of a third force between the ANP and the traditional opposition tendencies. The attempt failed while the opposition groups at last managed to present a united broad left front after the congress of the Democratic Opposition in Aveiro in April.

The dismal elections of October 1973, which were reminiscent of Salazarist days in as much as both sides knew that all the ANP lists would be elected and that the opposition would withdraw after taking advantage of the pre-electoral period to mobilise opinion against the regime, marked the definitive end of any hopes for dialogue. The MDP/CDE (Portuguese Democratic Movement/Democratic Electoral Committee), led by Pereira de Moura and José Tengarrinha, now included leftist and centrist Catholics, socialists, social democrats and even some monarchists, though its organisational core was the PCP. While the government camp, divided as it was between Caetanists and *ultras,* grew smaller, the forces of opposition were expanding to occupy more and more of the political spectrum. Though the post-electoral ministerial reshuffle was thought to be, on balance, progressive, the regime was already in crisis. It was not just that government and opposition were as polarised as in Salazar's time; because there had been relatively more freedom since 1968 repression would now be all the more difficult, if not impossible, given the unfavourable conjuncture of this political situation with a deteriorating economic situation and a worsening of the overseas problem.

If in the political sphere the Caetano regime by 1974 seemed to many to have taken away with one hand what it had given with the other, such a generalisation would not be altogether accurate if applied to the social and economic spheres, to developments to which Caetano (like Salazar before him) attached primary importance. Here, too, the idea was renewal in continuity, the aim being to reinvigorate and update the New State's corporative structure so as to bring about 'the social state'. 'The corporative state', Caetano claimed in 1970, 'has achieved, and can continue to give practical expression to, what the Socialist parties have aimed at in those countries where they existed.' The social state was not, however, to be socialist, but was to be quite different from the nightwatchman state of nineteenth-century liberalism: it was to be a Catholic-inspired third way between capitalism and socialism. Its general philosophy was described by Caetano as follows:

> In a market economy, like the Portuguese, one must seek to guarantee the role of free initiative and private enterprise, with the state reserving to itself the creation and amelioration of infrastructures and intervention at the key points of management to guarantee overall control so as to ensure respect for the national interest, observance of official plans and greater justice in the distribution of returns . . .
>
> The old freedom meant abstention by government, autonomy of the individual to solve his problems by himself. Today freedom necessitates that the state be active to the end that the right to health, the right to education, the right to insurance, the right to housing have real meaning. This is freedom as opposed to necessity, the freedom that arises from the struggle against misery, ignorance, sickness, the insecurity of the future . . .
>
> While maintaining private property and the freedom of initiative in a market economy, the state should intervene in strength in social life to correct the injustices in the apportioning of returns, directly through the adjustment of wages and indirectly through giving benefits and opportunities to allow the workers and their families to overcome obstacles to their advancement and to shorten social distances. The state, then, must be a permanent dynamiser of society, so as to assure all citizens, under the aegis of the general interest intransigently

defended and realised, harmonious progress in the moral sphere, on the cultural plane and in the material field.

In short, there was to be a change of emphasis from the Salazarist New State, an attempt in some respects to emulate the social ideals set out in the Federal German constitution.

Certainly social welfare was a theme which Caetano's administration liked to stress. In May 1969 family allowances were extended, as was old-age, sickness and accident insurance, to rural workers, tenants and smallholders. However, the network of *casas do povo* was inadequate for the purpose in 1969. This network was accordingly extended, the number of *casas* rising from 625 in 1965 to 736 in 1972, so that by the end of 1973 four-fifths of the country's parishes were covered by the network – at least on paper. In 1970 social insurance provisions were extended to fishermen, and later also to newspaper vendors and domestic servants. Pension schemes for state employees covered only a few thousand people in 1968, but by 1973 all military and civil service personnel had full pension schemes; in addition, Caetano introduced the thirteen-month year for pay purposes for civil servants to give them rough parity with the private sector. More hospitals (though never enough) were built, while attempts were made to deal with the housing shortage. Rents were frozen, a housing development fund for the construction of prefabs was set up and the low-cost housing schemes in operation since 1933, whereby rent payments were equivalent to mortgage payments, were continued. Although a law was introduced to permit expropriations of property for low-cost housing, and although visible signs of progress could be observed in the clearing of slums (for example, in Lisbon's Bairro Salazar), the influx of population into the cities meant that demand for housing always exceeded supply, a fact to which the growth of shanty towns bore witness. Nevertheless, for a significantly large section of the population living standards and conditions noticeably improved, so that even at the height of the revolutionary period after April 1974 Marcelo (Caetano) was still remembered by many with affection.

Another Caetanist reform was liberalisation in the sphere of industrial relations. By a Decree Law of 14 June 1969 the government relaxed its powers to approve the personnel elected by union assemblies to lead the *sindicatos nacionais*. One result of this new freedom of election was that control of some important *sindicatos,* including bank employees, textile and metallurgical workers, shopworkers, journalists and medical personnel, quickly passed to oppositionists who were members of, or close to, the PCP. This development led to some backtracking in 1970 when the government reasserted its powers to suspend union officials for activities 'contrary to social discipline' and to appoint the arbiter between management and labour in negotiations for collective bargaining agreements. In January 1971 about forty *sindicatos,* representing hundreds of thousands of workers, adhered to the recently formed unofficial inter-union body, Intersindical. Although the government became progressively more restrictive of union liberties, the labour shortage produced by the emigration of unskilled – and now also skilled – workers led to many wage increases being conceded. From 1972, however, the government increasingly set its face against wage increases because of their inflationary effects and refused to entertain the idea of a national minimum wage, which Intersindical leaders in early 1974 claimed should be 6 contos, a figure that many of these same leaders were explaining twelve months later was beyond the capacity of the Portuguese economy. In general terms it would seem that Caetano's premiership saw an important advance in the living standards and bargaining power of industrial and white-collar workers, but such benefits were increasingly reduced by the rising rate of inflation. The PCP's policy of gaining control of the *sindicatos* from within and exploiting all opportunities was, it may be noted, too much for ultra-leftists, who denounced such collaborationism.

Another aspect of Caetano's drive for modernisation was the emphasis on educational reform, a task over which Veiga Simão enthusiastically presided from 1970 to 1974. All official basic education was made free and new schools built, many new secondary schools (*liceus*) were created, new university faculties and two new universities were set up, as were polytechnics and institutes for social and business studies. Greater provision was made for scholarships and the waiving of fees in higher education, the declared eventual goal being complete equality .of opportunity. Attempts were made to remove the blockages in secondary education and teacher training which had become apparent in the 1960s. It was the biggest programme of educational reform embarked upon since that of the First Republic sixty years before, but critics remained unimpressed. However much was done, they argued that more should be done, and that what was being done was unacceptably bourgeois and perpetuated class divisions. In fact the criticisms reflected voguish educational theories then popular in other countries and the rising tide of student and academic protest in Portugal. There was a long tradition of student militancy in Portugal which had been continued during the Salazarist period, chiefly by the PCP. However, from 1968, the great year of Parisian and international student militancy which Caetano was later to describe as 'the great European epiphany of that romantic illness called anarchy', the universities and other institutes of higher education were afflicted by an unprecedented state of perpetual turmoil in which the 'right-wing' PCP was overtaken by trendier ideological manifestations of the contestatory mentality.

The incorrigibility of the self-styled new proletariat, i.e. the *jeunesse dorée* of the Portuguese bourgeoisie, in the universities represented the vanguard of other international tendencies which challenged the traditional ethos of the regime. The relative relaxation of authoritarian control during the Caetanist period perhaps helped to accelerate the process of cultural diffusion in Portugal, as did the impact of large-scale tourism and migration. As in Spain in the 1960s, the better-off young of the cities and tourist resorts responded eagerly to the latest international fashions in dress, behavioural style and music. New attitudes to parents in the home were paralleled by radicalism inside the church, and sometimes against it, on the part of younger priests critical of 'bourgeois structures'. Journalists took up the cause of ecological preservation while at the same time castigating the country's failure to achieve the materialist levels of more advanced societies. Women's liberation arrived with the publication in 1972 of *New Portuguese Letters*; though a mild work by international standards, the book was banned as an outrage to public decency and its authors, 'the Three Marias' (the poet Maria Teresa Horta, the novelist Maria Velho da Costa and Maria Isabel Barreno) were arrested. In this as in other respects the regime's only response to the cosmopolitan wave of libertarianism among the young and the educated was repression – which was counter-productive as it drew publicity and made martyrs.

If general socio-cultural change was one (unquantifiable) ingredient in the reasons for the growing crisis of the regime in 1973–4, the deterioration in the general economic situation was another. On the one hand industrial growth continued in the Caetanist period and, as the projected Fourth Development Plan (1974–9) showed, there was an increasing awareness on the part of government that social and regional problems should be taken much more into consideration. As usual the agricultural sector stagnated, achieving an annual average growth rate of only 0·7 per cent in 1970–3 (compared with 1·5 per cent in 1960–70); indeed, in terms of constant prices, the gross agricultural product in the years 1971–3 was down on the 1968 figure. The industrial sector, however, grew at an annual average rate of 9 per cent in 1970–3 (compared with 9·1 per cent in 1960–70) and the service sector at a rate of 7·1 per cent (compared with 5·9 per cent in the previous decade). Direct foreign investments in Metropolitan Portugal continued to increase (from 760,900 contos in 1969 to a figure of 2,726,600 for 1973), but the balance of capital movements was changing for the worse: whereas in 1967 the difference between capital coming in and capital flowing out was +2,797,000 contos, in 1972 and 1973 the figures were −2,689,000 and −1,465,000 respectively. The visible trade balance also deteriorated: the deficit was 10·25 million contos in 1967, but 28·42 million in 1973. Nevertheless, the overall balance of payments for 1973 still showed a 6·5 million conto surplus. Given Portugal's large gold reserve the escudo remained steady, as in Salazar's time. However, Caetano's intention of continuing the practice of balanced budgets was more difficult to realise. There were budget deficits of 1·6 and 3·6 million contos in 1972 and 1973, at least partly caused by military overspending. Recourse was increasingly had to borrowing and the public debt accordingly increased.

Clearly the world recession, the export of inflation by other countries and the rise in commodity prices, most obviously oil, contributed to the worsening of the Portuguese position, especially after the middle of 1973. For the Portuguese in the street, however, the dashing of expectations raised about ever-rising living standards was blamed on the government – as happened in other countries. The rate of inflation, already running at 11·7 per cent in 1971, was 20 per cent in 1973 – and in that year wages rose by only 12·5 per cent while the prices of foodstuffs increased rapidly. Meanwhile the tax structure remained basically unchanged and the well-informed were aware that indirect taxes accounted in 1973 for 42 per cent of taxes raised. As living standards took a dip and small firms went bankrupt in increasing numbers, it could be noticed that there still seemed to be plenty of money for the oligopolists to invest in property redevelopment for luxury flats and hotels, while on the stock exchange there was an ever more feverish speculative boom in share prices. Big firms were often exempted from profits taxes – often evaded anyway – to stimulate investment, but the investments made were increasingly speculative. Observers could note that in 1972 Siderurgia Nacional made a net profit of 88,289 contos but paid the Treasury 31,121 contos; in 1973 it paid only 8,593 contos in taxes, though the net profit was 406,752 contos. The rich, it seemed, were getting much richer while inflation was eating away the advances made by the poorer. The flow of emigration continued and the colonial wars dragged on; in 1972–3 the state spent three times as much on defence and security as on development.

Visitors to Portugal in 1970–3 did not sense deeply the growing crisis. Apart from a certain atmosphere of lassitude which some might have termed malaise, there were few signs of impending crisis, even though rising prices were noticeable. There was much talk, official and unofficial, about 'the overseas' and reports of occasional acts of sabotage. Along with the odd small bomb left by LUAR or ARA (Armed Revolutionary Action, an Algerian-based group dependent on the PCP) went some slogan-daubing, chiefly the work of ultra-leftist students. Nevertheless, despite the outward appearance of calm, the country was moving towards a major crisis centring on the unresolved overseas question.

This question overshadowed all others and played its part in exacerbating other difficulties. It was the principal bone of contention between government and opposition and between Caetano and his Salazarist critics. For the opposition, an end to the colonial wars was essential, even if this meant capitulation. For the government, the need to try and keep the home front steady meant that censorship and repression of subversion took precedence over dialogue with the opposition or liberalisation. For right-wing critics of Caetano, his policies towards overseas matters were suspect and possibly had treasonable implications. Large-scale military expenditure was a factor in causing inflation; in retarding Metropolitan social and economic development; and in encouraging emigration, especially among those of military age. Conscription was a contributory factor to the shortage of labour and to the growth of political disaffection. War-weariness created a psychological malaise which was spreading ever wider in Portuguese society, and from which the armed forces themselves were by no means immune. Without a solution to the African conundrum, or a resolution of it, stagnation on all fronts seemed a certainty, a crisis of regime an increasingly strong possibility.

On becoming Premier, Caetano had given the military assurances that he would not press his earlier federalist ideas and that he would 'defend the overseas in so far as we are able' to do so. In 1968–9 the military situation in Angola and Mozambique did not give cause for alarm; as Caetano later put it in a memoir: 'in 1968 it was not a question of negotiating with peoples who had risen up or of putting down national uprisings. The guerrilla bands were relatively small in number and were unrepresentative. To contain them was a matter of internal security.' After a visit to the three African territories in 1969 Caetano returned 'convinced that it would be an ignoble betrayal of the people there and the work done there to make pacts with the tiny groups [*grupúsculos*] which, out of mere adventurism, maintained solely through international support, were disturbing the general peace in odd localised points of the vast territories of Angola and Mozambique'.

However, he was aware that there had to be changes. Salazarist integrationism was internationally unacceptable, as would be any attempt to hand over power to the local settlers. Therefore, instead of federalism, but within the framework of the constitution so zealously upheld by Tomás and the *ultras*, the best that could be done was to choose the middle way of progressive and participatory autonomy for Angola and Mozambique, which meant in the short term decentralisation and in the long term an assured Portuguese future for the territories, i.e. a Brazilian-style society in which the interests of Portuguese settlers and business would be safe even if outright independence were the eventual outcome. Hence the constitutional revision of 1971 and its complementary legislation was put through, despite strong criticism and disapproval among the *ultras*, who saw such reforms as counter-productive concessions to the enemy. The *ultras,* who disapproved of the internal liberalisation process for the same reasons, remained committed to the idea of one nation from the Minho to Timor. For *ultras* Caetano's policy represented the slippery slope: 'autonomy,' wrote Fernando Pacheco de Amorim, 'colonial self-government, is the step that, logically and historically, precedes complete political independence and total decolonisation'.

Nevertheless, legislative assemblies were elected on a widened franchise in the colonies and, except in Angola, natives were elected in large numbers. The slow and gradual movement towards decentralisation also implied a loosening of economic ties, but it was to overcome increasing tardiness in paying for imports from the Metropolis that Caetano, to the annoyance of big business interests, decreed that each province should have its own exchange account which should balance annually: debts outstanding to the Metropolis, some 24 million contos in 1973, were to be paid in three years. Although the proportion of Metropolitan trade with the colonies was decreasing – the colonies accounted for 24·4 per cent of Portugal's exports and 14·3 per cent of its imports in 1967, but for 14·8 and 10·1 per cent respectively in 1973 – Caetano's autonomist middle way satisfied fewer and fewer people, a process accelerated by the rapidly worsening military situation in Guiné and Mozambique in 1973–4.

In economically prospering Angola there was still no cause for alarm in April 1974. Sporadic guerrilla activity continued, but was being successfully contained. Here Portugal was favoured by the continuing divisions among the 'liberation movements' and by the international position. In 1972 President Mobutu of Zaïre promised to allow the MPLA to use his frontier with Angola on condition that they joined forces with the FNLA, led by his brother-in-law Holden Roberto; but with Zaïre, like Zambia, dependent on rail communications through Angola, little serious trouble was to be expected. In the event Zaïre continued to intern MPLA militants and the MPLA/FNLA split remained. Furthermore the MPLA itself was dividing into three factions and some of its leaders were advocating some kind of compromise with the Portuguese, while in eastern Angola UNITA and MPLA guerrillas were more hostile to one another than to the Portuguese. If in Angola the chances of Portugal being given time to develop the 'progressive autonomist' solution seemed still quite good, this was in contrast to the situation on the other two fronts.

Guiné since the 1960s had been the thorniest part of the 'global problem of defence of the overseas'. With Spínola as Governor and Commander-in-Chief from 1968 until his retirement because of bad health at the end of August 1973, the area under Portuguese control was more or less held but little attempt was made to reconquer PAIGC-controlled areas: the general's 'anti-reactionary counter-revolution' was therefore confined to a part of the population. From 1972 the Portuguese position began to crumble when the United Nations accepted an investigatory report which said that the PAIGC was 'the sole and authentic representative of the people of the territory'. UNO recognition came in the context of increased support from the Eastern countries, the OAU, the World Council of Churches and the Scandinavian states, while the Vatican's desire that there should be peace dated at least from July 1970 when Pope Paul received Cabral, Neto and Marcelino dos Santos to tell them: 'We are on the side of those who suffer. We are for the peace, the freedom, and the national independence of all peoples, particularly the African peoples.'

The Portuguese response to this hostile tide took a number of forms. The possibility of a negotiated settlement was investigated through President Senghor of Senegal in 1971–2, the scheme proposed being that Spínola and Amílcar Cabral should meet to arrange a ceasefire and negotiate PAIGC participation in the government of a Guiné independent within the framework of a Luso-Afro-Brazilian community. With his exaggerated conception of his own charismatic powers, Spínola saw this as a way out in Guiné, but Caetano, conscious of the wider perspective and *ultra* opinion, rejected such a scheme: a ceasefire would be a victory for the PAIGC, to whom the population would rally as the victor, and the precedent created would be fatal to Portuguese aims in the other territories. Caetano expressed the view that a military defeat was preferable to a negotiated surrender in Guiné if the Portuguese could not win. This was a view which deeply shocked Spínola and, as rumours of Caetano's opinion spread in military circles, the fear grew that the civilian government wanted defeat and wanted to use the army as its scapegoat; lingering memories of Salazar and Goa were revived. Then, on 23 March 1973, into the midst of military feelings of resentment and defeatism in Guiné came a new surprise in the form of Soviet-made SAM-7 ground-to-air missiles which brought down two Fiat G91s.

The SAM-7 at a stroke transformed the military situation: with the Portuguese deprived of unchallenged control of the skies morale took a nosedive, with pilots often reluctant to fly; by March 1974 the PAIGC claimed to have shot down thirty-six aircraft. In May 1973 Portuguese forces also lost their Guiledje base in the south, close to the guerrillas' supply route from Guinea-Conakry. Efforts to combat the PAIGC by playing on its internal divisions and rivalries had already come to nothing on 20 January 1973 in Conakry in what President Sékou Touré denounced as a 'crapulous crime of imperialism'. The assassination of Amílcar Cabral, carried out (albeit with some Portuguese involvement) by war-weary opponents of Cabral within the PAIGC tempted by Portuguese talk of handing over Guiné to a black government if the

PAIGC got rid of its Cape Verdean *mestiço* leaders, did not, partly thanks to Sékou Touré, prove fatal to PAIGC unity. When independence was officially declared somewhere in Guiné on 24 September 1973 Amílcar Cabral's brother Luís became President with Aristides Pereira as Secretary-General of the party. To Portuguese embarrassment the non-aligned but strongly Soviet-supported 'phantom-state of Guiné-Bissau' was recognised by about sixty countries in the three weeks following the proclamation of its existence. Despite these developments Spínola was lionised after his return to Portugal in September 1973. When Caetano suggested phased withdrawal to his military confidant, the Chief of Staff, General Costa Gomes, he was told: 'In present circumstances Guiné is defensible and must be defended!' New circumstances were soon to arise, and from the process of transition from the 'present circumstances' of mid-1973 Costa Gomes was not conspicuously absent.

While the possibility of *débâcle* in Guiné had not been discounted by Portuguese ruling circles for some time, the rapid deterioration of the situation in Mozambique came as more of a shock. As the decade of the 1970s opened FRELIMO's activities were contained in the northern areas of Cabo Delgado and Niassa. Dissensions within FRELIMO after Mondlane's assassination and the dependence of Malawi and Zambia on rail communications through Mozambique provided some encouragement, as did the confidence of the Commander-in-Chief (1970–3), the *ultra* General Kaúlza de Arriaga, with his policies of psychological warfare, large-scale resettlement and increasing recruitment of native troops (60 per cent of the army in Mozambique by 1974). However, in 1971–2 FRELIMO with Zambian and Malawian connivance opened a new front in Tete with the aim of cutting communications in the province generally and particularly with the site of the Cabora Bassa dam. FRELIMO were not very successful, but the Portuguese had to divert a lot of their military resources into Tete to counter the guerrilla threat. It was during these operations, in December 1972, that some 300 to 400 villagers were massacred in the settlements of Wiriyamu, Chawda and Juwau near the town of Tete, apparently by black troops of the 6th Commando ('The Shadows') under DGS command. (In Mozambique the DGS ran counter-insurgency operations as well as the regular army.) Terror and counter-terror were inseparable from the type of warfare waged in Mozambique (FRELIMO had earlier executed dozens of village headmen in Tete), but the size of these massacres and the attempted documentation of them by missionaries were to make them notorious.

Early in 1973 the Papal Nuncio informed the Lisbon government of the allegations and Caetano asked Kaúlza to hold an inquiry. The massacres achieved international notoriety with a report in *The Times* in July, on the eve of Caetano's visit to Britain to commemorate the 600th anniversary of the Anglo-Portuguese alliance. Subsequent Portuguese investigations led to the dismissal of the Governor of Tete, but no charges were brought against military personnel. On the other hand the Burgos Fathers who had reported the affair were expelled, like the White Fathers before them in 1971, and like the Bishop of Nampula in 1974. The international publicity and condemnation were damaging to the regime and the affair strained relations with the church.

It was not adverse publicity which brought on the crisis in Mozambique but FRELIMO's penetration into the province of Manica e Sofala, which threatened in 1974 to disrupt communications with Tete and Rhodesia – the appearance of the SAM-7 missile being an additional adverse factor. FRELIMO's presence created panic among the white settler population with attacks on farms. In Vila Pery, Vila Manica and Beira white civilians stoned the military for not giving them adequate protection. Military men in turn became more resentful of the local settlers and of the DGS, who were now given some of the tasks previously entrusted to the army. The events of January 1974 indeed acted as a catalyst on junior officers in Mozambique and encouraged many to join the nascent 'movement of the captains' and avoid engagements with the guerrilla forces.

The younger officers engaged in conspiracy in Mozambique in early 1974 were not, however, the only ones threatening the *status quo* of Caetanist progressive autonomy. Apart from FRELIMO's threat, efforts were made in 1973 to form a third force between FRELIMO and Portugal. One of the chief proponents of an independent, multi-racial Mozambique, which would be anti-communist and safeguard the future of the white settlers and their business interests, was a well-known businessman and former *homme de confiance* of Salazar, Jorge Jardim. On good terms with President Banda of Malawi (he was Malawian Consul in Lisbon) and with Kaúlza de Arriaga, he had by 1973 come to the conclusion that, though Caetano's policy of progressive autonomy was basically right, in the case of Mozambique it needed a strong push. With Malawian help Jardim made contact with President Kaunda of Zambia with a view to achieving a negotiated settlement with FRELIMO on the basis of 'peace for all, without dishonour for anyone'. (Zambia, like Senegal, the Ivory Coast and, earlier, Tanzania, had been prepared to act as an intermediary with the liberation movements in achieving a negotiated settlement.) The so-called Lusaka Programme of 12 September 1973 envisaged Mozambique achieving peacefully its independence under majority rule with FRELIMO nationalists taking part in the process. However, Caetano thought that Jardim had gone too far, while FRELIMO's response was to open a new front in Manica e Sofala. Nevertheless, by the spring of 1974, Jardim was envisaging a unilateral declaration of independence, to be achieved with the connivance of senior Portuguese officers and the support of most of the 30,000 black troops. In the political sphere he had the co-operation of ex-FRELIMO men like Murupa, and was in touch with GUMO (United Group of Mozambique), a semi-clandestine movement of all races founded in 1973 to act as an internal front for the independence movement but really as a political alternative to FRELIMO. Jardim's plans, like those of so many others, were to be overtaken by events, i.e. the plans of army officers.

The armed forces had been the ultimate arbiters in Portuguese politics since the nineteenth century and throughout the period 1908–74 there had always been rumours that military conspiracies were afoot; that the armed forces were again going to put on the mantle of interpreters of the popular will and of the national interest. Sometimes the rumours had proved correct. Often nothing had happened. It was not until early 1974 that evidence of the preparation of a military movement began to present itself, and then only in an indirect way. It had until then generally been assumed by observers that any military movement would be the work of *ultras* disgruntled at Caetano's policy of progressive autonomy for the overseas possessions. It was also generally believed that Caetano had appointed General Costa Gomes, a former under-secretary of war under Salazar, who had been military commander in both Angola and Mozambique but who was known to have liberal views, to the post of Chief of Staff of the Armed Forces to keep *ultras* in line and promote non-*ultra* officers. Belief that the liberal wing of the military establishment was being strengthened seemed to be confirmed by the appointment of the prestigious ex-Governor of Guiné, General Spínola, as Deputy Chief of Staff of the Armed Forces in January 1974. In Guiné he had come out in favour of the 'reform [of] the structures on the home front' and against the *ultras*' integrationist ideas on the overseas question. Evidence that there was a divorce between government policy and the views of the top military men came on 22 February, with the publication of Spínola's book *Portugal and the Future*.

The book quickly became a best-seller and was given extensive coverage inside and outside Portugal, yet it was in no way a radical text. Full of florid, rhetorical statements whose meaning was often difficult to discern, the work's general thesis was that the overseas wars needed a political solution which lay somewhere between the *ultra*-integrationist line, signifying perpetual war, and outright and immediate independence, signifying a betrayal of the national past and advocated by the communist and socialist opposition. Social reform and political liberalisation were necessary at home and overseas, while purely military victory in wars of subversion was an impossibility. The age of dogmas was declared to be in the past. What was now needed was 'a vast Lusitanian community . . . in which moral ties will prevail over political statutes' and in which Brazil would play the major role, not Portugal.

This could be achieved, he argued, through a policy of progressive autonomy pursued in a new spirit: if the right to democratic self-determination of the overseas territories were recognised and plebiscites held, then this community would come into being, for Spínola believed that the overseas populations were still loyal. But would the nationalist guerrillas accept such a solution? If they did not accept the verdict of plebiscites then, he believed, they would be isolated because the neutral and the indifferent, including the increasingly alienated Free World, would rally to Portugal's side.

The present regime must not equate the 'national fact' with itself, taboos must go and 'the dogma of national *immobilisme*' be discarded in favour of a 'renovated conception of patriotism'. The old myths of the regime were now divisive and therefore 'anti-national'. The creation of daughter nations, like Brazil, was preferable to amputation, as had occurred in Goa. Portugal's future was

> only possible in an expanded context of plurality [built] on a community which keeps the fragments of the Portuguese whole united . . . Certainly we want one Fatherland of Fatherlands from the Minho to Timor, and one common Fatherland . . . It would be criminal and fundamentally anti-Portuguese to abandon to their fate those thousands of Europeans and millions of Africans who put their trust in us.

But what assurance could he give that self-determination would lead to his solution? In truth, none: yet he adhered to the dogma that 'the overseas' was an essential prerequisite

> of our survival as a free and independent nation . . . Without the overseas, we should be faced with the options of the poverty of the subjacent or absorption; and the old Iberian dream, or the suzerainty of the great non-European powers, or a Soviet thorn embedded in the West's back, would be in the long term the choices for our destiny.

A 'Portuguese Federal Republic' or 'State of Lusitania' was therefore essential to national independence, otherwise the African territories would be lost one by one. Such a federation, he had to admit, might break up, but this was a lesser evil compared with otherwise inevitable losses.

It was a strangely confused book, echoing many of the ideas put forward by Delgado, Galvão and Caetano in the early 1960s. Its very contradictions, however, allowed most people to find something in it to their taste. Its tone was no doubt more important than its content, though this was perhaps not the author's intention. Spínola at one point acknowledged that his 'federative thesis' was no more than an accelerated

version of Caetano's declared policy – and acceleration of this policy was
the declared aim of the new Overseas Minister, Baltasar Rebelo de Sousa.
Even though he did not read the final text until four days before
publication, Caetano was aware of its general thesis and sanctioned
publication on the recommendation of Costa Gomes, Spínola's military
superior.

In speeches before and after the book went on sale, Caetano spelt out
his own attitude. He had believed in Spínola-style federalism twelve years
before, but now knew that it was a chimera: 'The guerrillas and their
allies, the United Nations and the disunited, will not accept any other
political solution than the handover of power to the terrorist movements,
with [the] expulsion, immediate or after a short interval (as happened in
Madagascar and Zaïre), of the whites resident in the territories.'
Spínola's solution was therefore moonshine. Plebiscites among
populations incapable of understanding the issues would be 'a parody of
direct democracy'; if held under Portuguese auspices, no one would
recognise the results as valid, for 'the United Nations only consider
legitimate results which accord with their wishes'. Agreements
negotiated with so-called liberation movements for a federal solution
would be illusory, as the fate of the French Union and the British
Commonwealth demonstrated. In Caetano's view, Spínola's thesis was
far removed from reality and the illusions he was propagating could only
help the enemy by creating doubts, divisions and therefore weakness on
the key front, the home front. Progressive autonomy meant self-
determination in the long run. To assure a Portuguese future for the
overseas, people must have the will and make the sacrifices to hold on, for
the only real alternative was abandonment. By this time, however,
Caetano was well aware that the armed forces' will to resist was
evaporating.

The origins of the military movement which overthrew the regime on
25 April 1974 in fact pre-dated the appearance of Spínola's book and had
little to do with it or him. *Portugal and the Future* was only a symptom of
the war-weariness and disgruntlement felt in the officer corps. The
seemingly interminable colonial wars cost Portugal's armed forces 7,674
dead and 27,919 seriously wounded between 1961 and May 1974
(although roughly half the casualties resulted from accidents rather than
action). The cost in terms of morale was even more serious. The very fact
of being called upon to fight was too much for some long-serving regular
officers; one general was once heard to remark: 'I chose the military
career as a way of living, not as a way of dying.' Despite opening up the
Military Academy from 1958, both by lowering entry qualifications and
by waiving fees, recruitment to the regular army (as to the other services)
fell off progressively until only 137 career lieutenants could be attracted
into it in 1973. Reliance on conscript officers, often with radical ideas

picked up from their previous university attendance, became more and more marked; by 1973 it was forecast that there would soon be no regular subalterns and that within a few years there would not be enough regulars to fill all the higher and general staff posts in the army. A way had to be found of attracting conscript officers into regular service.

For some time past conscript officers (*milicianos*) who had completed their secondary education and had served overseas had been able to sign on in the Military Academy and keep the rank they had attained, though they were only deemed to hold that rank as of right from their date of graduation. This arrangement did not prove popular; older, decorated soldiers frequented the Academy alongside raw cadets and only some 200 officers of this type had been produced in ten years. The Ministry of Defence therefore decided to give conscript officers who had battle experience and re-enlisted a one-year crash-course in the Academy (instead of the full four years) on the theoretical side of officer training. These men would then go back into the army with their seniority dating from their appointment as conscript officers, while other ex-conscript regulars would now have this same rule of seniority applied to them. After opposition in Cabinet from the Minister of the Navy, the measure was approved as Decree Law No. 353/73 (13 July 1973).

Opposition to the Law from regular officers who felt aggrieved that they would be overtaken by *milicianos* – some captains would become lieutenant-colonels – led to the first signs that latent dislike of government policies was about to crystallise into a more serious and organised movement of military opinion. Already some junior officers resented having to bear the brunt of the colonial wars while senior officers (with rare exceptions) stayed in headquarters or in the Metropolis. Already younger regulars were being persuaded that something was rotten in the state of Portugal through contact in the mess with sometimes radical university-educated *milicianos* and in the bush with conscript soldiers from poor home backgrounds. As inflation became more marked, junior officers noted that their pay was at the level of office clerks who did not have to risk death, while senior officers collected lucrative sinecures from industry and commerce. Already, too, some disgruntled officers had noted with interest speeches made at the congress of the Democratic Opposition in April, which indirectly called on the military to dissociate themselves from the regime – in short to overthrow it. Four hundred military personnel also signed a public letter dissociating themselves from an *ultra*-inspired Congress of Servicemen held in Oporto at the beginning of June.

(Given the suspect direction of Caetanist policies and the Premier's attitude to the Portuguese Legion, associated with such *ultra* deputies as Tenreiro and Casal Ribeiro, the *ultras* were trying to create an alternative organised pressure group to the right of the government. Within the

Legion there still existed a small GII, nicknamed Red Handkerchiefs, though, in 1971 the 'commandos', who had attacked opposition buildings and personnel in the 1969 election campaign, were abolished as such, and Legionaries had to keep their firearms in police barracks.)

The government prohibited regular officers from taking part in the congress. Sensing the unpopularity of Law 353/73, a clumsy attempt was made to minimise the effects on seniority of that law by Decree Law No. 409/73 (20 August 1973), which effectively satisfied most of those with the rank of major and above that their seniority would be protected at the cost of further antagonising captains and subalterns, the overstrained men who were directly involved in the fighting. For the latter both Decree Laws were a calculated civilian-inspired insult aimed at humiliating professional soldiers. The 'movement of the captains' was therefore in origin an essentially professional protest movement, though it was almost certain to have wider political implications; however, as Caetano later wrote: 'Given the malaise existing in the armed forces any pretext would have served as an explosive detonator.'

The first attempt to organise the movement of military trade unionism took place on Sunday 9 September when 140 junior officers met at a farmhouse near Evora owned by a PCP member, a cousin of one of the participants, 26-year-old Captain Dinis de Almeida. At this meeting government policies were denounced from a professional standpoint and a document of protest against the decrees drawn up, a document subsequently supported by about 300 other officers. Protests reached Caetano from regular junior officers in Guiné, Angola and Mozambique, while the Chief of Staff, Costa Gomes, received a delegation led by Major Mariz Fernandes to protest about pay and conditions. Costa Gomes, who had been involved in Botelho Moniz's attempted *coup* in 1961, took it upon himself to be the spokesman of the movement in government but had to relay back to it Caetano's willingness to re-examine the question only when this incipient mutinous movement had dissolved itself. This it did not do. On 6 October, after meeting representatives from units overseas, the still somewhat informal leadership of the 'movement of the captains' decided to use the tactic of collecting documents of resignation from officers – with the date left blank – so as to blackmail the government into revoking the Decree Laws. Some 800 officers obliged, out of a total army officer corps of around 2,500, and sergeants in the air force followed suit. At another meeting at Oeiras (near Lisbon) on 24 November Lieutenant Coelho raised political, as opposed to professional, issues but this premature *démarche* was badly received. By this stage a loose co-ordinating committee was in existence which included conservatives such as Major Mariz Fernandes and more leftist elements such as Captains Dinis de Almeida and Vasco Lourenço. It was the latter element which kept up the momentum.

At an important meeting of eighty-six officers, representing all army units, and with observers from the air force, navy and parachutists, held in Óbidos on 1 December 1973, the future course of action was decided. To the disappointment of leftist and younger officers the idea of a *coup*, first put forward by Lieutenant-Colonel Ataíde Banazol, who understandably disliked being posted to Guiné again, was rejected in favour of a motion advocating continued protest until more support was forthcoming. Nevertheless, some decided that Costa Gomes was the favourite candidate for leadership in the event of a *coup*; others preferred Spínola or Kaúlza de Arriaga. Divergences on aims, tactics and allegiances within the co-ordinating committee were apparently growing and so at a meeting at Costa da Caparica on 8 December an inner steering committee of three was created: Colonel Vasco Gonçalves was the most senior; Major Otelo Saraiva de Carvalho (recently returned from Guiné) was to busy himself with military plans; Major Vítor Alves was to be in charge of the political side. Naval officers, among whom clandestine activity was also rife, still looked askance at a professional military movement and considered themselves more politicised. At this juncture, however, wires nearly got crossed. Some junior officers eager for action approached the former Commander-in-Chief in Mozambique, Kaúlza de Arriaga, asking him to launch a *coup* with paratroops. Known to be unhappy with government policy and an advocate of decentralisation in the overseas and not autonomy, he agreed to head a military movement. Anti-*ultra* members of the co-ordinating committee sabotaged these plans, in conjunction with Costa Gomes and Spínola: an announcement to officers in the School of High Military Studies that Spínola was not involved was enough, and the government transferred some officers. Ironically, Kaúlza de Arriaga, who had helped foil Botelho Moniz's *coup* in 1961, had, like Spínola, come round to the view that democratisation was necessary to strengthen the home front.

The revocation of the two contentious Decree Laws by the government on 21 December (by Decree Law No. 683/73) and the transfer of officers suspected of conspiracy did nothing to quell the movement. Conscript officers (the *espúrios* or illegitimate) – who tended to favour Spínola's leadership – were now furious and made common cause with the regulars (the *puros* or legitimate). Military tourism gave committed officers the chance to convert others in the garrisons to which they were reassigned. Meanwhile meetings continued. There was one in the house of Colonel Marcelino Marques in January 1974 to discuss a political programme for a *coup* drawn up by Major Alves, but there was no agreement. Some wanted to keep the movement purely professional. A new drafting committee was set up, consisting of Lieutenant-Colonel Costa Brás and two leftist officers, Majors Ernesto Melo Antunes (who had tried to be an opposition candidate in 1969) and Moreira de Azevedo.

Much mystery still of course surrounds the military conspiracy, but i would seem that it was plagued by divisions in January and February Some members of the movement were in touch with Costa Gomes, other with Spínola; the DGS suspected that conspiracy was afoot, but seems no to have been able, or not to have wanted, to discover too much, while the captains as a group virtually had veto powers over the governmen because of their key military role. Most of those involved had rudimentary political ideas of various types, though among the leader there was a clearer leftist line, albeit subdued for tactical reasons. Some wanted an immediate *coup,* others wanted to wait. Yet amid the clandestine confusion certain basic ideas could be discerned. A circula from the leadership in early March pointed out to fellow officers that the armed forces were the mainstay of an undemocratic regime which had made them the scapegoat for the failure of an impossible overseas policy More and more officers were becoming aware of the 'real divorce' between armed forces and nation. Increased pay could not compensate for humiliation, whether by the government or by settlers in Mozambique Conscious soldiers knew that a political solution must be found in the colonies, safeguarding the legitimate interests of Portuguese resi- dents while allowing black self-government; and such a solution was beyond the capacity of the regime, which had to be replaced by a democratic system. The minimal points on which all conspirators were agreed, it seemed, were the two Ds: democratisation and decolonisation.

The publication of Spínola's book on 22 February acted as a accelerator of events. For his supporters in the army, some of whom saw him as a new Sebastian, the event represented throwing down th gauntlet to the civilians in government. To the more left-inclined leader of the movement, however, the book was an embarrassment: their aim were far removed from his neo-colonialist ideas, even if some othe officers might now be less cautious. It would now be very difficult not to give Spínola a leading position after a successful *coup.*

The meeting which may be said to have given birth to the MFA (Armed Forces' Movement) proper (though it was still called the 'movement o officers') was a plenary session of some 200 officers from the army and ai force, and including observers from the navy, held in Cascais on 5 March to discuss the movement's political programme. The meeting wa somewhat inconclusive. About ninety participants signed the draf programme, which the air force and pro-Spínola men thought too left wing, while naval representatives found it too right-wing – also the view of one of its authors, Melo Antunes. Some wanted the movement to be led by Spínola and to adhere to the ideas in his book, but a compromise was reached whereby both Costa Gomes and Spínola were to be the leaders. Melo Antunes was to do another draft as part of Alves's politica committee; Major Otelo Saraiva de Carvalho was to press on with military arrangements.

By this stage the government was aware that something serious was afoot. Caetano's initial reaction to the publication of Spínola's book had been to call in Costa Gomes and Spínola and suggest that they arrange with President Tomás their assumption of power. This they declined to do, so on 28 February Caetano suggested to Tomás that a new government be formed, perhaps under Baltasar Rebelo de Sousa. Tomás favoured Caetano continuing. A debate was held in the National Assembly after which a vote of confidence was naturally expressed in the government's overseas policy. Caetano then tried to get his military leaders publicly to demonstrate their acceptance of government policy, but Costa Gomes, Spínola and Admiral Tierno Bagulho all refused to make a speech of loyalty and, in the event, failed to turn up to the televised ceremony in the São Bento Palace on 14 March at which the army Chief of Staff, General Paiva Brandão, pledged military subservience. Costa Gomes and Spínola, as Caetano had promised them, were dismissed, a development which, with the humiliating act of homage by the generals, enraged military opinion as a whole.

The ideal psychological moment for the MFA to strike seemed to have come, but things were not quite ready. The Army Minister, General Andrade e Silva, had been told of the conspirators' plans and no doubt the DGS had reported on the meeting in Cascais on 5 March. Three days after this, six important conspirators were either arrested or, like Captain Vasco Lourenço (in charge of liaison with overseas units) and Melo Antunes, transferred to other units. After the dismissal of Costa Gomes and Spínola, twenty-three more officers were arrested or transferred for protesting. All of this proved too much for some officers, especially when Costa Gomes's replacement was the *ultra* military commander in Angola, General Joaquim da Luz Cunha, Kaúlza de Arriaga's brother-in-law. In the commando training centre at Lamego on the 15th officers met to discuss a move on Lisbon, but they decided not to act on their own. Nevertheless news reached the military organiser of the movement in Lisbon, Otelo Saraiva de Carvalho, that a revolt had begun. Cashing in on the unexpected and premature incident, and safe in the knowledge that the air force had indicated that it would not act in the event of a *coup,* he set about getting other units moving. However, it was Friday, many officers had gone off for the weekend and transport was not to hand in Santarém. Only in the spa town of Caldas da Rainha (50 miles from the capital) was the garrison commander arrested; the pro-Spínola majors Casanova Ferreira and Monge set out for Lisbon with a 200-strong force from the 5th Infantry in the early hours of the 16th.

The DGS had been alerted, however, and shortly after dawn the 5th infantrymen were halted on the Santarém–Lisbon motorway as they

approached the airport. The rebellious detachment, faced with men of
the 1st Light Artillery and the 7th Cavalry, as well as men from the GNR,
returned sadly to Caldas where their barracks was surrounded by other
units. With no shots fired, they surrendered to the police in the afternoon.
The 200 rebels were arrested and the government announced that thirty-
three officers were to be detained; these included Lieutenant-Colonel
Almeida Bruno, a follower of Spínola, who had supported the revolt in
the Military Academy. Caetano and other ministers had taken
precautionary refuge in the headquarters of the 1st Air Region at
Monsanto, whence they emerged to find that only one unit had moved,
others had obeyed orders and there had been no popular participation.
There was a feeling of jubilation in some government circles that the
military abscess had been lanced, but Caetano realised that this was only
the beginning: the rebels would have to be court-martialled and this
fellow officers were most unlikely to permit.

Although some bewildered officers thought that Otelo Saraiva de
Carvalho might be an *agent provocateur,* the will of the conspirators was
strengthened: they must strike soon or risk seeing their plot broken up.
The movement's co-ordinating committee again met and decided to go
ahead as soon as practicable. Otelo Saraiva de Carvalho reported that the
Caldas affair had shown the confusion prevalent in the highest echelons
faced with a *coup,* and that it was possible to begin a *coup* with one unit
and then bring more troops into Lisbon: a new plan could therefore be
drawn up. As in previous successful *coups* a minority of the officer corps
would act, counting on the passive support or inactivity of fellow officers.
Formal contact with opposition politicians was shunned both on security
grounds and because the military themselves represented the mirror o
the nation; however some officers were in touch with MDP and PC
members.

On 18 March the MFA Committee, for 'the good of the nation and the
armed forces', issued another circular protesting against transfers and
arrests, 'the methods of administrative terrorism used for a long time now
by military pseudo-leaders far removed from the real problems of the
armed forces and whose only interest is in defending privileges
identifying themselves with the political and economic powers that be
and abandoning their younger comrades-in-arms'. Particularly out
rageous had been the government's use of the DGS, GNR and Portuguese
Legionaries against 'generous and selfless' fellow officers. The new draf
of the MFA's political programme was completed on 24 March by Melo
Antunes just before leaving for the Azores, and Costa Gomes and
Spínola were again contacted. While military planning and preparation
went ahead, with about half the units supporting the MFA, there was still
no general agreement on the political situation to be installed after the
coup or who was to preside over it. The common objectives were to bring

down the regime, decolonise and democratise, and redeem military honour. In 200 days the movement had matured fast since its birth as a 'reactionary co-operative in defence of privilege' (in the words of Melo Antunes).

For the conspirators it was essential that the blow be struck before 1 May, when the government was thought likely to use the army against popular disturbances being planned. By 23 April the military arrangements were complete and the 25th was the date agreed – coincidentally the anniversary of the Liberation of Italy in 1945.

As *coups* go, that of 25 April 1974 went well. The *coup* was timed to begin at 3.00 a.m. with the seizure of key points in Lisbon by picked teams of officers. The prearranged signals to these and other units went out, thanks to civilian collaboration, on time: the Eurovision Song Contest entry, Paulo de Carvalho's *E depois do adéus,* was played on the commercial station Emissores Associados de Lisboa at 10.55 p.m. on the 24th; at 12.30 a.m. on the 25th, on the Catholic Rádio Renasçenca, came the definitive signal, José Afonso's *Grândola, vila morena,* a protest song about popular resistance to the regime in a town in the Alentejo. With its martial rhythm it was to become *the* song of 25 April, almost a second national anthem, and its lyric gave vent to the populist aspirations of the more radical MFA leaders:

> Grândola, dark town
> Land of brotherhood
> The people are the ones in charge
> Within you, O city!

The main radio stations, Emissora Nacional and Rádio Clube Português, were taken before dawn and a communiqué from MFA headquarters in the 1st Engineers' barracks at Pontinha (on the outskirts of Lisbon) broadcast, which called on citizens to stay indoors and on the police forces not to put up opposition. Only at 7.30 a.m. did bemused listeners get an indication that the *coup* came from left of the government rather than, as many expected, from its right.

By this time Otelo Saraiva de Carvalho's plans were working smoothly. Captain Salgueiro Maia had taken over the Cavalry School in Santarém (50 miles from the capital) and had arrived in Lisbon's Praça do Comércio, on the bank of the Tagus, with 200 men and a few Patton tanks. Other units seized the airport and cut off the capital's road communications. As crowds began to gather, Salgueiro Maia, now reinforced by other units, set about taking over the ministries surrounding the square but the ministers of the Interior, Army, Navy and Defence escaped through a hole in one of the ministries' walls. Pro-government tanks arrived in the square during the morning and confronted his forces; true to form neither side fired and by midday the pro-government forces had yielded. A frigate in the Tagus was surrendered to MFA officers, while the air force did not oppose the movement. Salgueiro Maia's next task was to proceed to the GNR barracks half a mile away and he moved off after asking bystanders the way. The GNR's Carmo barracks should have been neutralised by a unit which failed to turn up and was now the refuge of Caetano and other ministers whom the MFA had expected to go to Monsanto. By late afternoon a tense situation had developed: though now surrounded and supported by a large crowd, Salgueiro Maia's forces were themselves hemmed in by other GNR units and the barracks refused to surrender.

In the end Caetano and colleagues surrendered to General Spínola, who was at home awaiting events until summoned by the Under-Secretary for Information, Feytor Pinto. Salgueiro Maia entered the barracks and met Caetano, who informed him that a *coup* was unlikely to solve overseas problems; asked what the MFA's politics were, the Captain replied truthfully that he did not really know. At 5.45 p.m. Spínola arrived at the barracks; Caetano had refused to surrender to anyone else while Spínola only agreed to take the surrender after an MFA member with the rank of colonel had sanctioned his action. After a brief meeting during which Caetano told the general that he feared power would end up in the hands of the mob, the outgoing Premier was taken to the Pontinha barracks by armoured vehicle, leaving Spínola to be acclaimed by the crowd (who supposed him leader of the *coup*) before following on. It only remained for the military commander in Évora to surrender and for President Tomás, almost forgotten in the excitement, to be arrested at home by paratroops under the newly released Colonel Bruno. Tomás, Caetano and other ministers were flown to Madeira next morning, Tomás and Caetano being flown on to Brazil a month later. The DGS headquarters in Lisbon held out against a siege till the next morning; five people were killed in incidents near the building.

Thereafter in Lisbon there was a carnival atmosphere. V for Victory signs were given constantly to shouts of 'Victory! Victory!' Red carnations were presented to the soldiers (some of whom had to be told that they were 'rebels' and on the right side). Soon the red carnation became the badge of respectability, new supplies being imported from the Netherlands; monarchists, however, preferred white carnations. Youthful leftists set the tone of the euphoria by popularising the Chilean slogan 'The people united never shall be defeated'. The mood of Lisbon was followed in Oporto, where the Commander of the Military Region was arrested by the forces of the Army Driving School at 5 a.m. Nothing happened until afternoon when clashes between police and youth began. The military then took over and the DGS were the last to surrender

Elsewhere, apart from vain appeals for resistance by pro-government people in Coimbra, nothing happened. As usual, it was in Lisbon that matters were decided; the rest of the country simply looked on. In another respect the revolution of 25 April ran true to form: like all successful twentieth-century *coups* (except for that of 28 May 1926) the rapid seizure of key points in the capital was the secret of success. As usual, too, the advent of a new 'situation' meant that allegiances changed rapidly. Caution on 25 April itself was not confined to civilians: many military units never left their barracks, including some that were supposed to, according to Otelo Saraiva de Carvalho's plans.

Such was the revolution of 25 April, 'the Revolution of the Flowers', which created a new Portugal. The year 1974 took its place alongside 1910 and 1926 as yet another attempt at regeneration, but in the first days of careless rapture it seemed rather as if Sebastian had returned. It was easy to see who had lost power, but who had gained it? Who played the part of Sebastian: Spínola, or the anonymous captains, or both?

6

A Revolutionary Process

The Fatherland is still sick; the Fatherland is still in danger. António de Spínola, 11 July 1974

Rumour is the national disease. *O Comércio do Porto,* 12 March 1975

'Madhouse under Self-Management' is one of the least offensive epithets with which Portugal has been insulted recently. *Expresso* editorial, 18 October 1975

Faced with the challenge of the military movement of 25 April 1974, the political and institutional edifice of the forty-one-year-old regime of the New State collapsed like the proverbial house of cards. It was not until the summer of 1976 that the vacuum was filled by a new constitutional democratic representative system. In the intervening period, to the increasing amazement of non-Portuguese and of many Portuguese, the country survived in what may properly be called a state of anarchy – an absence of government, during which those who nominally held power and those who for short or longer periods attracted support to themselves or their groups, jockeyed for advantage in the new situation. For almost two years after the liberation of 25 April 1974 the revolutionary process worked itself out in the context of global economic recession, yet bloodshed was minimal despite numerous prophecies of civil war; instead ideological and personal differences were resolved by politicians and military men in what, at least retrospectively, seemed a model of low-intensity operations. The political and economic élites of the old situation were swept peacefully away by the revolutionary tide; a vast colonial empire vanished; provisional governments came and went; the economy moved close to collapse; all variety of solutions for the political and social future were advanced; yet the outcome was constitutional government based on the popular will expressed through the ballot box.

A full study of Portugal in 1974–6 is a subject demanding several books and, especially in the present state of knowledge when the deluge of information available has yet to be digested and revelations continue to be made about key episodes and actors, no brief account can hope to capture all the changes of mood; to reflect adequately all the political complexities; to deal with all regional variations or to encapsulate all the details of these two years. Nevertheless, the main outlines are clear. From April 1974 until late 1975 the movement was politically to the left, the main stages on the route being symbolically marked by *coups* or attempted *coups*: 28 September (1974), 11 March (1975). Then 25 November (1975) revealed the definitive turn of the tide and the start of the counter-revolutionary process of returning to a new normality. Although ideological positions, economic developments and the influence of outside opinions also had their importance in the Portuguese revolutionary process, that process was essentially psychodynamic in character.

After half a century of authoritarianism, the Revolution of the Flowers, intentionally or otherwise, removed, as it were, from the Portuguese collectivity and from many of the individuals composing it, the superego of socio-political discipline. The activist ego was given free rein and the results were manifested in political, and to a lesser extent social, flights of fantasy which ignored or challenged the hard facts of economic and societal reality. By 25 November 1975 most of the libido was spent and the superego began again to take up its function. Until that time, however, the changing scenario to which the ego-tripping of the activists gave rise was, in the language of Portuguese journalism, surrealist – and indeed sometimes even dadaist. Yet if the great majority of Portuguese in 1977 felt thankful that the traumas of the recent past were over, some felt *saudades* for the time when everything seemed possible; when people's attitudes and positions were constantly being overtaken (*ultrapassado*) by events or other people, and when many political actors found themselves 'overtaken by themselves'. For the majority not emotionally involved in the revolutionary process there was, however, a darker side to the picture which will also doubtless remain in the popular memory: the exploitation of the naïvety of the many by the sophisticated few; the advancement of personal interests under the guise of political principles; the ways in which new vested interests sought to take the places of the old behind the masking slogans of democracy, *saneamento* and socialism.

In the early hours of 26 April 1974 the Portuguese public – after hours of waiting during which listeners to Emissora Nacional were treated to much playing of martial music, ranging from the National Anthem *A Portuguesa* through *Hearts of Oak*, *Rule Britannia* and *A Life on the Ocean Wave* to *Grândola, vila morena* – were finally told who had taken power and with what aims. At a meeting in the Pontinha barracks high ranking officers previously sounded out by the MFA co-ordinating committee to represent the armed forces were proclaimed as the new governing body, the JSN (Junta of National Salvation). The seven members of the Junta were: for the army, 64-year-old General António de Spínola, General Francisco da Costa Gomes and Brigadier Jaime Silvério Marques (whom the MFA had arrested hours earlier); for the navy, Commander Rosa Coutinho and Captain José Baptista Pinheiro de Azevedo; and for the air force, Brigadier Diogo Neto (absent in Mozambique as Air Force Commander) and Colonel Carlos Galvão de Melo (who had ceased active service in 1966 owing to disagreements with the regime). The six members present in Lisbon elected Spínola President of the Junta and it was he who announced that the JSN's role would be: 'To guarantee the survival of the sovereign nation in its pluri-continental entirety; to promote . . . the conscientialisation' (a favourite word) of the people by allowing full freedom of opinion 'in order to accelerate the creation of civic associations' which would participate in the free election, by direct suffrage, of a constituent assembly and, later, of the President of the Republic; to safeguard public order and fundamental civil rights and to uphold international treaties; and to hand over power to the new President when constitutional institutions freely chosen by the people had been established.

Thus it appeared that the new Portugal was under the safely conservative control of an elderly cavalry general famed for his attachment to monocles, African canes and kid-gloves. However, Spínola and his Junta accepted, albeit in a modified form in respect of the provisions on decolonisation, the programme of the MFA as its guide. The programme as published spelt out Spínola's undertaking in greater detail, promising a constituent assembly within twelve months; a civilian provisional government composed of political figures accepting the programme; the immediate abolition of the DGS (except overseas), Legion, *Mocidade* and ANP; an amnesty for political offenders; strict control of economic and financial transactions with foreign countries; replacement of the top office holders at home and overseas and the general 'cleansing' of Portuguese life; abolition of censorship – but with an *ad hoc* censorship committee to prevent 'ideological aggression' in the media; freedom of thought and association (including 'trade union freedom' and 'the formation of political associations, possible embryos of future political parties'). More controversially Point 6 stated that

The provisional government will create the bases for:
(a) A new economic policy serving the interests of the Portuguese people, especially the strata of the population most disregarded until now [and] having as its immediate concern the struggle against inflation and the excessive rise in the cost of living, which will necessarily involve an antimonopolist strategy.

(b) A new social policy which, in all fields, will have as its essential objective the defence of the interests of the working classes and a progressive, but accelerated, increase in the quality of life of all Portuguese.

Point 8 of the final version, edited by Spínola, read:

The overseas policy of the provisional government, bearing in mind that its definition will be the nation's task, will be guided by the following principles:
(a) Recognition that the solution of the wars overseas is political and not military.
(b) Creation of conditions for a frank and open debate, at the national level, of the overseas problem.
(c) Creation of the bases of an overseas policy leading to peace.

From the first, then, assuming the continuation of the MFA as a self-appointed watchdog over those ostensibly in power, the seeds of discord over interpretation of the programme were present. Would the victors be Spínola and the JSN, or the still hidden co-ordinating committee of the programme of the MFA, an increasingly autonomous group of seven leftist officers out of the previous twenty-one of the old co-ordinating committee: Vasco Gonçalves, Melo Antunes, Vítor Alves (army); Vítor Crespo, Almada Contreiras (navy); Costa Martins and Pereira Pinto (air force)? There was not at first serious disagreement.

Latent differences between the military men who had taken over the government were, however, to be only one of the factors making for a quickening of revolutionary momentum after 25 April. While euphoric crowds surged about Lisbon chanting the slogans of the new freedom, congratulating the soldiery and hunting down agents or alleged agents of the PIDE/DGS – who were usually saved from the most unpleasant of fates by the firm but good-natured efficiency of the military who took them into custody – the politicians quickly emerged or returned from exile to boost enthusiasm still further but also to act as restraining influences. With the return of Mário Soares from France and Álvaro Cunhal from Prague the idea of political parties being things of the future was immediately overtaken. Vast and orderly mass demonstrations on 1 May (now a national holiday), held under the auspices of Intersindical leaders and the MDP/CDE (the old opposition umbrella organisation whose precise relationship to other groups had yet to be defined), conclusively showed that neither the politicians of the Left nor the people (*o povo,* but rapidly coming to mean the urban followers of leftist movements) could be ignored. The lesson of this mobilisation of support was not lost on the officers of the MFA.

Though groups of the ultra-Left had already been calling for more radical solutions than so-called bourgeois democracy before that date, the mobilisation of 1 May seemed to release many city dwellers from the last of their inhibitions. Ideas of self-management (*autogestão*) became widespread as workers and employees occupied their factories, newspapers, broadcasting stations and other places of work. Demands for immediate wage increases mingled with theoretical discussions on self-management while *ad hoc* meetings effectively acted as revolutionary tribunals in demanding (and achieving) the 'cleansing' of unwanted and unpopular owners and managers. Though originating in a genuine desire to clean out the old order, the movement for cleansing progressively became broader in its scope: behind the spontaneity of assemblies demanding the dismissal of collaborators of the PIDE and fascists, more calculating minds set about using the process for settling old personal scores, for advancing their own careers, for ousting potential party political opponents in the future from key positions. To keep a modicum of order and administration, army officers found themselves called in or sent in to help restructure enterprises, and so they became even more directly involved in civilian affairs in an atmosphere of libertarian enthusiasm.

Quite apart from representing authority in a situation in which the normal bureaucratic processes and police functions had ceased to exist, military men by training prefer order to chaos. So it was that many of them began to develop a respect for the apparently more clear-sighted and disciplined workers' and employees' representatives – very often members of the PCP – and came to make contact with young leftist intellectuals who were only too willing to advise and serve soldiers in unfamiliar situations. Military vanity was flattered and, in the case of many officers, political education was both rapid and shallow.

From the point of view of Spínola and the conservatives in the JSN there was an urgent need to reassert some sort of control over a country which seemed to be disintegrating before their eyes: government organisms in a state of shambles; the productive process breaking down; local government passing into the hands of questionably representative opponents of the old regime; the capital covered with revolutionary slogans; old social disciplines and restraints being cast aside all over the place. For the personnel of the JSN liberation meant orderly rejoicing followed by sobriety and hard work and not open manifestations of Maoism or sexual liberation, solidarity with African enemies or demands for union recognition by Lisbon prostitutes. In an attempt to stabilise the situation, and in accordance with the programme of the MFA, Spínola became provisional President of the Republic in mid-May and the first provisional government was formed, whose work was to be approved by a Council of State, while the JSN was to continue as guardian of the programme of the MFA.

Since Spínola was to preside over the JSN and the Council of State, these interim constitutional arrangements were aimed at phasing out the MFA. The Council of State consisted of the seven members of the JSN; seven representatives of the armed forces who were the co-ordinating committee of the programme of the MFA; and seven citizens of recognised merit, appointed by the President of the Republic: Rui Luís Gomes, a former exile and pro-communist presidential candidate, now Rector of Oporto University; Azeredo Perdigão, President of the Gulbenkian Foundation; Isabel Magalhães Colaço of the Lisbon Law Faculty; Henrique de Barros, Caetano's socialist brother-in-law; Diogo Freitas do Amaral, *procurador* in the old Corporative Chamber; Colonel Rafael Durão, a cavalry officer; and Colonel Almeida Bruno, head of Spínola's military household. The Spínolist victory was not, however, complete. Though he might hope for a majority in the JSN and Council of State, the MFA leadership was still a force to be reckoned with and blocked presidential plans to provide an element of continuity with the past by appointing Caetano's Minister of Education, Veiga Simão, as Premier – he became Ambassador to UNO instead.

As Premier Spínola appointed Adelino da Palma Carlos, a respected 69-year-old lawyer of old-style republican views. In order to try to strengthen the hand of authority against the street, the fifteen-man government also included the MDP/CDE leader Pereira de Moura (without Portfolio), two communists (Cunhal without Portfolio, the bank employees' leader Avelino Pacheco Gonçalves at the Labour Ministry – formerly Ministry of Corporations), and three socialists (Soares at the Foreign Ministry, the lawyer, Salgado Zenha, at the Ministry of Justice and the editor of *República,* Raúl Rego, at the renamed Ministry of Social Communication, i.e. Information). Other ministers included two representatives of the PPD (People's Democratic Party, a centrist grouping springing from the former 'liberal wing' of deputies of the old regime): Sá Carneiro as Deputy Premier and Magalhães Mota at the Ministry of Internal Administration (as the Ministry of the Interior was now renamed); the ex-SEDES intellectual Mário Murteira in charge of Social Affairs, and a bevy of independents including the Mozambican Democratic lawyer, Almeida Santos, in charge of Interterritorial Co-ordination (the new name for Overseas) and Colonel Firmino Miguel (who had been abroad on 25 April) as Defence Minister.

This first provisional government lasted fifty-six days in all, and before that Palma Carlos had had enough. On becoming Premier he noted that he succeeded 'forty-eight years of dictatorship and three weeks of anarchy' and he quickly found that he had no means with which to assert authority: the police forces were not functioning, ministers found themselves barricaded in their offices by functionaries for hours at a time. 'It was absolutely impossible to impose authority', said Palma Carlos later. He concluded that the only way out was to get Spínola to stand for President in an immediate election by universal suffrage and to promulgate a provisional constitution under which the Premier could nominate his own ministers: only with popularly legitimated authority could President and Premier overcome the anarchic situation and resolve the colonial question, which was pressing. Spínola accepted his Premier's ultimatum with some reluctance, but Palma Carlos had in Cabinet obtained only the Premier's right to nominate his ministers and so he refused to form a new government after resigning on 10 July. In the ensuing crisis the co-ordinating committee of the programme of the MFA, the only people with any force at their disposal, vetoed the name of Firmino Miguel as Premier. In the end, on 17 July, Brigadier Vasco Gonçalves became Premier in a seventeen-man government, eight of whom were military men (including the Marxist, Major Melo Antunes) and four were socialists; Cunhal and Magalhães Mota represented the PCP and PPD respectively, while the rest were independents.

The governmental crisis had shown that power lay, if anywhere, with the MFA leadership and not with Spínola, and this power was given a more organised reality with the creation of a military intervention force based on the Lisbon military region, COPCON (Operational Command for Continental Portugal) under the command of Brigadier Otelo Saraiva de Carvalho, who could still be described as a pragmatic and politically uncommitted officer. Events were to show that the new distribution of nominal power was no more cohesive than its predecessor, though it lasted seventy-five days.

During the time of the second provisional government what it was fashionable to call the 'contradictions' inherent in the situation became more evident. The process of and demands for 'cleansing' in various aspects of national life continued, despite admonitions from on high that it was time to call a halt. Workers in the secondary and tertiary sectors had received wage increases under the previous provisional government, which had meant doubling wages in some sectors but had fallen far short of demands in others. There was still a vogue for self-management and further strikes occurred. The press of the cities and broadcasting, increasingly under the sway of journalists of the Left, looked quite different from that of the old regime but were equally uniform in their use of Marxist terminology and tirades against reaction and fascism, which were even held at least indirectly responsible for the spread of cholera throughout the country.

Until the end of September the advocates of pressing on with revolutionary change were the groups to the left of the PCP. Newspaper kiosks were filled with weeklies prominently displaying hammers and sickles and red stars. Walls and statues were sprayed with hammers and sickles, slogans against the government (military-fascist dictatorship), against imperialism and any continuation of fighting overseas (not one more embarkation) and against the revisionism of Cunhal's PCP. The number of *grupúsculos* of the ultra-Left to surface or be created – all, apparently, with adequate financial backing – was legion. In 1974 the lead was taken by the so-called Maoist MRPP (Reorganising Movement of the Party of the Proletariat), which had been founded in 1970 as an authentic Marxist-Leninist-Maoist revolutionary vanguard party to fight for the popular masses against fascism and the social-fascism of Barreirinhas Cunhal's PCP which had now become 'a party of the bourgeoisie'. MRPP militants, who advocated an intensification of the class struggle and a democratic and popular dictatorship, tested the new freedoms with increasingly provocative demonstrations which led to the suspension of their organ, *Luta Popular,* and the detention of their leader, Saldanha Sanches, in the fort at Elvas.

Other groups to the left of the PCP which sought to profit from the intoxicated atmosphere after 25 April to gain mass support for pushing forward the revolutionary process included the Trotskyist LCI (Internationalist Communist League), part of the Fourth International and founded in 1973, and the PRP/BR (Revolutionary Party of the Proletariat/Revolutionary Brigades), a group founded during Caetano's premiership advocating a rapid and violent revolution by organised people's power committees and in 1974 spraying slogans demanding death for the fascists accompanied by its insignia, a machine-gun. These and other groups bickered among themselves, modifying ideological positions to project different images at different times and to vilify personal and organisational competitors. Less exotic and containing many of the younger intelligentsia was MES (Movement of the Socialist Left), founded in May 1974 as an autonomous group adhering to the MDP/CDE, a group attempting to further the revolutionary process by the organisation of people's power bodies at the base while seeking to capture left-inclined MFA officers and perhaps become a new technocratic governmental élite. Though prone to schisms in the manner of the ultra-Left, the latter considered MES centrist.

Just as the MRPP waged a two-front campaign against fascism and Cunhalist social-fascism, so the PCP, the oldest and at first the only relatively well-organised political party, also waged war on two fronts. On the one hand, of course, it was opposed to fascism and reaction, i.e. anyone connected with the previous regime; since the vast majority of the population had collaborated in some way or other at some time with Salazarism-Caetanism, it remained to be seen how widely the PCP would cast the net of these terms. In general, until September, they were applied to those to the right of Spínola and the PPD, who were nevertheless on occasion accused of (at least objectively) engaging in reactionary manœuvres. While the PCP was alert to the threat of Bonapartism posed by Spínola's advisers, seen, for instance, in Palma Carlos's plans in early July, it set about making itself a respectable and responsible governmental party, supporting appeals for order, national unity, economic reconstruction, wage restraint and the need for all to get down to hard work. Cunhal was a member of the government which on 28 August issued a decree on the right to strike, which banned political stoppages and strikes in sympathy with other workers, as well as introducing a thirty-seven-day pre-strike period which, if violated by workers, would make a lock-out legal.

The PCP strategy of 1974 was in fact geared to the long term. As the programme of the 6th Congress of 1965 had said, the party's 'supreme objective . . . is the victory of the proletarian revolution and the construction of socialism and communism in Portugal', but the fall of the Salazarist regime would make for 'a historic turning-point' in the revolutionary process, namely, 'the realisation of the national and democratic revolution', an essential staging-post on the journey towards 'socialism' which could not be omitted. Thus the PCP found in the programme of the MFA just about all that was needed at this stage. Certainly there were to be no steps backward but a relative stabilisation of the political and social situation was required in the short term. Thus its representatives, whose experience and organisation gave them a dominant position in the trade union movement Intersindical which absorbed the structures if not the personnel of the old corporative system, set their face against strikes, some local experiments in self-management and 'unrealistic revindications' which could only 'create conditions favourable for reaction and counter-revolution'. From all this it naturally followed that the libertarian tendencies of the ultra-Left ('petty bourgeois radicalism with a socialist face') and of some socialists were 'objectively counter-revolutionary', and so advocates of revolutionary change out of line with PCP policy could only be 'objectively agents of [American] imperialism'.

Indeed, in the political sphere in general, the PCP mentality conformed to the Jacobin logic of Leninism – and indeed of Afonso Costa's Democrats during the years 1910–26. Since the PCP's analysis of the situation was 'scientifically' correct, only its leader knew what was in the best interests of the 'national and democratic' revolutionary stage, what measures should be taken by whom and when. Thus 'unity' was essential among workers, democrats and the armed forces, but this 'unity' could only be on the PCP's terms. He who was for 'unity' on terms different from those of the PCP was not 'really' for unity, was not 'truly' democratic, and therefore must 'objectively' be an enemy of popular unity and democracy and be treated as such. Since the PCP Central Committee was the repository of political truth, he who was not for the PCP must be against it.

Although for the time being these truths were not quite so clearly spelt out, PCP statements in the months following 25 April provided all the evidence anyone needed: there was no need to resort, as rightists and socialists were to do, to secret documents and conspiracy theories. Cunhal's tactics were to remain on good terms with his governmental partners, civilian and military, to castigate the objectively pro-fascist ultra-Left, to prevent the deterioration of the economic situation, to disarm the anti-communist fears of the problematical petty bourgeoisie, to end the colonial wars, to encourage a Portuguese opening to the East and to keep the MDP/CDE in being as the instrument of popular unity. As in Intersindical, so in the MDP/CDE, the PCP's men could accurately be said to occupy a hegemonic position. In the mid-summer of 1974 there seemed to be no hurry for the PCP to take over 'the commanding heights of power', for while Cunhal marked time the unrivalled organisation and discipline of the party, and its resistance record, allowed its members openly or under the MDP label to take advantage of the confusion of spontaneous assemblies to occupy key positions in trade unions, newspapers, broadcasting stations, local government and the state apparatus. Naturally it had its collaborators in those who saw in the PCP the situation of the future – and among those who might at any moment be 'cleansed' if certain revelations about them from PIDE/DGS files which had fallen into PCP hands should be made public.

No one ever thought that the PCP could win the majority of votes in a free national election; if elections there were to be, then the role of the MDP as a PCP-sponsored umbrella organisation was of great importance. Its leader, Pereira de Moura, had been a casualty of the governmental crisis of July since other ministers had found him very difficult to work with and, though a decade or so before a leading economist of the New State, he was given to startling public attacks on fascism, a term which he defined with breathtaking latitude. He toured the country to organise the MDP, explaining to journalists that those who adhered to the ideals of 25 April should present themselves to the electorate as one movement because, in rural areas in particular, people did not understand what political parties were and so might not vote, or vote for the wrong ones. Certainly he believed that the road to socialism ought to be opened, but for the foreseeable future a socialist Portugal was an impossiblity because of the country's economic and geographical situation. For the MDP/CDE to be a success it had to include not only the PCP but the Socialist Party, MES and PPD as well as non-party independents. MDP and PCP hopes of a united electoral front came unstuck when the PPD and Soares's socialists formally shunned the movement in August. The tetchy response of the PCP perhaps reflected its need to rethink its tactics, though Soares had since May opposed the idea of the MDP as 'a sort of national union . . . Democracy can only be organised through parties, so that everybody knows clearly "who's who".'

For those with an eye to the future and with a general belief in democracy plus social change the Socialist Party, a member of the Socialist International founded as a successor to the ASP in West Germany in 1973, was an obvious choice. Since it had virtually no organisation in April 1974, almost anyone was welcome; it was safely sufficiently leftist for any accusations of fascism or reaction not to stick, while at the same time it was the most credible obstacle to the advance of the PCP and had international respectability and support. What sort of 'socialist' party was this PSP (which quickly dropped its third letter to avoid confusion with the initials of the police force)? According to Soares (in May 1974), it was 'not a bourgeois party' but was open to all who 'do not dissociate [themselves] from the values of progress in the coherent struggle for democratic socialism; the Socialist Party is not a monolithic party, but rather seeks to bring together socialist tendencies, and in it all those who want socialism and liberty should find a place'. It was to develop from a 'cadre party' into 'a mass party with real roots among the common people'. It would never support 'any totalitarian adventures of any type' though it wanted 'fraternal dialogue' with the PCP. It wanted the 'consolidation of democracy through political pluralism', general social democratisation (including experiments in self-management) and 'total reform of the archaic structures of our economy', as well as independence for the colonies. 'The dictatorship of the proletariat is not for us . . . We are humanists. We are an open party' aiming to attract the majority of Portuguese of the Left and centre-Left. 'We must not alarm the bourgeoisie.' The PS was therefore flexible in its ideological boundaries: as the best counterweight to the organised PCP it sought to attract people from well into the centre of the political spectrum, while its ideas on self-management meant that it could claim in some ways to be to the left of the PCP. Manœuvres to maximise support led the PS to denounce the decree on the right to strike which the PCP said it respected.

To the right of the PS and also flexible in its ideological parameters, there appeared the PPD, a party evolving from SEDES and the liberal wing of 1969–73. Its aim was to rally moderate opinion – moderately progressive and moderately conservative – to prevent the PCP and the PS being left alone in the camp of 25 April. Its founders were mostly around 40 years of age, practising Catholics, and not averse to attracting non-*ultra* conservative elements into the new situation. Their programme was, like that of the PS, voter-oriented rather than ideologically dogmatic. The PPD adopted the UNO Declaration on Human Rights as the basis for its interpretation of personal and civic liberties, advocated co-partnership and profit sharing, greater social justice, political pluralism and democracy. As 'a social democratic party inspired by the principles of socialist humanism like the social democrat parties of Western Europe', it wanted a welfare state as well as orderly political liberty. A 'centre-left party, positioned for social progress and open to the non-Marxist Left', the PPD was 'not a revolutionary party . . . It rejects the importation of any foreign model of socialist development, since its design for social democracy must be put together in the light of Portuguese realities' – all of which did not stop PPD posters saying it wanted 'social democracy as in West Germany'. The new party had an established organ in the weekly *Expresso*.

Still in the centre of the emergent political spectrum was the PPM (People's Monarchist Party), founded in May from Monarchist Convergence, monarchists who had over the years broken with the old Monarchist Cause and the UN. Though officially headed by the veteran Francisco Rolão Preto, who at the age of 76 was able to recapture the radical excitement of his youth by declaring 'long live the monarchy of the soviets', other leaders were of younger generations, including the Under-Secretary for the Environment, Gonçalo Ribeiro Teles. The PPM showed that Portuguese monarchism had changed. The party stood for political pluralism and democracy, and it was for the people to decide whether they wanted a restoration, though the PPM advocated 'a democratic monarchy, analogous in its characteristics to the present-day monarchies of northern Europe'. It was therefore in favour of greater social justice, welfare services and experiments in co-partnership and self-management in industry. On the overseas issue, however, its position was more conservative: there was to be self-determination, the future of territories being decided by universal suffrage and not by abandonment to the liberation movements.

To the confusing and confused political spectrum of the summer of 1974 must be added the groups of the centre-right and right, which in any democracy have a right to exist but which so soon after the fall of the old regime were bound to be looked on with suspicion by the Left. Attempts to found a mass Christian democratic or conservative party at this time met with no success: since the Second Vatican Council Catholics were encouraged to join any party which was not anti-Christian and Catholics were indeed to be found in political organisations from the ultra-Left to the far Right. In their pastoral of 16 July, the episcopate came out in favour of 'the democratic way', but the faithful could not support Marxist or classical liberal parties. Together with the PPD, the new group that seemed to reflect the official Catholic outlook most closely was the CDS (Party of the Social Democratic Centre), a party founded in July by moderate conservatives who had often had connections with the previous regime, though some joined from SEDES. The principal figures were Diogo Freitas do Amaral (one of Spínola's Councillors of State), Adelino Amaro da Costa (high up in the Ministry of Education) and Basílio Horta of the CIP (Confederation of Portuguese Industry). 'Personalist humanism' was the basic Christian philosophy of this 'centrist party, open to genuine political creativeness'. Like other parties it was for pluralist democracy, greater social justice, civil rights, state intervention in the economy, free trade unionsim, welfare services and worker participation in industry. For the overseas it favoured a commonwealth solution, or as the CDS put it, 'a solid community of Portuguese-speaking independent states'.

For the ultra-Left and the PCP, though not for the PS, the CDS was evidence of the resurgence of reaction or fascism. Also unacceptable in the eyes of the Left was the appearance of rightist groups such as the PL (Liberal Party) and the PP/MFP (Party of Progress/Portuguese Federalist Movement) and their allied weeklies *Tempo Novo* and *Tribuna Popular*, which appeared to sell just as well as their left-wing opposite numbers at news-stands. Both groups had powerful financial backing and their cadres were said to owe much to those of the abolished ANP. The groups accepted the new situation of democratic liberty, but emphasised that this was not the same as anarchy. Generally conservative and capitalist, their main emphasis was on the rights of what they claimed was the silenced majority at home and opposition to abandonment in the overseas. Sticking to the revised, published – and therefore official – version of the programme of the MFA, they opposed decolonisation without prior consultation of the populations. In this and other respects their short-term aims converged with those of the provisional President of the Republic, a point exploited by revolutionary propagandists.

As this brief survey of the political spectrum in the summer of 1974 suggests, there was considerable confusion among the leaders of cadre parties as they tried to accommodate themselves to what they perceived to be the new situation. With the exception of the *exaltés* of the ultra-Left and a few ultra-rightists still at large but hopelessly compromised with the old regime, it seemed that everyone was now a political democrat, in favour of social changes (whether modest or far-reaching) and keen on a solution of the overseas question. Although in Portugal overseas developments seemed in the minds of the public to take second place to domestic changes – changes obvious in the capital but scarcely apparent in the conservative countryside of the north, where squares in small towns still went by the name 'Praça de Oliveira Salazar' – it was the overseas question which was to bring down Spínola as surely as it had brought down Caetano. What Spínola could never admit was that the downfall of the previous regime robbed the solutions he had propounded in his book of any serious possibility of success.

Despite his verbal victory in amending the final version of the pro-gramme of the MFA to exclude the word independence, his unrealistic solution was immediately overtaken by events. He could continue to argue that the will of the overseas populations must be respected, that a period of 'conscientialisation' was necessary before the right of self-determination could be meaningfully exercised, but the reality was that the guerrilla movements were still in the field while the Portuguese armed forces, or at least key sections of them, had carried out a *coup* because they were tired of fighting. Conscript officers and troops rejoiced at the overthrow of the regime because it meant they could go home, while many regulars were with the MFA in wanting to get things settled as quickly as possible. The liberation movements responded to Spínola's appeal to negotiate peace certain in the view that time was on their side. The will of most military units to resist had gone, removing with it the very bargaining counter upon which Spínola's hopes rested. Nor was it simply military morale and discipline that quickly disappeared; the hopes raised and the political vacuum created by 25 April signified, not the strengthening of the home front, but its collapse. That ultra-leftists could demonstrate for immediate capitulation to the 'liberation movements' was embarrassing and potentially corrosive of morale; more important was the fact that the main political heirs of 25 April, the PCP and PS, were committed to handing over to the PAIGC, FRELIMO and the MPLA.

Spínola had vainly hoped to rely on his charismatic powers and deal with the guerrilla leaders as if they were chieftains in Guiné; instead he found that he had virtually no power over anyone. His Foreign Minister, Soares, openly entered into negotiations with the PAIGC with the aim of giving the latter what it wanted on 25 May. As Head of State Spínola could withhold his approval of such an agreement, but there was little point in doing this when the army in Guiné was already ceasing fire and, indeed, fraternising with PAIGC forces. Spínola had sent a trusted officer who had served under him when governor, Major Carlos Fabião, to the colony with the aim of conducting a military holding operation during which a political third force would have the time to emerge, thus strengthening the Portuguese hand in the negotiations with the PAIGC. On arrival, however, Fabião found that such a policy was far removed from the realities of the situation and he became the spokesman of military opinion in the colony, demanding immediate abandonment to what was still supposed to be the enemy. Thus a frustrated and angry Spínola was overtaken by the realities of the new situation and, having suffered a defeat during the governmental crisis of early July, he found that on 26 July he had no alternative but to promulgate the Council of State's Constitutional Law No. 7/74. The next day, in a historic television address, he conceded his

... recognition of the right of the peoples of the Portuguese overseas territories to self-determination, including the immediate recognition of their right to independence ...

We are ready, starting now, to begin the process of transferring power to the populations of the overseas territories avowedly prepared for this, namely, Guiné, Angola and Mozambique.

In September Portugal formally recognised the independent Republic of Guiné-Bissau, under PAIGC rule. This was not what Spínola had hoped for, but the PAIGC had agreed not to demand immediate control of the strategically sensitive Cape Verde Islands. For the MFA and the parties of the Left, Guiné was a model for that 'novel' decolonisation of which Major Melo Antunes was to speak. For Spínola it was a depressing defeat. Asked, at an appropriately cold lunch given to celebrate the event, what were his thoughts on the process, the general morosely replied: 'I am thinking of the dead.' On taking over, the PAIGC reportedly shot several hundred people and the country retreated behind a wall of silence thicker than that of which pro-PAIGC journalists had complained when it was under colonial rule. Liberation had come to Guiné.

The next most pressing case to be dealt with was Mozambique, a territory in which the position was complicated by white settlement and Portuguese economic interests, though it was financially bankrupt. The *coup* of 25 April brought confusion to Mozambique. Spínola and the majority of the JSN wanted a firm new Commander-in-Chief and selected the rightist General Silvino Silvério Marques, while appealing to FRELIMO to cease fighting and prepare for normal political activity with a view to self-determination through popular consultation. However, in Mozambique the *coup* threw military loyalties into confusion and the visit in mid-May of the JSN member Costa Gomes, now again Chief of the Armed Forces' General Staff, seemed only to add to the confusion. One reason for his visit was to make indirect contact with the FRELIMO leadership in Dar-es-Salaam, and another to strengthen pro-MFA forces in the army and administration. As the Mozambican-born Major Otelo Saraiva de Carvalho, who accompanied him, noted, no one knew what to think in the territory. FRELIMO stepped up its activities while the Portuguese army was ordered to avoid clashes. Multi-racial groups such as GUMO began campaigning in Beira and Lourenço Marques, while tribal political groups were founded, such as Kavandame's UNIPOMO (Union for the Peace of the People of Mozambique, but Makonde-based) in Cabo Delgado. Poor whites in Lourenço Marques and small farmers rallied in fear of the future to the officially non-racial FICO (Remain Living Together, but also meaning 'I stay'), while, with the approval of Costa Gomes and the pro-MFA military who were already on bad terms with white settlers, the old MDM resurfaced under the title MUDM

(Movement of Democratic Unity of Mozambique). Chiefly led by white opponents of the old regime, it provided the new Governor and the new Minister for Interterritorial Co-ordination in Lisbon, António Almeida Santos. Sensing the way the wind of change was blowing, it made itself the favourite group of the new situation by moving leftwards and praising FRELIMO, with whose clandestine organisers it apparently sought to co-operate. Thus these democrats and the pro-MFA military in Mozambique outmanœuvred Spínola (Silvino Silvério Marques was sent to Angola instead), the nascent but disorganised political third force and Jorge Jardim, who took refuge in the Malawian Embassy in Lisbon for twenty-three days before escaping to Spain and then central Africa.

While Jardim and GUMO tried to negotiate with FRELIMO through Malawi and Zambia on the basis of the previous year's Lusaka programme, in early June Mário Soares and Otelo Saraiva de Carvalho met FRELIMO representatives in Lusaka. In Mozambique itself prices and unemployment soared, the economy came to a standstill, there were waves of strikes, white farmers moved into the towns, confused and apprehensive black troops deserted either to join FRELIMO or seek refuge in neighbouring countries. The indignation and fears of most whites and anti-FRELIMO blacks grew as Portuguese military units pulled out of the north and in some cases, with the approval of some in Lisbon, fraternised with advancing FRELIMO units.

In this situation FRELIMO could not lose by intransigence and Samora Machel held out for 'the liquidation of Portuguese colonialism . . . There is no such thing as democratic colonialism.' With MFA elements determined to ignore any third force as a complicating embarrassment in the haste to end hostilities, a new effort to get a face-saving formula for withdrawal was made by Major Melo Antunes, whose mission to Tanzania was approved by Spínola even though the latter denounced him to a visiting FICO delegation as 'a communist'. (Spínola, indeed, in his frustration and inability to control events entertained fantasies about American or South African intervention.) In the event the third force never got itself organised and could not rally support as the black population hastened to rally to the side of the victors. Soares and Melo Antunes signed the Lusaka Accord with Samora Machel on 7 September. The document said there would be a ceasefire the next day, that independence would be complete on 25 July 1975, and that a 'government of transition' under a FRELIMO premier would supervise 'the progressive transfer of power' in the meantime in conjunction with a Portuguese high commissioner.

An atmosphere of impending doom had pervaded most white Mozambicans since 25 April. Like the many blacks and *mestiços* who had served the Portuguese, they felt bitterly a sense of betrayal as the real victims of decolonisation: first they had been told Portugal would never leave, then that they could decide their own future by plebiscite and now that FRELIMO would decide it for them. When news of impending agreement reached Lourenço Marques on 3 September the Democrats and FRELIMO supporters began celebrating, while anti-FRELIMO elements milled about in anger and confusion. When a taxi flying a FRELIMO flag and trailing a Portuguese flag in the dust appeared shortly after the terms of the agreement became known, events took a dramatic turn. Angry crowds appealed for South African intervention, released DGS agents and took over Rádio Clube de Moçambique, the airport and telephone exchange. The anti-FRELIMO revolutionary movement, which took the name Movement of Free Mozambique, was a divided and *ad hoc* coalition, including the FICO leader Gomes dos Santos, the former ANP leader Gonçalo Mesquitela and the former PCP luminary Velez Grilo, Gumane of COREMO and ex-FRELIMO leaders such as Uria Simango. This more or less spontaneous revolt of despair collapsed within three days and was followed by a pro-FRELIMO backlash which may have cost as many as 9,500 lives. The Portuguese air force airlifted FRELIMO units into the country from Tanzania but under Vítor Crespo as High Commissioner and Joaquim Chissano as Transitional Premier the racial, social and economic situation worsened. The exodus of whites continued until the formal independence of the Marxist People's Republic of Mozambique in July 1975 and the assumption of power by Samora Machel as FRELIMO leader. Liberation had officially arrived, but for the peoples of Mozambique one tyranny had been replaced by another.

If the novel decolonisation of Mozambique was a bloodstained shambles, it was to pale into insignificance before the fate of Angola, the third territory named as ready for self-determination in Spínola's speech of 27 July. Initially there seemed to be little change in what was potentially one of the richest countries in Africa. A visit from General Costa Gomes resulted in the usual changes in commands but the new Governor-General, Silvino Silvério Marques (who had held the same post in the 1960s), seemed to want to preserve the *status quo*, to the dismay of the pro-MFA Commander-in-Chief, General Franco Pinheiro. Spínola's and the new governor-general's idea was to insist on the guerrilla movements – all in bad shape – ceasing fire and acting as normal political parties alongside the new multi-racial and white settler movements that were emerging. There were about three dozen of these, ranging from former anti-Salazarists to ultra-rightists. Among the more significant were the FUA (Front of Angolan Unity), led by the white Angolan industrialist Fernando Falcão, which sought accommodation with the guerrilla movements; the rightist PCDA (Christian Democratic Party of Angola), led by a known DGS sympathiser, António Ferronha, which sought to protect settler interests by force if necessary and which, despite its title, was to be disavowed by the church in Angola; and the FRA (Angolan Resistance Front), in essence a para-military group of ex-servicemen also prepared for violent resistance to any imposed decolonisation. At first FUA constituted the fourth force (the three main guerrilla movements were the other three) in the projected scenario of self-determination. However, with only UNITA accepting a ceasefire (on 14 June), with increasing violence in Luanda and other cities from mid-July as a result of racial incidents and the struggle for supremacy in the *muceques* between the MPLA and FNLA which may have cost 4,000 lives, and with the recall of Silvério Marques at the behest of MFA elements following the Portuguese governmental crisis of early July, frightened white opinion rallied to the newly founded FRA and settlers formed their own defence units.

From the viewpoints of the settlers, Spínola, UNITA and the FNLA, the situation worsened with the arrival in late July as Governor-General (now re-styled Head of the Governing Junta) of a leftist naval officer who had earlier been humiliated by the FNLA when their prisoner, the bald-headed Admiral Rosa Coutinho, soon nicknamed 'the Red Admiral' or 'Rosa *le rouge*'. Like leftist colleagues in the MFA and the Portuguese Left, he saw the ideal solution as a transfer of power to the MPLA, which had a progressive international image compared to the tribalist and black racist FNLA. No such simple solution was possible. Apart from the views of the settlers, who had often viewed the MPLA with less hostility than the FNLA in the past, the trouble was that the MPLA itself was in a state of internal crisis and had virtually no military force. What proved an unsuccessful attempt to knock the MPLA into credible shape was the patching up of differences, chiefly of a personal nature, at a congress held in Lusaka in August: Agostinho Neto remained President, but his faction failed to defeat the intellectuals of the 'active revolt' faction led by the Pinto de Andrade brothers, who wanted greater demo-cratisation of the movement and the widest united front with other groups, or the 'eastern revolt' faction of the former Benfica footballer, Daniel Chipenda, who led the movement's only guerrilla band in the north-east which was quite at odds with Neto's headquarters. Even had the MPLA been united, this would not have solved the problem, for it drew support from a minority of the population – the chiefly detribalised blacks of the *muçeques* and the Kimbundu. While the Soviet Union was ready to restart aid to the MPLA, the Bakongo-based FNLA (of the Duvalier-like Holden Roberto) had support from the Americans and the Chinese as well as the President of Zaïre and now showed signs of being willing to compromise with other forces, while endeavouring to boost its credibility with a new burst of military activity. The situation was further complicated by the reappearance of FLEC, one faction of which hoped to do a deal with Gulf Oil for an independent Cabinda under Zaïrean protection, while another sought to enlist French support.

The holder of the key card in this complicated situation was the UNITA leader Jonas Savimbi. Though his guerrilla movement was small, in the new situation it would be able to mobilise the largest ethnic group in Angola, the Ovimbundu. Savimbi was the first to cease fire so that the politicking could begin, and his apparent moderation and commitment to a multi-racial Angola through negotiated independence soon won him the tactical support of the white fourth force and the goodwill of Zambia and Zaïre (the Benguela Railway carrying their copper ran through his 'territory'). To international and Portuguese business interests UNITA and the FNLA seemed preferable to the MPLA, whose programme, though non-racial, called for the 'liquidation . . . of all traces of imperialist and colonialist relations'. Although Rosa Coutinho obtained a *de facto* ceasefire with the MPLA at the end of July, the violence and uncertainty continued in the cities of Angola: blacks migrated to the countryside, while whites and Cape Verdean traders started to leave.

By early September 1974 Angola had come to the forefront of politics in Lisbon and was the issue around which opinions, divided on many other counts, polarised. For Spínola, right-wing members of the JSN and the re-emerging right-wing groups, the loss of Guiné was regrettable, the loss of Mozambique a tragedy which should and could have been avoided, but the abandonment of Angola was unthinkable. For the sake of the white settlers and of Portuguese business interests, whose main source of capital accumulation came from the exploitation of Angolan resources, there had to be a solution by which these interests were safeguarded. For the Portuguese Left and MFA leftists, such neo-colonialist solutions were anathema: the new Portugal must not be a pawn of international capitalism and imperialism and since the MPLA was the only force which was not 'a puppet of reaction' it was the only one qualified to lead the territory to independence on a non-racial basis.

Believing himself increasingly surrounded by cowards and traitors, Spínola decided to take personal control of the Angolan question. In a controversial television address on 10 September, after the usual playing of his signature tune, Sousa's *Washington Post*, the President announced that

> . . . the process of decolonisation does not consist, as some flippantly think, in the pure and simple transfer of power to partisan organisations which carried on the armed struggle against the previous Portuguese regime . . . In our defence of the freedom of political choice and its consequent representative and institutionalised affirmation . . . in our fight for the liberty of pluri-party democracy, some will perhaps see an intransigent taking up of position which is an obstacle to the process of decolonisation . . . To defend the African territories from the

danger of this new enslavement (by certain ideologies and their corresponding totalitarian regimes) is an obligation of conscience which I draw to the attention of all those who serve the democratic ideology.

So one must distinguish between authentic decolonisation and hasty abandonment to satellitisation by third parties; that is, between authentic decolonisation and the deliverance of the populations of the African territories to the will of new dictatorships . . .

Therefore no person of good faith can believe that decolonisation is consubstantial with the fact that the Portuguese flag ceases to fly in African lands. Decolonisation will only be complete when democratic institutions safeguarding the interests of all citizens are fully and efficiently functioning.

He went on to say he believed the JSN's 'programme of action' for Angola was 'the one which best defends independence and democracy in that territory', and so he was going to stick to it. This 'programme of action' had been announced a month earlier and said that as soon as the liberation movements ceased fire, a provisional coalition government would be set up including their representatives alongside those of the most important ethnic groups, including the whites. This government should arrange free elections within two years on the 'one man, one vote' principle, if necessary with United Nations observers present, for a constituent assembly which would draw up a constitution and settle its relationship (which could be independence) with Portugal.

Four days after his television speech, Spínola met President Mobutu of Zaïre – who had some months before expelled the Portuguese community from his country – on the Cape Verdean island of Sal. Mobutu apparently put three points to Spínola: Spínola would support the Zaïrean President's brother-in-law Holden Roberto in Angola; Angola would be governed by a team dependent on both Spínola and Mobutu, while a detached Cabinda would be ruled by a FLEC team also dependent on them; Spínola would support the creation of a Zaïre-Angola-Cabinda federation under Mobutu and Roberto. Spínola is said to have accepted these proposals on three conditions: diplomatic support from Zaïre in Africa; Portugal should control concessions to all companies in Zaïre-Angola-Cabinda for twenty years; Mobutu should help Spínola regain Guiné and Mozambique through *coups*, assassinations, etc. Mobutu apparently agreed to the conditions. If this report of the Sal conversations is accurate, then both leaders seem to have moved rather far from reality. However, in late September FNLA forces did begin to move into northern Angola without Portuguese opposition.

Differences over the issue of decolonisation between the Left and MFA leaders on the one side, and Spínola and his allies on the other, were not the only source of tension in the confrontation of 28 September 1974. There were other internal reasons, too: political, social, economic and military. The world economic depression and internal confusion made for a worsening economic situation: inflation was increasing; productivity was falling; the trade gap was widening; cautious emigrant workers were not sending back remittances; there were fewer tourists; unemployment was rising and investment, whether Portuguese or foreign, was falling off – clear evidence for the Left of politically motivated 'economic sabotage' by capitalists of all nationalities. The first television address of Gonçalves as Premier announced an austerity programme. Meanwhile ultra-left groups stepped up their attacks on capitalism and casualties occurred when COPCON was called in to disperse demonstrators. The PCP still condemned ultra-left adventurism and opposed strikes as counter-revolutionary, but pressure from below suggested that the central committee of the party and its allies in Intersindical could not allow this attitude to become permanent. It was, however, necessary if the tactic of alliance with the MFA leaders was to be maintained, an alliance which the PCP saw as central to the furtherance of its aims. Thus in the Greater Lisbon area, where the daily press and media under broad left control showed increasing signs of uniformity, there was pressure for moving further to the left among political activists and workers.

While the first stirrings of popular demands for land reform could be discerned in the Alentejo, the rest of the country seemed increasingly alienated by the constant televising of rallies and political speeches. In country areas of the north and centre there were already those who began to wonder whether they had not been better off when they were worse off, while incomprehension and bewilderment at what was going on in Lisbon was widespread. Leftist students on self-appointed pedagogical missions found their ideas and themselves meeting with increasing hostility in villages, while MDP personnel holding what they called (in revolutionary newspeak) 'sessions of clarification' sometimes found themselves driven out of villages by residents armed with pitchforks and shotguns. The intellectuals of the capital were quick to condemn such behaviour: 'the people' did not include 'the peasants', one of them explained. In the north and the Islands, it was said that 25 April had not yet arrived.

When to this situation were added the misgivings of sections of the urban middle class about the way things were going, ranging from concern over the economic situation to alarm at the soaring crime rate and the breakdown of traditional social conventions, both Spínola and the Left sensed that there was the possibility of a backlash. Already, in July, Spínola had called on 'the silent majority' to assert itself; it was a theme to which he returned with greater emphasis in his address of 10 September:

> We inherited a sick country. Now that the euphoria of the first days of liberation is over, we must realise that we are still passing through a serious crisis which makes us vulnerable to extremist adventures . . .
>
> In truly democratic human societies, transformations must come about without sudden leaps or convulsions which contain within themselves the germ of new dictatorships, of the Right or of the Left. So the silent majority of the Portuguese people will have to wake up and actively defend itself against the extremist totalitarianisms that contend with one another in obscurity, making use of well-known techniques of mass manipulation to steer and condition the emotions and behaviour of a people perplexed and confused by half a century of political obscurantism . . .
>
> Either we understand and are capable of seeing the process of the country's democratisation through to a good conclusion, or a future of misery, blood and slavery awaits us . . .
>
> The Portuguese people has the right to demand that its freedom of choice of political regime be maintained intact . . . The President of the Republic will continue to be the intransigent defender of democracy . . .

The Gaullist style of this appeal by the general, who saw himself as Sebastian returned, reflected his frustration at not being able to get his own way, even within the armed forces. The still mysterious and amorphous MFA was his biggest bugbear. The inner circle, the co-ordinating committee of the programme, did virtually as they pleased, distrusted Spínola and opted for a policy of effective alliance with the PCP as an organised party of order. There was 'a coincidence of attitude', as the COPCON commander later put it, between the MFA and the PCP. However, not all MFA members were similarly left-inclined, let alone the rest of the officer corps. In August some MFA founder members led by Major Hugo dos Santos drew up a document critical of the leftist MFA leadership: it pointed out that the co-ordinating committee was not democratically elected and called for its abolition. As Chief of Staff, Costa Gomes at first approved the circular but then retracted his authorisation under pressure from members of the inner circle. Supporters of the document found themselves given overseas postings. It was another victory for the inner circle, which increasingly influenced promotions for its own political ends under a law decreed in July which abolished the criterion of seniority (the threat to which had prompted the MFA's creation a year earlier) and instituted a committee system to deal with such matters.

Democratisation and self-management therefore came to the armed forces – or rather to their officers. In the new situation, however, most officers found it advisable to be 'pro-MFA', i.e. to keep a situationist low profile so as not to be automatically passed over, while some boldly moved to the left to improve their career prospects. By September the inner circle were seeing themselves as the new élite with a new weapon at their disposal: the veteran conspirator of the 1960s, Colonel Varela Gomes, now began reorganising the psychological warfare section, the Fifth Division of the Armed Forces' General Staff, for indoctrination of military personnel and society at large with the MFA message. With the usual Jacobin logic the MFA represented the real will of the armed forces, while the leftist co-ordinating committee of the programme represented the real will of the MFA. Though not yet officially institutionalised, the MFA's revolutionary vanguard would be very difficult to dislodge. A new centre of power had emerged.

The occasion for the showdown between Spínola and the MFA and the Left was the organisation of a rally of the 'silent majority' in support of Spínola, to be held at Belém on the afternoon of Saturday 28 September. The organisers were a group of people, mostly ex-servicemen, with no known political past who obviously wanted to strengthen Spínola's position *vis-à-vis* the Left. A popular demonstration with people brought from all over the country would give him greater room for manoeuvre, perhaps a 'mandate' for reorganising the government and getting rid of the MFA's co-ordinating committee. Certainly this was how the forces of the Left viewed the planned demonstration. Most of the newspapers and other media under broad left control refused to advertise the rally and launched a propaganda campaign against what was seen as an attempted *coup*, a reactionary conspiracy aimed at putting back the clock. The PCP weekly *Avante!* called on 'the vigilant people', on 'all those who want to secure the road of democracy and decolonisation and prevent the regression to fascist tyranny', to 'take practical measures to provoke the failure of the counter-revolutionary demonstration'. Given the determination of the Left – from ultra-Left to PS – to stop the rally, the whole future of the interim regime installed on 25 April was at stake. Anxious not to appear too conservative, the PPD and CDS leaders came out against it, which meant that the proposed event took on a more right-wing character, supported only by the small PDC (Party of Christian Democracy), the PL, the PP/MFP and a few other groups which embarrassingly included the PNP (Portuguese Nationalist Party), a number of ex-Legionaries in Oporto whose organisation was immediately banned by the government.

The prelude to the rally was a bullfight on 26 September in the Campo Pequeno in Lisbon, organised by the rightist League of Servicemen. The guest of honour, Spínola, was given a standing ovation by the 15,000 present, who then just as loudly booed Vasco Gonçalves. In the presidential box a fierce argument between President and Premier was to be observed. Gonçalves told Spínola: 'As you see the ring is full of reactionaries.' At this Spínola exploded: 'Not reactionaries! Portuguese, patriotic Portuguese!' Outside the bullring there were clashes between demonstrators.

On the 27th the organisers of the rally got cold feet and thought of cancelling it, but General Galvão de Melo, the JSN member dubbed the Portuguese Pinochet by leftists for his conservative pronouncements and commonsensical handling of an earlier riot by PIDE prisoners, persuaded them to go ahead. Spínola was for continuing, but most of his government, led by Gonçalves, came out against it. On the night of the 27th members of the PCP, MDP, Intersindical, PS and ultra-Left – some of them with firearms – moved quickly and efficiently to block the roads into Lisbon. Unless the barricades could be removed there would be no rally. Spínola called a meeting of the Cabinet and the JSN at the presidential palace in Belém. Tempers rose and the air turned blue with barrack-room language as Galvão de Melo, Diogo Neto and Jaime Silvério Marques demanded Gonçalves's resignation – which he refused, in the name of the MFA, to give.

At 2 a.m. on the 28th Brigadier Otelo Saraiva de Carvalho was summoned to Belém from COPCON headquarters. Fed with rumours during the tension of previous days, he had authorised the arrests of about 200 people who had held high positions before 25 April or who were suspected of organising the rally. These arrests, often made by marines accompanied by PCP civilians working for the official Commission for the Abolition of the PIDE/DGS, went ahead. With Gonçalves and Otelo Saraiva de Carvalho virtually prisoners in Belém, the government issued a call for the vigilantes to abandon their barricades. When the PCP-controlled Rádio Clube Português (now also called Emissora da Liberdade – transmitter of freedom) continued calling on people to set up barricades, all broadcasting stations except Emissora Nacional were closed down and occupied by the GNR. Spínola appeared to be winning and was at one time ready to use force to get rid of the barricades. However, this was an illusion. COPCON forces under Captain Vasco Lourenço were prepared to advance on Belém if Otelo Saraiva de Carvalho were not freed. The possibility of a clash between opposed military units proved too much and the latter returned to COPCON. Spínola conceded defeat and agreed to the demands to cancel the rally.

All was not yet over. The barricades of popular vigilance were still in existence while the MFA inner circle met to discuss their next moves. On the morning of the 29th the JSN and the MFA leaders were summoned to Belém. Spínola proposed the abolition of the JSN while the MFA leaders demanded the dismissal of their three opponents on it (Galvão de Melo,

Diogo Neto, Silvério Marques). Meanwhile the Council of State had been summoned, but when it met it refused Spínola's proposal for the declaration of martial law (according to some accounts Spínola was thinking of calling in NATO support). Spínola now conceded definitive defeat and agreed to the institutionalisation of the MFA. COPCON troops moved on the vigilantes, who sang 'Soldier, friend, the people are with you', and fraternisation took place before people went home. A frenzied crowd, however, surrounded the Sheraton Hotel where Galvão de Melo was dining with international guests of the Portuguese Horse Club. He was rather tardily rescued by 300 COPCON troops.

On the morning of 30 September, as arranged, Spínola resigned. His farewell address was along now familiar lines:

> In this generalised climate of anarchy, in which everybody makes up his own law, crisis and chaos are inevitable . . . My sense of loyalty inhibits me from betraying the people to whom I belong and for whom, beneath the flag of a false freedom, they [anti-democrats of the Left] are preparing new forms of slavery.

It was a characteristically theatrical exit, even if the warnings which made moderate, progressive opinion smile were to be recalled by those same people with some embarrassment during the next twelve months.

As is the case with other events in recent Portuguese history, 28 September still has its shroud of mystery. Explanations and interpretations of the episode are perhaps better couched in terms of the attitudes, beliefs and fears of the participants than simply in terms of the unfolding of events. The Left as a whole, including the co-ordinating committee of the MFA, saw themselves as defending 25 April against an attempt by Spínola and right-wing forces to install, at least temporarily, a more Bonapartist or presidentialist regime. This would mean the marginalisation of themselves from the political process and probably violent confrontations between the militants of the Left and right-wing and military forces. The rally of the silent majority would be the beginning of a *glissement à droite*. On the other side, Spínola, Galvão de Melo and others thought the danger of allowing elements of the former regime to resurface in democratic garb, a danger they believed they could contain, a lesser evil compared with the continuation of a confused situation in which leftist pseudo-democrats had the initiative. Unless something was done, the *glissement à gauche* would continue, the motive forces being the communists – by which they meant the PCP, MDP, ultra-Left and MFA leaders.

Whatever the particular issues at stake, it was basically a psychological question of how the intentions of the other side were perceived: in the last resort Spínola and friends were objectively reactionaries for the Left, the

Left objectively communists for Spínola's camp. The basic degree of trust essential for the maintenance of a consensus broke down as each side saw the moves of the other in the most sinister light and an escalation of tension occurred. In this murky atmosphere an actor from the politics of the early twentieth century reappeared in a leading role: *o boato*, the rumour. In the episode of 28 September no participant could afford to discount even the wildest and unfounded piece of information; both sides thought in conspiratorial terms. In the MFA's subsequent 'Report on 28 September' there was nothing to substantiate the lurid press reports of the time about hearses loaded with arms, of party offices stacked with war material, of 40,000 armed rightists, of plans to assassinate the Premier, and indeed later Spínola himself, by ultra-rightists. The vigilantes' haul of arms was modest: several hundred hunting rifles and the absence of a single standard-issue Portuguese army G-3 rifle suggested the usual return from weekend hunting expeditions rather than preparation of a *coup de force*. The old problem so common between 1910 and 1926, of telling an *intentona* (a planned attempt to seize power) from an *inventona* (the invention by the opposing side of such a plan to further one's own purposes) remained, and still remains. Spínola's resignation, however, was a fact and an important turning-point: politics took a left turn.

The co-ordinating committee of the MFA replaced Spínola with the man they would have preferred from the first, General Costa Gomes. Nicknamed the cork for his ability to float with the tide, Costa Gomes had served Salazar and Caetano and been decorated by the PIDE but had conspired against both premiers. After 25 April he became Spínola's right-hand man as Chief of the General Staff, but saw his role as that of mediator between the provisional President and the MFA radicals, a role he attempted to play during the episode of 28 September. More than anyone else, perhaps, his priority was to avoid bloodshed, be it between soldiers and civilians or within the armed forces. The losers of 28 September, however, saw in Costa Gomes an exceptionally flexible opportunist with his eye on the main chance; some recalled that his nickname in the Military Academy had been Judas.

The new President of the Republic pledged himself to carry out the programme of the MFA: decolonisation would proceed as quickly as possible, while he interpreted democratisation as the creation of 'the social conditions allowing the people to choose their political institutions within the basilary concept of pluralist democracy'. He kept on as Premier the 53-year-old Vasco Gonçalves, who denounced the preceding episode as 'a first attack by way of reaction against the movement of 25 April', but which had had the salutary result of reinforcing the 'unity between the people and the armed forces' movement'. The MFA programme would be implemented and 'the real interests of the

Portuguese people' would be defended by the MFA, whose members 'put the unitary interests of their Fatherland above all else and lower partisan flags in the presence of these unitary interests'. They had 'made a revolution whose consequences are still in process of growth'. His fifteen-member third provisional government comprised seven MFA colleagues (including Melo Antunes and Vítor Alves), four socialists, a PPD and a PCP representative (Cunhal), and two independents.

However, real power, in so far as it existed, lay divided between the MDP and PCP militants who had demonstrated their ability to mobilise their forces quickly, and the MFA members of the co-ordinating committee and JSN with their COPCON ally. The situation was now clarified in some respects. There was to be no opportunity for those to the right of the centre-right CDS, whether connected with the old regime or not, to indulge in political activity. This limitation on democratic liberties some saw as Cunhal's first victory: two slices of salami, to use Rákosi's metaphor, one military and one civilian, had already been carved off the political spectrum. Press and broadcasting were firmly under 'broad left' – some said PCP – control, while it became clear that the 'MFA-People Alliance' (the new catch-phrase) meant only people on the left. The parties of the emergent Right were closed down and the old PIDE prison at Caxias was filled with suspects. Despite the astonishing claim of the socialist Minister of Justice, Salgado Zenha, in October 1974 that there were no political prisoners, four or five times as many people were now detained as before 25 April, detained without trial and indeed with no charges brought. Thus 28 September created a new situation of fear and apprehension among those not on the triumphant Left. While inside barracks politics were no longer discussed lest 'right-wing' opinions adversely influence career prospects, outside similar fears of denunciation by informers were widespread. Because of its powers of arbitrary arrest, justified by its commander, Brigadier Otelo Saraiva de Carvalho, on grounds of revolutionary legality, COPCON was cynically said by some to stand for 'How to Organise the PIDE With Another Name'. With Spínola removed some of the contradictions of 25 April were said by leftists to have been resolved.

One consequence of 28 September was the speeding up of the process of decolonisation. While the PCP stressed its fraternal links with movements such as the PAIGC, FRELIMO and MPLA, which gave rise to speculation by some on the PCP's role in Lisbon as an agent of Soviet global policy, MFA officers, such as Melo Antunes, had a rather different view of novel decolonisation. Composing a revolutionary variation on an old Lusotropicalist theme, they believed that a handover to the liberation movements would allow a fresh start in Portugal's relations with other Portuguese-speaking peoples. Portugal's position as a backward but

European country would mysteriously give her a special mission as the link between the advanced countries and the Third World, which Portugal was prevented from joining because of her geopolitical situation. In the case of African territories not named in Spínola's speech of 27 July as ready for self-determination, rapid progress was made. In November 1974 agreement was reached with the MLSTP for the independence of São Tomé e Príncipe on 12 July 1975 after a period of joint transitional rule on the Mozambican model. In December 1974 agreement was reached with the PAIGC for the independence of the impoverished Cape Verde Islands on 5 July 1975, after a period of joint transitional rule and the election of a constituent assembly. At the end of December 1974 a treaty was signed with the Indian Union which formally recognised the latter's incorporation of Goa, Damão, Diu, Dadrá and Nagar-Aveli.

Elsewhere, however, things did not proceed so easily. Spínola's fall came as a heavy blow to Portuguese business and settler interests in Angola and as a disappointment to the FNLA and its foreign sympathisers. Following 28 September the whites of FRA sought arms from the Portuguese army and outside sources. Some thought of a Rhodesian-style solution, while others tried to strengthen relations with UNITA and the FNLA. However, FRA never got its arms and the High Commissioner, Rosa Coutinho, who now had a freer hand, used his powers to harry or arrest FRA leaders. Meanwhile he also pursued a policy of favouring and building up the forces of the MPLA: the majority of the blacks in the Portuguese army were demobilised by incorporating them, often with their arms, into the MPLA's FAPLA (Angolan People's Liberation Armed Forces), while several thousand Katanguese *gendarmes,* whom the Portuguese had kept in a state of military preparedness as a bargaining counter with Zaïre, were also attached to FAPLA – to the chagrin of FRA, which had hoped to use them. Soviet aid to the MPLA was stepped up from October 1974.

However much Rosa Coutinho and the MFA may have wanted to hand over to the MPLA, reality demanded compromise and unity with the FNLA and UNITA. The latter built up its forces in the south while units of the former, in league with whites and coffee interests, set up their capital in Uíge (formerly Carmona). Having advanced its position on the ground, the FNLA called a ceasefire (15 October) and opened negotiations with the Portuguese, UNITA and Chipenda's 'eastern revolt' faction. While Portuguese and MPLA forces occupied Cabinda to stave off a takeover by FLEC in November 1974, the battle for control in Luanda between MPLA and FNLA supporters continued. Neto for the MPLA openly admitted that his movement's future depended on the Portuguese progressives staying in power and in December negotiated a ceasefire with UNITA which was the prelude to a summit meeting under President Kenyatta's auspices in

Mombasa (3–6 January 1975). There the FNLA, MPLA and UNITA leaders agreed that Cabinda was an integral part of Angola and that they were prepared to come to a joint agreement with the Portuguese on independence. The outcome was a meeting at the luxury Hotel Penina at Alvor (Algarve), at which agreement was reached on independence for the territory on 11 November 1975. Until then a quadripartite interim regime (Portugal, FNLA, MPLA, UNITA) would govern Angola (including Cabinda), elections would be held before independence, with only the three movements being allowed to put up candidates, and each movement would contribute equal numbers of men to a common army alongside Portuguese troops.

The Alvor accords of 15 January were only a paper agreement, as all parties knew. While Rosa Coutinho's policy had salvaged the MPLA' chances, elections (were they to take place) could not produce a majority for the MPLA, given tribal allegiances. The MPLA also lost its best ally when in late January Rosa Coutinho was replaced as High Commissioner – presumably the FNLA's price for signing the accords – by General Silva Cardoso, who was to pursue a more neutral policy *vis-à-vis* the three movements, a policy which came to be called active neutrality. From the Portuguese government's point of view, the accords constituted a face-saving formula giving them a date – the 400th anniversary of the foundation of Luanda – on which to be able to withdraw.

During 1975 the Angolan situation progressively deteriorated, a development almost independent of the marginalisation of FLEC which, with desultory Zaïrean and French support, declared Cabindan independence in Paris and in Uganda. As the months passed, aid to the MPLA from the Soviet bloc and other countries, such as Yugoslavia and Algeria, was increased and the battle between the FNLA and MPLA for control of Luanda and other cities continued with growing ferocity. An effort to patch up differences between the three movements at a summit meeting at Nakuru (in Kenya) in June was a meaningless gesture. Civil war and the partition of the country into zones of influence had in fact begun. With the MPLA victory over the FNLA in Luanda complete by August, UNITA was well entrenched in the south with its 'capital' at Huambo (formerly Nova Lisboa), while the FNLA, which now included Chipenda's 'eastern revolt', was entrenched in the north and planning to reconquer Luanda. Portuguese forces kept out of the way as much as possible and made rather haphazard attempts to protect and evacuate white settlers, hundreds of thousands of whom struggled to leave before independence. In Luanda in particular, murder, rape, pillage and arson became the norm. Western governments had to provide much of the transport for the desperate white refugees who told horrifying stories of the most terrible atrocities. (As in Guiné and Mozambique, the

Portuguese authorities cared even less about the plight of blacks and *mestiços* who had obeyed their earlier injunctions to 'serve Portugal'.) In July the Portuguese government admitted it had totally lost control of the situation, but in August announced that it was nominally resuming direct control in the face of the breakdown of the transitional arrangements and would oppose the FNLA's march on Luanda. The OAU attempted mediation but was split down the middle in its ideological sympathies.

When the Portuguese flag was hastily lowered on 11 November, full-scale civil war was already under way. The MPLA, backed by Soviet aid, Cuban troops, the revenues of Gulf Oil (Cabinda) and some African countries, proclaimed the People's Republic of Angola in Luanda. The FNLA and UNITA, in tactical alliance, proclaimed a rival Democratic Republic of Angola in Uíge and Huambo, counting on support from Zaïre, South Africa, former Portuguese army officers and some African countries. Covert aid came from some Western countries and China, infuriated at the designs of Soviet social-imperialist aggression. In February 1976 Portugal, like the EEC countries, recognised the 'Marxist' MPLA government which had won thanks to Cuban support. However, the MPLA still contained competing factions, the FNLA and FLEC still existed, and UNITA soon reasserted its presence over large stretches of southern Angola. In that unhappy country in 1977, in the language of liberation movements, the struggle goes on.

The decolonisation of its African territories left Portugal with a legacy of over half a million embittered and largely destitute colonial refugees (*retornados*), about whom successive governments wanted to know as little as possible. Colonial markets and sources of commodities at prices below the international level were gone, while the Angolan contribution to the well-being of the escudo was removed. The novel decolonisation of the African territories turned out to be a chaotic and bloodstained exercise in capitulation: whether there was any alternative is still a lively theme of discussion in Portugal.

The withdrawal from Africa, to the accompaniment of tens of thousands of dead, was not to be the end of the sad story of imperial liquidation. One outpost of empire still remains, because of the wishes of the Chinese regime, in the form of the enclave of Macao. The 25 April was slow in reaching Macao and for some months the Governor, General Nobre de Carvalho (appointed by Salazar in 1966) was not changed. This was because of the wishes of Peking expressed through their principal local representative, the entrepreneur Yo Hin. Mindful of the usefulness of Macao as a channel through which to import precious metals from southern Africa and dismayed at the objectively pro-Soviet turn of events in Portugal, the Chinese declined to establish diplomatic relations with the new Portugal but informally agreed to the continuation of

Portuguese rule in Macao through a special statute in late 1974. Article 306 of the Portuguese constitution of 1976 incorporated Law No. 1/76 (17 February 1976) which delegated certain powers to the Legislative Assembly of Macao.

The prolonged episode which further streaked Portugal's imperial sunset with blood was the frightful case of Timor, the least-remembered remnant of the colonial empire. After the *coup* of 25 April 1974 three political groupings emerged in Timor: the UDT (Timorese Democratic Union), representing the élite of administrators, tribal chiefs, plantation owners and Chinese traders, advocating progressive autonomy while preserving the Portuguese connection; APODETI (Timorese People's Democratic Association), supported by other elements of the local oligarchy, advocating integration with neighbouring Indonesia; and FRETILIN (Revolutionary Front of Independent East Timor), a group advocating outright independence, led chiefly by radicals in their twenties newly returned from Portugal, modelling itself on the PAIGC and FRELIMO and with possibilities of popular support from dockers in Díli and sections of the backward rural population. In June 1975 Vítor Alves and Almeida Santos, for the Portuguese government, reached agreement in Macao with the leaders of the UDT and APODETI on a formula for progressive self-determination.

The radicals of FRETILIN, whom the Portuguese had been trying to persuade to compromise with the UDT, refused to attend the meeting in Macao. Tension mounted in the colony and there were rumours of an impending *coup* by FRETILIN, with the result that power was seized in an allegedly pre-emptive strike by the UDT on 11 August 1975. They declared the independence of the territory and set about eliminating communist FRETILIN opposition. Civil war ensued, with the Portuguese Governor Colonel Mário Lemos Pires, withdrawing to the offshore island of Ataúro. Within a month FRETILIN, organising a rising of the lower orders in Díli and the villages, had become the dominant force and carried out their own massacres. The Portuguese, who favoured the UDT, turned a deaf and embarrassed ear to FRETILIN demands for formal recognition of independence for the economically non-viable territory, with the result that on 28 November 1975 FRETILIN proclaimed the total independence of the Democratic Republic of East Timor. Fearing that East Timor could become some sort of Micronesian Cuba, the Indonesians invaded the territory in early December with the support of UDT and APODETI politicians. *De facto* occupation was subsequently formalised into *de jure* integration with Indonesia, but FRETILIN resistance was continuing in 1977. Portugal did not recognise the Indonesian *fait accompli* and the question remains on the agenda of the United Nations. The casualties in this bloody episode are estimated at 60–70,000 dead, or 10 per cent of the East Timorese population.

One of the reasons for the confused nature of decolonisation was that the development of the process was dependent upon the shifts and changes in Portuguese domestic politics, which meant that, whatever the shortcomings of personnel overseas, it was almost impossible for them to pursue a consistent line or get decisions taken in Lisbon. It is to developments in domestic politics that we must now return. The general tendency of the period from 28 September 1974 to 25 November 1975 was a quickening shift to the left in government and the armed forces. At least until the fall of Vasco Gonçalves from power in mid-September 1975, which ushered in a period of particular uncertainty, the political motto, at least in Lisbon, could be described as: 'Always to the left'. Talk of democracy gave way to talk of making the transition to socialism, though still under the banner of the programme of the MFA with its ambiguities and potential contradictions; talk of the transition to socialism gave way to talk of socialism and then to talk of people's power. Among civilian activists and members of the armed forces the vogue for outflanking or overtaking the situation and its personnel was dominant. The maintenance of the momentum of revolution opened up vistas not only of political and social experimentation but opportunities to further careers in meteoric fashion, and to set up new centres of influence and patronage.

As the revolution progressed, so more and more political figures, civilian and military, found themselves marginalised. While the general tendency until the hot summer of 1975 was to make desperate efforts to keep oneself within the revolutionary process in order to survive, thereafter, rather like a Newtonian law of physics, revolutionary activism created an opposite reaction from those marginalised, a reaction which enlisted the support of the majority of the population. Given the generalised climate of anarchy which Spínola had earlier divined, it was in the logic of the revolutionary process that the initiatives should come from farther and farther left but that these initiatives should become increasingly counter-productive as the hostile and the marginalised were driven to defend themselves. The abstract logic of the revolutionary process, given Portuguese realities, seemed to point to the reaction resulting in the return to power of right-wing authoritarianism, but in practice such an outcome was averted by the firmness at critical junctures of the moderates, so that on 25 November 1975 the then somewhat tarnished ideals of 25 April were rescued from potential oblivion.

If such was the general drift of events, it is still necessary to examine in greater detail the actions of groups and personalities, the changing balance of forces and the importance of particular episodes within this suggested framework. Following 28 September the still mysterious and amorphous MFA was not, as many expected, fully institutionalised. One reason for this was to be located in the uncertainty of its radical leaders – who successfully marginalised conservatives such as Major Sanches

Osório, the former Minister of Social Communication loyal to Spínola –
as to the political views of the officer corps as a whole. Immediate
institutionalisation might mean genuine democratisation with anti-
radicals marginalising the radical leadership. In this situation time was
needed for the services' promotion committees to do their work, putting
the politically reliable (including new revolutionaries who had been
apolitical before 25 April) into key positions. In addition Colonel Varela
Gomes' Fifth Division set about making psycho-social warfare on the
armed forces with a view to winning hearts and minds within the services,
enlightening and dynamising all ranks so that they would possess
revolutionary consciousness as the MFA understood it. In all services
'cleansing' proceeded in a confused and haphazard way, being least
extensive in the air force and most extensive in the navy, some of whose
officers were eager to emphasise its left-wing tradition. Politicisation and
favouritism went hand in hand under the watchful eye of the new MFA
élite, the military new class.

Yet if the MFA were to legitimise its position within the armed forces,
some semblance of democratic structures was necessary. In national
politics the JSN, now MFA-dominated, remained the supreme organ
institutionalised by the revolution, but the co-ordinating committee was
still the key body even though more or less formally merged into a new
Supreme Council of the MFA (the Council of Twenty) which consisted of
President Costa Gomes and the other six JSN members, the five military
ministers in the provisional government, the co-ordinating committee of
seven and the Commander of COPCON. The precise relationship of this *ad
hoc* military coalition to the General Assembly of the MFA, set up in
December 1975 to represent the armed forces through delegates from the
councils of the three services chosen by largely unknown methods, was
left vague. Anyhow, 'the Movement of the Armed Forces is the same as
the armed forces in movement', it was explained; 'the MFA will last as long
as the armed forces exist' and the MFA's 'formal institutionalisation'
would be 'a natural phenomenon resulting from the current dynamic
itself'.

In other words, those who had power were going to keep it; the General
Assembly was designed as a democratic façade for this reality, while it
also served as a means of indicating the state of the armed forces' feelings
to the top people of the MFA. That the 5th Division's internal
dynamisation was not quite obtaining the results it had set out to achieve
was revealed in elections to the three service councils in the first week of
March 1975: in the artillery for example, a secret ballot of all officers
failed to result in the re-election of Melo Antunes or the COPCON
Commander, Otelo Saraiva de Carvalho. Genuine freedom of choice
seemed to work against the more revolutionary elements, but then, as
some MFA leaders maintained, such elections were not really free since

those who voted against the furtherance of the MFA's revolution thereby demonstrated their lack of enlightenment and 'conscientialisation'. By this time the MFA leadership was showing a lack of internal cohesion and a divided will, although it still claimed to represent the real will, not only of the armed forces, but of the Portuguese people.

Developments in the armed forces and within the MFA did not of course take place in a vacuum. At a party-political level, with elections promised at the end of March, the months from September to March were a time for organisation, clarification and jockeying for position within a changing situation. In general the ultra-Left, the PCP and its allies in the MFA attempted to keep up the momentum of 28 September and progressively marginalise those to their right on the political spectrum. Popular mobilisation to prevent the organisation and propaganda of centrist and rightist groups was the tactic used. Despite its hatred and contempt for the pseudo-radicals of the ultra-Left, the PCP found that in this respect left adventurism could be tolerated since the longer-term aims of the PCP for the marginalisation of the parties of reaction were being realised without the PCP itself having to take the lead. That the only group surviving which had supported the rally of the silent majority, the PDC, would not be allowed to operate was made plain by the breaking-up of attempts by the party, now led by the conservative ex-MFA Major Sanches Osório, to hold meetings in Lisbon and a congress in Figueira da Foz (1 February 1975). The centre-right CDS, linked with European Christian democrat parties and the British Conservatives, found its meeting in Lisbon broken up by ultra-leftists (4 November 1974). The same fate befell its congress in Oporto in January 1975, when foreign participants could see for themselves to what extent anti-democrats of the Left held sway; as usual, COPCON forces fraternised with the demonstrators against the besieged, but adverse international publicity on this occasion caused order to be restored by parachutists flown in from the south.

The centre-left PPD, still in the provisional government, held its first congress in Lisbon in late November, and its conclusions reflected the flexibility which had to be employed to keep within the revolutionary process and yet maintain its image as the least leftist government party. It now stood for the building of a democratic and socialist society by the road of social-democracy and sought affiliation to the Socialist International. Its anti-fascist credentials were further advanced by the adherence of close supporters of the dead Delgado and veteran oppositionists of the old ADS. Its leader, Sá Carneiro, said the PPD, stood for 'an integral, not a formal or bourgeois, democracy', yet the emphasis on the electorate deciding on what it wanted left open the options. Sniped at in some MFA and leftist circles as the party of the bosses, the PPD hoped to recruit the support of conservatives as well as social democrats and to

strengthen the democratic tendencies within the MFA. Yet the threat of
marginalisation was underlined by the attack on its meeting in Setúbal on
7 March by ultra-leftists.

While the PPD sought to project a more leftist image to avoid
marginalisation in Lisbon and therefore survive as a national grouping
offering shelter to conservatives, the PS indulged in similar manœuvres
from a position farther to the left. Flexibility, opportunism and
ambiguity were what the situation demanded and Soares was not to be
outdone by Sá Carneiro in providing these commodities. Like the PPD,
the PS was a coalition of different tendencies. In the wake of 28 September
(which took place when Soares was abroad) the image of the party
remained ill defined. At its first congress in mid-December 1974, Soares
fought off a challenge from the Left led by the veteran oppositionist
Manuel Serra, who had brought his MSP (People's Socialist Movement)
into the PS in May 1974. Serra advocated a more Marxist line, closer
contact with the PCP and the MFA; when his move to take over the PS
failed, he and other left-wingers left to found the FSP (People's Socialist
Front). The PS remained a socialist rather than social democratic party,
but was insistent on the right of the electorate to choose its own future. Its
official programme spoke of 'socialist democracy', 'a classless society',
'socialism in freedom', 'guaranteeing ideological and political pluralism':

> The Socialist Party considers Marxism its theoretical inspiration
> Marxism permanently rethought as a guide for action and never
> conceived of as a corpus of dogma . . .
> Registering itself against the totalitarian and bureaucratic models
> which . . . socialism has followed in certain countries, the Socialist
> Party seeks to find . . . the Portuguese way to grassroots socialism
> (*socialismo de base*) . . .
> The Socialist Party repudiates the road taken by those movements
> which, calling themselves social-democrat or even socialist, end up by
> conserving, deliberately or *de facto,* the structures of capitalism and
> serving the interests of imperialism.
> Conscious that capitalism is an oppressive and brutal force the
> Socialist Party is fighting for its total destruction . . .

In day-to-day practice, however, the PS saw the 'salami tactics' of the PCP
as the main threat, since these meant the 'marginalisation' of the PS.

The PCP itself felt pleased with the outcome of 28 September: to
compress its propaganda into paradox, the episode represented a great,
defensive step forward. The new tasks were, according to the
PCP, to 'reinforce the unity of action of the middle bourgeoisie, in
the struggle for a democratic Portugal'; 'to reinforce unity' between the
PCP and other 'democratic parties'; and 'to reinforce the alliance between

the popular movement and the Movement of the Armed Forces, indispensable condition for the successful prosecution of the revolutionary process'. If the successfull defence of a regime of liberty and democracy necessitated the liquidation of the economic power of monopolies and big landowners through nationalisations and agrarian reform, it also meant sacrifices and hard work from the workers to stabilise the economy – hence the resurrection of the French Communist Party slogan of the mid-1940s, the battle for production. Contrary to ultra-left maximalism, Cunhal wished to reassure the petty bourgeoisie and religious interests, in the manner of Togliatti, lest they be driven into the arms of reaction. At the brief 7th Congress of the PCP in October 1974 some changes were made to the party programme. The demand for Portugal to leave NATO immediately was dropped, as was the dictatorship of the proletariat:

> In the alterations to the programme, certain expressions currently employed in Marxist terminology are suppressed . . . No ideological significance must be attributed to the fact . . .
> This is the case, for example, with the dictatorship of the proletariat . . . The word dictatorship, employed now in Portugal after fifty years of fascist dictatorship . . . would not facilitate understanding of the party's policy, nor would it facilitate the realisation of its tasks.
> We are not altering anything in our concepts nor our doctrine. Let this be quite clear so that mistakes are avoided . . .
> The Portuguese Communist Party is the revolutionary vanguard of the working class and the popular masses. Its role is irreplaceable . . .

One step backwards was worth two forwards. Still at loggerheads with the infantile revolutionism of ultra-leftists – the so-called civil war between PCP and ultra-left students paralysed universities and caused more and more trouble in secondary education – Cunhal gave first priority to the MFA alliance. The Premier, Gonçalves, pursued policies in line with the party's needs and, even if not in 1974–5 a card-carrying member of the PCP, which he had certainly once been, allowed PCP influence in the media and the state apparatus to grow. As new MFA actors appeared on the political stage, many of them naval officers, the emergence of a potentially dominant Gonçalves faction or 'pro-PCP' faction became clearer. This potential predominance was, however, challenged by other MFA luminaries, once considered more radical than Gonçalves, but now beginning to have doubts about the wisdom of too close a convergence of aims with the PCP and sensing that they were in danger of being overtaken by newcomers. To get the better of the Gonçalvists (such as Costa Martins, Correia Jesuíno, Varela Gomes, Miguel Judas, Ramiro Correia), others began to enter into objective tactical alliance with the PS (such as Majors Alves and Antunes) or to adopt ultra-leftist language (as COPCON's Otelo Saraiva de Carvalho was to do).

From October 1974 Varela Gomes's 5th Division, in which the strong naval presence was perhaps reflected in its adoption of *A Life on the Ocean Wave* as its signature tune, set about a largely self-intoxicating programme of cultural dynamisation and political clarification among the least enlightened groups of the population, especially in rural areas. Meanwhile the 'Gonçalvist'-PCP alliance was threatened with its first setback in January 1975 on home territory in Lisbon. The occasion for confrontation was the debate over trade-union structures. The PPD was for pluralism, the PS for trade union unity but against legal recognition of complete oneness (*unicidade*) as advocated by the PCP and Intersindical. If *unicidade* were accepted by the MFA, then one all-powerful trade union structure would be created under the control of the pro-PCP bureaucrats of Intersindical. Intersindical, of course, advocated PCP-style socialism and had incurred the hostility of workers in many important enterprises for its stand against strikes, for wage restraint and the battle of production. The MFA Council of Twenty voted by a small majority for *unicidade,* but the PS, in alliance with the Maoists of the chemical workers' union, came out against it. The PS turned their campaign, which showed an unexpectedly large potential for popular mobilisation, into an attack on the PCP's dictatorial pretensions with the result that while the principle of *unicidade* remained, pro-PCP members of the government had to agree to small print saying that the law would be reviewed after a year, that union elections were to be by secret ballot, that affiliation to Intersindical was not compulsory and that closed shops were illegal. Workers' committees – some of them federated in the unofficial Inter-Empresas – continued to function, while the strength of anti-PCP and anti-Intersindical feeling spearheaded by the PS caused confusion within the MFA.

The month of February saw the decision-making powers of the MFA grind to a halt. Some officers were for postponing the general elections promised in March; some complained of all political parties and wanted the MFA to become a kind of superparty; others maintained the elections must be held (Costa Gomes said they were to be on 12 April); most were agreed that the MFA should institutionalise itself, but could not agree how. Then came the internal elections to the service councils at the beginning of March, which suggested that military opinion was tending to want a return to barracks or a change of political leadership. While Melo Antunes proudly presented a revolutionary economic plan which did not include nationalisation of banking and insurance, but promised agrarian reform, more housing and better social services, political disorder was growing, rural workers in the south were starting to occupy estates, squatters moved into empty houses and neighbourhood committees began to appear. It was to this mixture of chaos and self-help that the name of General Spínola was prominently added.

The episode of 11 March (1975) is in some respects more mysterious than 28 September. Rumours that Spínola was about to make a political comeback and that a military *coup* was being prepared were current from late February, so that when the abortive *coup* came on 11 March it did not come as a great surprise; that something was being prepared was an open secret. While the victors of 11 March were to claim another triumph over a reactionary conspiracy, the losers – or some of them – claimed that they had been manipulated by the other side. It would seem that discussions had been held between Spínola and right-wing officers and civilians. Contacts were also made in the air force and the GNR, with the parachute regiment stationed at the Tancos base in the central military region and with the cavalry school at Santarém. By 8 March MFA and COPCON elements apparently knew quite a lot about the conspirators' plans, and on that same day the businessman, Miguel Champalimaud, and Lieutenant Nuno Barbieri (son of a former PIDE officer) informed officers that an ultra-left group, LUAR, in conjunction with elements of the most left-wing unit, the 1st Light Artillery, were planning an Easter massacre in which 500 officers and 1,000 civilians would be eliminated. Whether or not such a plan existed is not known, but Spínola and others gave it credence as the French and Spanish intelligence services vouched for its authenticity; nor were anonymous threatening telephone calls unusual. The effect of the Easter massacre bombshell was to stampede events from the stage of leisurely and rather theoretical conspiracy into execution of an inadequately prepared plan. The headquarters of the movement was the Tancos base, 80 miles north of Lisbon, where Spínola arrived around midnight (10/11 March).

The hastily drafted plans of the conspirators envisaged an air and ground attack on the 1st Light Artillery barracks near Lisbon Airport, the seizure of the Porto Alto transmitter of Rádio Clube Português and of Rádio Renascença as well as the GNR's Carmo barracks in Lisbon, and the knocking-out of Emissora Nacional. The conspirators at Tancos presumably hoped that most units would stay neutral, though they tried unsuccessfully to get the armoured unit at Santarém and the commandos at Amadora to join the movement. The whole episode was a fiasco. At 11.50 a.m. the Light Artillery barracks came in for desultory strafing by two Harvards, while Lisbon Airport was taken by 160 paratroops ferried from Tancos by helicopter and Noratlas transports. The paratroops then encircled the Light Artillery barracks, while pro-Spínolist GNR officers took over the Carmo barracks and the squad sent to Porto Alto put that transmitter off the air. However, COPCON had already been alerted, and Intersindical and the 5th Division led the move for popular vigilance and

the erection of barricades as on 28 September. A broadcast from
Gonçalves at 2.45 p.m. showed that the existing regime was still in charge,
precipitating the fraternisation of the paratroops with the artillerymen
they had been besieging (though themselves by then besieged by civilians)
and a rising by sergeants and other ranks against their officers at Tancos.
The unsuccessful conspirators surrendered or fled – General Spínola and
his party being whisked off to Spain, as an Intersindical leader put it, 'by
the helicopters of reaction'. Despite COPCON appeals for calm, mobs
attacked Spínola's house, wrecked the CDS and PDC offices in Lisbon and
the PPD offices in Oporto as well for good measure. Unity was the order of
the day and the PS demonstrated alongside the PCP and ultra-Left, as did
the PPD, though its procession in Lisbon was broken up as reactionary.
As COPCON set out to make an unknown number of arbitrary arrests,
Gonçalves jubilantly declared that 'the alliance between the people and
the armed forces' demonstrated that 'the revolution is irreversible'. The
death of an artilleryman was avenged by the unexplained shooting of a
youngish man and his girlfriend near the Light Artillery barracks in front
of TV cameras.

The episode of 11 March recharged the batteries of the most radical
elements in the MFA and strengthened, at least in the short term, the
position of Gonçalves. The *saneamento* of Spínolist officers was carried
out and the cultural dynamisers of the 5th Division given their head. In a
confused situation in which reasoned opposition, whether within the
armed forces or in national politics, could easily be denounced as
counter-revolutionary, the leftward tendency of the situation reasserted
itself with renewed vigour. A meeting of the General Assembly of the MFA
decided on its immediate institutionalisation. Law No. 5/75 of 14 March
abolished the JSN and Council of State and vested full powers in a new
Council of the Revolution, including the President and Premier, the
Commander of COPCON, the co-ordinating committee of the programme,
the service chiefs and others nominated by the MFA – twenty-nine
members in all, after the failure of an attempt to marginalise Melo
Antunes, Vítor Alves and Vítor Crespo. The Council of the Revolution
was responsible only to a reorganised 240-member Assembly of the
armed forces' movement, which introduced internal democratisation by
including *milicianos,* NCO's and other ranks in line with the concept of
revolutionary discipline which the dynamisers began to propagate.
Regular officers noted that some elections were nominations by the 5th
Division; that the whole concept of professional hierarchy and cohesion
within units was being undermined; that the navy was over-represented
and that relatively conservative units in the north and centre were under-
represented. The MFA, President Costa Gomes announced, was the
motor of the revolution and the Council of the Revolution would not feel
constrained by conservative legalisms in its decisions.

The Council of the Revolution's first acts were the nationalisation of private banking and insurance (Decree Laws of 14 and 15 March), with the exception of foreign-owned concerns. By these decrees, some 50–60 per cent of the economy fell into the public sector. Since banks were formerly owned by the monopolists, who were mostly in gaol either for alleged participation in the movement of 11 March or for economic sabotage (the justification for a wave of arrests by COPCON in December), the decision meant automatic state ownership of the major industries and firms, of some of the main newspapers and even of hotels and restaurants. The divorce between economic and political power condemned by Marxists was thus ended, Melo Antunes and his economic plan overtaken and the MFA's promise of an anti-monopolist strategy effected in its most radical form at a stroke. The patronage of the state, which meant the MFA, was vastly increased and elements of the left-wing intelligentsia saw their career prospects widened: the MFA's choice of the socialist option perhaps would signify the arrival of Djilas's new class. Spoliation, and the redistribution of the spoils among the new élite, was always a feature of revolutionary political change. Nationalisation was most unlikely to mean workers' control, rather jobs for the boys, including Intersindical bureaucrats.

Another consequence of 11 March was the installation, with less power than before, of the fourth provisional government (on 26 March), headed again by Vasco Gonçalves. Of the twenty-one ministers, eight were officers (including Melo Antunes at Foreign Affairs and Correia Jesuíno at Social Communication); two were representatives of the PCP, three of the MDP, two of the PS, two of the PPD; the rest were independents. Despite continued PS and PPD presence in the government, a generalised atmosphere of fear and apprehension persisted: CDS leaders received threats to kidnap their families, while Soares summed up the situation in three words: 'fear, anxiety and opportunism'. The PCP leader Cunhal accused the PS and PPD of 'facilitating, by their action, the preparation of the political conditions for the unleashing of the reactionary *coup*', and called on them to indulge in public self-criticism, of which he did not think them capable. He described the PPD as 'obviously against the revolutionary process' and demanded its expulsion from government, while some MFA leaders sought to implicate the independent weekly *Expresso* in the episode. Inside and outside Portugal, fears were expressed that the MFA, intentionally or otherwise, was paving the way for a PCP takeover on the model of Czechoslovakia in 1948. (Had Spínola won on 11 March, his address to the nation would have been about how he had saved Portugal from such a fate.)

As it was, the image presented after 11 March was one of renewed MFA cohesion and dominance. Doubts as to whether general elections would be held were resolved when the main parties were required to agree to a 'platform of constitutional accord' at the start of the electoral campaign. Some groups, however, had already been banned: the PDC on the right, and on the far left the MRPP and the Maoist AOC (Worker-Peasant Alliance), whose revolutionism was as hostile to the KGB and social-imperialism as to the CIA and imperialism. The PS and PPD, who signed the accord along with the CDS, PCP, MDP and FSP, felt that they had no alternative and feared that otherwise the capricious MFA leaders might still cancel the elections on 25 April.

The accord put the MFA in overall control for a period of transition of from three to five years and made it clear that these elections were solely for a constituent assembly, which would have to incorporate the accord in its constitution. Contrary to the original programme of the MFA, the President of the Republic was to be chosen by an electoral college composed of the eventual Legislative Assembly and the Assembly of the MFA. The MFA was to keep key ministries (Defence, Internal Administration, Economic Planning) for itself. It was made clear that there was to be no going back on the chosen path of socialist revolution leading to a truly Portuguese socialism. Some officers still seemed to prefer a supra-party MFA regime inspired by Third World examples and a new political star was discovered in Admiral Rosa Coutinho who, after his return from Angola in January, charted a zig-zag course between Third World liberationism and alignment with the PCP as Gonçalves's potential successor. As Coutinho put it:

> The country is going to continue on the line to socialism, but all parties have the right to board the train ... The MFA will be the train's engine, the locomotive ... We shall pick up all the carriages so long as they don't act as a brake.

In the new situation passengers vied for the best seats. While presenting himself as the best bulwark against the PCP Soares emphasised that the PS had the goodwill of the Spanish and Italian Communists, that it was Marxist and to the left of any European Socialist party: 'social-democracy is not applicable in Portugal'. One PPD leader, Pinto Balsemão, told his party not to indulge in 'sterile nostalgia for the loss, at least in the short or medium term, of the formal democracy of which we dreamed ... Formal democracy has been overtaken.' The PCP was still, of course, for unity and therefore against the heresy of divisionism, as was its ally the MDP, one of whose speakers declared: 'He who is against the MDP is a fascist.'

The polling for the Constituent Assembly on 25 April 1975 passed off almost without incident, in contrast to the election campaign in which meetings of the PPD and CDS (especially those of its semi-independent candidate, Galvão de Melo) were the targets for disruption by ultra-leftists, who saw them as Marcelo Caetano again in Portugal. The country was divided into constituencies coinciding with the boundaries of *distritos* and candidates were elected on the very fair de Hondt system of proportional representation. The turn-out of voters (both sexes over 18) was surprisingly high on the mainland and in the Islands, averaging 91·7 per cent. Blank voting papers, called for by members of the MFA as a sign of non-partisan solidarity with the revolutionary process, totalled only 6·9 per cent (MFA radicals had hoped for 40 per cent). On the mainland and the Islands the results were as shown in Table 6.1.

Table 6.1   *Results of the Election of 25 April 1975*

Party	% of vote	No. of seats
PS	37·9	115
PPD	26·4	80
PCP	12·5	30
CDS	7·6	16
MDP	4·1	5
UDP	0·8	1

In addition the PS won the seat for Portuguese in Mozambique, the PPD the seat for emigrants and an independent sat for Macao. Six groups (five of the far Left and the PPM) failed to win any seats, though the FSP and MES polled over 1 per cent each.

The elections, whose results were broadly in line with previous opinion polls, revealed the regional strengths of the parties. The PPD, which had incorporated elements of the old ANP network, was predominant in the Islands, with votes ranging from 54·8 to 67·6 per cent according to constituency. In the Beiras and the north, the PPD headed the poll in eight out of the eleven *distritos,* the PS winning in Oporto, Castelo Branco and Coimbra. In the southern constituencies the PS topped the poll everywhere except in Beja, won by the PCP; while the PS ran the PCP a close second there, the PCP ran the PS a very close second in Setúbal and Évora. In Lisbon the PS scored 46·1 per cent of the votes against the PCP's 19, the PPD's 14·9 and the CDS's 4·8. The PS emerged as the major national party, coming second in all the constituencies in which it did not win: it got its highest vote (52·4 per cent) in Portalegre, its lowest in Funchal (19·4 per cent). The PPD's strength obviously lay mostly in the north, centre and Islands (it polled under 10 per cent in Setúbal and the Alentejo), while its rival for the conservative vote, the CDS, showed a similar geographical distribution of support. The PCP vote, however, was heavily circumscribed to sections of the rural and industrial working class: it polled over 30 per cent in Beja, Évora and Setúbal, but recorded less than 10 per cent everywhere else except for Faro, Lisbon, Portalegre and Santarém. MDP strength followed no particular pattern, but its five deputies were elected in Lisbon, Setúbal and Faro. The UDP (People's Democratic Union), a fusion of Marxist-Leninist groups priding itself on the slogan 'To the left of us there is no one', won its single seat in Lisbon.

Interpretations of the election results were legion. The triumphant PS could claim that the people had rejected reaction and revolutionary minorities, and had voted for pluralism, socialism and democracy. The PPD and CDS could say that the electorate had rejected the PCP and its MFA allies. The MFA and PCP could argue that it was an overwhelming vote for the socialist option, with over half the electorate voting for Marxist parties. For them it was a glorified public opinion poll which showed that many voters had yet to be enlightened or culturally dynamised: Jacobin logic led them to the conclusion that only votes for the PCP and its allies were really valid, while opponents could point out that the PCP's rural strength came, paradoxically, from the most backward area of the Alentejo if one took literacy rates as a guide to social progress.

However, whatever the composition of the Constituent Assembly which began to meet in June, the MFA leaders were determined not to be worsted by electoralism – a new heresy. As the premier, General Vasco Gonçalves, said: 'The election will not decisively influence the revolutionary process.' The intentions of the government, Intersindical and PCP were demonstrated on May Day: ugly clashes between rival processions were narrowly averted when attempts were made to ban PS demonstrations and Soares was refused admission to the official Intersindical-PCP-MFA rally. Cunhal informed an Italian journalist in June 1975:

> We are effecting a revolution with the armed forces . . . We communists do not accept the game of elections . . . Elections have nothing or very little to do with revolutionary dynamics . . . The solution to problems lies with the revolutionary dynamics . . . In Portugal there is now no possibility of a democracy like the one you have in West Europe . . . There are two options here: either a monopoly with a strong reactionary government or the end of monopoly with a strong communist democracy . . . We do not wait for the results of elections to change things and destroy the past . . .

'The revolutionary dynamics' were indeed the key to the situation during the hot summer of 1975. As the MFA moved from one position to another and then virtually disintegrated, the revolutionary process entered its surrealist phase of increasingly frenzied activity, with political groups and figures shifting their ground, breaking alliances and forming new alliances with dizzying speed. The extreme fluidity of the political and military situation had as its backcloth a deteriorating economic situation and another upsurge of popular movements of protest and despair which varied in character from region to region. In the Greater Lisbon area, workers' committees, revolutionary committees and neighbourhood committees sprang up which MFA radicals and ultra-leftists tried to use as a new basis for power. In the Alentejo the pace of occupations of farms increased, a movement which the PCP tried to make its own, though the initiative seems to have come from ultra-leftists, socialists and local PCP militants impatient with the Central Committee. In the north, centre and Islands the movement of protest took the form of a violent reaction against the politics of Lisbon, an assertion by the patronised that they had views of their own which must be respected: this movement was to varying extents encouraged and used by political groups from the PS to the extreme Right, by farmers' organisations and by the church. Political ideologies and old and nascent networks of patronage and influence interacted with rising prices, rising unemployment, the return of settler families from the colonies and the hopes and fears of foreign opinion and foreign powers. Behind the dustcloud raised by this growing chaos could be discerned the drawing of battle-lines for full-scale civil war should compromise prove impossible.

The first act in this new, post-electoral phase in the revolutionary drama may be said to have ended on 10 July, when the socialists withdrew from the government, a move which was followed shortly afterwards by the PPD, whose new Secretary-General, the veteran anti-Salazarist exile and collaborator with Delgado and LUAR, Emídio Guerreiro, brought to the party a new anti-capitalist and semi-libertarian image: for him the Russian Revolution of 1917 was 'the most marvellous and magnificent revolution', but it had gone off the rails after Lenin's death. The reasons for the withdrawal of the PS and PPD from Government were basically three: fear that civil liberties, especially freedom of the media, were being eroded; opposition to the MFA's attempt to bypass the majority parties; and the realisation that the international aid needed for the economy would not be forthcoming if pluralist democracy were not assured.

From 11 March MFA control of the media had been slanted against parties to the right of the PCP and this tendency was accentuated after the nationalisations. While MFA personalities came out more and more for censorship, major dailies such as *Diário de Notícias* and *O Século* came effectively under PCP management and the workers' committee of the PS paper *República* called for a change of political orientation and the ousting of the PS editorial staff. Denounced by the PS as a PCP takeover, the motivation of printing workers and others seems to have been farther to the left; for Soares and others, however, the point was that the last independent voice of the Lisbon daily press was being silenced and the government should uphold its own press law. The workers' committee barred the building to the PS editorial staff and the paper was closed by COPCON on 19 May. When the paper reopened it was in the hands of the workers' committee. Having enlisted the support of the Socialist International and the Italian and Spanish Communist parties, Soares found that the issue of press freedom was the best one to use in his attempt to bring about the reorganisation of the government.

The *República* affair rumbled on for the rest of the year, as did the parallel dispute over the Catholic Rádio Renascença, taken over by another workers' committee on 27 May. Neither the PCP nor Gonçalves were happy at this move, which threatened to alienate the church, and indeed did so. The hierarchy had accepted 25 April with varying degrees of enthusiasm and apprehension, while many of the rural clergy and their parishioners were alarmed by 'the communists' in power in Lisbon – an alien place now ruled by alien people. The hierarchy felt disquiet at 28 September, but the Vatican co-operated with the regime in negotiating a change in the concordat to allow divorce (the Decree Law was published on the day the workers' committee took over the church's radio station in Lisbon). After 11 March the scene changed as church leaders condemned the threats to political pluralism and civil rights. The anti-Salazarist Bishop of Oporto condemned those sowing the seeds of hatred and division, such as those who howled for revolutionary justice or the people's justice for conspirators, pointing out that it would scarcely be progressive to reintroduce the death penalty after more than a century. While the Vatican appealed to Catholics to vote against Marxist parties in April, some ecclesiastics, such as the Cardinal-Patriarch and the Bishop of Oporto, explained that this advice did not necessarily apply to the PS, though others, such as the traditionalist Archbishop of Braga, interpreted it as meaning a vote for the CDS. The MFA got itself off the Rádio Renascença hook by appointing an interim management committee pending nationalisation. The issue of the radio station, still run by its workers' committee, and the harrying of Catholic demonstrators in Lisbon, which brought formal Vatican protests, led the hierarchy into informal alliance with the PS and those to its right in defence of civil rights and pluralistic democracy, albeit in association with social reforms. This could only mean the mobilisation of the rural north and centre against MFA policies.

Socialist and Catholic actions were so far responses to MFA moves, or the absence of these in the face of leftist direct action. With strikes and occupations growing in number and the advent of revolutionary discipline in some COPCON units (most notably in Captain Dinis de Almeida's Lisbon Artillery Regiment), what little power the authorities controlled was being eroded. Although, under the command of the vain and increasingly publicity-conscious General Otelo Saraiva de Carvalho, COPCON was the weaponed arm of the MFA, it was becoming doubtful to what extent its soldiers would obey orders and to what extent its commander would obey governmental decisions. On some occasions, however, COPCON could still show arbitrary verve: such was the case on 27 and 28 May when, using ex-PIDE files, COPCON and PCP militants arrested over 400 members of the ultra-left MRPP. COPCON and the MRPP had been sparring partners since 1974, but, given the MRPP's attacks on social-fascism (i.e. the PCP) which were leading it into tactical alliance with the PS and PPD, many found the timing of the swoop significant. Ultra-left detainees were to testify to ill-treatment, in some cases torture, like right-wing prisoners of 'the new PIDE'.

Meanwhile, with a view to bypassing those awkward political parties with their majority electoral support, and with a view to harnessing for their own purposes the wave of popular protest, the MFA set out to find some new formula with which to legitimate their rule. To some MFA elements the poor performance of the PCP at the polls and the successes of anti-PCP lists in Intersindical elections suggested that the prevailing wind was now blowing from the ultra-Left. From late May onwards the MFA's organisms debated new plans to relate military rule to non-party popular organisms. Ideas were put forward for a kind of leftist version of corporativism, with networks of committees of revolutionary soldiers, sailors, workers and residents as the basis for a new revolutionary state. While the MFA declared itself the liberation movement of the Portuguese people, the disputes over whether workers' revolutionary councils (a PRP/BR-inspired idea) or committees for the defence of the revolution (supported by the PCP as a lesser evil) should be the new base were set aside with a programme of political action in June, which reiterated that the pluralist path and the platform of constitutional accord would be respected. However, it went on in its contradictory way to say that parties would only be tolerated if they went along with the MFA's 'transition to socialism' and that pro-MFA 'base units' would 'form the embryo of an experimental system of direct democracy . . . The MFA considers . . . it is extremely important . . . to strengthen and dynamise these [unitary people's basic] structures [for] overcoming the contradictions existing at the level of summit political structures.' In short the MFA was divided between ultra-leftist anarcho-populist structures (under military control) and a limited pluralistic socialist democracy.

On 9 July however a guide document was approved by the MFA's Assembly which shifted the balance towards the ultra-Left. Within the context of the programme of political action, the armed forces and police would have their own assemblies at unit level and these would cause to be set up workers' and residents' committees where none existed. All these would be unitary (in the sense of independence from party political links) and would, with the military unit assemblies, form a pyramid of representative structures culminating in an eventual People's National

Assembly. If taken seriously, it made a nonsense of the balance attempted in the programme of political action and all parties would be marginalised. Hence those on the ultra-left were jubilant – especially the PRP/BR; the MDP, PCP and *Intersindical* supported it, though without euphoria, while other parties rejected the scheme, Soares dubbing it a 'totalitarian manœuvre'. In fact it was a hopelessly utopian scheme which represented the figleaf hiding the nakedness of authoritarianism, a left-wing version of the New State.

When the socialists and PPD withdrew from the government, a new phase of confrontation began. The disquiet of Costa Gomes and Gonçalves at the new turn of events was reflected in their respective references to 'pseudo-revolutionary opportunism and adventurism' and 'the continuous escalation of leftism', but such phrases were buried in verbiage supporting the exciting new developments. The groups of the ultra-left were overjoyed, for the guide document seemed to indicate that the parties (including the PCP) were being marginalised and that revisionism was being overtaken in the revolutionary process. The vanguard of the MFA now seemed to be constituted by Otelo Saraiva de Carvalho of COPCON, Dinis de Almeida and the 5th Division, all of whom showed signs of increasing revolutionary intoxication: Gonçalves would have to move with the tide, would have to overtake his former self if those who had joined his faction in the MFA were not to desert him for new patrons. On 16 July members of the Lisbon Artillery Regiment joined an ultra-left demonstration demanding abolition of the bourgeois Constituent Assembly. The capital seemed increasingly to be in the hands of those to the left of the PS, while in the Alentejo over 200,000 hectares had been taken over by workers by early August.

Elsewhere in the country it was a very different story. On Sunday 13 July Catholics paraded in Aveiro with placards demanding freedom of information and no arbitrary arrests – reactionary slogans as the state radio described them – while on the same day a crowd organised by the League of Small and Medium-Sized Farmers attacked and destroyed the PCP and FSP offices in the market town of Rio Maior (50 miles north of Lisbon). These events were followed by a whole wave of repudiation of the turn events were taking in Lisbon on the part of people in the Minho, Trás-os-Montes, the Beiras and northern Ribatejo. By the end of the summer PCP and other leftist offices in almost every town in northern and central Portugal had been destroyed or attacked in what the MRPP saw as a peasant uprising against social fascism. Cunhal's last attempt to hold a meeting in this area was at Alcobaça on 16 August, an unsuccessful attempt which ended in shooting and injuries. In the north the PCP had virtually to go underground, its members threatened and harried as right-wingers and centrists had been earlier by the Left.

That there was a genuine movement of popular feeling in the north seems incontestable, whether prompted by fear of communism, alienation from the capital or protest against unemployment, rising prices and a novel decolonisation which brought back distressed and embittered relatives from Africa. The uneasy coalition of forces supporting, encouraging, canalising and on occasion organising the movement of opinion was broad. In the forefront was the socialist Soares, who called for Gonçalves to go and who held mass meetings in Oporto in July, despite PCP attempts to organise barricades to stop him and prohibitions from COPCON. (The army indeed showed that it was as powerless to control demonstrations in the north as it was in Lisbon.) Nevertheless Soares kept his options open, calling for a 'government of national union'. His aim was to gain bargaining power by demonstrating that 'the people are not with the MFA'. In rural areas, however, if not in Oporto, PS and PPD members were likely to find themselves ranged alongside the CDS, monarchists and undercover militants of the clandestine rightist organisations MDLP (Democratic Liberation Movement of Portugal) and ELP (Portuguese Liberation Army). In the battle to save the country from the threat of a communist dictatorship the broadest front was necessary for tactical reasons.

To what extent the avalanche of anti-communist activity in the north was organised by the Right's underground and to what extent it was a spontaneous outburst, directed against the PCP and its fellow travellers in local government (who discriminated against farmers on political grounds when giving credit or who tried to set up new networks of patronage), will long remain a matter for debate. Lisbon leftists' charges of reactionary manoeuvres are likely proudly to be given substance by the exaggerated claims of the rightist resistance. Here it is sufficient to record that smuggling of small arms occurred and that a role was played by ex-servicemen, *retornados* and civilians of the MDLP and ELP. These latter organisations remain largely mysterious. The MDLP was led by the exiled Spínola, whether from Brazil or from Western European countries which he visited in order to enlist support and contact Portuguese opinion from the PS rightwards. It was a movement founded by Spínola and other refugees from 11 March such as the naval officer, Alpoim Calvão, and Sanches Osório in May 1975, which incorporated elements of the PL and PP/MFP, banned after 28 September. It sought, if necessary, to create a government-in-exile, but otherwise to organise (and arm) a common front against the installation in Portugal of the Marxist military dictatorship. It pledged itself to carry out the programme of the MFA as announced by Spínola on 26 April 1974 and to create the conditions for a free, pluralist and social democracy. It still adhered to Spínola's programme for Angola, where some of its members fought with the FNLA, as did ELP members.

Though distinct from the ELP founded in Spain in late 1975 from refugees from 25 April as well as 28 September, the cadres of the two movements seem to have overlapped. The MDLP claimed to have incorporated many ELP members but said it could find no common ground with ELP. ELP leadership remains a mystery but it seems to have contained ex-PIDE and Legionary members who, on the model of the French OAS, and indeed of LUAR and ARA during Caetano's premiership, organised themselves into cells for guerrilla warfare and terrorist bomb attacks. ELP's ideology seems to have been minimal, but anonymous spokesmen claimed that it was the only group 'not identified with 25 April ... The ELP is not a party, and knows no other party than Portugal' – a country 'betrayed by Caetanism and late Salazarism'. Whereas the ELP leadership wished to be out on its own, the MDLP could be seen by the CDS, PPD and PS as a necessary ally in the event of civil war. While some churchmen favoured the PPD or a moderate PS, the voice of most of the rural clergy was probably that of the Archbishop of Braga:

> To conquer the masses, the communists begin the struggle against the Church. She must accept the struggle not in terms of man against man but Christ against Satan ... We are called upon to fight for God or against Him. To draw back would be betrayal. And betrayal would be death!

The situation in northern Portugal was paralleled in the Islands, where PCP and other leftist offices were attacked. The instigators would seem to have been rightists who, financed by emigrants in the Americas, preferred separation from Portugal to Gonçalvism. Thus the latter phenomenon in Lisbon stimulated the movement for autonomy which developed a separatist fringe in the FLA (Azorean Liberation Front) and FLAMA (Madeiran Archipelago Liberation Front). As in the case of the MDLP, FLA and FLAMA had hopes of channelling economic protest and anti-communist feeling to their own advantages, hopes which were to be dashed by the PS, PPD and moderate officers.

Meanwhile, back in Lisbon in July, the 5th Division explained disarmingly that 'the programme of the MFA was never intended to be the definitive and unique guide to the Portuguese Revolution'. The leftward shift in power was recognised by the Council of the Revolution at the end of July with the nomination of a triumvirate with sweeping powers. The new Directory was made up of President Costa Gomes, the Prime Minister (Gonçalves) and the Commander of COPCON. 'Otelo-Fidel' Saraiva de Carvalho had just returned from Cuba with very useful lessons for Portugal: apart from putting reactionaries in bullrings, these were, that a socialist society was a happy one in which everyone turned their backs on a consumer society and had 'a tremendous liking for work', and that 'the most politicised classes' had the duty to indoctrinate 'the least politicised classes' correctly. Gonçalves stressed the need for a 'unitary front in support of our revolution', but had an unpleasant message for the socially expectant: it was still necessary to keep the urban and rural middle classes within the revolutionary process. On the other hand, he argued:

> We have to build socialism, we have to sacrifice ourselves, it isn't possible to maintain the levels of a consumer society . . . Is a man freer for having a car, a fridge, a house, etc. if he has to live within the canons of capitalist society, with liberties, or with false liberties; would the life of such a man or of one who has a much lower standard of material life not be better if he took part in the building of his fatherland, if he debated with others in residents' committees?

In a speech to the MFA's Assembly on 25 July, Costa Gomes also had sobering thoughts:

> We are the fulcrum of the revolutionary process: but we are strongly influenced by the political macrocephaly of the city of Lisbon . . .
> We have in Lisbon a political microcosm, quite ready to absorb the revolutionary advances, but its circle of influence in the industrial belt is about 30 kilometres in radius.
> The rest of the country runs the risk of losing contact with the front of the column, with some areas where already appreciable discontent is growing and with others living in the past and attracted by re-actionism . . .
> The march of the Revolution accelerated to an extent that the people could not take . . .

Furthermore:

> Our external trade . . . is 80 per cent dependent on the West . . . It is my sincere belief that national independence cannot be achieved in the short term by any route that involves making an enemy of the West.

Mário Soares responded with conciliatory words:

> What divides us is not Marx or the construction of a classless society . . .
> What divides us is Stalin, the totalitarian concept of the state, the all-powerful single party, the rights of man and the problems of liberty . . .

The time for reconciliation on the terms of the PS had not yet come. On 8 August Companheiro Vasco (Gonçalves) replied by forming a new government with eighteen ministers. It was a scratch affair, with a PCP Foreign Minister (Mário Ruivo), four faithful MDP followers, seven military men and independent civilians including, as Vice-Premier, the well-known corporativist ideologue of three decades before, Teixeira Ribeiro.

This stop-gap fifth provisional government was to last thirty-five days during which decisions were taken by others. Divisionism was about to triumph for the new government's installation coincided with the appearance of the Document of the Nine. This open letter to Costa Gomes and Otelo Saraiva de Carvalho was drawn up by all those who had drafted the original progamme of the MFA except for Gonçalves and Almada Contreiras. The signatories were Vasco Lourenço, Melo Antunes, Vítor Alves, Sousa e Castro, Charais and Pezarat Correia for the Army (the two latter being the central and southern regional commanders), Canto e Castro and Costa Neves (of the air force) and Vítor Crespo (navy). It quickly gained majority support in the regular officer corps of all three services, weary of indiscipline and politicking. The Nine announced that 'a crucial point . . . the moment of the great options' in the revolutionary process had come. The middle and petty bourgeoisie were finding that their forms of social and economic organisation were disintegrating. 'The progressive decomposition of the structures of the state' was a reality and chaos was invading the armed forces, too. Each day saw the widening of the breach between 'a certain "revolutionary vanguard"', based on a small social minority in Lisbon and the Alentejo, and the rest of the country violently resisting the imposition of revolutionary changes. A law of censorship was being prepared while the state of the press could be gauged by the popular rush to hear foreign news broadcasts.

The Nine wanted the MFA to return to its genuinely supra-party image so that its social base could be broadened. While rejecting Western European social democracy, they also rejected the Eastern European socialist model: the answer was to go slower with a 'model of socialism . . . inseparable from political democracy'. They pointed out that the crisis was of the MFA's own making, for it had destroyed any idea of unity of command:

It is necessary vigorously to denounce the fascist spirit underpinning the scheme which, though calling itself socialist, will culminate in the practice of a bureaucratic dictatorship directed against the inert and uniform mass of the country's citizens.

It is necessary energetically to fight off the anarchism and the populism which inevitably lead to the catastrophic dissolution of the State, during a stage of social development when, without the State, no

political scheme is viable . . .
    It is necessary to regain the confidence of the Portuguese . . .

The Document of the Nine was supported by the PPD, the Maoist PCP (M-L) and, of course, by the PS, but opposed by the PCP. Soares also wrote an open letter to Costa Gomes warning that the country was 'near the abyss' and condemning minority government as well as violence, whether against the PCP or against the PS, MRPP or CDS.

The Document of the Nine (or Melo Antunes's Document) drew a response from the far Left on 13 August in the form of a revolutionary self-criticism by COPCON. Owing much to the ideas of the PRP/BR and the UDP, the document accused the Nine of adding to the confusion while admitting that cultural dynamisation had been counter-productive. It attacked the PCP by name for *dirigisme* and trying to gain control of the state apparatus, yet blamed parties to its right as well and said Melo Antunes's suggestions would lead to a recovery of the Right and increased dependence on foreigners. There were few new ideas: alignment with the Third World, new structures of decision making through village committees, more self-management in military units so that discipline would be by general consensus after free debate – and on top of all this a 'transitional executive power . . . constituted by the MFA and all truly revolutionary political organisations which demand and defend power for the workers' (i.e. certain ultra-left groups).

To complete the three-sided struggle, Gonçalves spoke at Almada (on the south bank of the Tagus) on 18 August in paranoid style. 'The Portuguese Revolution's moment of truth has at last arrived', he said. The Nine and Soares were accused of treason as well as acting out of frustrated ambition. Only Vasco Gonçalves and his allies were true socialists and all workers should unite with them to save Portugal from the danger of fascism. Gonçalves's days were numbered, however, for on 19 August Otelo Saraiva de Carvalho and the Nine, in tactical alliance, told Costa Gomes to find another Premier or himself be ousted. While the search began an ultra-left demonstration in favour of the COPCON line was supported by the PCP who attempted to turn the occasion into a pro-Gonçalves demonstration.

Five days later the anti-Nine position was given a boost with the formation of FUP (People's Unitary Front), being an amazing alliance of the Stalinist PCP (and its associates MDP and FSP) with MES, LUAR, the Trotskyist LCI and a Maoist *grupúsculo*. The PCP wanted to get support, if not for Gonçalves, then for a possible spell in opposition. However, FUP broke up almost immediately, while the PCP was formally excluded from it on 2 September. Internal tensions were too great to make it last, if only because the PCP at the same time showed willingness to enter a coalition with the PS as it became clear (on 27 August) how things were going when the 5th Division was closed down after issuing tendentious communiqués at odds with those of Costa Gomes. That, at least, was the official version, but it seems that Otelo Saraiva de Carvalho had already agreed to send in Neves's commandos on the previous day. With other COPCON units preventing land seizures in the Alentejo, it seemed that a new situation was on the way. On 29 August Costa Gomes announced that General Vasco Gonçalves was now Chief of the General Staff and the 57-year-old Admiral José Baptista Pinheiro de Azevedo was Premier: the latter had kept a low profile during the political manœuvring.

This new arrangement at the top in fact solved nothing, for the Nine would not accept Gonçalves as Chief of Staff, a position which would allow him to rebuild his position in the army. The initiative remained with the Nine as the army and air force assemblies voted against Gonçalves's appointment and voted to boycott the MFA assembly. Gonçalves therefore conceded defeat and the Council of the Revolution was reconstructed to cut down naval representation and shift power towards the Nine. The navy remained under the control of the leftists with Rosa Coutinho in the van pushing a Third World orientation for Portugal and Vítor Crespo (of the Nine) ousted from the navy assembly. Faced with a refusal to obey orders on the part of the military police and the emergence of SUVs (Solders United Will Win), groups of soldiers under leftist influence pledged to democracy within the barracks to paralyse military units, regular officers increasingly feared the total breakdown of discipline within the armed forces. While the SUVs demonstrated for a people's revolutionary army and linked up with the revolutionary Left to declare that 'Portugal will not be the Chile of Europe', the Nine scored another success with the replacement as commander of the northern military region of the staunch Gonçalvist Brigadier Eurico Corvacho by Brigadier Pires Veloso after units in the north had put themselves under the command of the central region. Such successes would, however, prove useless if military discipline were to cease to exist.

While all this was happening, negotiations for re-establishing the quadripartite MFA-PCP-PS-PPD coalition were under way. The PCP had no wish to be isolated, while the PS was willing to re-enter government if the *República* and Rádio Renascença affairs were settled; if freedom of expression were guaranteed, and if there were some 'cleansing' of leftist anti-democrats. The Council of the Revolution refused to help *República*'s ailing finances (its former socialist editorial staff had founded a new paper, *A Luta*), agreement was reached between the PCP and PS on freedom of information and, with the prospects for economic aid from the EEC looking brighter, the sixth provisional government took office on 19 September under the pragmatic Pinheiro de Azevedo. It contained five other officers (including Melo Antunes at Foreign Affairs and Vítor Alves at Education, later joined by Admiral Crespo as Minister of Co-operation), Veiga de Oliveira for the PCP (Environment), four socialists, two PPD representatives and three independents. Pinheiro de Azevedo pledged his government of unity to uphold democratic socialism and pluralism in accordance with the platform of constitutional accord; to defend the revolution and its conquests; to reinforce the authority of government; to defend democratic order and legality; to combat counter-revolutionary activities, etc. Consolidation, normality and pluralism were the watchwords, but it remained to be seen whether it could govern. The PCP was now again to co-operate with the PS, but in fact it adopted a double tactic: while defending the revolution in government, through its intermediaries in the MDP it kept up opposition from the left *via* FUR (Revolutionary United Front, composed of the PRP/BR, MES, LUAR, the LCI, FSP and the MDP) and through its support for the SUV movement. With the loyal Gonçalves ousted, there was no need any more to support the concept of military hierarchy – rather the reverse.

Under the sixth provisional government the state of anarchy continued. Revolutionary demonstrations and incidents did not abate, the anti-communist campaign in the north retained its impetus, in the Alentejo seizures of land proceeded at an ever quickening pace, radio stations supported revolutionary demonstrators against the government and the military remained divided and paralysed. The frequency of mass demonstrations in the capital increased, with the PCP using them to strengthen its position in government and those to its left hoping, no doubt, to wean support from the PCP by direct contact with its rank and file. A key figure in this phase of the revolution was General Otelo Saraiva de Carvalho of COPCON, the idol of the ultra-Left, who nevertheless vacillated. The units which he had commanded began to go their own way: the commandos at Amadora under Colonel Jaime Neves, whom the PCP had earlier tried to oust from his command, moved in a rightist direction, while the Lisbon Artillery Regiment of Major Dinis de Almeida moved farther leftwards, seeing itself as the vanguard of some ultra-leftist people's army. Otelo Saraiva de Carvalho had come to an understanding with the Nine to help oust the Gonçalvists, but now showed no inclination to be the instrument of the new situation. The Nine therefore set about creating a COPCON of their own in late September, the AMI (Military Intervention Grouping), to be spearheaded by the commandos, infantry units in Setúbal and Mafra and uncontaminated units returning from Angola. The marines and parachutists showed their hostility to the idea so that stalemate continued. On 29 September COPCON was ordered to occupy the broadcasting stations, but its troops fraternised with the ultra-Left, as they had during the burning of the Spanish Embassy two days before.

Rumour, as usual, played its part. According to the PS the Lisbon Artillery and the ultra-Left were preparing a *coup,* while the PPD (now again led by Sá Carneiro) saw Lisbon as having been surrendered by the authorities to 'so-called people's power which is in fact dominated by the PCP'. The Left, however, talked of right-wing *coups* being prepared with the connivance of the Nine and the provisional government. While in Lisbon demonstrators shouted 'Vasco will return', in Oporto Pires Veloso was faced with mutinies in the Army Driving School and the Heavy Artillery Regiment. Clashes between demonstrators for and against the mutineers resulted in violence and shooting, but the revolt in the two barracks eventually petered out through lack of support. While the PS in alliance with Maoists made gains in trade-union elections in the service sector to the disadvantage of the PCP, the capital seemed to be beyond anyone's control. Among most regular officers and politicians to the right of the PCP, the removal of the weak General Fabião as Army Chief of Staff and perhaps of Costa Gomes as President, as well as the closing of COPCON, were seen as prerequisites for bringing the situation under control. While the PCP showed that it still commanded the support of most workers in heavy industry in the Greater Lisbon area, Cunhal advocated exclusion of the PPD from government and a PS-PCP-FUR political alliance topped by a reconciliation of the Nine, the Gonçalvists and military ultra-leftists: neither the PS nor the ultra-Left, however, wanted to restore the PCP's hegemonic position. In late October Rádio Renascença came back on the air as an ultra-leftist voice in defiance of the government while the Nine speeded up demobilisation of conscripts in an effort to weaken leftist units.

Matters slowly reached their painful climax in November. On the 7th parachutists moved into Rádio Renascença and the transmitter was blown up on the orders of the Council of the Revolution. This firm action resulted in criticism from COPCON, which went on full alert, while NCOs of the Parachute Regiment paralysed its activities and led the occupation of the Tancos base on the 11th. The next day 20,000 building workers besieged the government and Constituent Assembly in the São Bento Palace. No military units came to their rescue and after thirty-six hours the government capitulated to demands for higher wages, collective contracts and a commission of inquiry. On the 16th, in Lisbon, a PCP-FUR-SUV-UDP mass demonstration demanded the resignation of the government, while the PS, PPD and CDS made plans to set up their Constituent Assembly in Oporto. On the 18th a member of the Council of the Revolution, sensing that opinion in the country was moving rightwards, declared that Otelo Saraiva de Carvalho, Fabião and Costa Gomes would have to be ousted, if necessary by force. The provisional government demanded 'the military means to govern' and martial law, while at Tancos the officers walked out of the base in protest against insubordination. On the 20th the government went on strike until the President re-established order and authority.

While there was talk of a Lisbon Commune seconded by a PCP Beja Commune, the Nine and the PS made plans for resistance to any leftist *coup*. The Nine insisted that COPCON would have to be controlled and pressed Costa Gomes to agree to Major Vasco Lourenço becoming commander of the Lisbon military region. Otelo Saraiva de Carvalho refused to step down from this post and a COPCON-Gonçalvist manifesto called for the politico-military crisis to be resolved through the creation of a revolutionary regime. The PS and the Nine, with military opinion hardening behind them and rumours rife of contacts between exasperated officers and the exiled Spínola for a real right-wing *coup*, refused to give way: both Soares and Melo Antunes were convinced that the PCP was intent on seizing power after a prolonged period of utter chaos during which military discipline would be thoroughly subverted, thus eliminating the armed forces.

The road to clarification of the situation still led to Otelo Saraiva de Carvalho and COPCON. He was something of an enigma: flattered by the ultra-Left, he had since 11 March developed an emotional commitment to their camp, while never quite losing feelings of solidarity with fellow officers now politically on the other side. At the time of the occupation of the radio stations on 29 September the PRP/BR had urged him to stage an impromptu *coup*, but he declined, agreeing with the UDP that the time was not right. Nevertheless he had not objected to the redirection of 1,500 G-3 weapons from the arms depot at Beirolas into the hands of ultra-leftists: they were in good hands. Time was not to be given for this Hamlet of the revolution to resolve his 'internal contradictions': the ousting of Otelo Saraiva de Carvalho would allow the disbanding of the Light Artillery (whose members as a sign of revolutionary discipline swore to 'fight . . . for people's power, for the victory of the socialist revolution') and the closure of the Gonçalvist stronghold of the SDCI (Information Control and Detection Service) whence still came instructions for media-manipulation.

The showdown began on the evening of 24 November. The Council of the Revolution (boycotted by Otelo Saraiva de Carvalho) confirmed Vasco Lourenço's appointment as commander of the Lisbon military region, its will stiffened by Soares's announcement that the PS would not shirk civil war and by news that farmers of the conservative CAP (Confederation of Portuguese Farmers, an interest group representing landowners of all sizes), meeting in Rio Maior, wanted action against wildcat occupations and were cutting off road and rail communications to Lisbon with felled trees. Threats to cut off the capital's water and electricity were also made. The scene was set for the confused episode of 25 November.

In the early hours of 25 November officers opposed to the Nine called on Otelo Saraiva de Carvalho to defy the Council of the Revolution. He declined and went home to bed, leaving the revolutionaries (including personnel of the closed 5th Division) to get on with it. By morning the air bases at Tancos, Montijo, Monte Real, Ota and Monsanto were in the hands of the revolutionary paratroops who demanded the dismissal of their commanders. The revolutionaries also used men of the Army Administration School to take over broadcasting stations and could count on marines at the Alfeite naval base. By this time a state of emergency had been declared and Colonel Ramalho Eanes, seconded by Major Lourenço, took over anti-revolutionary operations. The great mass mobilisation of civilians never occurred and the disciplined commandos of Colonel Neves moved from one revolutionary position to another, accepting their surrender. Ultra-leftist civilians were confused, while the PCP limited its support to strike action: Cunhal would not back a leftist adventure which would lead to a civil war in which the PCP was bound to be on the losing side. Three casualties occurred before the military police surrendered, followed by the air bases at Tancos and Montijo on the 26th. Martial law had been declared and the provisional government had won. It turned out that a great bluff had been called. COPCON, abolished after the episode, had failed to organise resistance, the SUVs had been totally ineffective and the Lisbon Light Artillery hardly stirred out of its barracks. In truth, no one really wanted civil war.

The events of 25 November, like those of 11 March and 28 September before it, still hold many mysteries, perhaps the biggest being the role of the PCP. Their significance, however, was immediately apparent. The leftward drift of the revolutionary process had been halted and, through the sixth provisional government and its military vanguard of commandos, the will of the majority had at last prevailed. The capacity of the groups of the ultra-Left to organise for action was shown to be virtually nil, while the effective removal of the ultra-Left from the political scales spelt objective defeat too for the PCP and its leader, 'the Nazi Cunhal, Brezhnev's running dog, the new Hitler' as the 'official' Maoists of the PCP (M-L) put it. The self-intoxicated revolutionaries of the ultra-Left were left with their post-revolutionary hangovers, indulging in mutual recriminations and rethinking their correct analyses. The ego-trip of the MFA's ultra-radicals and Gonçalvists was also over: some 200 were arrested, including Otelo Saraiva de Carvalho and Dinis de Almeida, giving them time to reflect on the past. The latter (who was close to the UDP) came to the conclusion that 'a thousand Maos and Lenins betrayed us', while the former had already come to the sad conclusion that he lacked 'political co-ordinates', otherwise he could have been 'the Fidel Castro of Europe'. The revolutionary dynamics had resulted, not in a brave new world of military-led anarcho-populism, nor in a Gonçalvist-PCP regime of order, but in the self-destruction of the MFA.

The sixth provisional government of Pinheiro de Azevedo remained in being, albeit with PCP and PPD ministers who demanded the exclusion of each other. The return to normality did not come overnight, but the tide of popular mobilisation ebbed quickly: 25 November, in fact, showed that the rank and file were suffering from revolutionary exhaustion after such a crowded timetable of mass demonstrations. With the worst of the political uncertainty removed – though not the infinitely dexterous Costa Gomes – minds could now be concentrated on constitution making; on the phasing out of the military from politics; on the critical economic situation; on regaining the confidence of other Western nations and on consolidating the gains of the revolution, for Gonçalves's governments left behind them a considerable volume of social reformist legislation. Despite the fears of those who denounced the victors of 25 November as counter-revolutionaries and reactionaries, the democratic Left stabilised the situation before the movement against Gonçalvism turned into a movement against the ideals of 25 April. The political mood was now more sober and realistic. The days were past when regional military commanders would opine in all seriousness: 'It seems that we are entering the age of Aquarius, which, they say, will turn out to be a golden age for mankind.'

7

Post-Revolutionary Portugal

If you wish to preserve liberty, re-establish authority.
André Tardieu

The episode of 25 November 1975 was a major turning-point in Portuguese evolution: the revolutionary process turned into the democratic process as Admiral Pinheiro de Azevedo's sixth provisional government endeavoured to steer a neutral and pragmatic course between critics to its left and right. The PS was the political fulcrum of the government, balancing the PCP and the PPD who, though governmental partners, were nevertheless critical of its progress. While the ultra-Left demonstrated its disapproval of the counter-revolutionary detention of their leftist military allies and clashed with the forces of authority, the PCP tended rather to concentrate on economic issues, such as collective bargaining for workers and protests at the rising cost of living, and warned against pseudo-revolutionary leftist provocations. The PCP also campaigned against the new wave of 'cleansing' in the state apparatus. As those who had become newspaper editors or gained good positions in the bureaucracy were replaced, the old difficulty of separating expertise and politics reasserted itself: those who were the losers in the process complained that they were being discriminated against on ideological grounds, while those making the changes maintained that those being replaced were lacking in competence. The gyrations of the wheel of political fortune made 1974–6 a very difficult time for patrons and clients.

While the PCP and ultra-Left played the role of conservatives, in the sense that they wanted no rightward revision of the situation, Pinheiro de Azevedo sought to put the ship of state on a course acceptable to the majority: 'We have been trying to create an unrealistic "Portuguese-style" socialism which is meaningless as far as I can see . . . Making revolution to make things worse is not a good revolutionary process.' Though 'a man of the Left', he did not 'subscribe to any dogmatic scientific political programme, much less a Marxist one'. The tendency was certainly to shift the political centre of gravity towards the middle of the political spectrum and the PPD and CDS therefore began to move away from the more leftist image they had presented, at least in the capital, during 1975. The CDS, no longer afraid of closure, declared itself a party in opposition, while in early February 1976 the PPD leadership's attacks on the social-Marxism of Soares, as well as the dictatorial pretensions of the PCP and military leftists like Melo Antunes, brought about the departure from its ranks of Emídio Guerreiro and others, who formed the MSD (Social Democratic Movement).

Meanwhile a spate of bomb attacks occurred, which were the work of ultra-rightists with no interest in the stabilisation of the situation. The politics of the illegal Right remain mysterious. Spínola's MDLP was still in existence, though plagued with dissensions. PPD and CDS leaders, as well as Councillors of the Revolution, had contacts with MDLP representatives, but whether these were of any sinister significance is very doubtful. ELP was still said to be active, though its relationship to other clandestine bands said to be operating was unclear. Spínola himself apparently thought 25 November a move in the right direction, but it did not go far enough and he seems to have feared that the PCP would recover lost ground. In February and March 1976 he was still thinking of a *coup d'état* and negotiating for the purchase of munitions in Western Europe. He hoped to count on military personalities such as Pires Veloso (commander of the northern military region), Ramalho Eanes and Morais e Silva (Chiefs-of-Staff of the Army and Air Force), with whom he may have had contact through the CDLs (Freedom Defence Committees of non-MFA officers) in 1975. Pinheiro de Azevedo, however, knew all about Spínola's efforts, which came to nothing. The MDLP was formally wound up at the end of April 1976 and Spínola was permitted to return in August. Apparently senile and increasingly out of touch with reality, he would lose his usefulness as a cover for the extreme Right if he were not in exile.

The main preoccupation was not, however, the threat of a rightist *coup* but the future relationship of the armed forces with the political parties. From December 1975 the Council of the Revolution – on which the navy's representatives had been replaced (Rosa Coutinho resigned, Almada Contreiras was detained) – was engaged in reformulating the platform of constitutional accord of 11 April 1975, which had been largely the work of Rosa Coutinho. After 25 November, however, military opinion moved away from the idea of permanent political involvement, a view shared by the main political parties. On 26 February 1976 a second pact between the military and the parties was signed after a lot of argument and manoeuvring. The views of the operational rather than the political soldiers – a distinction more and more frequently made – prevailed and the platform of 1975 was scrapped. The new pact envisaged a role for a military Council of the Revolution for another four years as guarantor of democracy. The document was a defeat for Melo Antunes, now the main political soldier, as it contained no reference to the MFA (which had in fact disappeared), nor to the armed forces as the motor of the revolution, nor to any military commitment to socialism. The PS, PPD and CDS were all agreed that it was for the electorate to choose whatever government it wanted. Legislative elections were to be held on 25 April, followed by a Presidential election on 27 June. The latter was now to be by direct suffrage and not (as envisaged in the platform of 1975) by electoral college. The days of the MFA were definitely over.

The election campaign for the new Assembly of the Republic attracted rather less interest than that of 1975, although it was hard fought. There were some violent clashes and incidents – the worst being the assassination of a candidate of the UDP in Vila Real – but the parties to the right of the PS had more freedom to hold meetings in Lisbon and the south, the PCP rather less in the north. Fourteen parties presented candidates. The PS campaigned as a party of respectable democratic socialism, in contrast to the slogan of 1975: 'Socialist Party! Marxist Party!' To the annoyance of the PPD it also projected itself as *the* party of Europe: 'Europe is with us' was the slogan launched at a grand international reunion of socialists and social democrats in Oporto. Soares announced that he would not be party to a coalition, particularly a PS-PCP coalition. The PCP, for its part, condemned ultra-leftists as agents of reaction, campaigned against the PPD and CDS as parties of reaction and for a left-wing majority and a left-wing government. Cunhal thus kept open the option of a coalition with the PS, an option which had the secondary aims of bringing the party, now supported by the MDP (which did not stand), back into the parliamentary arena and possibly acting as a pole of attraction for the Left of the PS.

The PPD and CDS both campaigned as conservative parties in their different ways and there was talk of a possible coalition government between them. As the CDS leader Freitas do Amaral put it: 'the CDS is a party of the centre which says it is and the PPD is a party of the centre which says it is on the left'. The PPD had circumstantial support from pro-Chinese Marxist-Leninists, since it campaigned against the PCP's social-fascism and the PS's social-Marxism, while the CDS could hope to pick up right-wing votes from *retornados* and others since it had not been in government and had voted against the new constitution. To the right, the reorganised PDC was standing and it remained to be seen what effect the hierarchy's injunction not to vote for 'parties opposed to the Christian conception of man and society' would have on the faithful.

The turnout on 25 April 1976 was high, though down on the previous year. On the mainland and the Islands 83·8 per cent of the voters went to the polls, and 4·8 per cent of these cast blank or spoiled ballot papers. The results for the mainland and Islands are shown in Table 7.1.

In addition four candidates were elected by emigrant Portuguese,

though only an estimated 4 per cent of these registered as voters. The PS
and PPD won the two European seats, the PPD and CDS the two for the rest
of the world. The general geographical pattern of voting of the previous
year was confirmed by the results, though, with a lower poll, the total vote
of both the PS and the PPD fell. The PCP vote increased by 80,000, but
given the fact that the MDP was not standing this was possibly misleading
(the latter pro-PCP group had polled 233,000 votes in 1975). The CDS
doubled its total vote to become the third largest party. The UDP vote also
doubled, but it was supported in 1976 by other Marxist-Leninist groups
which had gone to the polls with their own lists in 1975. All the nine
parties unsuccessful in returning any candidates polled less than 1 per
cent of the vote each (MES, FSP, MRPP, PPM, LCI, PDC, AOC, PCP[M-L] and
the Trotskyist newcomer the PRT (Workers' Revolutionary Party). In the
Islands and the north the PPD was predominant, though the CDS topped
the poll in Guarda and the PS again came first in Coimbra, Castelo
Branco, Oporto and Braga – in the last-mentioned the CDS took votes
from the PPD to allow this outcome. In the south the PCP (without
competition from the MDP) showed that it had more than held its own in
proletarian constituencies and topped the poll in rural Beja and Évora as
well as industrial Setúbal. In the Assembly of the Republic no party
commanded a majority so that, given Soares's independent stand, the
new constitutional system would be tested to the full with a minority
government.

Table 7.1   *Results of the Election of 25 April 1976*

Party	% of votes	No. of seats
PS	35·0	106
PPD	24·0	71
CDS	15·9	41
PCP	14·6	40
UDP	1·7	1

Before the new constitutional system could begin to function it was
necessary to have another election for the President of the Republic. The
choice of candidates gave rise to much debate and politicking in both
military and civilian circles. It seemed possible at one time that the 62-
year-old Costa Gomes would succeed in standing as a candidate of the
broad Left, but his vacillations and changes of direction had become too
much for important sectors of opinion although they had perhaps helped
to avert bloodshed at critical junctures in the past. In the event there were
four candidates. The candidate picked by the PPD (which had wanted to
be rid of Costa Gomes for some time) and supported by the CDS and the
PS, enjoying the approval of the consensus in the Council of the

Revolution and acceptable to the operational military, was the unsmiling 41-year-old General Ramalho Eanes, then Army Chief of Staff. Eanes was very much a professional soldier. He had had contacts with the MFA before 25 April 1974, at which time he was in Angola. He subsequently became the MFA's supervisor of the state television service, but was 'cleansed' by the Gonçalvists after 11 March for lack of revolutionary zeal. He supported the Nine in the summer of 1975 and commanded operations for the government on 25 November. As Army Chief of Staff, he set about planning the restructuring of the army with a view to making it a small professional force, with new equipment and integrated with NATO requirements. A friend but not a political follower of Spínola, he was seen by the ultra-Left as the man of 25 November, the Portuguese Pinochet:

> Sealed lips, dark glasses, a face of stone, an impeccable uniform, a liking for Wagner and poetry. A man of good breeding, defender of the professional army, of the pride of the officer corps, of the obedience of the soldiers, of discipline; in short, a solid defender of the bourgeoisie.

Though backed by parties which had got three-quarters of the votes in April, Eanes competed against three other candidates on 27 June. Hoping to get support from the PS rank and file and others worried by Eanes, the Premier, Admiral Pinheiro de Azevedo, decided to stand, with the result that the election nearly had to be cancelled when he had a heart attack – but it did not prove fatal. The PCP were not impressed by the Premier and put up a member of their Central Committee, Octavio Pato, as a candidate of leftist unity. Apart from the ease with which Pato (meaning duck) could be ridiculed, their plans were further spoiled by the openly divisionist character of the candidate of the ultra-Left, the candidate of the people, Otelo Saraiva de Carvalho. He had been released from detention in March as part of a general policy of emptying the gaols which applied not only to those held after 25 November, 11 March and 28 September but also to nearly all the ex-PIDE men (against whom no charges were brought, to the protests of the Left). His charismatic personality provided a focus for ultra-leftists (though Trotskyists were for Pato and official Maoists for Eanes): FSP, UDP, MES, PRP, the Syndicalist *Base*-FUT and other sets of initials and individuals came together in GDUPs (Dynamising Groups of Popular Unity). The candidate of the people defined his ideological position as that of some kind of Robin Hood.

The campaign was lively – so lively that one person was killed when a stone-throwing episode in Évora ended in gunfire. Eanes believed that UDP militants had tried to assassinate him. It was clear who would win, but the results contained surprises. There was a lower turnout than in

April: 75·4 per cent and 1·3 per cent of these voted with blank or spoiled ballot papers. The order of the candidates was: General Ramalho Eanes, 61·5 per cent of the valid votes; Major Saraiva de Carvalho, 16·5 per cent; Admiral Pinheiro de Azevedo, 14·4 per cent; and Comrade Pato, 7·6 per cent. Eanes managed over 70 per cent of the votes in the Islands and all the northern constituencies except Oporto. With the exception of Setúbal, where he was beaten by Otelo Saraiva de Carvalho, he topped the poll everywhere. Otelo Saraiva de Carvalho seems to have attracted much of the PCP vote, an indication of the attractions of personality rather than dogma. Pato, in fact, trailed behind him in every constituency except Ponta Delgada (Azores). On 14 July Eanes took over from Costa Gomes and pledged himself to 'assure and develop the conditions which have to guarantee the primacy of the democratic, law-bound state and the bases of a socialist society'. Constitutional legality replaced the revolutionary legitimacy of the previous two years. What sort of constitutional legality was this?

The new constitution of the Portuguese Republic was approved by the Constituent Assembly on 2 April 1976, with the respresentatives of the CDS voting against it on the grounds that it was insufficiently pluralistic and democratic and too socialistic: nevertheless, they emphasised that they would respect it. The constitutional text was the usual mixture of ambiguous platitudes and firm guidelines. It attempted to strike a balance between the powers of the President, the Assembly, the government and the courts, without forgetting the (at least transitional) importance of military influence in the shape of the Council of the Revolution. While the interpretations based upon the text will doubtless vary, according to the personalities and views of those holding particular offices, many commentators have categorised it as a semi-presidentialist constitution. In the Preamble of 'Fundamental Principles', Article 2 set the tone:

> The Portuguese Republic is a democratic state, based on popular sovereignty, on the respect for and the guarantee of fundamental rights and freedoms and on the democratic pluralism of expression and political organisation, which have as their objective the assurance of the transition towards socialism through the creation of conditions for the democratic exercise of power by the working classes.

Articles 3 and 10 acknowledged the role of the 'Movement of the Armed Forces' in constitutional arrangements, while Articles 9 and 10 spoke of the socialisation of the means of production and wealth and 'the collective appropriation of the principal means of production'.

In Section I civil rights were outlined in accordance with the Universal

Declaration on Human Rights. The death penalty was forbidden, as were violation of the right of *habeas corpus* and censorship. Freedom of religion, education, emigration, assembly and association was proclaimed, as was the state's commitment to full employment, equality of opportunity and regulation of wages and hours of work. The creation of workers' committees was recognised as a right, as were democratic trade union structures (but not compulsory membership), the right to strike, the illegality of lock-outs and the right to comprehensive social services. Co-operatives and experiments in self-management were encouraged, while expropriation of property had to be compensated. Section II, on economic organisation, stressed socialist relationships of production and committed the state to agrarian reform, balanced regional development and a system of democratic planning of the economy. Article 82, contrary to Section I, allowed expropriation without compensation of large estates, firms and shareholdings, while Article 83 said that 'all nationalisations effected since 25 April 1974 are irreversible conquests of the working classes', though these conquests could be reversed in the case of 'small and medium-sized enterprises indirectly nationalised'. Private enterprise was to be respected in principle but forbidden in the basic sectors. Planning was institutionalised and was to be in consonance with the construction of a socialist economy. Control of prices and advertising by the state was enunciated.

Section III concerned the organisation of political power. The President of the Republic was also President of the Council of the Revolution and Supreme Commander of the Armed Forces. Presidents had to be over 35 and could not seek re-election for a third five-year term; They were to be elected by universal suffrage and had to get over half the total votes. The President's power of dissolution of the Assembly, like his other important functions, was subject to the agreement of the Council of the Revolution. The Council of the Revolution – composed of the President, the Chief and Deputy Chief of Staff, the three service chiefs, the Premier (if a military man) and fourteen officers (eight chosen by the army, three each by the navy and air force) – was to advise the President, guarantee the functioning of democracy and the Constitution in line with 'the spirit . . . of 25 April', and be the political and legislative organ in military matters. In other words the Council was a democratic watchdog on President and government, while politicians could not interfere with the armed forces.

Regarding the Assembly of the Republic, deputies, elected by the de Hondt system of proportional representation for a four-year term, could not take their seats if they were public servants or members of the government. Legislation could be initiated by deputies or by government, while the Assembly could debate any Decree Law it thought fit. The government, however, was the policy making body, bound (by

Article 185) to carry out policies in line with the objectives of democracy and the construction of socialism. The Premier was appointed by the President, bearing in mind the advice of the Council of the Revolution and the composition of the Assembly, and the Premier put the names of ministers to the President for approval. The government was responsible both to the President and to the Assembly. Some attempt to prevent instability was to be found in the limitation on the number of motions of censure permitted. The independence of the judicial power was proclaimed and the jury system introduced for serious offences.

It was made clear that politico-administrative autonomy for the Azores and Madeira did not limit the unitary state's sovereignty. Regional assemblies were very much bound by the Assembly's decisions, while the powers devolved to regional assemblies and governments were supervised by a minister of the republic. (As it has worked out, the Azores and Madeira have PPD governments, but there is sufficient discontent with the restrictions placed on regional autonomy to keep alive separatist groups like FLA and FLAMA – illegal because regional, according to Article 311 – who argue that tourist and emigrant remittances and a guarantee of protection [presumably from the USA] would make independence viable.) The powers of local government or local autarchies, their method of election and their finances, were defined. The traditional administrative divisions were maintained with the additional provision that some powers could be delegated by the local autarchies to neighbourhood committees (territorially based popular organisations).

'The Portuguese armed forces', said Article 273, 'are part of the people and, identified with the spirit of the programme of the Armed Forces' Movement, ensure the continuation of the revolution of 25 April 1974'; furthermore the armed forces had 'the historic mission of guaranteeing the conditions permitting the pluralist and peaceful transition . . . towards democracy and socialism'. Nevertheless the armed forces were to be 'rigorously non-partisan' and were not to 'influence or impede the selection of a particular democratic path' (Article 275). Here, as elsewhere, a great deal depended on what was meant by socialism and who decided on the definition. Section IV gave a clue to the answer by saying that the Council of the Revolution decided what was or was not constitutional. Alongside the Council of the Revolution was a Constitutional Committee, five of whose nine members had to be jurists, whose function it was to advise the Council. The rules for revising the constitution – a function of the Assembly – were complex and rather obscure and were to be inoperative before the autumn of 1980.

It was the longest constitution in Portuguese history and is likely to be put to the test if ever the electorate chooses a non-socialist government, for the intention of the text, formulated under MFA influence, was clearly to make an anti-socialist government impossible. All parties were equal, but some parties were more equal than others. Clearly it was a document which best fitted the PS, the new dominant party of the regime. With President Eanes in office, the 52-year-old Mário Soares could now form the first constitutional government. He preferred to risk a single-party minority administration rather than enter into a coalition which would restrict his freedom of manœuvre more closely than negotiating the support or abstention of other parties on individual issues. The government was composed mostly of PS members, the numbers being made up by independent civilians such as Almeida Santos (Minister of Justice) and military men who had also served in previous provisional governments, such as Colonel Costa Brás (Internal Administration) and Colonel Firmino Miguel (Defence).

Soares presented his programme of government to the Assembly in August 1976. It was a long and detailed document promising legislation to give effect to the provisions of the constitution and concentrating, like the programmes of governments elsewhere during the world recession, on economic and social questions. It was a programme which struck an uneasy balance between keeping down public expenditure and going ahead with social reforms. The difficulties to be faced were many and varied, and external factors rather than the confusion of the revolutionary process were the cause of many of them. As governments discovered in other countries, how best to cope with the situation was problematical. Soares, like Gonçalves before him, found that one austerity programme after another was called for to try and cut consumption, and they both urged the virtues of hard work, wage restraint and discipline. Gonçalves, hard-working and austere like Salazar, combined his appeals for the spirit of sacrifice in economic affairs with a stress on national independence reminiscent of the New State's early years. The difference between Salazar and Gonçalves was not just that between corporativism and socialism, but also in the circumstances in which they operated: the 'legacy of fascism' was a less underdeveloped economy more heavily dependent on foreign trade than half a century before. While anxious to find new markets, which could mean some diversification of dependence, the *bon viveur* Soares was an enthusiast for Portugal's integration into the EEC: he was more of an internationalist than Gonçalves.

The aspirations and actions of the first constitutional government need to be seen in the light of economic and social policies pursued by the six provisional governments. In the field of social policy the aim had been to extend the scope of Caetano's 'social state' so as to realise a complete system of social welfare. Retirement and disability pensions in the private sector were increased, as were the more generous provisions for state and local government employees. The social insurance system for farm workers, family bonus schemes and maternity provisions were improved and tentative steps taken towards the creation of a national health service. Innovations included the introduction of a social pension, unemployment subsidies and a national minimum wage, which was progressively increased with the rise in the cost of living. However, it is as yet difficult to tell to what extent these have remained paper reforms: it has been estimated that half the workforce are paid less than the minimum wage, a situation accepted by many workers in small firms which would go bankrupt and bring unemployment were they to pay it.

In 1975 an institute for assistance to national refugees was created to cope with the influx of *retornados* from the colonies, many of whom arrived destitute. The exact number of *retornados* is unknown, but was officially estimated at 650,000 in May 1976: since then the numbers have been increased by further arrivals from Mozambique. The *retornados* have presented an enormous social problem, particularly at a time of economic recession. They swelled the ranks of the unemployed and added to the movement of protest against the government. While it would seem that up to 90 per cent found accommodation with or through relatives, the remaining 10 per cent had temporarily to be put up in hotels or lived in wretched conditions in refugee camps or overcrowded housing. The programme of assistance was another drain on the state's finances, but the shoddy way in which *retornados* have been treated has been criticised not only by the refugees themselves but also by international relief organisations. Evidence of continuity between the new and the old Portugal was provided by the scandalous revelation that a fifth of the funds for 1976 were misappropriated (and 12 per cent of the funds allocated were provided by the USA). The *retornados* have also added to the housing problem. The construction of low-cost housing is a high priority of government and has the added advantage of cutting unemployment through the revitalisation of the building industry. State funds are, however, short and this is another area where foreign aid plays a part.

As in other countries, the increase in unemployment in Portugal has been the result of a combination of factors. Apart from the *retornados,* the figures have been swollen by the release of conscripts from the armed services, roughly 100,000 by March 1976. With the decreased demand for labour resulting from the world depression, the flow of emigrants also decreased: 122,000 emigrated in 1973, but only 70,000 in 1974 and 44,000 in 1975. Unemployment has resulted from decreased investment, international and national, due in part to political uncertainty: while investment by the state rose from 6·4 million contos in 1973 to 14·6 million in 1975, overall investment fell by 40 per cent in 1974–5 (in 1973 private investment had been 81 per cent of the total). Lay-offs and redundancies were inevitable, but were naturally resisted by the workforce, and with considerable success in some cases. This was partly reflected in the losses made by public-owned concerns in 1975: CUF made a loss of 400,000, Siderurgia Nacional a loss of 700,000 contos. The highest rates of redundancies were in the textile industry (hit by the fall in international demand), electronics (where foreign investors had been drawn to Portugal by low wages in earlier years) and the building trade. Yet the exact number of unemployed was unknown – in part a reflection of the confusion into which public services were thrown after April 1974. It is also said that official figures understate the problem. Compared with the official figure of 90,000 in 1970, official figures for unemployment at the end of 1975 suggested around 330,000, or about 10 per cent of the active working population. However, unofficial estimates suggested that 500,000 (about 15 per cent) was a more realistic figure then. Official figures suggested a 16 per cent level of unemployment at the end of 1976 and 25 per cent was a round figure mentioned unofficially in mid-1977.

Apart from the general effects of the fall in demand occasioned by the world depression which would have prompted foreign companies to cut back in Portugal anyway, the country became a high-risk area for the outside investor from April 1974. In an effort to reassure the private investor, a foreign investments code was promulgated in April 1976. After the fall of General Gonçalves in August 1975 substantial aid was forthcoming from the EEC countries (especially West Germany), Portugal's EFTA partners and the United States (which had started giving aid in late 1974). Much of this aid was tied to specific development projects with which the disorganised bureaucracy found difficulty in coping. The world recession is not yet over and confidence has not yet been restored, which is perhaps not surprising in view of unbalanced budgets, the balance of payments crisis and general 'stagflation'.

A budget deficit of 3·6 million contos in 1973 became one of 7·1 million in 1974; in 1975 it rose to 29 million and in 1976 to 59 million. The rise in commodity prices, especially oil, and the fall in demand for Portuguese exports hit the balance of trade hard: a trade deficit of 28·4 million contos in 1973 rose to 55·8 million in 1974, but decreased to 48·3 million in 1975 (owing to cutting back on and taxing heavily non-essential imports, falling investment and difficulties in obtaining credits). Nevertheless, it rose again in 1976 to 63·3 million. Portugal's usual sources for balancing her payments – colonial profits, tourist and emigrant remittances – suffered in varying degrees from the effects of revolution. The benefits of the Angolan trade surplus disappeared, while the world recession was probably the major cause of the fall in tourist receipts (13·5 million contos in 1973, 13 million in 1974, 9·5 million in 1975). Emigrants' remittances fluctuated with the political uncertainty (28·1 million contos in 1973, 29·1 million in 1974, but down to 25·3 million in 1975). Both these sources of revenue showed signs of rapid recovery in 1976–7. The main weakness, as usual, lay in exports, where a fall in value (from 58·1 million to 49·5 million contos) was recorded in 1974 and 1975. Higher costs and falling foreign demand were among the causes, though increased competition in agricultural produce from Spain, Italy and the Third World also played a part. In 1976 the value of exports rose to 54·8 million contos. The imposition of quotas on Portuguese textiles (the main export) by Britain and Sweden have hit the country badly (in 1974–75 textile exports alone fell in value from 16·2 to 12·6 million contos).

With the chaos of decolonisation and the breakdown of the Angolan and Mozambican economies, former colonial markets shrank, while attempts were made to find new markets in the Eastern bloc to help the situation and also to lessen dependence on the West, with which Portugal does four-fifths of its trade. A tentative indication of the success, or lack of success, of these policies is given in Table 7.2 (the figures are percentages of the total of imports and exports).

Table 7.2   *The Changing Patterns of Trade, 1973–1975*

	1973		1975 (January–November)	
	Imports	*Exports*	*Imports*	*Exports*
EEC and EFTA	56·5	62·5	48·8	65·5
Other OECD countries	20·2	16·4	21·0	14·2
Soviet bloc and Yugoslavia	1·4	0·6	2·3	2·2
Colonies and ex-colonies	10·1	14·8	5·3	8·8

With the fall of Gonçalves relations with the EEC improved, resulting in an interim agreement between Portugal and the Common Market in September 1976 which helped some Portuguese exports and allowed the country to postpone the tariff reductions agreed in 1972. Financial help was forthcoming but only served to keep Portugal's trade going and no more. The country has about 800 tons of gold left from the New State (worth 28 million contos at the offical exchange rate), of which in 1976 some 40 per cent was collateral for loans. The real weak point was the shortage of liquid reserves, which by mid-1976 were equivalent to a month's imports. (Total reserves fell from 62·7 million contos in March 1974 to 39·6 million in December 1975). How increasing foreign debts were to be paid was problematical. The once hard escudo, like other once proud currencies, began to depreciate (for example 15·5 per cent against the German mark between February and July 1976). In February 1977 the escudo was formally devalued by 15 per cent against the pound sterling and in August the decision to allow it to float downwards was made. Though this should help exports if costs can be kept down, it will also have the effect of increasing the cost of essential imports of food, oil and raw materials.

A final combination of economic factors which suggested that Portugal's problems had more to do with the world recession than with the disturbance of the revolutionary process was the phenomenon of stagnation coupled with increasing inflation. Whereas in 1973 gross domestic product grew by 6 per cent and the figure for 1974 was 5·3 per cent, 1975 saw a diminution of 2·7 per cent (a phenomenon observable also in Britain, France, West Germany, the USA, etc.). Portuguese extractive industries showed diminutions of 4·3 and 7·1 per cent in 1974 and 1975, while the index of industrial production rose by 2·5 per cent in 1974 but fell by 4·7 per cent in 1975. The rate of inflation, already 20 per cent in 1973, rose to 25 per cent in 1974; after slowing somewhat due to price controls on food, rents, etc., in 1975, by the end of that year it was estimated at 30 per cent and in 1976 the official figure was 26 per cent. In mid-1977 unofficial estimates (always higher than official figures) suggested inflation was running at a rate of 40 per cent.

Wage increases in 1974–5 suggested, on official figures, a rise in real wages, even though popular opinion subjectively adhered to the belief that this was not so. Since 1975 determined efforts to slow down or freeze wage increases would suggest a fall in real wages. In the post-revolutionary period this has probably contributed to the growth of political apathy and cynicism, a development paralleled by the demobilisation of working-class militancy. While the government revised the trade union *unicidade* imposed in 1975, socialist hopes of creating a viable rival to Intersindical have not so far been fulfilled. While the PS, with the PPD and MRPP, control many unions in the service sector, the steam has escaped from the syndicalist momentum of non-PCP industrial workers in the Greater Lisbon area. The pro-PCP Intersindical in January 1977 held a congress attended by unions representing 85 per cent of workers, which was a major blow to the PS-supported 'Open Letter' movement which had hoped to found a successful rival with the support of Maldonado Gonelha (who replaced the left-wing socialist Marcelo Curto as Minister of Labour in March 1977). Intersindical, under its new title of CGTP/IN (General Confederation of Portuguese Workers/National Intersindical), therefore remained the powerful spokesman of workers in a time of falling living standards.

The attempts of the socialist government to hold down wages and rectify the hurried legislation decreed by Gonçalves's government have, of course, been opposed by Cunhal and the PCP. To them, government policies for economic recovery have been equivalent to policies for capitalist recovery, policies by definition anti-working class. Heading a minority government needing the goodwill of the PPD and/or CDS in order to survive, and still rejecting PCP offers of coalition, the pragmatic Soares has had a stormy passage. He was confirmed in his views on Cunhal by the 8th Congress of the PCP (November 1976) at which the latter made it clear that he was not going to evolve towards any Euro-Communist position. Though not considering the PS reactionary, Cunhal noted its reliance on the PPD (reactionary and in favour of capitalist recovery) and condemned the CDS as merely the legal face of potential dictatorship. The PS itself, like other Socialist parties, is a coalition of tendencies which do not always find co-existence easy. The 2nd Congress of the PS was also held in November 1976, coinciding with the resignation of the Minister for Agriculture, Lopes Cardoso. Soares and his moderate wing successfully fought off a challenge presented by the Marxist Left of the party, whose list for its national committee got a quarter of the votes (and therefore 38 out of the 151 places), compared to the 38 per cent obtained by Manuel Serra's list in 1974. As could be expected, some left-wingers have left the party since the congress.

Apart from arguments over economic reconstruction and the favouritism shown to socialists when civil governorships or other posts had to be filled – 'the party system . . . works among us [Portuguese] as a clientelism of government', noted one journalist – the most controversial legislation so far has concerned the demarcation of the public and private sectors of the economy and agrarian reform in the south. The wave of ill-prepared nationalisations decreed by Gonçalves's governments after 11 March marked the demise of the old plutocracy but left behind considerable confusion. If the economy was to be kept in working order, it was necessary to restore confidence and find an adequate number of trained personnel to run the public sector. After 11 March there was an economically extremely serious exodus of skilled managerial strata as well as owners of small enterprises with business know-how. Workers' control and/or public ownership could not, of themselves, keep factories operational, nor was the state's capacity to provide credit unlimited. With the advent of Pinheiro de Azevedo's government things began to change and the flow of managerial talent was reversed. A number of smaller enterprises, such as textile mills, were handed back to their previous owners in early 1976, while workers' committees in many enterprises themselves petitioned former owners or managers to come back in a managerial capacity: without managerial skills to keep firms going, workers' committees discovered that continued losses meant increasing unemployment. The problems faced by Soares's government included the need to curb public expenditure (and therefore stop pouring precious financial resources into the bottomless pit of inefficient enterprises) and the need to prevent bureaucratic proliferation by putting smaller enterprises, indirectly nationalised through the takeover of banking, back into the private sector. In mid-May 1977, with PPD support, PCP opposition and CDS benevolent abstention, a law was passed redefining the limits of the public sector. State intervention was to be confined to the key sector of banking and insurance, basic industries, public utilities and transport. The rest of the economy was open to private investment. The PCP denounced yet another onslaught on the revolutionary conquests which it was integrally defending, and feared that up to two thirds of state-controlled firms would be denationalised.

Undoubtedly the hottest political issue so far has been the question of agrarian reform. In 1975 (principally between 11 March and 25 November) approximately 1 million hectares of land south of the Tagus in the Alentejo and Ribatejo were occupied by agricultural workers, often led by PCP militants. The promise of agrarian reform was made in Melo Antunes's ill-fated economic plan of February 1975. With occupations already under way Gonçalves's government produced hasty Decree legislation during the summer which endeavoured to describe, by means of a complicated points system, the maximum size of holdings which could not be expropriated (the lower limit depending on the quality of land and whether or not it was irrigated). Those occupying the lands either formed co-operatives or, much more frequently, organised themselves under the aegis of the PCP into people's *herdades* or units of collective production which took names such as Wall of Steel, Cry of the Revolution, Unity and Happiness, Álvaro Cunhal, Heroic Plain – or, more simply, It's Hard but it's Ours. These collectives and co-operatives were financed by the emergency credit arrangements of the Institute of Agrarian Reorganisation, which also aided small and medium-sized farmers north of the Tagus.

After 25 November some efforts were made by the socialist Minister of Agriculture, Lopes Cardoso, to tidy up the loose ends. Expropriations were confined to the southern half of the country and a complaints' system created as first stages. The total area expropriable under Gonçalves's laws was about 1·6 million hectares, of which 1·3 million were occupied in early 1976. Pressure against the wildcat occupations, as they were not inaccurately called, came from the farmers' association CAP, which on 24 November 1975 and again in January 1976 threatened to take direct action by cutting off the capital's food supplies unless occupations and expropriations ceased and compensation to owners was guaranteed. Meanwhile CAP members, who included many *minifundiários,* were also upset by the Decree Law on rural tenancies of April 1975 which represented an effort to increase the security of lessees. However, written contracts were unpopular and after a year only a fifth of the estimated 300,000 agreements had been drawn up in all parts of the country. Emphyteutic tenure was abolished and Lopes Cardoso authorised the return of common lands in certain areas.

Lopes Cardoso's policy was to proceed slowly to the expropriation of land designated under the Decree Law of 1975, after adjusting the points system to protect slightly larger private farms than those covered by the Law of 1975. He also promised to have land not scheduled for expropriation returned to its owners – about two-thirds of the area actually occupied in February 1976. The communist Under-Secretary for Agriculture Vítor Louro, however, said that the existing occupations would be legalised: he was dismissed when he urged workers to resist eviction. Lopes Cardoso remained as Minister of Agriculture under Soares and began evictions of the occupiers of 101 farms, some of them foreign owned, at the end of September 1976. As could be expected, violent clashes sometimes ensued with the GNR or the army, and Lopes Cardoso apparently came round to the view that a number of token evictions could be followed by legalisation of other occupations. In November 1976 he resigned and was replaced by a less leftist socialist, António Barreto, who intended to implement party policy. This led to more confrontations and dissidence among Gonçalvist-appointed members of the Institute of Agrarian Reorganisation.

A new law of agrarian reform was introduced and inquiries made into the use to which state credit had been put by the units of collective production. Apart from technical considerations influencing the new law, the whole southern agrarian question was a trial of strength between the PS government, supported by the CAP, PPD and CDS, on the one side, and the PCP on the other. It is difficult to assess how successful the collective units of production have been. The PCP naturally claimed success and could point to the fact that a much larger area was collectively worked by their agricultural workers' union than by the socialist-supported 'movement of co-operative unity'. Agricultural production had also risen. Critics argued that the units of collective production were PCP fiefs characterised by the use of intimidation, that the state's credit was supporting surplus labour and paying for the PCP, that the rise in production was spurious because marginal land was being put under cereals and would soon be exhausted, that olive trees were not properly cared for and that the number of livestock slaughtered could lead to serious depletions of the national herd in the longer run, even if it boosted meat production figures in the short run. The new law, said by the PCP to be unconstitutional, was passed in July 1977. The PPD/PSD supported the government in exchange for repeal of the law on rural tenancies, the CDS objected to socialist land reform, while the PCP and PS dissidents (including Lopes Cardoso) opposed it. The new text enlarged the area of non-expropriable farms, promised compensation to owners, favoured co-operatives of small farmers (which the PCP pointed out had proved failures in the past) and restricted the size of collectives, which had to be run in co-partnership with the state, and not by trade unions, to the maximum size allowable for other individual holdings. It remained to be seen whether such a law could be enforced without further violence.

The passage of the law indicated the growing tendency of the socialist government to ally with the PPD which, since the autumn of 1976, went by the name of PSD (Social Democratic party). The dissidence of left-wing PS members was interpreted by some as a further sign of decay in that party: true socialists, it was argued, were leaving what was increasingly a social democratic party of government whose motive power came from patronage rather than conviction. In this respect the PS was said by some to resemble the Democrats of the First Republic, while the PSD and CDS were like the other two republican groups of that time. The CDS, whose leader described the socialists as the new conservatives, practised a policy of selective opposition and had its gaze on constitutional revision after 1980. Its leader, Freitas do Amaral, in the summer of 1976 successfully prevented his party being drawn into a right-wing broad front (Kaúlza de Arriaga's MIRN – Independent Movement of National Reconstruction) and defended his position against the right-wing challenge of Galvão de Melo within the party.

All this, despite the importance of the issues, sounded like 'normal parliamentary politics'; while manoeuvres and deals were bound to provoke cynicism and apathy, they did not necessarily represent symptoms of disease within the democratic political system. A relative decline in poltical interest could be observed in the lower turnout (64·6 per cent) for the local government elections on 12 December 1976 – partly because it was the fourth election in eighteen months. The main contestants were the PS, PSD, CDS and the PCP, which allied with MDP and other elements in FEPU (United People Electoral Front); other contestants included the monarchists of the PPM and the GDUPs, whose subsequent efforts to turn themselves into a united ultra-leftist movement were frustrated by the usual fissiparous tendencies. The results for the municipalities are shown in Table 7.3.

Table 7.3   *Results of the Local Government Elections of 12 December 1976*

Party	% of votes	No. of councillors	No. of mayors
PS	33·2	691	115
PSD	24·3	623	115
FEPU	17·7	267	37
CDS	16·6	317	36
GDUPs	2·5	5	—
PPM	0·2	3	1

The results were further confirmation of the political pattern observable in the previous elections if the results were examined by *distritos*. The PSD swept the Islands with over 50 per cent of the votes and topped the poll everywhere in the north except for Guarda (CDS) and Oporto, Coimbra and Castelo Branco (PS). The PS also topped the poll in Lisbon and Santarém but got its highest percentages (over 40 per cent) in Portalegre and Faro. As expected FEPU topped the poll (47 per cent in each case) in Beja, Évora and Setúbal. The monarchists managed to elect a mayor in Vila Real, which was perhaps consoling for Duarte Nuno who was to die a fortnight later, being succeeded as claimant by his son Duarte João.

In the Portugal of 1977 less was heard about the armed forces. Their spectacular eruption onto the political scene in 1974-5 had at last, it seemed, been succeeded by a return to barracks. The Council of the Revolution created by the constitution of 1976 could still have an important role to play in a political crisis, but the tendency has been towards its marginalisation. The restructured Council of 1976 included General Eanes (as both President and Chief of the General Staff) and the three service chiefs of staff as well as some familiar names from the days of the MFA and the Nine: Vítor Alves, Melo Antunes, Vasco Lourenço, Vítor Crespo, Franco Charais, Pezarat Correia. Something of a stir was created when Pires Veloso wrote a letter from Oporto suggesting that the Councillors who were not *ex officio* represented no one and rumours of dissension were still reported. Politically President Eanes, who reiterated his opposition to any form of dictatorship, seemed to keep a balance. The restructuring of the armed forces proceeded towards a small professional army of 32, 000 including an armoured brigade for NATO to be based at Santa Margarida (90 miles north-east of Lisbon).

Re-equipment with American tanks and aircraft from West Germany accompanied a firmly pro-Western stance in foreign policy. While in 1975 such as Rosa Coutinho placed emphasis on a Third World non-aligned position for Portugal to prevent people saying its citizens were 'lackeys of Europe', the commitment of the PS, PSD and CDS is to a European future in the political as well as in the economic sense. (The PCP, unlike its major West European counterparts, bitterly opposed this line.) On 28 March 1977 Portugal formally applied to join the EEC, following Greece but anticipating Spain. While countries like Britain and West Germany talked of investing in democracy in southern Europe by aiding the country economically, Italian and French agricultural and wine interests viewed an enlargement of the EEC with considerable apprehension. Any transition period to full Portuguese membership is likely to be lengthy. Nevertheless Europe is the obvious answer to a certain crisis of national identity following upon decolonisation. There are those who ask whether Portugal can live without its colonies and that perennial minority of 'Iberianists' now argue that the loss of empire means the loss of independent Portugal's *raison d'être*. Though the old Iberian Pact has gone, relations with Spain remained correct during the revolutionary process – Portugal was dependent on Spain for overland trade and 30 per cent of its electricity. In 1976–7 relations were again warmer, while Portuguese, always sensitive to foreign opinions, wrily observed how quickly Soares was eclipsed by Suárez in the world's press.

It is impossible to say with any precision what outside forces influenced events in Portugal in 1974–6. Clearly the need for foreign economic help was one factor keeping the country in the Western orbit: there was a time when Portugal saw itself as the Romania of NATO and that coincided with a Romanian grant of credit. What the outside world said and wrote was still important. Foreign criticism was resented by those criticised just as much as it was by the rulers of the New State, while foreign praise was welcomed and sought after; Soares's international stardom was a definite domestic asset. At another level of contact revolutionary tourists found an enchanting welcome (at least initially) on the far Left which boosted their egos as they experienced a revolution. From the Lisbon ultra-Left viewpoint they were useful contacts and could swell demonstrations in the summer of 1975: the pronunciation of slogans was carefully rehearsed by those who protested one night against international capitalist interference in Portugal's internal affairs, and the next against international capitalism's boycott of Portugal. The fact that civil war did not break out robbed the country of its opportunity to become the Spain (or the new Vietnam) of the younger generation in Western Europe. The Portuguese Revolution turned out to be rather disappointing in the end for the ideologically highly-motivated. Nevertheless there were outside forces at work whose operations were, by definition, covert. Though the details will probably never be known, it seems certain that the PCP was heavily subsidised by the countries of the Soviet bloc, while the PS and other anti-communist democratic forces were aided by the Americans and West European Socialist parties (channels for American funds). Right-wing forces in 1975 would seem to have had contacts with the French and West German intelligence services, and possibly the CIA (who were also accused of financing 'Maoist' ultra-leftists). Conservatives, by contrast but just as reasonably, speculated on the role played by the Soviet Ambassador (Kalinin, fresh from Cuba), the KGB and the Cuban intelligence service. The beauty and usefulness of conspiracy theories lies in the ease with which they can be invented, while, by definition, they can never be satisfactorily refuted.

How much change and how much continuity there has been in Portugal since 25 April is a question which could be endlessly, and possibly fruitlessly, debated. Some would argue that socio-cultural change has been the most important aspect. The usually turbulent universities were thrown into further confusion after 25 April and here 'cleansing' was perhaps more thoroughgoing than anywhere else.

Faculties became revolutionary communes and the excitement infected secondary schools where novel experiments in self-management also took place. True to advanced educational ideas, notions of hierarchy, élitism and unequal ability were consigned to the proverbial historical dustbin. Curricula and texts were changed, political intoxication was general and chaos ensued: the government admitted no new students to university for the 1974–5 academic year. From 1975, however, there was something of a backlash and in 1976, as in other spheres of social activity, revolutionary exhaustion and a certain 'demobilisation' of militancy became apparent. Sottomayòr Cardia, socialist Minister of Education in the first constitutional government, set about restoring some order. Inevitably this led to clashes which mirrored the evolution of the situation in other spheres. There was a kind of counter-cleansing of the victors of 1974–5 in universities and the ministry, and the phenomenon of bureaucratic recovery was manifest. Students still demonstrated, but in May 1977 the University of Coimbra was closed. Students, like other demonstrators, discovered that the return of the military to barracks was accompanied by the re-emergence of police forces willing to obey orders. Some wondered whether the old methods had not returned.

For the intellectual world, however, cherished freedom had at last come, and the events of 1975 underlined for many just what a scarce commodity it could be. The most obvious cultural change after 25 April – apart from that of vocabulary – was the flood of leftist and Marxist literature in bookshops and on news-stands, fairly quickly followed by an apparent vogue for pornography. The liberation process extended to the cinema, where there was lost time to be made up: films such as Eisenstein's *Battleship Potemkin* vied for popularity with the commercial film-makers' latest salacious offerings. A French visitor concluded that this was a Marx-*Emmannuelle* revolution. Despite the increasing parrot-like uniformity of the Lisbon press in 1974–5 and somewhat curious content of television transmissions, strange anomalies could be found. Caetano's defence of his premiership was openly sold in Portugal, but for some months typographers refused to print translations of such works as Solzhenitsyn's *August 1914*. Rádio Clube Português juxtaposed condemnations of capitalist imperialism with commercials urging people to drink Schweppes lemonade. After 25 November ideological pluralism became more of a reality as new publications started up and the typographers abandoned their claims to censorship. Broadcasting was nationalised, which meant the end of the PCP-dominated Rádio Clube Português/Emissora da Liberdade. Only Rádio Renascença, returned to the church at the end of 1975, remained outside the state's Radiodifusão Portuguesa. A 'counter-cleansing' of state-owned newspapers and broadcasting took place to ensure 'ideological pluralism', but it was soon noted that the party in government, the PS, received a disproportionate amount of broadcasting time: to be on the side of the situation helped job security, as always. After 25 November *fados* were again heard on the radio, having been banished on the grounds that they encouraged listlessness and fatalism and were therefore inimical to social progress and enlightenment. Symbols are important: the significance of the change brought by 25 November was possibly most vividly demonstrated by the Braganza studio of Emissora Nacional playing *Land of Hope and Glory,* adopted by the CDS as its anthem, late that night.

Certainly the period since 25 April has seen a burst of creativity. Exiled intellectuals have returned, new plays have been staged, new literature written in the heat of the moment. The most obvious sign of this release of artistic energy has been the profusion of (more or less) spontaneous wall paintings and poster art (this latter, if officially sponsored, could be very lucrative). While people's artists expressed their distaste for the Gulbenkian Foundation as a purveyor of imported culture, they themselves often manifested their indigenous talents with stylised portraits of Lenin or Che Guevara or cloth-capped workers bearing large red flags. Portuguese humour became more politicised and it too took to the walls in paint. A collection of the *graffiti* of 1974–5, whether serious or not (it was sometimes difficult to tell), would be fascinating. Perhaps two examples of spontaneity in Lisbon in 1975 deserve special mention. With decolonisation in full swing and the threat of separatism in the Adjacent Islands, someone wrote: 'Independence for the Berlengas' (a cluster of granite rocks just off the west coast of Portugal). With the fear of a new authoritarianism in the air, someone else wrote: 'We apologise for this democratic interlude. Normal dictatorship will be resumed as soon as possible.'

The third anniversary of 25 April in 1977, which to most people seemed more like the thirtieth because of the amount of history crammed into such a short space of time, naturally provided the occasion for stocktaking. In his Easter homily, the Bishop of Oporto recalled that 25 April was 'something which three years ago promised to be a dawn of flowers and hope', but 'now the flowers have wilted and in many faltering hearts the hopes seem to have died'. The cleric who had spent ten years in exile for his criticism of social injustice and authoritarianism concluded: 'To put essential order back into [people's] spirits is what Portuguese society needs more than bread to eat.'

The influential Lisbon weekly *Expresso* headed its editorial 'A country at the crossroads':

Commented on in the most diverse places, 25 April comes more and more to be the excuse for every person, every group, every faction to try and sing their own praises and register their own complaints, to assert their own opinions and make their own criticisms, to assert their own indispensability and the dispensability of the others.

Few are those who do not claim for themselves, each in his own way, the reviving spirit of April, participatory activism in the struggle against the fallen regime, a coherent position during the three crowded years that have gone by. Few are those, however, who can, with a clear conscience, lay claim to this spirit, this coherence, this participation.

In fact 25 April is surrounded with a lot of forgetfulness, a lot of appropriation and little truth . . .

To each his own truth? Perhaps, but also to each his own theoretical construction and practical application thereof on the sometimes devious road to the gaining and retention of power.

With forgetfulness, appropriations and various truths, and the clashes to which they give rise, Portugal has changed a lot in the last three years. Political freedom has been won, some social injustices have been put right, the financial and economic situation has become complicated or deteriorated. Decolonisation (for some exemplary, for others criminal, for others the only one possible) has been achieved and the constitution (for some a perfect and infallible primer, for others an absurdity, for others what was possible at the time, taking into account the pact(s) and the political situation) has been made. There have been four elections and the institutions have begun to function. We have not reached the 'oasis of Europe' of which Mário Soares speaks, but, particularly since 25 November . . . a slow normalisation of national life has taken place.

Yet the positive side of the account was counterbalanced by its negative side:

One historical cycle has closed without an immediate and possible alternative in terms of national identity. Outwardly many things have changed, from dress to language, from the capacity to make demands to the liberation of the expression of thought, but no renewed cultural foundation has been laid nor, in diverse aspects, have mentalities changed (we continue to work harder abroad than at home; the need for paternal guidance remains, albeit clothed in new apparel; the gulf between town and country is still there; the centralism of Lisbon has been accentuated).

Three years later, the intentions of the PCP having been thwarted, the novel way to socialism having failed, we are still a country at the crossroads . . . It is true that absolute national independence does not exist, but it is no less true that, with the passage of time, we are heading for almost complete economic (and, therefore, political) dependence. . .

Meditation in depth on how to get off the crossroads in time becomes more and more urgent. Otherwise, because mental structures have changed little, we shall go on putting off solutions and accepting, passively, the consequences of our proverbial fatalism.

Once again in Portuguese history, a burst of feverish activity had given way to gloomy listlessness. Neither Spínola's Sebastianism, nor the regenerationism of Vasco Gonçalves and the MFA, nor the cosmopolitan triumphalism of Mário Soares had been able to inspire a widespread sense of national revival.

Poets, it is sometimes said, have a sensitivity to atmosphere and powers of divination not given to ordinary mortals. The changes of mood in the country were reflected and anticipated in some short pieces by the poet **Sofia de Melo Breyner Andresen**. *25 April* was written two days after the event:

> This is the dawn that I awaited
> The daybreak whole and clear
> When we emerge from the night and the silence
> And live free in the substance of time

Although written in June 1974, *With Fury and Rage* anticipated the excesses of the revolutionary process:

> With fury and rage I accuse the demagogue
> and his capitalism of words
>
> For one must know that the word is sacred
> That long long ago a people brought it forth
> And in it put their trusting soul
>
> Long long ago in the beginning
> Consciousness was formed by the word
>
> . . . .
>
> With fury and rage I accuse the demagogue
> Who furthers himself in the shadow of the word
> And with the word makes power and sport
> And transforms words into money
> As is done with wheat and with land

Project, dated 4 July 1974, was perhaps appropriate to the needs of Portuguese in 1977:

> Long white wall of Alentejo
> Long line of billowing wheat
> Fair perfection of each ear
> I believe in the purity of the earthy
>
> I believe in the project
> Rational clear and poetic

The future holds no certainties save uncertainty.

Guide to Further Reading

This guide is not intended as a complete checklist for the specialist but rather, as befits the purposes of the text, as a select bibliography for the reader who wishes to follow up aspects of the subject. It is weighted in favour of books rather than articles and in favour of works available in English. For convenience of reference, it is divided (somewhat arbitrarily) into sections rather different from the chapters of the text.

BACKGROUND AND GENERAL

Those seeking a reliable general history of the country should consult A. H. de Oliveira Marques, *History of Portugal* (2nd edn, New York, 1976). Cast in a more traditional mould are H. V. Livermore, *A New History of Portugal* (2nd edn, Cambridge, 1976) and Charles E. Nowell's shorter *Portugal* (Englewood Cliffs, New Jersey, 1973). Sarah Bradford, *Portugal* (London, 1973) provides a good introduction.

On geography, the detailed wartime Admiralty Geographical Handbooks on *Spain and Portugal*, Vols I, II and IV (London, 1941-5) are still useful. More recent texts placing Portugal firmly in its Peninsular setting include J. Vilá Valentí, *La Péninsule ibérique* (Paris, 1968) and Michel Drain's brief *Géographie de la Péninsule ibérique* (3rd edn, Paris, 1972). A good tourists' introduction is Franz Villier, *Portugal* (London, 1963 but now updated in its original French version: Paris, 1976) which contrasts with more romantic examples of the genre such as Marie Noële Kelly, *This Delicious Land, Portugal* (London, 1956). The south coast is described by Charles E. Wuerpel, *The Algarve, Province of Portugal* (Newton Abbot, 1974) while border areas are examined in Antonio Pintado and Eduardo Barrenechea, *La raya de Portugal: la frontera del subdesarrollo* (Madrid, 1972). A standard Portuguese geographical text is Orlando Ribeiro, *Portugal, o Mediterrâneo e o Atlântico* (2nd edn. Lisbon, 1963).

Social life, conditions and folklore are surveyed by Paul Descamps, *Le Portugal: la vie sociale actuelle* (Paris, 1935); by J. Leite de Vasconcellos, *Etnografia portuguesa*, Vols III and IV (Lisbon, 1941-58); and by Rodney Gallop, *Portugal: A Book of Folk-Ways* (Cambridge, 1936). José Cutileiro, *A Portuguese Rural Society* (Oxford, 1971), is a revealing social anthropologist's study of a community in the Upper Alentejo. Those interested in ethnopsychology will enjoy Fernando Pessoa, *Análise da vida mental portuguesa: ensaios críticos* (Oporto, no date) and A. Jorge Dias, *Portuguese Contribution to Cultural Anthropology* (Johannesburg, 1964).

THE NEW STATE: POLITICS AND RELIGION

General surveys of the period include Hugh Kay, *Salazar and Modern Portugal* (London, 1970), sympathetic to the regime, and António de Figueiredo, *Portugal: Fifty Years of Dictatorship* (Harmondsworth, 1975), hostile to the regime; Peter Fryer and Patricia McGowan Pinheiro, *Oldest Ally: A Portrait of Salazar's Portugal* (London, 1961) is still useful and is more than a political history. Possibly the best sympathetic biography of the dictator is Jacques Ploncard d'Assac's *Salazar* (Paris, 1967), while some insight into his thinking may be gleaned from António Ferro, *Salazar: Portugal and her Leader* (London, 1939) and António de Oliveira Salazar, *Doctrine and Action: Internal and Foreign Policy of the New Portugal, 1928–1939* (London, 1939), a collection of speeches. Publication of what promises to be a standard biography has begun: Franco Nogueira, *Salazar, Vol. 1: a mocidade e os princípios, 1889–1928* (Coimbra, 1977). On the years preceding the New State one may consult the somewhat idiosyncratic account by the Goan V. de Bragança-Cunha, *Revolutionary Portugal, 1910–1936* (London, 1937) and Jorge Campinos's straightforward *A Ditadura Militar 1926/1933* (Lisbon, 1975).

The corporative aspects of politics are rather controversially discussed in Howard J. Wiarda's *Corporatism and Development: the Portuguese Experience* (Amherst, Massachusetts, 1977). The New State's constitutional arrangements are studied in F. I. Pereira dos Santos, *Un État corporatif: la Constitution sociale et politique* (Paris, 1935), while the text of 1933 and its subsequent revisions are put in historical perspective in Marcello Caetano, *História breve das Constituições portuguesas* (3rd edn, Lisbon, 1971). The political history of the New State has yet to be written but a preliminary analysis is the essay by H. Martins, 'Portugal' in S. J. Woolf (ed.), *European Fascism* (London, 1968). Josué da Silva, *Legião Portuguesa, força repressiva do fascismo* (Lisbon, 1975) is a sketch of that paramilitary body.

A basic starting-point for studying the opposition is an article by Hermínio Martins, 'Opposition in Portugal', *Government and Opposition*, vol. IV (1969). Memoirs of oppositionists include Henrique Galvão, *Santa Maria: My Crusade for Portugal* (London, 1961); *The Memoirs of General Delgado* (London, 1964); Fernando Queiroga, *Portugal oprimido* (reprinted Lisbon, 1974); Vasco da Gama Fernandes, *Depoimento inacabado* (Lisbon, 1974); and Mário Soares, *Portugal's Struggle for Liberty* (London, 1975), a particularly useful guide first published in France in 1972. On communist activities and views one can refer to some documentary selections, such as *O PCP e a luta sindical 1935–1973* (Lisbon, 1975) and *Documentos do Comité Central do Partido Comunista Português 1965–1974* (Lisbon, 1975); Álvaro Cunhal, *Portugal: l'aube de la liberté* (Paris, 1974) is another selection of texts. The views of ex-militants are stated in J. A. Silva Marques, *Relatos da clandestinidade: o PCP visto por dentro* (Lisbon, 1976) and Francisco Ferreira's slight *Álvaro Cunhal, herói soviético* (Lisbon, 1976).

Whatever its shortcomings, Marcello Caetano's *Depoimento* (Rio de Janeiro, 1975) is essential reading on his premiership. Some insight into his thinking can be gleaned from António Alçada Baptista, *Conversas com Marcello Caetano* (Lisbon, 1973). A useful general survey from the perspective of the end of the regime is Ezequiel G. Díaz-Llanos, *Portugal en la encrucijada* (Madrid, 1974).

On Catholicism, a hostile account is contained in Paul Blanshard's *Freedom and Catholic Power in Spain and Portugal* (Boston, Massachusetts, 1962). Two articles may be consulted: Thomas C. Bruneau, 'Church and state in Portugal: crises of cross and sword', *Journal of Church and State*, vol. XVIII (1976), and R. A. H. Robinson, 'The religious question and the Catholic revival in Portugal, 1900–30', *Journal of Contemporary History*, vol. XII (1977), which explains the background. Joaquim Maria Lourenço, *Situação jurídica da Igreja em Portugal* (Coimbra, 1943), is the basic book on church–state relations, whilst Catholic criticism of the regime is introduced in José da Felicidade Alves (ed.), *Católicos e política de Humberto Delgado a Marcello Caetano* (2nd edn, Lisbon, 1969) and José Geraldes Freire, *Resistência católica ao Salazarismo-Marcelismo* (Oporto, 1976). The findings of an opinion poll are presented by IPOPE, *Estudo sobre liberdade e religião em Portugal* (Lisbon, 1973).

EMPIRE, DECOLONISATION AND FOREIGN RELATIONS

On Portugal's third empire there is unfortunately no equivalent to C. R. Boxer's *The Portuguese Seaborne Empire, 1415–1825* (Harmondsworth, 1973), but its creation is studied in R. J. Hammond, *Portugal and Africa 1815–1910: A Study in Uneconomic Imperialism* (Stanford, California, 1966).

General surveys of the African empire are provided by James Duffy, *Portugal in Africa* (Baltimore, Maryland, 1963) and Ronald H. Chilcote, *Portuguese Africa* (Englewood Cliffs, New Jersey, 1967), while David M. Abshire and Michael A. Samuels (eds), *Portuguese Africa: A Handbook* (London, 1969) is a mine of information. John A. Davis and James K. Baker (eds), *Southern Africa in Transition* (London, 1966), and Christian P. Potholm and Richard Dale (eds), *Southern Africa in Perspective* (New York, 1972), are also useful compilations. On the wars in general there are Neil Bruce, *Portugal: The Last Empire* (Newton Abbot, 1975); and Arslan Humbaraci and Nicole Muchnik, *Portugal's African Wars* (London, 1974); Eduardo de Sousa Ferreira is critical of Portuguese rule in his *Portuguese Colonialism in Africa: the End of an Era* (Paris, 1974).

Angola is the territory best served in the literature. Douglas L. Wheeler and René Pélissier, *Angola* (London, 1969) is the best history, while a pro-MPLA view is presented in Basil Davidson's *In the Eye of the Storm: Angola's People* (2nd edn, Harmondsworth, 1975). John Marcum, *The Angolan Revolution, Vol 1: the Anatomy of an Explosion, 1950–1962* (Cambridge, Massachusetts, 1969) is a detailed account. Useful volumes in French include Mário de Souza Clington (Ary Kemtiow Zirka), *Angola libre?* (Paris, 1975); J. P. Cosse and J. Sanchez, *Angola: le prix de la liberté* (Paris, 1976); and Groupe Afrique centrale du Cedetim, *Angola: la lutte continue* (Paris, 1977). Amadeu José de Freitas, *Angola: o longo caminho da liberdade* (Lisbon, 1975) contains much evidence, while a settler's view of decolonisation is given by Pompílio da Cruz, *Angola: os vivos e os mortos* (Lisbon, 1976).

Mozambique is much less well served, but Keith Middlemas, *Cabora Bassa: Engineering and Politics in Southern Africa* (London, 1975) is wider than the title suggests. The views of FRELIMO's founder are set out in Eduardo Mondlane, *The Struggle for Mozambique* (Harmondsworth, 1969). Some light on decolonisation is cast in Jorge Jardim's memoir *Moçambique, terra queimada* (Lisbon, 1976) and by the eye-witness account of Giancarlo Coccia, *The Scorpion Sting: Moçambique* (Johannesburg, 1976).

There is no proper history of the other territories. The best book on Guiné is now Lars Rudebeck, *Guinea-Bissau: A Study of Political Mobilization* (Uppsala, 1974). Also from the PAIGC side is Basil Davidson's *The Liberation of Guiné* (Harmondsworth, 1971), while the party's views are given directly in Amílcar Cabral, *Revolution in Guinea* (2nd edn, London, 1971), a selection of texts, and the PAIGC's own *História da Guiné e as ilhas de Cabo Verde* (Oporto, 1974).

Carlos Benigno da Cruz (ed.), S. *Tomé e Príncipe: do colonialismo à independência* (Lisbon, 1975) has the merit of existing, a verdict applicable to what little there is on the Asian territories. Botelho da Silva (ed.), '*Dossier' Goa – Vassalo e Silva: a recusa do sacrifício inútil* (Lisbon, 1975) deals with the loss of the State of India. On the decolonisation of Timor, the FRETILIN view is presented in Denis Freney, *Timor: Freedom Caught between the Powers* (Nottingham, 1975) and its own documentary *Timor-Leste: uma luta heróica* (Lisbon, 1976); the anti-FRETILIN view is given in Sá Pereira (ed.), *O pavoroso caso de Timor* (Lisbon, 1976).

Defences of the old regime's stand include Marcello Caetano, *Razões da presença de Portugal no Ultramar* (Lisbon, 1973), and Franco Nogueira, *The United Nations and Portugal* (2nd edn, London, 1965). From the other side there is William Minter's *Portuguese Africa and the West* (Harmondsworth, 1972).

On foreign relations, Luc Crollen's useful *Portugal, the US and NATO* (Leuven, Belgium 1973) is like an oasis in a desert. British policy towards Portugal during the Second World War can be studied in the offical histories: W. N. Medlicott, *The Economic Blockade,* Vols I and II (London, 1952-9) and Sir Llewellyn Woodward, *British Foreign Policy in the Second World War,* Vol. IV (London, 1975).

THE NEW STATE: ECONOMY AND SOCIETY

On corporative structures, apart from the very full study by Howard Wiarda, *Corporatism and Development: The Portuguese Experience,* there is Philippe C. Schmitter, *Corporatism and Public Policy in Authoritarian Portugal* (Beverly Hills, California, 1975) while Freppel Cotta's work on the early years of the system, *Economic Planning in Corporative Portugal* (London, 1937), still has its uses. The recognised standard work is Manuel de Lucena, *A evolução do sistema corporativo português* (2 vols, Lisbon, 1976).

Useful introductions to the economy in the 1930s and 1940s are provided by the successive HMSO reports on *Economic and Commercial Conditions in Portugal* (London). A full economic survey is V. Xavier Pintado, *Structure and Growth of the Portuguese Economy* (EFTA, 1964), while criticism of Portuguese development can be found in Francisco Pereira de Moura, *Por onde vai a economia portuguesa?* (4th edn, Lisbon, 1974). Information on the monopolies is conveniently gathered in Maria Belmira Martins, *Sociedades e grupos em Portugal* (reprinted Lisbon, 1975). Luís Salgado de Matos has made a thorough study of foreign investment in his *Investimentos estrangeiros em Portugal* (Lisbon, 1973). Portugal's relations with the EEC are examined in Carlos Roma Fernandes and Pedro Álvares, *Portugal e o Mercado Comum* (Lisbon, 1972).

The main facts and figures on the agricultural sector are succinctly presented in José Carvalho Cardoso, *A agricultura portuguesa* (Lisbon, 1973). Longer detailed works are Eduardo de Freitas, João Ferreira de Almeida and Manuel Villaverde Cabral, *Modalidades de penetração do capitalismo na agricultura: estruturas agrárias em Portugal Continental, 1950–1970* (Lisbon, 1976) and, by the communist leader, Álvaro Cunhal, *Contribuição para o estudo da questão agrária* (2 vols, reprinted Lisbon, 1976).

A fundamental demographic work going up to the 1960s is Massimo Livi Bacci, *A Century of Portuguese Fertility* (Princeton, New Jersey, 1971). The high emigration of recent years is put in historical perspective by Joel Serrão, *Emigração portuguesa: sondagem histórica* (Lisbon, 1971), and is ably analysed by Eduardo Sousa Ferreira, *Origens e formas da emigração* (Lisbon, 1976). For social structure, the essay 'Portugal' by Hermínio Martins in Margaret S. Archer and Salvador Giner (eds), *Contemporary Europe: Class, Status and Power* (London, 1971) is essential reading.

'THE NEW PORTUGAL'

Surveys of events include 'Insight' team of the *Sunday Times, Insight on Portugal: the Year of the Captains* (London, 1975); Michael Harsgor, *Portugal in Revolution* (Beverly Hills, California, 1976); and, the best so far, 'written from an explicitly libertarian communist viewpoint', Phil Mailer, *Portugal: the Impossible Revolution?* (London, 1977). On the military, Rona M. Fields, *The Portuguese Revolution and the Armed Forces Movement* (New York, 1975), has now been largely overtaken by Douglas Porch, *The Portuguese Armed Forces and the Revolution* (London, 1977). Works in French include Pierre Audibert and Daniel Brignon's dramatic and rather breathless *Portugal: les nouveaux centurions* (Paris, 1974); Márcio Moreira Alves, *Les soldats socialistes du Portugal* (Paris, 1975), pro-MFA by a Brazilian leftist; Jean-Marc Dufour, *Prague sur Tage* (Paris, 1975), notable for being one of the few right-wing accounts; Jacques Frémontier, *Portugal: les points sur les i* (Paris, 1976), an incisive communist view; and, from the ultra-Left, Comité Portugal pour l'information et le soutien, *L'expérience portugaise: un bilan après le 25 novembre 1975* (Paris, 1977).

Most accounts give adequate coverage, in as much as this is possible, of the military conspiracy, but the basic, much-quoted book is Avelino Rodrigues, Cesário Borga and Mário Cardoso, *O Movimento dos Capitães e o 25 de Abril* (Lisbon, 1974); a further contribution is Dinis de Almeida, *Origens e evolução do Movimento de Capitães* (Lisbon, 1977). Documentary works on the early stages include Henrique Barrilaro Ruas (ed.), *A revolução das flores* (Lisbon, 1974), and Orlando Neves (ed.), *Textos históricos da revolução* (Lisbon, 1975) which includes the official reports on 28 September and 11 March. Turning-points are examined in António Maria Pereira, *A burla do 28 de Setembro* (Amadora, 1976); Jorge Feio, Fernanda Leitão and Carlos Pina, *11 de Março: autópsia de um golpe* (Lisbon, 1975); José Gomes Mota, *A resistência* (Lisbon, 1976), on the Nine; L. Pereira Gil, *Novembro 25: anatomia de um golpe* (Lisbon, 1976); and *Relatório do 25 de Novembro de 1975* (2 vols, Lisbon, 1976), official documents. The latter episode is investigated from the ultra-Left in Jean-Pierre Faye (ed.), *Portugal: The Revolution in the Labyrinth* (Nottingham, 1976).

Apart from Sanches Osório's dictated memoir *O equívoco do 25 de Abril* (Aveiro, 1975), contributions to the literature by or about military politicians take the form of interviews, speeches or documents. More than ephemeral examples of the genre include: Otelo Saraiva de Carvalho, *Cinco meses mudaram Portugal* (Lisbon, 1975); M. Manuela de S. Rama and Carlos Plantier, *Melo Antunes: tempo de ser firme* (Lisbon, 1976); Vasco Gonçalves (ed. Augusto Paulo da Gama), *Discursos, conferências de imprensa, entrevistas* (Oporto, 1976);

Manuel Duran Clemente, *Elementos para a compreensão do 25 de Novembro* (Lisbon, 1976); and António de Spínola, *Ao serviço de Portugal* (Lisbon, 1976). Contributions by civilian politicians are of similar type. The PS leader's views are set out in Mário Soares, *Democratização e descolonização: dez meses no Governo Provisório* (Lisbon, 1975) and his interviews with Dominique Pouchin, *Portugal: que revolução?* (Lisbon, 1976). For the PPD, there are Francisco Sá Carneiro's *Por uma social-democracia portuguesa* and *Poder civil, autoridade democrática e social-democracia* (both Lisbon, 1975). The PCP leader's pronouncements to early 1975 are in Álvaro Cunhal, *A revolução portuguesa* (Lisbon, 1975); further pronouncements by Cunhal and the Central Committee have been published at intervals in the series 'Documentos políticos do Partido Comunista Português' (Lisbon, 1975 onwards).

Given its numerical strength, the ultra-Left is comparatively well served. Some light is cast on some groups in the following: Fernanda Leitão and Carlos Pina, *LUAR: o que é?* (Lisbon, 1975); *O que é a UDP?* (Lisbon, 1976); Judith Balso (ed.), *MRPP: le Portugal de près* (Paris, 1976), and (an attack by a former leader) J. L. Saldanha Sanches, *OMRPP, instrumento da contra-revolução* (2nd edn, Lisbon, 1976). Glimmers of light are shed on the clandestine Right in Alpoim Calvão's memoir *De Conakry ao MDLP* (Lisbon, 1976); Carlos Dugos, *MDLP-ELP: o que saõ?* (Alfragide, 1976): and Günter Wallraff's controversial *A descoberta de uma conspiração: a acção-Spínola* (Amadora, 1976).

The first election is analysed with admirable thoroughness in Jorge Gaspar and Nuno Vitorino, *As eleições de 25 de Abril: geografia e imagem dos partidos* (Lisbon, 1976), while a very useful annotated edition of the constitution is that of Victor Silva Lopes, *Constituição da República portuguesa, 1976* (Lisbon, 1976). Tentative introductions to the President and Prime Minister are made by Paulino Gomes, *Eanes: porquê o Poder?* (Lisbon, 1976), and B. Díaz Nosty, *Mário Soares, um combatente do socialismo* (Lisbon, 1975).

An account of economic affairs is written by Eugénio Rosa, *Portugal: dois anos de revolução na economia* (Lisbon, 1976). Documentation on the popular movement is contained in F. Ávila *et al., Portugal, l'autre combat: classes et conflits dans la société* (Paris, 1975), and in Maria de Lurdes Lima Santos, Marinús Pires de Lima and Vítor Matias Ferreira, *O 25 de Abril e as lutas sociais nas empresas* (3 vols, Oporto, 1976–7); these contrast with the PCP / Intersindical viewpoint in Albano Lima, *Movimento sindical e unidade no processo revolucionário português* (Lisbon, 1975). On land reform there is the contribution of the socialist minister António Lopes Cardoso, *Luta pela reforma agrária* (Lisbon, 1976).

A useful compilation of ecclesiastical texts is Miguel de Araújo (ed.), *Dicionário político, 1: os Bispos e a revolução de Abril* (Lisbon, 1976).

Glossary of Political Terms

ADS	Democratic-Social Action
AEV	Accão Escolar Vanguarda (fascistic students' movement)
AMI	Military Intervention Grouping
ANP	People's National Action
AOC	Worker Peasant Alliance
APODETI	Timorese People's Democratic Association
ARA	Armed Revolutionary Action
ASP	Portuguese Socialist Action
Base- FUT	*Base*-United Workers Front
CADC	Academic Centre of Christian Democracy
CAP	Confederation of Portuguese Farmers
CCP	Portuguese Catholic Centre
CDE	Democratic Electoral Committee(s)
CDLs	Freedom Defence Committees
CDS	Party of the Social Democratic Centre
CED	Democratic Electoral Committee
CEUD	Electoral Committee of Democratic Unity
CGL	General Confederation of Labour
CGTP/IN	General Confederation of Portuguese Workers/National Intersindical
CIA	(U.S.) Central Intelligence Agency
CIP	Confederation of Portuguese Industry
CONCP	Conference of the National Organisations of the Portuguese Colonies
COPCON	Operational Command for Continental Portugal
COREMO	Mozambique Revolutionary Committee
DGS	Directorate-General of Security
DRIL	Iberian Revolutionary Directorate of Liberation
EEC	European Economic Community
EFTA	European Free Trade Association
ELP	Portuguese Liberation Army
FAC	Motorised Shock Force/Anti-Communist Force
FAO	Food and Agriculture Organisation
FAP	People's Action Front
FAPLA	Angolan People's Liberation Armed Forces
FAPLE	Antitotalitarian Front of Free Portuguese in Exile
FEN	Nationalist Students' Front
FEPU	'United People' Electoral Front
FICO	Remain Living Together
FLA	Azorean Liberation Front
FLAMA	Madeiran Archipelago Liberation Front
FLEC	Enclave of Cabinda Liberation Front
FLING	Front of the Liberation and Independence of Portuguese Guinea
FNAT	National Foundation for Happiness in Work

FNLA	Angolan National Liberation Front
FPLN	Patriotic National Liberation Front ⎫ (Delgado's two Algerian-
FPLN	Portuguese National Liberation Front ⎬ based revolutionary
	⎭ organisations)
FRA	Angolan Resistance Front
FRAIN	African Revolutionary Front for National Independence
FRELIMO	Mozambique Liberation Front
FRETILIN	Revolutionary Front of Independent East Timor
FSP	People's Socialist Front
FUA	Front of Angolan Unity
FUP	People's Unitary Front
FUR	Revolutionary United Front
GDUPs	Dynamising Groups of Popular Unity
GII	Intermediate Intervention Group
GNR	Republican National Guard
GRAE	Revolutionary Government of Angola in Exile
GUMO	United Group of Mozambique
ILO	International Labour Office
JMLN	Military Junta of National Liberation
JSN	Junta of National Salvation
KGB	Komitet Gosudarstvennoi Bezopasnosti (Soviet Union Committee of State Security)
LCI	Internationlist Communist League
LUAR	League of Revolutionary Union and Action
MAC	Anti-Colonialist Movement
MANU	Mozambique African National Union
MCAD	Christian Movement of Democratic Action
MDLP	Democratic Liberation Movement of Portugal
MDM	Democratic Movement of Mozambique
MDP/CDE	Portuguese Democratic Movement CDE (q.v.)
MES	Movement of the Socialist Left
MFA	Armed Forces' Movement
MIRN	Independent Movement of National Reconstruction
MLSTP	São Tomé e Príncipe Liberation Movement
MND	Democratic National Movement
MNI	Independent National Movement
MPLA	Angolan Popular Liberation Movement
MRPP	Reorganising Movement of the Party of the Proletariat
MSD	Social Democratic Movement
MSP	People's Socialist Movement
MUD	Movement of Democratic Unity
MUDJ	Movement of Democratic Unity Youth
MUDM	Movement of Democratic Unity of Mozambique
MUNAF	National Anti-Fascist Unity Movement
NATO	North Atlantic Treaty Organisation
OAU	Organisation of African Unity
OAS	(French) Organisation of the Secret Army
OCN	National Civic Organisation
OECD	Organisation for Economic Co-operation and Development

ONS	National-Syndicalist Organisation
PAIGC	**Guiné and Cape Verde African Independence Party**
PCDA	Christian Democratic Party of Angola
PCP	Portuguese Communist Party
PCP (M-L)	Portuguese Communist Party (Marxist-Leninist)
PDC	Party of Christian Democracy
PIDE	International and State Defence Police
PL	Liberal Party
PNP	Portuguese Nationalist Party
PNR	Republican Nationalist Party
PP/MFP	Party of Progress/Portuguese Federalist Movement
PPD	People's Democratic Party
PPM	People's Monarchist Party
PRP	Portuguese Republican Party
PRP/BR	Revolutionary Party of the Proletariat/Revolutionary Brigades
PRT	Workers' Revolutionary Party
PS. PSP	Portuguese Socialist Party
PSD	Social Democratic Party
PSP	Police of Public Safety
PVDE	Vigilance and State Defence Police
SDCI	Information Control and Detection Service
SEDES	Social and Economic Development Study Group
SNI	National Secretariat of Information
SPN	National Propaganda Secretariat
SUV	Soldiers United Will Win
UDENAMO	Mozambique Democratic National Union
UDT	Timorese Democratic Union
UDP	People's Democratic Union
ULR	Republican Liberal Union
UN	National Union
UNAMI	African Union of Independent Mozambique
UNESCO	United Nations Educational, Scientific and Cultural Organisation
UNIPOMO	Union for the Peace of the People of Mozambique
UNITA	National Union for the Total Independence of Angola
UNO	United Nations Organisation
UON	National Workers' Union
UPA	Union of the Populations of Angola
UPNA	Union of the Populations of North Angola
USA, US	United States of America
USSR	Union of Soviet Socialist Republics

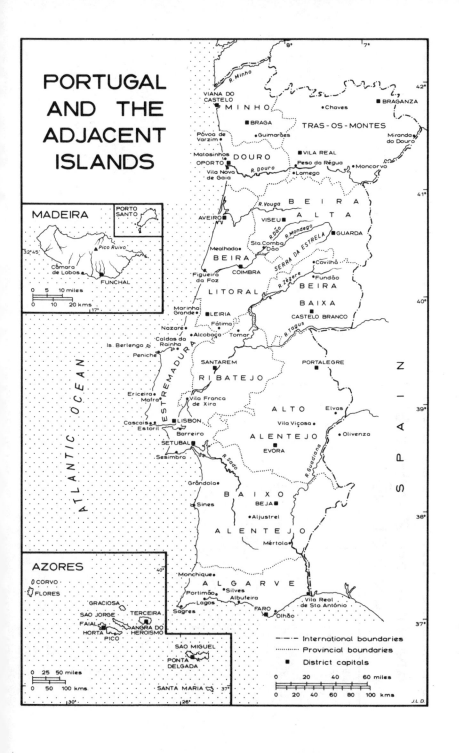

PORTUGAL
AND THE
ADJACENT
ISLANDS

MADEIRA

PORTO SANTO

32°45'
Pico Ruivo ▲
Câmara
de Lobos ●
FUNCHAL ■

0   5   10 miles
0   10   20 kms
17°

ATLANTIC   OCEAN

AZORES

40°
○ CORVO
○ FLORES
GRACIOSA
SAO JORGE   TERCEIRA
FAIAL   ■ANGRA DO
HORTA ■   HEROISMO
PICO
SAO MIGUEL
PONTA
DELGADA

0   25   50 miles
0   50   100 kms.

SANTA MARIA ○   37°
30°   26°

R. Minho
VIANA DO
CASTELO
M I N H O   ● Chaves   ■ BRAGANZA
■ BRAGA   TRAS - OS - MONTES
Póvoa de
Varzim ●   ● Guimarães   Miranda
Matosinhos ●   DOURO   ■ VILA REAL   do Douro
OPORTO ■   Peso da Régua
Vila Nova   R. Douro   ● Moncorvo
de Gaia   ● Lamego

B E I R A
R.Vouga   A L T A
AVEIRO ■   VISEU ■
R.Dão   R.Mondego
B E I R A   Sta Comba ● GUARDA
Mealhada ●   Dão   SERRA DA ESTRELA
● Covilhã
Figueira   COIMBRA ■
da Foz   ● Fundão
LITORAL   R.Zêzere   B E I R A
B A I X A
Marinha
Grande ● ■LEIRIA   CASTELO BRANCO ■
● Fátima
Nazaré ● ● Alcobaça ● Tomar
Caldas da   R. Tagus
Is.Berlenga ○ Rainha
Peniche ●

● SANTAREM   PORTALEGRE ■
R I B A T E J O

Ericeira ●
Mafra ●   ● Vila Franca   A L T O   Elvas ●
de Xira
Cascais ● ● LISBON   Vila Viçosa ●
Estoril   A L E N T E J O   ● Olivenza
Barreiro
SETUBAL ■   ● EVORA
Sesimbra ●
R. Sado
● Grândola

● Sines   B A I X O
BEJA ■
● Aljustrel
A L E N T E J O
● Mértola

Monchique ●
A L G A R V E
Portimão ● ● Silves
Lagos ●   Albufeira   Vila Real
Sagres ●   FARO ■ de Sta António
● Olhão

S P A I N

R.Guadiana

—·—·— International boundaries
·········· Provincial boundaries
■ District capitals

0   20   40   60 miles
0   20   40   60   80   100 kms

J.L.D.

42°
8°   7°
41°
40°
39°
38°
37°

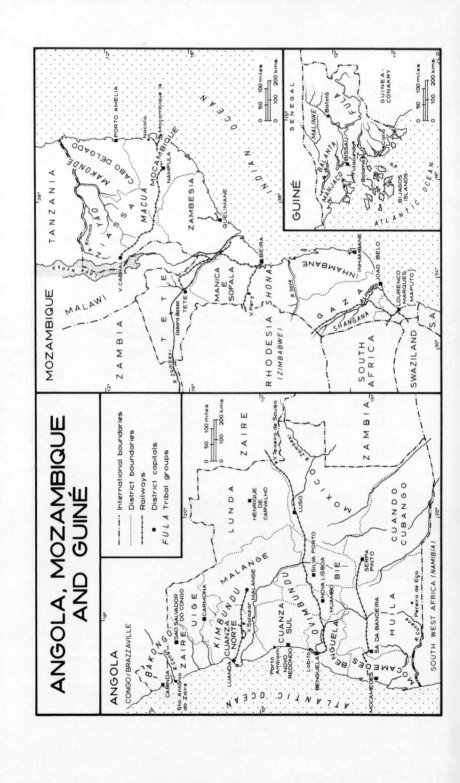

Index